PSYCHOANALYSIS ONLINE 2

Library of Technology and Mental Health

Series Editor: Jill Savege Scharff, MD

Distance Psychoanalysis: The Theory and Practice of Using Communication Technology in the Clinic (2011) by Ricardo Carlino, translated by James Nuss

Psychoanalysis Online: Mental Health, Teletherapy, and Training (2013) edited by Jill Savege Scharff

Screen Relations (2015) by Gillian Russell

PSYCHOANALYSIS ONLINE 2
Impact of Technology on Development, Training, and Therapy

Edited by
Jill Savege Scharff

KARNAC

First published in 2015 by
Karnac Books Ltd
118 Finchley Road
London NW3 5HT

British Library Cataloguing in Publication Data

A C.I.P. for this book is available from the British Library

ISBN-13: 978-1-78220-321-6

Typeset by V Publishing Solutions Pvt Ltd., Chennai, India

Printed in Great Britain by TJ International Ltd, Padstow, Cornwall

www.karnacbooks.com

For digital natives, Emme, Ethan, Coco, Anabel, Ben and Chloe

CONTENTS

ACKNOWLEDGEMENTS

I gratefully acknowledge permissions received from the following publishers:

Chapter Three was published in Italian as "La Seduzione della magia digitale" in *Rivista di Psicoanalisi*, 59 (pp. 1041–1052) and appears by permission of the journal's director.

Chapter Four was mainly inspired by Chris Kraft's perspective on Internet sexuality and also presents opposing views.

Parts of Chapter Six by Adela Abella were published previously in 2014 as "De quelques conditions nécessaires à la sublimation" in *Perspectives psychosomatiques*, 2: *Sublimation*, pp. 145–158, Genève: Georg, and are published courtesy of the publisher.

Chapter Nine by Lin Tao was modified and expanded from a paper read by Lin Tao at a Scientific Meeting of the British Psychoanalytical Society on January 16, 2013.

Chapter Eleven by David Scharff is modified from "Conquering geographic space: teaching psychoanalytic psychotherapy and infant observation by videolink", in M. Stadter and D. E. Scharff (Eds.) (2005), *Dimensions of Psychotherapy, Dimensions of Experience* (pp. 115–125), and appears by permission of Taylor and Francis Publishing.

Chapter Twelve by Michael Buchholz and Horst Kächele is an adapted and revised version of a German version in *Journal of Psychotraumatology Psychotherapy Science, Psychological Medicine* 11: 49–61. (Kächele, H., & Buchholz, M. B. (2013). Eine Notfall-SMS-Intervention bei chronischer Suizidalität—Wie die Konversationsanalyse klinische Beobachtungen bereichert. ZPPM Zeitschrift für Psychotraumatologie, Psychotherapiewissenschaft, *Psychologische Medizin*, 11(2), 49–61.) This revision appears courtesy of *Psychologische Medizin*.

Chapter Eighteen was given as a paper by Glen Gabbard on a panel at the winter meeting of the American Psychoanalytic Association, New York, January 18, 2014.

These chapters owe everything to the efforts and creativity of the contributors and the team at Karnac in London. Oliver Rathbone, who conceived of the series Library of Technology and

Mental Health, and his team including Rod Tweedy and Cecily Blench, have been consistently delightful to work with. As editor and series editor, I am grateful for their personal attention and responsiveness and their excellent production values. At my office in Chevy Chase, MD, USA, Anna Innes and Angela Moorman worked kindly and efficiently to keep me on schedule. Last but not least, I thank David Scharff for his constant support.

CONTRIBUTORS

Adela Abella, MD (Switzerland) is an IPA training and supervising adult and child analyst in Geneva, and past president of the Centre de Psychanalyse de la Suisse Romande, Switzerland. She serves as a member of the IPA committee on culture and as a reviewer of the *International Journal of Psychoanalysis*. She writes on child analysis and on the interface between analysis and art, and co-authored *La Construction Psychanalyse* with Juan Manzano (Paris: PUF).

Carl Bagnini, LCSW, BCD (USA) is a senior and founding faculty member at the International Psychotherapy Institute in Washington DC and in Long Island, NY, where his private practice is in Port Washington, NY. He is a clinical supervisor at the Ferkauf Graduate School of Psychology, faculty at The Derner Institute at Adelphi University, and New York University Graduate Certificate Program in Child and Family Therapy. Mr. Bagnini is a featured presenter at national and international conferences and video-conferences, and has written many papers and book chapters on object relations topics. His recent book is: *Keeping Couples in Treatment: Working from Surface to Depth* (Lanham, MD: Jason Aronson, 2012).

Becky Bailey, PhD (USA) is a psychoanalyst and psychologist in private practice in Salt Lake City, Utah, USA where she also leads the rehabilitation psychology/neuropsychology services department at the Neuroscience Institute at Intermountain Medical Center. She is a faculty member of the International Psychotherapy Institute (IPI) and a member of the Teaching Faculty at the International Institute for Psychoanalytic Training at IPI in Chevy Chase, MD, USA.

Nancy Bakalar, MD (USA) is a supervising analyst, International Institute for Psychoanalytic Training; faculty member, the Denver Institute for Psychoanalysis and the University of Colorado School of Medicine; chair, infant observation program, International Psychotherapy Institute; distinguished fellow, the American Psychiatric Association; and psychoanalyst practicing in Denver, CO and Rockville, MD.

Sharon Zalusky Blum, PhD (USA) is a psychologist and psychoanalyst in private practice in Los Angeles. She is a senior faculty member at the New Center for Psychoanalysis in Los Angeles and author of numerous articles on telephone analysis and the impact of technology on the practice of psychoanalysis.

Michael B. Buchholz, Dipl-Psych (Germany) is a training analyst in Goettingen, full professor for social psychology (microanalysis) at International Psychoanalytic University (IPU), Berlin. He is the author of many publications in psychoanalysis, supervision research, qualitative methods, and clinical topics. He is interested in empathy and musicality. See http://journal.frontiersin.org/Journal/10.3389/fpsyg.2014.00349/abstract

Glen O. Gabbard, MD (USA) is clinical professor of psychiatry at Baylor College of Medicine and training and supervising analyst at the Center for Psychoanalytic Studies in Houston. He is the author or editor of twenty-seven books and has published over 350 scientific papers and book chapters. He was the joint editor-in-chief of the *International Journal of Psychoanalysis* from 2001 to 2007, the first non-British editor to hold that position. In 2000 he received the Sigourney Award for outstanding contributions to psychoanalysis.

Horst Kächele, MD, PhD (Germany) is a specialist in psychosomatic medicine and a psychoanalyst. He now is professor at International Psychoanalytic University Berlin (2010-) and was chair of the department of psychosomatic medicine and psychotherapy at the Faculty of Medicine, Ulm University (1997–2009). He is known for his research in psychoanalytic process and outcome, psychosomatics, clinical and neurobiological aspects of attachment, and error in psychotherapy. He is a collaborator in the single case archive with the department of psychology at Ghent University. He co-authored with H. Thomä the three-volume textbook *Psychoanalytic Practice*, now in more than fourteen languages.

Luca Nicoli, PhD (Italy) is a psychologist, psychotherapist, and psychoanalyst, member of the Società Psicoanalitica Italiana and the International Psychoanalytical Association, and member of the editorial board of the *Rivista di Psicoanalisi*. He is in private practice in psychoanalysis and psychotherapy with adults, adolescents, and children in Modena and Ferrara. His books are *Amare senza perdersi* (Foschi, 2009), *L'arte di arrabbiarsi* (Foschi, 2012), *Il sogno* (Foschi, 2014).

Andi Pilecki, MS, LPC (USA) is a psychotherapist in private practice in Pittsburgh, Pennsylvania. She is a member of the International Psychotherapy Institute and the Association for Women in Psychology. She has taught at Carlow University, and facilitates trainings and workshops in the Pittsburgh area on gender and sexual diversity and psychodynamic psychotherapy.

David Scharff, MD (USA) is co-founder, former director, and chair of the board of the International Psychotherapy Institute (IPI); supervising analyst at the International Institute for Psychoanalytic Training at IPI; teaching analyst at the Washington Center for Psychoanalysis; clinical professor of psychiatry at the Uniformed Services University of the Health Sciences and at Georgetown University, and former director of the Washington School of Psychiatry (1987–1994). He is in private practice in psychoanalysis and psychotherapy in Chevy Chase, MD. His most recent books are *Psychoanalysis in China* (ed. with S. Varvin, 2014), *Psychoanalytic Couple Therapy* (ed. with J. S. Scharff et al., 2014) and *The Interpersonal Unconscious* (with J. S. Scharff, 2011).

Jill Savege Scharff, MD, MRCPsych (USA) is co-founder, board member emeritus, and formerly co-director of the International Psychotherapy Institute (IPI); founding chair and supervising analyst at the International Institute for Psychoanalytic Training at IPI; teaching analyst at the Washington Center for Psychoanalysis; clinical professor of psychiatry at Georgetown University. She is in private practice in psychoanalysis and psychotherapy with adults, children, couples, and families in Chevy Chase, MD. Her newest books are edited volumes: *Psychoanalysis Online* (2012) and *Clinical Supervision of Psychoanalytic Psychotherapy* (2014).

Caroline M. Sehon, MD (USA) is chair, Metro Washington Center of the International Psychotherapy Institute (IPI-Metro), chair, Teleanalysis Research Group of the International Institute for Psychoanalytic Training (IIPT) at IPI, teaching analyst at IIPT, trustee, Accreditation Council for Psychoanalytic Education, clinical associate professor of psychiatry and past director of the child and adolescent psychiatry program at Georgetown University, and member, American and International Psychoanalytical Associations. She is in private practice in psychoanalysis and psychotherapy in Bethesda, MD.

Lea Setton, PhD (Panama, RP) is an IPA training and supervising analyst in Panama City, Panama RP. She is a faculty member of the International Institute for Psychoanalytic Training at the International Psychotherapy Institute in Chevy Chase MD, USA and formerly chair of IPI-Panama. Her book in press is *Enrique Pichon-Rivière*, co-edited with Roberto Losso and David Scharff (Jason Aronson, 2015).

Lynn Stormon, PhD, (USA) is a psychoanalyst in private practice in Syracuse, NY, a faculty member of the International Psychotherapy Institute and the International Institute for Psychoanalytic Training, and a direct member of the American Psychoanalytic Association and the International Psychoanalytic Association.

Lin Tao, MD (China and UK) is a vice-chief psychiatrist in Beijing and the first qualified psychoanalyst in China. He is a direct member of the International Psychoanalytical Association (IPA) where he is a member of both the China committee and the international working group on couple and family psychoanalysis. He is on the Board of the China Psychoanalytic Association. In the UK he is a qualified couple psychoanalytic psychotherapist and a member of the British Psychoanalytic Council (BPC) and the British Society of Couple Psychotherapists and Counsellors (BSCPC) and visiting psychotherapist at the Tavistock Centre for Couple Relationships (TCCR). He is a guest member of the British Psychoanalytical Society (BPAS). He was director of the ward for patients with neurosis and associate director of the Department of Clinical Psychology at Beijing An Ding Hospital, affiliated to the Capital Medical University in China.

Virginia Ungar, MD (Argentina), a full member and training analyst at the Buenos Aires Psychoanalytical Association, is president-elect of the International Psychoanalytic Association. Specializing in child and adolescent psychoanalysis, she is the former chair and current consultant on the IPA Committee of Child and Adolescent Psychoanalysis (COCAP). She is also chair of the IPA Integrated Training Committee and a member of the Latin American Board of the *International Journal of Psychoanalysis*. She has published numerous papers in journals and chapters in some books.

Donna Vanderpool, MBA, JD (USA) is the vice-president of risk management at Professional Risk Management Services, Inc. in Arlington, VA. She is responsible for the development and implementation of risk management services for professional liability insurance programs for psychiatrists and other mental health professionals. She has consulted, written, and spoken nationally on healthcare law, telehealth, and other risk management topics.

Yolanda de Varela, PhD (Panama, RP) is an IPA didactic analyst, IPA direct member, and chair of the scientific committee for the Grupo de Estudios Psicoanalíticos de Panamá-IPA. She is a faculty member of the International Institute for Psychoanalytic Training at the International Psychotherapy Institute (IPI) in Chevy Chase, MD and a founding faculty member of IPI. Yolanda Varela is the founder of IPI-Panamá.

Ernest Wallwork, PhD (USA) is a psychoanalyst in private practice in Washington, DC and Syracuse, New York, professor of religion and ethics at Syracuse University, and a teaching analyst at the Washington Center for Psychoanalysis. His many publications on ethical topics include *Psychoanalysis and Ethics* (Yale University Press), *Durkheim: Morality and Milieu* (Harvard University Press), and *Critical Issues in Modern Religion* (Prentice-Hall).

Janine Wanlass, PhD (USA) is director of the International Psychotherapy Institute (IPI), Chevy Chase, MD, and professor of psychology and counseling at Westminster College, Salt Lake City, Utah, USA. She teaches psychoanalytic couple therapy in the videoconference course of IPI and the Tavistock Centre for Couple Relationships in London, UK, and in the continuous course of the Mental Health Association and Peking University in Beijing, China. She is a psychoanalyst and psychologist in private practice, treating children, adults, couples, and families. Her research interests include the use of technology in psychotherapy and psychoanalysis, clinical applications of object relations theory, and the treatment of trauma.

INTRODUCTION

Jill Savege Scharff

This volume continues the effort of the Library of Technology and Mental Health to confront the challenge posed to analysts and therapists by the digital age. Analytic teachers who were educated in the predigital age tend to prefer relating to a live person rather than an image, reading the printed word rather than electronic text, and doing one thing at a time. The Internet is changing all that, because myriad streams of information and requests for communication and response come at us in all directions. Will we adapt to the pace of change, the rapid multitasking, the diffusion of attention across many networks in this new world of liquid modernity? The authors address this fundamental question concerning the impact of technology and the Internet in four parts: on development, on the training of therapists, on professional ethics, and on the provision of psychotherapy and psychoanalysis.

In Part I, I introduce the question: How is the Internet affecting the minds of members of the digital-age generation, their language, and way of being in the world, and how, as analysts of the predigital era, can we adapt our methods to their needs? Becky Bailey reviews the literature as she asks: How are we changing our social attunement, our capacity to connect, create, and love when we spend increasing numbers of hours intimately attached to our devices? Luca Nicoli weaves personal and professional experience to consider the new landscape, finds that it looks like an unknown planet with confused inhabitants dealing with aliens landing on it, and then asks us to scrutinize our way of insisting on the centrality of traditional in-person consultation. Unlimited social interaction, sexual fantasy, online sexuality, and pornography are widely available on the Internet. I describe a continuum of behavior from healthy to problematic to at-risk and argue for a balanced point of view from which to reflect on the deeper issue that concerns me: What is the impact of online sex on the unconscious and its fuelling of manic defense, flight from anxiety, and sadistic part-object relating? The Internet offers an antidote for loneliness and alienation. Andi Pilecki shows how marginalized gender non-conforming people use the Internet as an uncommon venue in which to meet others with shared experience and perspectives. Adela Abella looks at the impact on relationships, including therapeutic relationships, of living in a world filled with quickly evolving and all-embracing communication technologies that reshape thinking and relating.

Part II deals with ethics of teletherapy, those external ethics of rules, licensing, and standards, and the internal ethics of maintaining a respectful, open-minded position dedicated to concern for the patient as well as for the profession. Ernest Wallwork ask us to assess with our patients the values and risks of using the Internet in treatment and to arrive at truly informed, voluntary consent, and he gives two case examples to stimulate debate. Then Donna Vanderpool contributes her legal expertise to increase therapists' awareness of the shifting legal environment and various legal issues relevant to patients and professional practitioners in whichever states they live. Back in the clinical arena, Lin Tao asks whether a secure connection on the Internet can offer a "good enough" setting for psychoanalysis, with enough oxygen in the atmosphere for the survival of the analytic couple and the analytic process? Or does it indulge an omnipotent fantasy? He is honest about the limitations of working online but he shows how these experiences can be analysed to deepen the process.

In Part III Janine Wanlass introduces a discussion of the use of technology in clinical supervision or consultation conducted either regularly or intermittently via telephone, tablet, desktop computer technology, or videoconferencing system. David Scharff considers the technical challenges of equipment and broadband connection, the opportunities and challenges to in-depth communication, and the dynamics of teaching when technology is needed to overcome the barriers of geographic separation in large and small group seminars, and in long-term group supervision. Michael Buchholz and Horst Kächele bring their renowned research skills in conversational analysis to an experimental short message-based therapy for a chronically suicidal patient.

Part IV brings an immersion in the issues of clinical work with adults in analysis, children in analysis and therapy, and couples in analytic couple therapy. Chapters cover ongoing, intermittent, and occasional teleanalytic sessions. David Scharff asks: Could a session of teleanalysis be more effective *at times* than a session in person for some patients in ongoing in-person analysis, and perhaps even lead to a turning point? He illustrates his answer with process notes. Lea Setton moves beyond Freud's and Pichon-Rivière's view of the analyst's office as the only special space for psychoanalysis and shows that the patient can create the setting and use technology to create the metaphorical space. She challenges us to figure out which of the individual analytic sessions she presents is conducted in person and which on the telephone. Lynn Stormon and Caroline Sehon, both members of the telanalysis research group at the International Psychotherapy Institute and both experienced in conducting teleanalyses, comment on the differences between, and similarities of, the sessions. Carl Bagnini applies his experience in domiciliary care to guide his way in the uncharted territory of online couple therapy, and offers an example of an effective interpretation addressed to the couple's presentation for online sessions. One indication for teleanalysis is the relocation of the analyst. In the case that Nancy Bakalar describes, working online with web camera introduced a negative transference that could have ended the treatment but, with effective interpretation, allowed for a deepening of the treatment. Bakalar tells us why and shows us how she flexibly expanded the frame of the treatment to include the patient's infant as part of her containment, since that is what the patient's needs dictated and Bakalar's expertise allowed her to make the accommodation. Speaking of the needs of children, Caroline Sehon asks a number of questions, including whether it is possible to play therapeutically with a child screen-to-screen, and if so how does the child's body participate in the session. She gives two illustrations to let us judge for ourselves. In their commentaries, Sharon Blum, a noted innovator in the field of teleanalysis, and Virginia Ungar, a prominent child and adolescent specialist, argue that working analytically with a child is clearly possible. These children appreciated having their remote sessions, but they preferred to meet in person when possible. We are now facing a generation of adults who prefer to communicate across cyberspace. Yolanda de Varela considers that preference as an indication for prescribing online treatment, because she has found that with some schizoid personalities, cyberspace is a space where something that has not yet taken place is recreated in all that is missing in online communication, and, once understood, then that which did not happen in early life may happen in the future of the analytic relationship. The book concludes with Glen Gabbard recounting a senior analyst's experience of coming to terms with the impact of cyberspace, accepting the loss of anonymity in the world of Google Search, and adapting to change while preserving analysis as a sanctuary for reflection.

PART I

TECHNOLOGY AND CHILD AND ADULT DEVELOPMENT

CHAPTER ONE

The impact of technology on development, community, and teletherapy

Jill Savege Scharff

The impact of technology on individual development

Computer technology is with us, like it or not. For some of us it arrived during our middle age. For others it is there from the beginning. This realization occurred when I went to visit a new-born and her parents. I was given the privilege of wakening the three-day-old baby and bring-ing her for her next feed. I entered the bedroom where her mother and father were resting. The father was on his iPhone, shopping for diapers online. There were two iPads at hand on the bed, and on a side table was the video baby monitor. The mother had her personal cellphone in hand and her business phone on the bedside table. She asked me to hold the baby for another minute, saying that she needed time to wake up. Of course, I was happy to comply, but she did not mean that she needed time to wake herself up before taking the baby in her arms. She needed time to wake up "the app!" She has long used iPhone apps to order groceries for delivery, buy a cup of coffee at Starbucks, board a plane, and unlock her front door to let a tradesman in when she is at work. Now she has an app to track her baby's feeding times, sleeping times, and frequency of elimination. It even makes bar graphs of the data. To me, the graphs were an amusement or a demand, but to the mother the app is a convenience for remembering what is happening with her baby, for updating her husband on the baby's activities, and giving information to her pediatrician, lactation consultant, and babysitter. It is part and parcel of the process of tuning in and adjusting to the baby's rhythms. To her, it is as natural as breast-feeding.

Then it was time for the mother to put the baby down in the bassinet in the nursery, to the accompaniment of a short piece of soothing electronic music. Back in the master bedroom, the mother checked on the baby's waking and sleeping on a video monitor especially developed to give a clear picture in the dark. To me this seemed like spying on the baby's privacy, intrud-ing into her being in the world, and conveying a lack of trust in her ability to stay alive when separate. And how do the parents know that the data they are collecting remains private and for their use alone? "Mass data collection is becoming 'designed in' to everyday life as we increasingly rely on technologies capable of monitoring, storing and distributing information about us … People continue to use the technologies and applications implicated in data collection even as they express outrage over such activities" (Shklovski, Scott, Mainwaring, Skúladóttir, & Borgthorsson, 2014). But how can the baby object? Then again, concepts of privacy are changing in the digital age. To the parents, the video monitor is simply a device of convenience to ensure that they will hear their baby cry or see her stir, without the intrusion of entering her room to check on her. To them it is a better way of staying connected than staying home, or co-sleeping with their infant as many young parents now do.

The picture I have of life in this young family is typical of the scene in the home of young parents. Many of them use the baby app and the monitor. If the parents cannot afford a video monitor, they may leave one parent's iPhone in the baby's room in communication with the others in the room where the parents are. Like many babies in this decade, this one is growing up, from birth, with technology, not as a substitute for her parents but in support of their efforts to offer her the most sensitive, responsible care. Some parents whose children are in day care install video monitors there, and those who use a babysitter have hidden nanny cams at home to check in on their children or check up on the quality of care they are receiving. Technology plays a major role in the baby's facilitating environment, and will continue to do so in various ways as she grows.

Because of access to the Internet, free Skype software, and visual transmission using an inbuilt web camera, the baby gets to know significant others beyond her nuclear family. Grandparents in another city or country are only a click away. They can develop gaze interactions and vocal communication sequences with the new baby. I watched as this baby, as young as three days, never having met her grandmother in person, actually looked at and reached out for the image of her face on the iPad. Just as an older baby will turn to watch an older child on a swing at the playground, the newborn turned to the iPad with excitement at hearing the high-pitched voice of a toddler cousin. Even the small image on the iPhone generates interest. The baby who looks at a grandparent or an uncle in virtual reality on the screen manages the situation because he is being held in the arms of the parent who is really there, and who interprets the experience for the baby and for the relative who is at a distance. The virtual bridge to the Other is supported by the human bridge to the One. The baby is growing up connected.

By the time a baby is one year old, she will, simply by having watched the parent manipulate the icons on the phone or iPad hundreds of times a week, imitate the parent's behavior with digital devices (Bailey, Chapter Two). A one-year-old becomes proficient at opening the digital device and pressing buttons and icons to get the desired effect. The device becomes like a teddy bear, not a soft cuddly one, but a hard object with hidden wonders and endless entertainment. This is the precursor for interaction with many cyber objects over the course of a lifetime (Gabbard, 2001, 2014, and Chapter Eighteen). I think of our adult attachment to digital devices: "They are now our pals, and although we may find ourselves addicted to them, they are ultimately indispensable. You love your iPhone, yet, in the blink of an eye you can exchange it for something newer, better, more desirable" (Nafisi, 2014, p. 171). Fickle, we discard them like a worn-out teddy bear that no longer serves its purpose.

To avoid a premature attachment to digital stimulation, some mothers hold off on exposing their infants to television and video until after the age of two. Others allow occasional viewing, say on a car trip or at a boring family dinner, when the device functions as a digital babysitter. Others use the television and the iPad regularly, as a part of everyday life in keeping with cultural norms. By the time they are in preschool, the child is exposed to computer games in order to develop technological readiness, akin to reading readiness activity in preparation for more specifically skill-based learning in first grade. These three to five-year-olds are totally comfortable in the digital world. They can operate a television remote, a cellphone, and an iPad—and many of them actually do. They are growing up in the culture of the D-Gen, the Digital Generation. As Prensky (2001) says, they are "digital natives".

Moving on to the elementary school years, we see children learning to read, write, and count with the help of educational programs that make words and numbers fun. They learn to print, but for many of them handwriting instruction stops there. Because computer software has been developed to convert printing into type face, and because children have been hunting and pecking on keyboards since they were toddlers, they might as well move on from printing to typing. So there is a trend away from teaching cursive handwriting. Being pushed to be ready for the advantages that the computer can bring to writing creative narratives or reports, robs the child of the bodily experience of making fluid shapes and the mental experience of connecting letters to form words. To me, as a person of the predigital generation, there is a disadvantage here in the access to technology, because email expression tends toward language that is cryptic or disjointed and goes against coherence, logical flow, and style. Nevertheless, technology offers experiences of wonder and edutainment that stimulate curiosity and thinking beyond the confines of academic instruction. For the older child in late elementary and middle school, computer games crowd into their social life. As the child spends more time on gaming, time spent in physical activity decreases, to the detriment of the development of a well-rounded, healthy child. Frequent arguments ensue over how much time on the computer is allowed, and it is often difficult to distinguish between time needed on the Internet for homework and research versus time for games. Texting, chatting, and instagramming enable children to maintain their social connections, but, again, these activities can become all-consuming. Just as the parents help the infant to self-regulate, they help their child to regulate work and social life, time on screen and time reading or playing music or sport. Parents can support one another to develop standards by which the whole community abides.

Adolescence is a time of upheaval, as bodies change into new shapes along with secondary sexual characteristics and uncontrollable functions such as menstruation and spontaneous emission. Some adolescents turn to the Internet to escape the constraints of a body with which they cannot come to terms. They can enter the Internet without any bodily constraint or anxiety, present themselves as avatars with desired characteristics, and enter a world of pretence. Working with the immense anxieties of adolescents who hate their uncontrollable, changing bodies, Lemma (2014) developed the hypothesis that these adolescents long to merge with the maternal object that eludes them, except in cyberspace. Where cyberspace is a temporary retreat or an area of self-discovery and rehearsal for adult relationships, there is no cause for alarm. But it may become for them a psychic retreat or, more seriously, a psychotic enclave in which to escape the terrors of corporality (Lemma, 2014).

By the time the child is adolescent, self-regulation needs to be in place, because by then it is too late to impose standards, the battles are louder and more violent, and, with the approach of college application, the anxiety about academic disruption is more acute. College applications are made mainly online—another area in which technology has entered the everyday life of young people. The adult learning environment is now quite different than it was for me in the predigital age.

In Scotland, when applying to school in the 1960s, we had to handwrite our applications. Once in medical school, I had to handwrite my exam papers, and marks were deducted for poor penmanship. By the time I was training as a psychoanalyst, candidates had to submit case summaries that we typed ourselves or paid someone to type them for us. Few of us had ventured into the world of personal computers, but by the late 1990s many of us had a Mac that looked like a little television, or perhaps an IBM laptop for those not averse to DOS, and modems for accessing the internet (very slow). Soon after that came email and search engines such as Google (very fast). Many of us were halting in our response to technology and felt bamboozled by the "unnerving promiscuity of digital information" (Nunberg, 2014). We feel unsure, rushed by the pace of response, and flummoxed much of the time. We try to catch up. We try to adapt but we are never completely natural, our language and our way of thinking always bearing the stamp of our education in the singularity mode of the predigital age. We are what Prensky (2001) calls "digital immigrants".

Now, as an analyst, I am a member of a professional organization, the International Psychoanalytical Association, in which the average age of members is 63.27 years. Most of us are therefore digital immigrants. A few of us do not use email. Some of us do not type. Most American analysts who are now over fifty used a manual typewriter to produce their graduation papers, or paid to have them typed. Contrast this with the mindset of younger analysts who grew up with technology, learning to use a computer in elementary school, and proceeding to communicate by text rather than email. Their peers in medicine are consulting to colleagues in other states and countries over videoconference; their peers in business attend meetings on videoconference with an interface so advanced that they feel they are on the opposite side of the desk with their associates although they are miles and time zones apart. This generation learned to use the computer in kindergarten; the next generation is being introduced to technology at birth, like the baby I described earlier, or even before birth, as sonograms now yield baby pictures that show the face, and electronic monitors record the frequency and intensity of contractions that the woman, having had a routine epidural, cannot see or feel.

What has technology done to the value of touch? The physician does not have to feel the abdomen to find the height of the fundus of the uterus any more than he needs to percuss the chest to detect fluid in the lung. As a medical student in the clinical years, I was trained to begin by shaking the hand of patients and looking them in the eye. I was taught that you could gather diagnostic information from that ordinary human contact, and at the same time reassure the patients of your willingness to connect and put them at the center of your attention. Then you engage in conversation to take the history of the symptoms, the medical, family, and social history, and begin to develop hypotheses. With a relationship established, you could then proceed to the physical examination: take the pulse at the wrist and measure the blood pressure; check for lymph nodes in the armpit; check the pulse in the neck and on the feet;

examine the head and neck before approaching the more vulnerable areas of chest, abdomen, and genitals. The point is to begin with social greeting, establish a relationship, extend that human connection at the physical level, and begin examination at the periphery and progress to the center. With the history and physical examination complete, you would then decide on any technology needed—such as basic blood chemistry specific to the tentative diagnosis, electrocardiogram, and X-ray—only if indicated. Based on those results, further tests might then be ordered. Nowadays when I go as a patient for an annual physical, the first thing that happens is that a nurse takes my blood pressure, plugs me into an electrocardiogram machine, and takes a blood sample for a general screening for abnormalities. Whereas, formerly, seeing the doctor might lead to the need for technology to complete diagnosis, now passing through the portal of technology leads me to the doctor. I do see my doctor in person, but in the summer of 2014 it was predicted that very soon one in six visits will be virtual (Deloitte, 2014).

It is not only in medicine that technology has taken away the pleasure of sensation in the actual hand, but also in every area that calls for reading and writing. Certainly, for the writer, there is the pleasure of touching fingertips to keyboard and seeing words spill across the screen; and for readers there is pleasure in tapping and swiping on a digital device, as they read a novel or tune in to the latest news (some of them choosing to get their news from social media rather than traditional news sources). But older writers are attached to paper. "The computer offers an illusion of freedom, but it is only when you print out and you have several hundred pages that you can say, well, these 50 pages go here, these 20 pages go there, and these 100 pages go into the round file under the desk. I love the tactile sense of the pages, and you can't quite do that with a computer" (Verghese, 2014). And older readers feel that they know where they are with a book in hand. They can mark their place.

And what effect does access to the Internet have on the storage of memories? Gone are the scrapbooks and photo albums of pasted-in printed snapshots. Albums are stored electronically on iPhone, iPad, and computer, or in professionally printed books and calendars made from personal photos sent to and stored on a website. Having lost access to files on floppy disc from years ago that my computer can no longer open, I became worried about the loss of shared memory. A young man assured me, "The data will be there for all time in the cloud, readily accessible from any hand-held device."

Internet as community

The Internet conquers the constraints of geography and cuts across class, race, and gender difference. It offers an antidote to isolation by facilitating the creation of multiple diverse communities across the globe. Social networking sites such as Facebook offer a potential space in which to catch up with old friends, maintain contact with family members, and interact with others who find or "like" you. Second Life offers more anonymity. Those who go there present many versions of themselves, as avatars to interact with other avatars. For some, Second Life may be a potential space for rehearsing social roles in a protected environment, an opportunity to relate without the constraints of psychological limitations, reduced finances, and unattractive physical endowment (Scharff, Chapter Four). For instance, the avatar of a man who is married in real life may marry in virtual reality an avatar that appears to be female but may be one of the avatars of a man. For some, it remains a playground. For others, it becomes a parallel universe of "inauthenticity, perversion, the avoidance of mourning, a mirage of the infinite imagination made material, and the substitution of autistic aloneness for community" (Freeman quoted in Stevens, 2014, p. 1106). Hartman described the internet as a space in which "all kinds of part-object relationships, perverse and otherwise, can rapidly be brought to life as activated introjects and then just as rapidly be relinquished or transformed" (Hartman paraphrased in Stevens, 2014, p. 1111). Strangely, on Second Life Freeman met a Lacanian analyst for these part-objects. The Lacanian complained that his avatar patients dropped their personas and brought in real details of their traumas. They had only been "pretending to pretend" (Freeman quoted in Stevens, 2014).

The internet as a space for community has been particularly useful for people who are non-conforming in society or who have had trouble finding people with whom to share their interests. Transgender, non-conforming people have found internet community a place to share and develop comfort in their identity (Pilecki, Chapter Five). As much as it provides information and support, the Internet can also be overwhelming. A questioning man said, "I was looking at a video on the Internet that asks: are you a cross dresser or a transgender variant? I don't know, I just don't know. How do people know what they want? For me one of the worst things is to discover on the Internet that there are so many possibilities."

The Internet provides a lifeline for those who are dislocated. Immigrants can find one another and communicate with their loved ones in the old country. Ahktar views email, fax, and Skype as "'electronic tethers' that reduce the separation anxiety and grief of the migrant" but he notes that they also "become 'new objects' … they stir up fantasies, evoke affects, and become targets of displacement and projection" (Ahktar, 2004, p. 201).

What role does the Internet play in the lives of those who cannot migrate? Traveling to teach analytic couple and family therapy in China for the last six years, I have seen the role of the Internet in a totalitarian society. All our students use digital devices and they access Baidu, the Chinese version of Google, and the microblogging site Weibo. Many of them are in teleanalysis and telepsychotherapy with a member of the China-America Psychoanalytic Alliance, never having met their analyst in person. They all complain about the Great Firewall that blocks access to Twitter, Facebook, and newspaper articles critical of the government and human rights abuses. So, many of them know how to get "over the wall", as they put it, for instance, by connecting to a service in Hong Kong, and they get their news from social media, not just newspapers.

New technology has stirred a fugitive political culture in China in which "things once secret are now known; people once alone are now connected" (Osnos, 2014, p. 5). Even with the controls in place, dissidents have been able to communicate more safely than if they were to gather in a public place to share their views. As one prominent Chinese activist wrote, "The Internet is like a magic engine, and it has helped my writing to erupt like a geyser" (Liu Xiaobo qouted in Osnos, p. 160). But others felt that the "Web provided only an illusion of openness, and a weak sense of community: that it strengthened authoritarian governments by creating a safety valve and defusing the pressure for deeper change" (Osnos, p. 160). Another downside to the ubiquity of the Internet—Liu's email records and online chats were monitored and that led to his arrest and conviction as a dissident.

There are pros and cons to the Internet. It seems to offer unlimited access to information, a stimulating international work environment, and a free play space with all manner of stimulation and entertainment. It is not a passive medium. It encourages active participation. It speeds up response and helps us to get lots done. But it raises doubts too. "What if the efficiency that we so worship, rather than paving the way for the actualization of passions, has become a tool for easy escapes, inviting less thinking, less confrontation with real pain and actual impediment?" (Nafisi, 2014, p. 288). There are healthy ways of using the Internet (to support a lively attitude of curiosity and sharing) and unhealthy ways (to shut out relationships and productivity). The non-problematic user is open about his online activity and shares information about his online life with his partner or friend; the problematic user hides what he is doing online and how much time he spends there. Drawing on the idea that mental health depends on and reflects integration of the intrapsychic and social aspects of life, Suler (2004) concluded, "Dissociating online and in-person living is associated with psychological problems. Integrating online and in-person living is associated with psychological health" (p. 361).

The impact of technology on therapy

The globalization of trade has meant that patients move from one location to another within a multinational corporation, and they travel internationally from those locations. This makes it extremely difficult for them to be in ongoing psychotherapy, and impossible to be in analysis four times a week. Technology provides a means of maintaining continuity of treatment for them (Lin, Chapter Nine) or of reaching people in disadvantaged areas and those who cannot spend hours in traffic in a big city (Setton, Chapter Fourteen). Analysts wishing to respect the traditional setting for psychoanalysis have resisted their patients' requests for teletherapy because of fear of the unknown or possible censure. They did not know the rules to follow (Vanderpool, Chapter Eight), nor how to take an ethical stance in the absence of guidelines (Wallwork, Chapter Seven), so accepted the limitation to which patients they could treat. Others have acquiesced, usually with trepidation, some then finding that it is possible to do good analytic work in a virtual setting.

It is time we admitted that, like Prensky's (2001) digital immigrant instructors "who speak an outdated language (that of the pre-digital age)" and "are struggling to teach a population that speaks an entirely new language" (p. 2), we analysts are struggling to adapt to the needs of D-gen patients. Prensky continues: "Digital Natives are used to receiving information really fast. They like to parallel process and multi-task. They prefer their graphics before their text rather than the opposite. They prefer random access (like hypertext). They function best when networked. They thrive on instant gratification and frequent rewards. They prefer games to 'serious' work" (p. 2). "They grew up on the 'twitch speed' of video games and MTV. They are used to the instantaneity of hypertext, downloaded music, phones in their pockets, a library on their laptops, beamed messages and instant messaging" (p. 2) whereas we proceed "slowly, step-by-step, one thing at a time, individually, and above all, seriously" (p. 3). We sat solo at a desk, not in a group at a Harkness table. We listened to instruction, looked at a blackboard, and then asked questions. We went to the library: it did not come to us. We did not grow up networked all our life. We did not grow up multitasking, connecting, living in a hive mentality. It is difficult for us to adapt our brains to the new way of thinking and relating (Hayles, 2012; Turkle, 2012). But adapt we must if psychoanalysis is to remain vibrant and relevant (Nicoli, Chapter Three; Abella, Chapter Six). We need to embrace technology that can extend psychoanalytic treatment and teaching (Wanlass, Chapter Ten; Scharff, D., Chapter Eleven).

Nevertheless, the use of technology in psychoanalytic psychotherapy and psychoanalysis is still a matter of controversy. I am referring to teleanalytic treatment in which the patient and analyst/therapist are not in the analyst's room, but meet by appointment in a private location in cyberspace. In this situation, the analyst works from the usual office, while the patient is responsible for creating a private setting in which to have the treatment session without interruption. This may be a consistent setting for the patient in ongoing teleanalysis (Lin, Chapter Nine; Varela, Chapter Eighteen), a temporary one for the patient in in-person analysis who alternates in-person and teleanalytic sessions (Setton, Chapter Fourteen), or an occasional one for the person who travels (Scharff, D., Chapter Thirteen). Opponents say that the setting for teleanalysis breaks the frame, ignores resistance, magically overcomes separation anxiety, and cannot possibly support analytic process. Proponents describe a new frame, just as firm, but adapted to the needs of the patient at a distance. They give examples of unconscious communication among internal objects, unconscious fantasy, transference and countertransference experienced in the analyst's body, and response to interpretation, so as to demonstrate that teleanalysis is as effective as in-person analysis (Scharff, 2012, 2013; Sehon, Chapter Seventeen). A more realistic position is that it works well for some patients and for some analysts but it does not suit everyone, any more than psychoanalysis is possible with every patient.

Telephone-based therapy

The practice of telephone-based therapy has a long history, beginning with its use in consultation and crisis intervention and extending into psychotherapy and psychoanalysis in private practice (Leffert, 2003; Lindon, 2000; Saul, 1951). With the advent of the Affordable Care Act, funds have been made available to support a huge growth in community-based telemedicine services using the telephone or videoconference. The Veterans Administration, Armed Forces Health Services, and Medicaid have been in the lead because, being federal programs, they avoid the problems of state regulations constraining service across a distance. To give just one example of a telephone-based treatment service, I might mention a properly researched, randomized controlled trial of short-term interpersonal psychotherapy for the treatment of postpartum depression (Dennis et al., 2012). Trained nurses under supervision provided interpersonal psychotherapy (I.P.T.) over the phone once a week for twelve weeks to 240 clinically depressed mothers across Canada. The mothers' convenience determined the time of the therapy appointment and, with that arrangement in place, compliance rates were greater than eighty-five percent. Statistics on the effectiveness are still in press but the mothers reported great benefit (Dennis, personal communication).

Psychoanalytic psychotherapy has been conducted on the telephone since the 1950s, reported on, and discussed at study groups and panels of the American Psychoanalytic Association (Stevens, 2014), and published separately in journals, and collected in books (Aronson, 2000; Scharff, 2013). Some therapists prefer the telephone to an online connection with web camera because they feel that not seeing, and being seen by, the patient is most similar to the way they work in person, privileging spoken language for communication, and drifting in a state of freely hovering attention, not looking at anything. Others, who rely on body language, prefer to work online with a web camera showing them the patient's movements. I let the patient choose the medium, and if the telephone is preferred, I find that as I listen in a state of reverie, the patient's words come to me and so does an image of the patient's face and body: I feel we are in the same interpersonal space even though we are miles apart (Scharff, 2013).

Text-based therapy

It is a far cry from teleanalysis and teletherapy to text-based therapy, consisting of email chat between patient and therapist. Yet Carlino (2011) predicted the development of chat-based therapy occurring during a regularly scheduled appointment time. Kächele and Buchholz (2013) studied a two-month-long short message stream between a therapist and patient during a crisis while both were out of town (Buchholz & Kächele, Chapter Twelve). Some patients tend to engage in text chat that is definitely not short, but the therapist's ability to read the voluminous material and construct a response is necessarily limited by schedule. The therapist decides how much he can take in, what to write in response, and when to write it, just as he has to dose and time his responses when listening in person. Text-based therapy services have now entered the equation. They advertise a subscription service online in which they offer their subscribers unlimited text-chat with licensed mental health professionals for $25–$40 per week. Having sampled such a service, Fruhlinger (2014) enthused, "the process was identical to what I had experienced in traditional treatment, except I had access to it any time I pulled out my iPhone". The advantage of text-based therapy is accessibility from any location on any hand-held device, no appointment schedule, reduced cost, open-ended ongoing communication, and response on a once-a-day basis.

In my view, the disadvantage of text-based therapy is that without regularly attended and anticipated sessions there is no structure to the process. Instead, treatment becomes an impulse driven by written expression, interrupted by a daily text response from a therapist. One of the claimed advantages, the encryption of messages to keep them private, may not be as secure as patients think, and these services do not claim HIPAA (Health Insurance Portability and Accountability Act) compliance. Another supposed advantage, the archiving of the sessions, could be a disadvantage if the whole session history can be accessed by hackers or curious family members who are able to guess at a password. Text-based therapy services claim greater privacy in that patients are not exposed to questions about where they are going and why they were absent. Patients never have to sit on a couch. I can see that highly mobile, constantly connected people (including therapists who prefer to be out of the office) really appreciate this innovation, but I doubt that they realize that they are subjecting their psyches to a solution-based, instant information cycle of input and response that avoids the slow pace of feeling and thinking in the presence of a trained therapist, leading to the eventual stillness of a deeply examined life. Anonymity of communication, accuracy and speed of response, and easy access become more important than an enduring therapeutic relationship that is itself the object of study and the fulcrum of personal change.

Skype analysis

Many patients who have to relocate, or who live in a remote area, ask for treatment on Skype. They are familiar with it, already use it with friends and family at a distance, and it is free. For the therapist, there is the same advantage of convenience and affordability. And there is the added benefit of seeing the patient's facial expressions and body movements, which counters the objection to teleanalysis on the grounds that the non-verbal communications of the patient are lost. Nevertheless, there are problems with both the audio and the video on Skype, because the connection is subject to dropped calls, junk on the line, and pixilation of the image. So, communicating on Skype is certainly not the same as communicating in person, but it offers a reasonably manageable experience for those who prefer it over a landline telephone. And the reaction to technical interferences connects to earlier experience that generates grist to the analytic mill.

It has been thought that computer-to-computer Skype is totally secure. But major concerns have arisen about the level of security that Skype offers. It is a consumer-grade platform, its encryption has not been independently tested, it cannot claim to be HIPAA complaint, and it is not a medical-grade platform. It is much safer for the therapist to sign a business agreement as an associate of a videotechnology services provider (VTC) that can claim to be HIPAA compliant, and to pay the yearly fee as a business expense (TeleMental Health Institute, 2015). The patient then is given an individual address in order to access the therapy session through a portal that is completely private, secure, and there is no recording or storage of data. In the unlikely event of a breach, say, by hackers getting through the company's advanced security system, the company will report the breach and appropriate steps can be taken. The extra step and the cost of signing up with VTC means that many therapists continue to use Skype, and some patients push them into it, disregarding the risk of intrusion to their privacy.

Opponents of teleanalysis are usually arguing against it without having tried it. They worry that virtual reality is no reality at all. But the transference/countertransference dialectic of the analytic relationship is itself a virtual reality, an "as if" construction of the infant at the breast and in the Oedipal triangle, fostering the expression of love, lust, and aggression in the pursuit of the other and the formation of the self. Indeed the analysis is destroyed if that virtual reality becomes real. "For example, do we move too quickly to defend the 'real' of interpersonal exchange as opposed to what is most often called the 'virtual' that occurs in technological exchange? And if we move too quickly to separate the interpersonal and the virtual might we also lose hold of the fantastic potential of psychic equivalence—the potential of psychic reality as it blends and bends material reality?" (Corbett, 2013).

Adapting our way of thinking to the style of the digital generation is hard, as is adapting our way of offering analysis to the reality of the changing needs and ways of communicating of patients in a rapidly changing culture. And it is particularly hard when the analytic establishment reacts by maintaining traditional standards, based not on assessment of clinical effectiveness but on the need to maintain consensus with regard to the quality of institutional power (Aryan & Carlino, 2013). So, analysts tend to hide what they are doing, to stay under the radar, to avoid attack from colleagues, in the name of ethics. "Any pace of change in the psychoanalytic world takes too long or it may even have to occur 'secretly' before unusual or unconventional methods of working become common knowledge and thus influence or are endorsed in our clinical practice" (Caparrotta & Lemma, 2014, p. 18).

I admit to being reluctant to embrace technology. I began teleanalysis because colleagues in another country requested it, first by phone, then by Skype, and now using a dedicated line from a videotechnology company. I found that even though the analysand's body is not in the same physical location as the analyst, daily communication of unverbalized feelings are, nevertheless, transmitted, whether on the phone or online. Whether in individual analysis or couple and family therapy, the frame gets attacked, resistance develops, interpretations occur, as they would in in-person analysis (Bakalar, Chapter Sixteen; Bagnini, Chapter Fifteen). The person going online for therapy may be projecting various false selves, as they would be when meeting in person. David Scharff (Chapter Thirteen) found that in the anonymity of the Internet session, where the analyst's reactions are not as immediate, the patient may feel freed to reveal more of his true self. In teletherapy or teleanalysis, an intimate relationship develops, and patient and therapist achieve deep unconscious communication. Whether meeting with an analyst in the same room or online, there is intimacy and there is distance. "The combination of these two elements, of intimacy and distance, conspires to create moments of immense frankness" (Nafisi, 2014, p. 127). In-person analysis and teleanalysis both use the paradoxical effect of intimacy and distance to therapeutic advantage. The boundary has to be set and accepted, so that the analytic process can unfold with confidence within the frame's ability to support it.

Rilke's words on marriage are apt for the functioning of the teleanalytic pair: "Once the realization is accepted that even between the closest human beings infinite distances continue to exist, a wonderful living side by side can grow up, if they succeed in loving the distance between them which makes it possible for each to see the other whole and against a wide sky" (Rilke, 1972, pp. 28–29). Analyst and analysand need to acknowledge, and to accept, that they live in different towns, countries, seasons, and time zones. They need to mourn the lost object of in-person analysis with all its untethered pleasures of welcome, sameness, reliability, and nuances of visible bodily communication. Then they can co-create something new, relevant to our times, something meaningful and therapeutic.

References

Ahktar, S. (2004). Editor's introduction. *International Journal of Applied Psychoanalytic Studies*, 1: 200–201.

Aronson, J. (Ed.). *Use of the Telephone in Psychotherapy*. Northvale, NJ: Jason Aronson.

Aryan, A., & Carlino, R. (2013). The power of the establishment in the face of change: psychoanalysis by telephone. In: *Psychoanalysis Online: Mental Health, Teletherapy and Training* (pp. 161–170). London: Karnac.

Caparrotta, L., & Lemma, A. (2014). Introduction. In: A. Lemma & L. Caparrotta (Eds.), *Psychoanalysis in the Technoculture Era* (pp. 1–21). Hove, Sussex: Routledge.

Carlino, R. (2011). *Distance Analysis* (translated from Spanish by James Nuss). London: Karnac.

Corbett, K. (2013). Shifting sexual cultures, the potential space of online relations, and the promise of psychoanalytic listening. *Journal of the American Psychoanalytic Association, 61*: 25–44.

Deloitte (2014). eVisits: the 20th century house call. http://www2.deloitte.com/content/dam/Deloitte/global/Documents/Technology-Media-Telecommunications/gx-tmt-2014prediction-evisits.pdf Accessed September 29, 2014.

Dennis, C. -L., Ravitz, P., Grigoriadis, S., Jovellanos, M., Hodnett, E., Ross, L., & Zupancic, J. (2012). The effect of telephone-based interpersonal psychotherapy for the treatment of postpartum depression: study protocol for a randomized controlled trial. *Trials, 13*: 38.

Fruhlinger, J. (2014). Textual healing. *Wall Street Journal*, October 18–19, p. D11.

Gabbard, G. O. (2001). Cyberpassion: E-rotic transference on the internet. *Psychoanalytic Quarterly, 70*: 719–737.

Gabbard, G. O. (2014). One analyst's journey through cyber-space. Contribution to Panel "Online and On the Couch Virtuality: The Real, the Imagined, and the Perverse" at Winter meeting of the American Psychoanalytic Association, January 18, 2014.

Hayles, N. K. (2012). *How We Think: Digital Media and Contemporary Technogenesis*. Chicago: University of Chicago Press.

Kächele, H., & Buchholz, M. B. (2013). Eine Notfall-SMS-Intervention bei chronischer Suizidalität— Wie die Konversationsanalyse klinische Beobachtungen bereichert. ZPPM Zeitschrift für Psychotraumatologie, Psychotherapiewissenschaft, *Psychologische Medizin, 11*: 49–61.

Leffert, M. (2003). Analysis and psychotherapy by telephone. *Journal of the American Psychoanalytic Association, 51*: 101–130.

Lemma, A. (2014). An order of pure decision; growing up in a virtual world and the adolescent's experience of the body. In: A. Lemma & L. Caparrotta (Eds.), *Psychoanalysis in the Technoculture Era*. Hove, Sussex: Routledge.

Lindon, J. (2000). Psychoanalysis by telephone. In: J. Aronson (Ed.), *Use of the Telephone in Psychotherapy* (pp. 3–13). Northvale, NJ: Jason Aronson.

Nafisi, A. (2014). *The Republic of Imagination*. New York: Viking Adult.

Nunberg, G. (2014). Linguist's commentary. *Fresh Air (NPR)*, 12–10–2014.

Osnos, E. (2014). *Age of Ambition: Chasing Fortune, Truth, and Faith in the New China*. New York: Farrar, Strauss & Giroux.

Prensky, M. (2001). Digital native, Digital immigrants. *On the Horizon, 9*: 1–6. Retrieved from http://www.marcprensky.com/writing/prensky%20%20digital%20natives%20immigrants%20-%20part1.pdf. Last accessed Dec 10, 2014.

Rilke, R. M. (1972). Rainer M. Rilke *Letters* 1892–1910 (translated by Jane Barnard Greene and M. D. Herten Norton). New York: Norton.

Saul, L. J. (1951). A note on the telephone as a technical aid. *Psychoanalytic Quarterly, 20*: 287–290.

Scharff, J. S. (2012). Clinical issues in analysis over the telephone and the internet. *International Journal of Psychoanalysis, 93*: 81–95.

Scharff, J. S. (2013). *Psychoanalysis Online: Mental Health, Teletherapy, and Training*. London: Karnac.

Shklovski, I., Scott, D., Mainwaring, S. D., Skúladóttir, H. H., & Borgthorsson, H. (2014). Leakiness and creepiness in app space: Perceptions of privacy and mobile app use. Retrieved from http//:www.scottmainzone.com/pubs/14-leakiness-creepiness.pdf. Last accessed Dec 10, 2015.

Stevens, D. (2014). Report of panel "Online and on the couch virtuality: The real, the imagined, and the perverse" featuring panelists Vera Camden (chair), Philip Freeman, Glen Gabbard, and Stephen Hartman. Winter meeting of the American Psychoanalytic Association, January 18, 2014.

Suler, J. (2004). Computer and cyberspace "addiction". *International Journal of Applied Psychoanalytic Studies*: 359–362.

TeleMental Health Institute. (2015). Video Teleconferencing Companies Claiming HIPAA Compliance. Retrieved: www.telehealth.org/video, January 10, 2015.

Turkle, S. (2012). *Alone Together: Why We Expect More from Technology and Less from Each Other*. New York: Basic Books.

Verghese, A. (2014). Interview. *Medscape One-on-One*, October 9, 2014. http://www.medscape.com/viewarticle/832853?src. Accessed December 10, 2014.

CHAPTER TWO

The impact of electronic media and communication on object relations

Becky Bailey

"Mommy, Mommy! Angela let her baby die!" the little girl wailed as she burst through the front door. "She didn't check on her or feed her, and in the morning she was dead!" This rather ominous announcement was fortunately not about the death of another human being, but rather about the death of a pet baby featured on a small electronic toy named a Tamagotchi. This miniature hand-held device in a variety of colors is popular for children as young as six. The game involves having to carefully monitor and tend a tiny electronic infant creature deposited on earth by aliens. The child must protect the abandoned pet infant by selecting foods for consumption, playing with the infant at regular intervals, and cleaning up the excrement, which is deposited conspicuously on the screen, complete with steam. The infant evolves differently depending on how well it is cared for. If the infant creature is not happy enough, it begins to get sick and must be given medicine and entertainment until it recovers. When angry, the little baby provides dangerous "gifts" such as snakes and fecal matter for the caregiver. The device is active 24/7, just like a real infant, and if not properly tended to, simply perishes, leaving only a halo behind.

No subtle signs about the raising of an infant are to be found in this game. No reading of facial and bodily cues, holding or rocking, reciprocal gaze interactions, odors, audible expressions of distress or delight, and unconscious to unconscious relating. Admittedly, the game captures the persistent need to hold the infant in mind and the unrelenting responsibility of performing rudimentary nurturing activities to ensure survival, which mirrors some aspect of the raising of a human child. But there is little affective attunement involved in the raising of this Tamagotchi infant, whose upbringing illustrates a schema that provides only an empty scaffolding of elements necessary for the development of a human being. The game places the infant in a context bereft of the intense, emotional interplay and rich complexity necessary for the raising of a psychologically adaptable human infant in a world now threatened by the vast, exploding electronic universe.

In this chapter, I want to raise the alarm about our electronic milieu, not only in terms of its immediate effects on the mental health of children and the parents who raise them, but also in its potential to affect physical fitness, life expectancy, brain function, mood, and attachment, to increase vulnerability to addiction, and to collapse the space for personal interaction and creativity. In short, it can alter the quality of family life and have a profound influence on the object relations set of the personality.

The ubiquitous use of electronic media

Proponents of technology might argue that little disaster has befallen the human race following the developments in technology and in social media during the last fifty years. As mental health professionals, we need to become aware of the scope of electronic media and of the current research on its influences on the human mind, in order to identify the potential effects on relationships, especially those in the formative years. The introduction of access to information and entertainment on a screen delivered into our homes began when black and white television, invented in the 1920s, became affordable for American households in the 1950s. Then, on September 2, 1969, scientists connected two computers with a fifteen-foot cable so that the machines could communicate with each other, and the Internet was created. This means of communication became accessible to all when the first consumer computers were introduced in 1974. The advance of new technology then produced the cellphone (1983), texting (1995) when Sprint began providing mobile to mobile service, Facebook (2004), Twitter (2006), and the iPad (2010) (all dates from Wikipedia).

Here are the questions I want to raise: Can we really know, after one generation or less, about the widespread effect of technology on our brains and our interpersonal functioning? How are we changing our social attunement, our capacity to connect, create, and love when we spend increasing numbers of hours intimately attached to our devices? What is being missed when we are all gazing down at the image in our hand-held device or are glued to the computer screen? What is happening to unconscious to unconscious communication? How is the diversion of our gaze going to alter affect regulation? Could it change our ability to manage loss, separateness, and disconnection? Will we retain a capacity to self-soothe without attachment to a device? Will we be hurt by the erosion of our privacy and personal boundaries? How will we cope with the alteration in our fantasy life as technology becomes a pervasive part of our object world?

The rapid widespread adoption of media technology in a few short years is stunning. In 2009, seventy-eight percent of the world's households owned at least one television set and television broadcasting became digital (Wikipedia). No longer a device with a few channels received by an antenna, a television set, fed by cable or satellite dish, now allows for viewing hundreds of channels, recording for later replay, and streaming the internet. According to the Census Bureau (2012), seventy four point eight per cent of Americans own a home computer, and ninety four point eight per cent use it to connect to the Internet. Of the ninety-one percent of adults who own a cellphone, fifty-six percent have a smart phone, which allows for immediate connection to the Internet and seventy-eight percent of teenagers carry some sort of mobile phone (Pew Research, 2013). Phones are rarely being employed for their original purpose—a tool to converse with others—but are being used to connect to the Internet and for texting. Pew Research (2012) reports that teens are sending an average of sixty text messages per day, and that only thirty-nine percent of them make phone calls daily and only thirty-five percent of them communicate face-to-face. In a short period of time, interpersonal communication has changed from oral to written and is composed of short segments of words, with the rare scattering of an emoticon or hashtag, conveying a limited, two-dimensional expression of affect.

Use of electronic media in very young children is no exception. The Tamagotchi is only one of many electronic toys that alter interpersonal contact with others. In 2006, ninety percent of parents said that their children younger than two years of age used some form of electronic media (Rosin, 2013) despite ongoing advice from the American Academy of Pediatrics (2011) which discourages media use in young children and cautions that children require contingent interactions with parents and other adults. The use of technology by children has exploded, with an estimated two-thirds of children ages four to seven having used an iPhone (Joan Ganz Cooney Center, 2010). More than 40,000 games are available on iTunes alone, with thousands more on Google Play, all targeted specifically at children (Rosin, 2013).

The amount of time that people spend engaged with technology is astounding. In the eight to eighteen-year-old bracket, children spend an average of seven hours and thirty-eight minutes using various forms of entertainment media during a typical day, which amounts to more than fifty-three hours a week, more than a full-time job for an adult. Cell phone users between the ages of eighteen and twenty-four exchange an average of 109.5 text messages per day, which results in more than 3,200 texts per month. The average number of hours Americans ages thirteen to sixty-four spent watching television in 2012 was five hours and five minutes per day, in addition to three hours and seven minutes spent on the Internet and another forty-eight minutes on videogames (Kaiser Family Foundation, 2010; Gfk and Interactive Advertising Bureau, 2013). Another study notes that three-fourths of married parents report spending all or most of their non-work time with their children (Rainie & Wellman, 2012). Putting that finding together with the entertainment media statistics reported above, we have to conclude that when parents are spending time with their children, they are engaged in the use of technology in one form or another. This shared preference for interacting with a screen alters the landscape of parents' and children's interactions with one another in a number of important dimensions, especially with respect to gaze and nonverbal communication. Some might argue that time spent on electronic media is not necessarily in lieu of time spent with one another, but in light of the studies I have cited, we have to acknowledge that the quality of human interaction is changing.

Media effects

In the past, parents spent time with children engaged in housework—a calm, ordinary experience. Although when parents are engaged in housework they might be somewhat preoccupied with their chores, they can be interrupted. Parents who are surfing the Internet or sending texts are far more inaccessible to the child. There is something enthralling, captivating, and preoccupying about entering the online environment and the digital universe.

The title of Nicholas Carr's (2011) comprehensive book summarizing research on the effects of the Internet—*The Shallows: What the Internet is Doing to Our Brains*—warns us as to what is happening. Carr captures the conditioning aspects of engaging with various forms of electronic media in a chapter aptly entitled "The juggler's brain." He states that the Internet

> provides a high-speed system for delivering responses and rewards ... which encourage the repetition of both physical and mental actions. When we click a link, we get something new to look at and evaluate, a keyword, we receive, in the blink of an eye, a list of interesting information to appraise. When we send a text or an instant message or an email, we often get a reply in a matter of seconds or minutes. When we use Facebook, we attract new friends or form closer bonds with old ones. When we send a tweet through Twitter, we gain new followers .... The Net's interactivity gives us powerful new tools for finding information, expressing ourselves, and conversing with others. It also turns us into lab rats constantly pressing levers to get tiny pellets of social or intellectual nourishment .... (p. 117)

In addition to describing the highly addictive nature of the positive reinforcement inherent in using the Internet and social media, Carr remarks crucially that:

> When we are on line we're often oblivious to everything else. The real world recedes as we process the flood of symbols and stimuli coming from our devices .... The Net seizes our attention only to scatter it .... The Net encourages constant distractedness, rather than allowing our mind long enough for a break to think deeply about a problem. (p. 118)

Consider the implications of this description. Getting immediate responses to pressing buttons on our electronic devices shapes us to be impatient and intolerant of space between interactions. This reduces our ability to delay and strikes at the heart of our capacity to reflect on experience. Interpersonal object seeking is exchanged for electronic object seeking.

Carr goes on to describe work by Dijksterhuis (2004), who studied the unconscious in a series of experiments that showed that unconscious thought not only improved the quality of complex decisions, but led to more integrated representations in memory. In a later study, Dijksterhuis found that "unconscious thought is an active thought process" and that people who are asked to think further about a problem made more integrated decisions than those who were merely distracted by looking at numbers on a computer screen (Bos, Dijksterhuis, & Baaren, 2008, p. 586). This study raises the question as to whether the rapid barrage of information flowing from the Internet and our electronic devices disrupts our deep reflective capacity, which is central to affective processing and psychological growth.

Repeatedly, researchers present evidence that shows that technology not only interrupts the unconscious flow of associations through demanding attention to bursts of busy, electronic detail, but also directly alters the cerebral activation of our brains. Carr discusses the work of Gary Small (Small & Vorgan, 2008) who discovered that Internet search tools "simulate brain cell alteration and neurotransmitter release, gradually strengthening new neural pathways in our brains while weakening old ones" (Small & Vorgan, 2008, p. 1). Small speculates that the brains of those children raised in the new electronic age will function differently from the brains of those from earlier generations. He was able to show that within five days, Internet-naive subjects began to demonstrate the same neural activation patterns in their prefrontal cortex as people who used the Internet regularly. He suggested that a very different form of brain activity occurs when people search the Internet instead of reading a book. Surfing the Internet seems to activate prefrontal regions associated with problem-solving whereas reading books stimulates the areas for language, memory, and visual processing. It appears that the brains of people surfing the Internet are overstimulated (Small, Moody, Siddarth, & Bookheimer, 2009). Carr (2011) points out that "by allowing us to filter out distractions, to quiet the problem solving functions of the frontal lobes, deep reading becomes a form of deep thinking. The mind of the experienced book reader is a calm mind, not a busy one" (p. 123). He goes on to say that when we use the Internet, "our ability to make the rich mental connections that form when we read deeply and without distraction remains largely disengaged" (p. 122).

In addition to our mental capacity for deep thinking being lost by not reading books, those of us who spend many hours every day on digital devices are, obviously, more sedentary. We spend less time interacting with green space. Leisure time spent outdoors contemplating nature improves cognition. A psychologist examined test performance on a rigorous cognitive measure before and after having subjects walk in either a tree-lined park or a downtown street. He discovered that those in the group that spent time in the park significantly improved their test performance, but those who walked in the city did not. Furthermore, simply looking at pictures of nature had similarly restorative benefits. Brief interactions with nature improved both directed attention and cognitive control (Berman, Jonies, & Kaplan, 2008).

Another study compared the effects of exercising outdoors in a woodland area to exercising indoors in a shopping center. The outdoor exercise statistically improved self-esteem, energy, and mood, and reduced anger, confusion, depression, and tension (Peacock, Hine, & Pretty, 2007). Additional research demonstrates that children function better cognitively and emotionally in environments with vegetation (Taylor, Kuo, & Sullivan, 2001; Wells, 2000) and they have better self-esteem, social relationships, and school functioning (Crisp & Hinch, 2004). The restorative influence of nature appears to be mediated by the components of "fascination," "being away" [immersion], "extent" [scope of the experience], and "compatibility" [of the experience with wishes and desires] (Kaplan, 1995, p. 173). A group of naive hikers, who spent four days in the wild with no access to technology, improved their performance on a task of creativity and problem solving by a full fifty percent (Atchley, Strayer, & Atchley, 2012). The authors conclude that

> our results demonstrate that there is a cognitive advantage to be realized if we spend time immersed in a natural setting. We anticipate that this advantage comes from an increase in exposure to natural stimuli that are both emotionally positive and low-arousing and a corresponding decrease in exposure to attention demanding technology, which regularly requires that we attend to sudden events, switch amongst tasks, maintain task goals, and inhibit irrelevant actions or cognitions. (Atchley, Strayer, & Atchley, 2012, p. 1)

Mental illnesses are becoming more common in young people and at younger ages (Raphael & Martinek, 1996; Roszak, 1995). Disconnection from the natural world is believed to be one of the factors responsible for this decline in mental health in young people.

The interaction of physical and mental well-being

Since ancient times we have known of the overlap of physical and mental well-being. Any discussion of the effects of technology would be incomplete without mention of this convergence. A WHO/World Bank report has predicted that cardiovascular disease and poor mental health are likely to be the two largest causes of disease by the year 2020 (Murray & Lopez, 1996). These causes should not be considered mutually exclusive given the effects of inactivity on mood and cognition. Use of electronic media increases *sitting disease*, a leading risk factor for heart disease and metabolic syndrome (Edwardson et al., 2012). Heart disease risks doubled in those who sat for at least five hours a day (Young et al., 2014). In fact, sitting for more than three hours per day can reduce life expectancy from all causes of death by two years, even in people who exercise regularly. Another 1.4 years can be shaved from the life expectancy of those who watch television for more than two hours per day (Katzmarzyk & Lee, 2012). Regular cardiovascular exercise is one of the few preventative measures for dementia, a powerful threat to mental health in the aging population (Elwood et al., 2013). The inactivity, together with the effects on cognition and related mood associated with seven and a half hours of technology use per day, is beginning to take a staggering toll on physical and mental health.

Potential effects on infant development

Having established the widespread use of technology and having discussed the potential effects on psychological health, brain function, and cognition, I want to shift to my concern about its effects on early emotional development. I connect the effects on a child of a parent gazing at a screen to the effects of the lack of gaze interaction between mother and baby as shown in the still face experiment, developed by Edward Tronick in 1975. In this experiment, a lively, engaged mother is asked to hold her face still for a couple of minutes. She turns her expressionless face to her baby. The infant quickly tries to re-engage her, gesturing, smiling, and then increasingly becoming more frustrated and frantic, looking away, turning away, slumping, and finally crying. Tronick has found that this experience can be remembered for as long as two weeks, and when repeated, rapidly produces physiological changes in the infant not produced under the first exposure (Tronick, Adamson, Als, & Brazelton, 1975). The experiment shows that even very young babies are able to read their mothers and use them for reciprocal interaction to regulate their own emotions and behavior, and that without this possibility, they suffer.

A still face looks like that of a depressed mother, and infants of depressed mothers show decreased responsiveness to faces and voices even in the first month of life. In addition, mothers' depression seems to affect the prenatal development of their children (Murray & Cooper, 1997). Infants of depressed mothers showed less orienting to a live face/voice stimulus and were less alert. They scored lower on cuddliness and hand to mouth activity. The authors conclude that newborns of depressed mothers are more aroused, less calm, and less attentive, and their mothers demonstrate less empathy (Field, Diego, & Hernandez-Reif, 2009). Infants of depressed mothers suffer a number of consequences, including emotional dysregulation, insecure attachment, aggression, non-compliance, attention deficits, poor self-esteem, poor peer relations, and depressed mood. These children develop a "working model" of their mother as "insensitive, unresponsive, and even harsh and abusive" (Gelfand & Teti, 1990, p. 342).

How different, then, is the still face of the disengaged or depressed mother from the mother who is engaged compulsively with her cell phone? How does the mother's absorption in electronic media interfere with the visual, auditory, tactile, olfactory, and motor interactions necessary for the developing infant?

Hofer (1996) studied how the physiological aspects of caretaking (sensorimotor, thermal, and nutrient-based events) have long-term consequences for the developing infant, contributing not only to an ability to learn, but providing a direct role in regulating the susceptibility to disease later in life. The two- to three-month-old infant is already focusing on the face and voice of the mother in a contingent response pattern (listen and reply) and becomes visibly perturbed if the listen and reply sequence becomes unsynchronized (Trevarthen & Aitken, 2001). During this *protoconversation* mothers and infants are "looking at and listening to each other ... mutually regulating one another's interests and feelings in intricate, rhythmic patterns, exchanging multimodal signals and imitations of vocal, facial and gestural expression" (Trevarthen & Aitken, 2001, p. 5). Visual contact with the mother is central for infant attachment (Bowlby, 1982), and touch is important in communicating distinct emotions. We can actually decode whether tactile stimulation conveys anger, fear, disgust, love, gratitude, or sympathy (Hertenstein, Keltner, App, Bulleit, & Jaskolka, 2006a; Hertenstein, Verkamp, Kerestes, & Holmes, 2006b). Furthermore, the development of empathy is related to neurophysiological processes, including, but not limited to, visual affective stimuli (Brothers, 1989). During all of these exchanges the infant is communicating its inner state to the mother in a rich, rapid verbal/nonverbal interplay that I believe to be highly vulnerable to the distraction and preoccupation produced by electronic media.

During the first six months of life "as mother and infant match each other's temporal and affective patterns, each recreates in himself a psychophysiological state similar to that of the partner, thus participating in the subjective state of the other" (Beebe & Lachmann, 1988, pp. 321–322). The infant–mother dyad mutually regulates affect intensity through gaze, facial expression, head position, and vocalization. Matching is a way of accessing the subjective state of the other, which provides a foundation for feeling known and understood. This research involves the film microanalysis of mother–infant interactions where affect is communicated in fleeting, subtle responses not visible to the "naked eye" (Beebe & Lachmann, 1988, p. 317).

These highly nuanced, affect laden interchanges between baby and mother promote the growth of brain circuits involved in high intensity affect regulation (Schore, 1994; Stern, 1985). A critical period between six months to one year occurs for the wiring of the prefrontal cortex, a part of the brain involved in regulating affect. For adequate development of dopaminergic axon terminals during this period the "infant must engage in mutually responsive face to face, gaze, vocalization, and smiling interactions with the caretaker" (Pally, 1997, p. 590). The mother's oxytocin response, a hormone involved in lactation and bonding, is directly related to the amount of time that the mother's gaze is directed toward her infant (Kim, Fonagy, Koos, Dorsett, & Strathearn, 2013). Mothers who demonstrated a lack of response to their infant's distress also produced less oxytocin. The authors note that mothers of infants who "develop profoundly insecure attachment at 12 months were characterized not by their global failure of attunement, but rather by a remarkably specific failure to attend to their infant's distress" (Kim, Fonagy, Koos, Dorsett, & Strathearn, 2013, p. 6).

Verbal and nonverbal interaction in conjunction with various sensorimotor modalities (tactile, olfactory, visual) are critical variables for the development of the infant's brain, affect regulation, sense of self, object relations, and capacity for relating as an adult sexual being. The visual distraction of the electronic world reduces vital, scarcely discernible interchanges, causing the baby to react to the unresponsive, distracted mother as if she were depressed and, at the very least, misattuned. Reduced interchange time due to technological preoccupation affects the number of opportunities for the infant to feel deeply understood. In our increasingly technology-driven world, alteration in the mother's capacity for unconscious to unconscious responding leads to emotional difficulty in the infant and the child.

Vulnerability to addiction

We must also consider the developing brain's vulnerability to addiction in some young children who have widespread and largely unregulated access to the Internet. Rapidly appearing, brightly colored, surprising, and erotic and perverse images provide readily available, virtually free "substances" for addiction. The widespread exposure to sexual and pornographic images primes the vulnerable child for the development of compulsive behavior. We see the same destructive pattern of events unfolding from media addiction as we have done over the course of our longer experience with addiction to substances.

Natural rewards to the brain such as food and sex provide pleasure by stimulating dopamine release (Di Chiari et al., 1999)—and so do interactions with electronic media. For example, a study of videogamers revealed that dopamine was released when participants played a game (Koepp et al., 1998). Even more concerning is that dopamine is more likely to be released when the use of rewards is variable or random, such as in gaming, when people get a "like" for something they have posted on Facebook, or when they receive unexpected email or messages (Henn, 2014). Variable reward systems are the most powerful for eliciting compulsive responding. Dopamine D2 receptors in the brain decrease over time in drug abuse, requiring more and more of the drug for the same pleasurable effect (Volkow et al., 2010; Koob & Volkow, 2010). Not surprisingly, men addicted to the Internet were shown to have decreased dopamine D2 receptor availability in the subdivisions of the striatum including the bilateral dorsal caudate and right putamen (Kim et al., 2011).

Fantasy/phantasy

A final consideration in a dense matrix of influences that electronic media has on the developing infant involves fantasy/phantasy regulation and the integration of good and bad objects. Donald Winnicott (1945) describes the process by which the infant moves from phantasy to reality on the basis of micro-interactions with the parent during which the baby has a need, receives satisfaction, and develops a fantasy about the satisfactory fulfillment of that need that he keeps with him. If that need is left unsatisfied, the child feels the parent to be persecutory, and the child is left alone to deal with the distorted reality and contend with his/her bad objects. Winnicott states,

> the infant comes to the breast when excited and ready to hallucinate something fit to be attacked. At that moment the actual nipple appears and he is able to feel it was that nipple that he hallucinated. So his ideas are enriched by actual details of sight, feel, smell, and next time this material is used in the hallucination. In this way he starts to build up a capacity to conjure up *what is actually available*. (Winnicott, 1945 p. 140, italics added)

The experience of sameness, ordinariness, and expectability, built up over numerous interactions with the mother, is a necessary element of the process of building fantasy based on tangible reality. Exposed to a world of internet fantasy, where the reality of the other cannot be ascertained through tangible means, the child runs the risk of having an altered view of the other and of the self. Fantasy is left unregulated by in person interaction.

The collapse of space

In the current social environment, we have immersed our infants and children in a complex web of media, sometimes referred to as "digital babysitting." Instead of turning to fantasy or to one another for comfort and soothing, children are turning to electronic devices. A play date is increasingly spent in parallel play around a screen or screens, with young children involved in games on digital devices and older children engaged in movies, YouTube, or Facebook. Sometimes they use multiple devices simultaneously. When teens interact, it is often through text messaging, and actual conversations are thought to be unnecessary. It is not unusual to see a group of teens sitting together looking at their phones, sometimes texting to others who are across from them in the same room. Socially awkward moments can be addressed by seeking solace with a cell phone. On social media sites, where people not uncommonly have hundreds of friends with access to intimate information about them, the boundaries between self and other are eroded. Furthermore, the available information is unreliable and may be totally falsified, such as when a pedophile poses as a teenager. Inherent in these "Facebook friendships" is the illusion of connection or closeness to people who are scarcely known or knowable. Filling every moment with a digital interaction deprives us of the sanctuary of our own minds and those of others, and robs us of the pleasure of getting to know them as real human beings rather than fantasy constructions. In psychoanalysis we have learned that it is the authentic relationship that matters to recovery, and that the silences, the pauses, and the spaces are as important as the interpretations for facilitating reflection, depth, linking, and understanding.

What we know

Due to the relatively recent and rapid global proliferation of technology and electronic media of unlimited variety, researchers have not yet had time to conduct longitudinal studies on the effects of this immersion in electronic media across a human lifespan. We do have some information about the short-term effects, but even these studies are only at their beginning. Nevertheless, we can usefully extrapolate from data that is available on the effects of television, Internet, and videogames, since these have been around for a more extended period.

When television was spreading through North America, homicide rates from 1957 to 1971 doubled (Anderson & Gentile, 2008). When television was introduced to South Africa in 1974, there was a one hundred thirty per cent increase in homicides between 1974 and 1991, a similar fourteen-year period (Centerwall, 1992). The amount of violent videogame viewing time predicts the rate of aggression and severe violence in children and adolescents (Anderson, Gentile, & Buckley, 2007; Gentile & Gentile, 2008). Adolescents who often viewed sexual content on television were more likely to initiate sexual behavior, including intercourse (Collins et al., 2004). Mildly increased exposure to television and videogames at nine months and two years of age is associated with early childhood self-regulation problems (Radesky, Silverstein, Zuckerman, & Christakis, 2014).

In addition, research shows that the use of electronic media affects mood. People who spend a large amount of time surfing the Internet have higher rates of depression (Belanger, Akre, Berchtold, & Michaud, 2011; Lam & Peng, 2010; Morrison & Gore, 2010). Compulsive internet use leads to higher levels of anxiety and poor well-being (Mazer & Ledbetter, 2012). Heavy use in teenagers, defined only as more than two hours per day, was associated with an increase in depression in thirty-three percent of males and eighty-six percent of females (Belanger, Akre, Berchtold, & Michaud, 2011). A study of Facebook users shows that two key components of well-being—how people feel moment to moment and how satisfied they are with their lives— are undermined rather than enhanced by Facebook use (Kross et al., 2013). In persons classified as web addicts, multiple structural changes in the brain have been identified. They have been found to have a decreased volume of gray matter in the bilateral dorsolateral prefrontal cortex, the supplementary motor area, the orbitofrontal cortex, the cerebellum, and the left rostral anterior cingulate cortex (Yuan, Qin, Wang, Zeng, & Zhao, 2011).

What we need to know

My purpose in this chapter has been to highlight and present evidence for some of the potential effects of technology, especially electronic media, on the development of infants and children and to discuss the implications these encounters may have for object relations. Although I am aware that there are some constructive effects from an interconnected world, with rapid access to information and social networks, I am concerned here with the effects on early development. There are risks to the infant of the preoccupied mother distracted by her electronic device. There are consequences to the very young having widespread access to electronic devices, which reduces the opportunity for rich multisensory, interpersonal interactions between the child and parent. Increasingly, electronic media are being used as substitutes to regulate affect, manage loss through constant connection, provide self-soothing through immediate connection to keystrokes, and create an alternative universe through social networks. All this minute to minute technological activity reduces our reflective capacity for deep thought, diminishes our interpersonal interaction, and alters our fantasy lives and our inner object world. The costs of our electronic immersion are as yet unknown. In the meantime, while we live with the ramifications of electronic media, let us not be Tamagotchi parents, who substitute a false technical world for the intricacies of human interaction.

References

American Academy of Pediatrics (2011). http://www.aap.org/en-us/advocacy-and-policy/aap-health-initiatives/Pages/Media-and-Children.aspx

Anderson, C., & Gentile, D. (2008). Media, Violence, aggression, and public policy. In: E. Borgida & S. Fiske (Eds), *Beyond Common Sense: Psychological Science in the Courtroom*. Malden, MA: Blackwell.

Anderson, C. A., Gentile, D. A., & Buckley, K. E. (2007). *Violent Video Game Effects on Children and Adolescents: Theory, Research and Public Policy*. New York: Oxford University Press.

Atchley, R., Strayer, D., & Atchely, P. (2012). Creativity in the wild: Improving creative reasoning through immersion in natural settings. *Public Library of Science, (7)* 12.

Beebe, B., & Lachmann, F. M. (1988). The contributions of mother–infant mutual influence to the origins of self and object representations. *Psychoanalytic Psychology, 5*: 305–337.

Belanger, R., Akre, C., Berchtold, A, & Michaud, P. (2011). A U-shaped association between intensity of Internet use and adolescent health. *Pediatrics, 127*: 330–335.

Berman, M., Jonides, J., & Kaplan, S. (2008). The cognitive benefits of interacting with Nature. *Psychological Science, 19*: 1207–1212.

Bos, M., Dijksterhuis, A., & van Baaren, R. (2008). On the goal-dependency of unconscious thought. *Journal of Experimental Social Psychology, 44*: 1114–1120.

Bowlby, J. (1982). *Attachment:* (Second Edition). New York: Basic Books.

Brothers, L. (1989). A biological perspective on empathy. *American Journal of Psychiatry, 146*: 10–19.

Carr, N. (2011). *The Shallows: What the Internet is Doing to Our Brains*. New York: W. W. Norton.

Census Bureau (1984–2012). http://www.census.gov/hhes/computer/files/2012/Computer_Use_Infographic_FINAL.pdf.

Centerwall, B. (1992). Television and violence: The scale of the problem and where to go from here. *Journal of the American Medical Association, 267*: 3059–3063.

Collins, R., Elliott, M., Berry, S., Kanouse, D., Kunkel, D., Hunter, S., & Miu, A. (2004). Watching sex on television predicts adolescent initiation of sexual behavior. *Pediatrics, 114*: 280–289.

Crisp, S., & Hinch, C. (2004). *Treatment Effectiveness of Wilderness Adventure Therapy*. Melbourne: Neo Publications.

Di Chiara, G., Tanda, G., Bassareo, V., Pontieri, F., Acquas, E., Fenu, S., & Carboni, E. (1999). Drug addiction as a disorder of associative learning: role of nucleus accumbens shell/extended amygdala dopamine. *Annals of the New York Academy of Sciences, 877*: 461–485.

Dijksterhuis, A. (2004). Think different: The merits of unconscious thought in preference development and decision making. *Journal of Personality and Social Psychology, 87*: 586–598.

Edwardson, C., Gorely, T., Davies, M., Gray, L., Khunti, K., Wilmot, E., Yates, T., & Biddle, S. (2012). Association of sedentary behavior with metabolic syndrome: a meta-analysis. *PLoS ONE, 7*: e34916.

Elwood, P., Galante, J., Pickering, J., Palmer, S., Bayer, A., Ben-Shlomo, Y., Longley, M., & Gallacher, J. (2013). Healthy lifestyles reduce the incidence of chronic diseases and dementia: Evidence from the Caterphilly cohort study. *PLoS ONE, 8*: e81877.

Field, T., Diego, M., & Hernandez-Reif, M. (2009). Infants of depressed mothers are less responsive to faces and voices: A review. *Infant Behavioral Development, 32*: 239–244.

Gelfand, D., & Teti, D. (1990). The effects of maternal depression on children. *Clinical Psychology Review, 10*: 329–353.

Gentile, D.A., & Gentile, J. R. (2008). Violent video games as exemplary teachers: A conceptual analysis. *Journal of Youth and Adolescence, 9*: 127–141.

GfK and Interactive Advertising Bureau. (2013). Social, digital video drive further growth in time spent online. http://www.emarketer.com/Article/Social-Digital-Video-Drive-Further-Growth-Time-Spent-Online/1009872#uhlFMwwuUkd1IRe7.99.

Henn, S. (2014). Online marketers take note of brains wired for rewards. *NPR: All Tech Considered. Tech, Culture and Connection.* July 24, 2014.

Hertenstein, M., Keltner, D., App, B., Bulleit, B., & Jaskolka, A. (2006a). Touch communicates distinct emotions. *Emotion, 6*: 528–533.

Hertenstein, M., Verkamp, J., Kerestes, A., & Holmes, R. (2006b). The communicative functions of touch in humans, nonhumans, primates and rats: A review and syntheses of the empirical research. *Genetic, Social, and General Psychology Monographs, 132*: 5–94.

Hofer, M. (1996). On the nature and consequences of early loss. *Psychosomatic Medicine, 58*: 570–581.

Joan Ganz Cooney Center (November 10, 2010). Parents pass-back mobile devices to children but are skeptical of educational benefits. http://www.joanganzcooneycenter.org/press/parents-pass-back-mobile-devices-to-children-but-are-skeptical-of-educational-benefits/

Kaiser Family Foundation (2010). Daily media use among children and teens up dramatically from five years ago. http://kff.org/disparities-policy/press-release/daily-media-use-among-children-and-teens-up-dramatically-from-five-years-ago/

Kaplan, S. (1995). The restorative benefits of nature: Toward an integrative framework. *Journal of Environmental Psychology, 15*: 169–182.

Katzmarzyk, P., & Lee, M. (2012). Sedentary behavior and life expectancy in the USA: a cause-deleted life table analysis. *British Medical Journal, Open; 2*: e000828.

Kim, S., Fonagy, P., Koos, O., Dorsett, K., & Strathearn, L. (2013). Maternal oxytocin response predicts mother to infant gaze. *Brain Resarch,* http://dx.doi.org/10.1016/j.brainres.2013.10.050.

Kim, S., Baik, S., Park, C., Kim, S., Choi, S., & Kim, S. (2011). Reduced striatal dopamine D2 receptors in people with internet addiction. *Neuroreport: Motivation, Emotion, Feeding, Drinking, 22*: 407–411.

Koepp, M., Gunn, R., Lawrence, V., Cunningham, V., Dagher, A., Jones, T., Brooks, D., Bench, C., & Grasby, P. (1998). Evidence for striatal dopamine release during a video game. *Nature, 393*: 266–268.

Koob, G. F., & Volkow, N. D. (2010). Neurocircuitry of addiction. *Neuropsychopharmacology, 35*: 217–238.

Kross, E., Verduyn, P., Demiralp, E., Park, J., Lee, D., Lin, N., Shablack, H., Jonides, J., & Ybarra, O. (2013). Facebook use predicts declines in subjective well-being in young adults. *PLoS ONE, 8*: e69841.

Lam, L., & Peng, Z. (2010). Effect of pathological use of the internet on adolescent mental health: a prospective study. *Archives of Pediatric and Adolescent Medicine, 164*: 901–906.

Mazer, J., & Ledbetter, A. (2012). Online communication attitudes as predictors of problematic Internet use and well-being outcomes. *Southern Communication Journal, 77*: 403.

Morrison, C., & Gore, H. (2010). The relationship between excessive Internet use and depression: A questionnaire-based study of 1,319 young people and adults. *Psychopathology, 43*: 121–126.

Murray, C., & Lopez, A. (1996). *The Global Burden of Disease: a comprehensive assessment of mortality and disability from diseases, injuries and risk factors in 1990 and projected to 2020.* Cambridge, MA: Harvard School of Public Health (Global Burden of Disease and Injury Series, Vol. I).

Murray, L., & Cooper, P. (1997). Effects of postnatal depression on infant development. *Archives of Disease in Childhood, 7*: 99–101.

Pally, R. (1997). I: How brain development is shaped by genetic and environmental factors: Developments in related fields Neuroscience. *International Journal of Psychoanalysis, 78*: 587–593.

Peacock, J., Hine, R., & Pretty, J. (2007). Got the blues, then find some Greenspace: The mental health benefits of green exercise activities and green care. University of Essex report or Mind week. www.psykinfo.regionsyddanmark.dk/dwn1

Pew Research Center (2013). http://www.pewresearch.org/fact-tank/2013/06/06/cell-phone-ownership-hits-91-of-adults

Pew Research Internet Project (2012). http://www.pewinternet.org/2012/03/19/teens-smartphones-texting/

Radesky, J., Silverstein, M., Zuckerman, B., & Christakis, D. (2014). Infant self-regulation and early childhood media exposure. *Pediatrics, 133*: e1172-e1178.

Rainie, L., & Wellman, B. (2012). *Networked: The New Social Operating System.* Cambridge, MA: The MIT Press.

Raphael, B., & Martinek, N. (1996). Psychosocial wellbeing and mental health into the 21st Century. In: Furnass, B., Whyte, J., Harris, J. & Baker, A. (Eds.), Survival, health and wellbeing into the twenty first century—Proceedings of a conference held at The Australian National University, 30 November—1 December 1995 (pp. 31–46). Nature and Society Forum, Canberra.

Rosin, H. (2013). The touch screen generation. *The Atlantic, 4*: 1–12. http://www.theatlantic.com/magazine/archive/2013/04/the-touch-screen-generation/309250/

Roszak, T. (1995). Where Psyche meets Gaia. In: Roszak, T., Gomes, M.E., & Kanner, A.D. (Eds.), *Ecopsychology: Restoring the Earth, Healing the Mind* (pp. 1–17). San Francisco, CA: Sierra Club Books.

Schore, A. N. (1994). *Affect Regulation and the Origin of the Self.* Hillsdale, NJ: Lawrence Erlbaum.

Small, G., & Vorgan, G. (2008). *iBrain: Surviving the Technological Alteration of the Modern Mind.* New York: Collins.

Small, G., Moody, T., Siddarth, P., & Bookheimer, S. (2009). Your brain on google: patterns of cerebral activation during internet searching. *American Journal of Geriatric Psychiatry, 17*: 11–126.

Stern, D. (1985). *The Interpersonal World of the Infant.* New York: Basic Books.

Taylor, F., Kuo, F., & Sullivan, W. (2001). Coping with ADD: The surprising connection to green play settings. *Environment and Behavior, 33*: 54–77.

Trevarthen, C., & Aitken, K. (2001). Infant Intersubjectivity: Research, theory, and clinical applications. *Journal of Child Psychology and Psychiatry. 42*: 3–48.

Tronick, E., Adamson, L. B., Als, H., & Brazelton, T. B. (1975). Infant emotions in normal and pertubated interactions. Paper presented at the biennial meeting of the Society for Research in Child Development, Denver, CO, April 1975.

Volkow, N. D., Wang, G. J., Fowler, J. S., Tomasi, D., Telang, F., & Baler, R. (2010). Addiction: decreased reward sensitivity and increased expectation sensitivity conspire to overwhelm the brain's control circuit. *Bioessays, 32*: 748–755.

Winnicott, D. (1945). Primitive emotional development. *International Journal of Psychoanalysis, 26*: 137–143.

Wells, N. (2000). At home with nature effects of "greenness" on children's cognitive functioning. *Environment and Behavior, 32*: 775–795.

www.Wikepedia.org

Young, D., Reynolds, K., Sidell, M., Brar, S., Ghai, N., Sternfeld, B, Jacobsen, S., Slezak, J., Caan, B., & Quinn, V. (2014). Effects of physical activity and sedentary time on the risk of heart failure. *Circulation: Heart Failure, 7*: 21–27.

Yuan, K., Qin, W., Wang, G., Zeng, F., & Zhao, L. (2011). Microstructure abnormalities in adolescents with Internet addiction disorder. *PloS ONE, 6*: e20708.

CHAPTER THREE

The seduction of digital magic

Luca Nicoli

"Primitive man had an immense belief in the power of his wishes. The basic reason why what he sets about by magical means comes to pass is, after all, simply that he wills it"

—*Freud*, 1913, p. 83

Having heard I was working on this chapter, a woman friend of mine told me a story about the power of the digital world. "Last night I was at the pub with some friends," she said. "One of them enters a chat room, and he just *turns off*. An hour or so later he *turns back on* and utters: 'Well, friends, I'm going!'" My friend concluded, "Obviously he'd scored." The man was more connected to his virtual world than to his friends in the pub. This is one of many such weird stories. I found myself flooded with material about the effects of the digital world. I did not need to leaf through session notes with patients to look for material for this chapter. It was experience in everyday life—made of personal habits, friendships, radio news, and, of course, clinical work with patients—that led me to talk about pervasive seduction by digital devices: cell phones, tablets, and laptops. The seduction is all around me all the time, including in my clinical practice.

For instance, Broglio, age thirteen, lives in a private world of monsters and fantasy stories. In the first session he whisks me up in a vortex of mannered gestures and affected words about school and family. He takes out his cellphone, and he's nonchalantly playing with it. I prudently ask him if he'd rather play than talk. He replies candidly, "I'm listening to you *while* I'm playing!" It takes me a few minutes to realize he's doing the same thing that some of my friends do on Saturday nights at the pub.

Here in my office, I am writing on my iPad and browsing online articles that just a few years ago would have filled the whole room (assuming I could even find them in journals from all around the world). As I think about attending one of many international conferences, making my online reservation and flight confirmation, choosing a hotel based on reviews, contacting faraway colleagues, I am struck that the Internet has sparked a revolution in what we can do, how we do things, and how we think, not just as consumers but as analysts. Of course we were able to do our psychoanalytic reading, writing, and conference networking before we had access to the Internet, but now it's *different*.

We listen through earbuds relieving us of the hassle of holding the phone. We look up emails, street addresses and directions, photos and videos, translate instantly on cellphone or laptop, or look through augmented reality glasses that pack the potentialities of a smartphone inside a lensless frame. The Internet offered a simultaneity of desire and satisfaction (Civitarese, 2012); mailing lists and social networks brought us a continuous connection with our professional groups (Hartman, 2011); we could manipulate our image through avatars, nicknames, and profiles; but now, with mobile devices, we have continuous accessibility to the digital world, where we enjoy the certainty of having *anything* at our disposal, *anywhere* and *anytime*—even in a psychoanalytic session.

From a psychoanalytic point of view, these innovative and surprising capabilities represent outright magical powers. As Freud said of primitive forms of thinking, "It may be said that the principle governing magic, the technique of the animistic mode of thinking, is the principle of 'omnipotence of thoughts'" (Freud, 1913, p. 85). In Freud's day, omnipotence referred to thought associated with dream, fantasy, and myth.

Today, because of technological enhancement of the human capability for connection that eliminates the limits of time and distance, the omnipotent idea becomes real immediately. Instant access to information and companionship via digital devices favors the reemergence of primary process thinking, feeds the pretense of keeping pain and frustration out of the way, and creates a kind of delusion. The analyst of the third millennium will have to deal, both in theory and in technique, with an enormous extension of the virtual, potential space, with aspects of omnipotent thought that will be more and more part of the mind, and may even be embedded in the body.

Everything right now: the magic wand

Holding a communication device conveniently miniaturized to pocket or handbag size, accessing personal archives, global knowledge, and interaction, or experiencing audiovisual messages from an outer shell or membrane on which are displayed messages and from which music may emerge, leaves us feeling as if we own a *magic wand*. I am describing an omnipotent fetish. Yet this omnipotence is anything but illusory. The payment of bills, the making of reservations, and attendance at videoconferences are ways to actually affect the real world.

The concept of *virtual* as a synonym of *simulated*, as opposed to *real*, is losing its meaning. I believe we need to redefine *virtual* as *potential*, that is, as describing a generator of endless possibilities.

Dariush, an impulsive and dynamic sixteen-year-old who has been in therapy for a few years, enters the consulting room, ignores the armchair in which he usually sits facing me, and lies on the couch. He says: "I lay down because I have to tell you something I feel deeply ashamed of. So I'll try to tell it from here. A few days ago, as a joke, my friends and I went on the Chat-roulette site to meet girls. But now I always go there, every time my parents are away and I'm home alone. I turn on the PC and I can chat with a lot of different girls, even though I'm supposed to be eighteen to join that site. It's like a drug, but what's better than getting to know a few girls for a boy of sixteen?"

I ask him if his problem is struggling to find a limit when he's alone.

"I'm afraid I can't stop! In real life I can't even ask a girl her name, but here I get to know a bunch of them. Girls from Lombardy, maybe if they come to my city we can meet. There's an older girl, a woman, she's twenty-five. Then there's a Russian girl who asked me to play a game. We found ourselves practically half-naked."

Stories like Dariush's are anything but rare and force us to question how the continued use of digital technology alters the psychic functions that psychoanalysis is used to dealing with. Dariush describes the persecutory fear of being trapped in a here and now where Bion's well-known concept of *being without memory or desire* is de-metaphorized, made cartoonishly real.

The endless potential of an always accessible and limitless container, a mother with an inexhaustible breast, a holding environment that ignores the paternal function, favors the shrinking of desire and the progressive loss of the ability to wait. The difficulties in symbolization and in construction of a container for the internal world, by now amply pointed out (Curtis, 2007; Guignard, 2010; Szekacs-Weisz, 2007) are destined to increase exponentially—gratification always at hand!

Back to the clinical vignette, the contact with any girl, many girls, is immediate and seems to allow a deep and idealized intimacy. The ambivalence experienced seems to be very limited, since one can immediately move on. The Internet, an other place where memory proceeds by substitution or accumulation, becomes the seat of choice for an emotional evacuation. Without any direct experience of consequences, it becomes harder to build an integrative memory and thus to develop processes for bearing intrapsychic conflict, such as entering the depressive position and developing a capacity for concern, both of which force us to tolerate our finiteness and experience ambivalence. Difficulties in refining competencies inside a relationship and in integrating reactions to frustration and pain, can lead an individual to repeatedly, compulsively, seek the channels of evacuation. Process and review of experience is by-passed. How do we feel after a sexual encounter, and when seeing each other again? And how do we feel meeting the girl that turned us down again?

Questions like these, markers of intrapsychic dynamics, are more and more at risk of being evacuated instead of dreamed (Bion, 1962; Ogden, 2003). New rites, such as frantically checking email or profiles on various social networks, or repetitive group or solitary gaming, are frantic, consuming activities that, by blocking boredom and blanking space and time, obliterate silence and reflection. They take us away from reviewing our concerns and encountering and reintegrating our estranged Self.

Mirror, mirror on the wall …

Panfilo, a strapping young man of twenty who brings to his sessions themes related to the sense of limit and guilt, says he's good at texting girls, but he wimps out in real life. The toughest time of the day for him is between midnight and 2 a.m. Since all of his friends are asleep and he can't text anybody, he feels lonely.

Fernando Riolo neatly sums up the panorama offered by the current crisis of the symbolic and by its consequences on a psychic level: "We wonder, from time to time, where did the neuroses of old go? Neuroses are the expression of a world centered on psychic reality and its meanings: desire, forbiddance, conflict, impotence, passion, guilt. The pathologies that replaced them—sociopathy, drug addiction, bulimia, anorexia—are rather the expression of a fault in the symbolic order and of a 'normalized' use of hallucinatory productions and actions, whose end is the evacuation of anguish but also of the meaning of self. Because 'terror' is recognizing oneself, being inside oneself, responsible for one's own psychic reality and its irreducible contradictions" (Riolo, 2008, p. 902).

Terror, Panfilo might say, had he words to give voice to his anguish, is being offline, separating from one window of experience without immediately opening another window/room/chat to replace the one he just closed. Digital magic would not be so alluring if it did not allow us to avoid facing consequences and continually hide from ourselves.

One of the main refuges of the Self is the group. The relationship with others in a group is completely revolutionized by massive use of digital devices. Thanks to the dizzying development of telecommunications, we are less bound by geography in choosing and associating with groups. Above and beyond the obvious practical advantages of getting together cheaply, the Internet allows everybody to build their own clique of narcissistically invested "friends", almost parts of themselves. From time to time, these internal and external friends can offer support, sharing, or company. Being able to choose, one by one, contacts, friendships and groups to belong to, to connect to and disconnect from at leisure, being able to delete them with a click—all of this makes it possible to limit disagreements and frustration and to enjoy feeling part of a whole. Being able to continually exchange text messages, phone-calls, photos of the food we are eating, and sharing current feelings, signifies ample space for a "fusional Us" that is hard to give up. "Sense of belonging to the group moreover represents an important narcissistic gratification, since the individual partly forgoes his Ego and expands himself in a fusion that widens his boundaries and takes him away from finiteness and solitude" (Usuelli, 2008).

We are faced with an object, the virtual community, which belongs more to the intermediate area than to the outer world. It allows everybody to use it as needed, even performing functions that should otherwise be performed by inner structures. Taking a look at some Facebook pages, we will find some typical posts: "I miss you …", "Falling down …", "First day in Paris …", "Two things that go well together … my full belly and the sea view restaurant in Venice!" What stands out is the need to leave sentences suspended, incomplete. There is an unconscious request to receive from the "mirror" reverie, containment, dreaming, sharing, envying admiration. It is as if the writer of the post were expecting enquiring responses, a group working-through of the experience: "How is it in Paris? Does it feel good or not? And what's the danger in falling down? How is it terrible?"

Using the impersonal form of the phrases, I want to highlight that the responses quoted above do not address a subjectivation process, but rather foster the illusion of standing in an intersubjective/group experiential space for working-through.

Continuous accessibility to influence from the other prevents the achievement of psychological balance between object-relating and narcissistic defense, thus hampering the capacity to be alone, especially for the current and future generations of digital natives, those young people who have not known a world without information technology. Outsourcing part of our psychic functions of mirroring and emotional containment means not being able to trust ourselves fully (Bolognini, 2004). In cases where this fragility is more pronounced, the need to prop up the sudden collapses during moments of crisis, existential voids, separations, and losses can manifest through a continuous clinging to the "good" object that's right there, in one's pocket, in an intermediate area, at hand, on the bridge between transitional object and fetish (Greenacre, 1969, 1970; Winnicott, 1953).

> At the end of the session Panfilo and I get up. I walk ahead of him and, when I turn back to say goodbye, I see him fiddling with his cell phone, reading the precious messages he received in these forty-five minutes. He absentmindedly looks up, says goodbye and leaves, online again.

The picture of Dorian Gray

Anybody who works with a teenager is used to considering the cell phone not just as an object, but as part of the Self, a membrane linking him with his peers and his Self. But the digital world is not only the province of the young, as the next example shows.

> "Doctor, would it be unusual if I asked you to read my profile?" asks Svevo, a forty-year-old professional man, single, and among the most popular in dating chats. Sometimes he makes it to the top ten most-clicked profiles in his city. "Since in my notes I wrote some deep things that really represent me, I'd like to know if they could help us understand how I present myself to others!"

The profile Svevo is talking about is the virtual business card he uses to introduce himself in dating-site chat rooms, in which most of his social life originates. Svevo pictures that interface with the digital world as a privileged access to his Self. His business card is like a sign of his identity, like a Maori tattoo whose function is "not only to imprint a drawing onto the flesh but also to stamp onto the mind all the traditions and philosophy of the group" (Levi-Strauss, 1963, p. 257). The fantasy, from which the proliferation of avatars, profiles, nicknames, and blogs come forth, is that digital magic power allows us to shape ourselves to our own liking. The need to *tattoo* the authentic Self on our digital skin is expressed through processes of avoiding, splitting, or disavowal of the uncontrollable unconscious aspects of body and mind. In virtual reality, self-representations are consciously managed, giving a sense of control and defense, made possible by the avoidance of the less controllable, nonverbal aspects of communication and the absence of visible otherness.

Customized communication interfaces, ringtones, and webpage contents appear to allow us to present our individual identity, but really we are creating an illusion of appearing to be who we are not (Turkle, 1997). Incidentally, some authors value the potential of an interactive identity, because they view virtual role-playing as a way to escape the bonds of excessively harsh superego demands (Gabbard, 2001; Sand, 2007). New, ideal, or partial self-images are projected onto the screen of the other and experienced more and more frequently. When is it integrative play and when is it contrived fiction?

For these kinds of identity explorations to evolve into a more confident, stable identity, with a capacity for flexible interactions, there must be enough ego strength to integrate unpleasant or embarrassing parts, without avoiding or splitting them. Otherwise, like postmodern Dorian Grays, the individuals that depend more heavily on digital devices present a fabricated face to perpetuate the illusion of successful self-functioning, but the illusion lasts only as long as they keep the neglected parts of themselves locked up.

> "Last time we met, I wanted to give you my profile," says Svevo at the beginning of the session, "and you told me to read it aloud. I felt ashamed like … a goat. Today I copied it on my cell phone, but then I turned it off. Maybe we can come to the same results differently."

This exchange led me to a hypothesis that could apply in other cases. Instead of indulging the patient's request to read a profile or email from a cellphone, the analyst requires a communicative act such as asking the patient to tell him about it, or read it aloud, and then the patient might be helped to make contact with "the goat", his own feeling of inadequacy—a bad feeling otherwise hidden, as in that famous painting of the handsome Dorian Gray, until its integrity is corrupted by his inner hedonistic Self.

Wonderland

> Cristoforo is facing a summer separation from his young son. He began: "I bought the little one a SIM card too, since this summer he's often going to be away from home. If we need him, or if he needs us …" Cristoforo, a fairly traditionalist middle-aged father, seems to struggle with who needs whom, the parent or the child. Then he adds: "Last evening we were dining with our pre-teen daughter, Anselmina, and some friends who have a boy her age. Both of those kids are very reserved. When they got home, our friends took it out on their son because he hadn't talked to Anselmina. He replied that she had been texting on her own all the time. The day after that, the son forgot his phone at home on the table, and they checked his messages, even though it was a bit of an intrusion on his privacy. Checking the chronology and time of the messages, they realized that he and Anselmina had actually been texting each other. Well, I'd like it if my daughter felt like telling me things like that, so I could help her."

To me, this vignette from Cristoforo illustrates society's massive use of digital devices as an expression of a fantasy of control of the environment, the other, and the relationship.

I am reminded of Freud's description of the omnipotence of thought of primitive people and children as "their unshakeable confidence in the possibility of controlling the world and their inaccessibility to the experiences, so easily obtainable, which could teach them man's true position in the universe" (1913, p. 89). As the trends I am describing shape our future, we can expect a world in which instant gratification will rule over desire, telepathy among members of a group over individual reflection, potential over commitment to a choice. The regression offered by virtual reality promotes the construction of a predictable, narcissistic world in which to curtail frustrating relationships and promote gratifying relationships with partial or idealized objects to the detriment of the dialectic encounter-clash with otherness—be that of the other in an interpersonal sense or as the internal other of unconscious elements.

In our work as analysts, I believe it is essential to ask ourselves how the permanence of a virtual condition, that is, one of infinite, timeless potential with the resulting burden of inaccessibility to real experience, changes the mental functioning of individuals. I wonder if we can describe this situation as a dilation of potential space to the detriment of object-relating (Ogden, 1985; Winnicott, 1963, 1967, 1971). The object is always right before us, but we can never reach it, because it is perpetually consumed and recreated, but we never possess it, and we are never possessed. The compulsive avoidance of pain and frustration and the illusion of a group working-through promoted by technological innovations can hamper the full development of individual working-through.

Extreme cases of this process pave the way to hallucinosis, a Bionian concept recently claimed by Italian authors (Civitarese, 2012; Marzi, 2013; Riolo, 2010) to describe certain psychotic configurations found within non-psychotic individuals. In the absence of a container able to contemplate and metabolize the projections (Bion, 1965; Grinberg, Sor, & Bianchedi, 1975) the hallucinating activity becomes continuous. This ongoing hallucinosis in relation to objects that are neither fully desired, committed to, nor mourned in virtual reality deprives objects of their libidinal value.

In the near future, where the union of man and machine will enable permanent connectivity, I imagine that relationships with others will tend more and more to rest on transitional gradients, and that the individual mind will be more and more in need of virtual prostheses, continuous action, and evacuation to limit the dizziness of uncertainty.

Conclusion: leaving fairyland?

Given current market data, it is unlikely that man will shed digital technology at any time soon. On the contrary, in the future, psychoanalysts will have to accept *homo digitalis* as an object of study, if psychoanalysis wants to keep its standing as a model for understanding the mind. Some efforts are underway on the path to a large-scale theoretical and technical revision without abandoning the rigor of our method (Carlino, 2010; Guignard, 2010; Lemma and Caparrotta, 2013; Scharff, 2013). I believe that the first duty of psychoanalysis, when faced with the seduction of digital magic, is to scrutinize our concepts and retain those that are relevant to the twenty-first century. As for me, I conclude by leaving a few open questions and suggestions for paths of exploration.

How do digital devices interact with a given patient? To what extent do they represent external objects and to what extent parts of self? How do they interact with the capacity for elaborating experiences? What is our countertransference reaction when patients turn to digital devices in sessions? Are we in tune, are we disrupted, or are we not even noticing anymore because the habit is so pervasive that it flies under the analytic radar?

To what degree is the setting changed by our use of digital systems? To what extent can the analytic couple tolerate uncertainty? Do we accept or refuse text messages, emails, cell phone calls, and requests for sessions on Skype? Which unconscious elements in us lurk below this permeability or impermeability?

Would it be useful to apply findings from studies on autism and hallucinosis with patients who are compulsively attached to digital communication, patients who, though they do not have seriously pathological structures, show defective functioning in symbolization, mentalization, and desire?

Are we at the threshold of a world in which the very relationship between perception, representation, and hallucination needs to be rethought, starting from a systematic study of psychic development in young people who have grown up with technology from birth?

In the current socio-cultural environment, how is a relationship of strong emotive dependence, such as the analytic relationship, received by patients increasingly less able to understand the meaning of separation? Should we expect an increase in narcissistic aspects in transference? Should we deepen our thoughts on the centrality of the consultation phase that is looking more and more like the landing of confused aliens on an unknown planet?

References

Bion, W. R. (1962). *Learning from Experience*. New York: Basic Books.

Bion, W. R. (1965). *Transformations*. London: Heinemann.

Bolognini, S. (2004). Fidarsi di sé. Pseudomaturità e disarticolazione Io-Sé negli attacchi di panico. *Psicoterapia Psicoanalitica*, 11: 47–68.

Carlino, R. (2010). *Psicoanalisis a Distancia*. Buenos Aires, Argentina: Lumen. (Reprinted as *Distance Analysis*, London: Karnac, 2011.)

Civitarese, G. (2012). Internet e la vita simultanea. *Quaderni de Gli Argonauti*, 24: 33–44.

Curtis, A. E. (2007). The claustrum: sequestration of cyberspace. *Psychoanalytic Review*, 94: 99–139.

Freud, S. (1913). Totem and taboo. *S. E.*, 13: 1–162. London: Hogarth.

Gabbard, G. O. (2001). Cyberpassion. *Psychoanalytic Quarterly*, 70: 719–737.

Greenacre, P. (1969). The fetish and the transitional object. *Psychoanalytic Study of the Child*, 24: 144–164.

Greenacre, P. (1970). The transitional object and the fetish with special reference to the role of illusion. *International Journal of Psychoanalysis*, 51: 447–456.

Grinberg, L., Sor, D., & de Bianchedi, E. T. (1975). *Introduction to the Work of Bion*. Strath Tay: Clunie Press.

Guignard, F. (2010). Lo psicoanalista e il bambino nella società occidentale di oggi. *Rivista di Psico-analisi*, 56: 901–920.

Hartman, S. (2011). Reality 2.0: When loss is lost. *Psychoanalytic Dialogues*, 21: 468–482.

Lemma, A., & Caparrotta, L. (2013). *Psychoanalysis in the Technoculture Era*. London: Routledge.

Levi-Strauss, C. (1963). *Structural Anthropology*. New York: Basic Books.

Marzi, A. (2013). Cyberfantasmi del profondo. In: *Psicoanalisi, Identità e Internet*. Milano: Franco Angeli.

Ogden, T. H. (1985). On potential space. *International Journal of Psychoanalysis, 66*: 129–141.

Ogden, T. H. (2003). On not being able to dream. In: *This Art of Psychoanalysis*. London: Routledge, 2005.

Riolo, F. (2008). Identità: la giubba e il filo. *Rivista di Psicoanalisi, 54*: 897–903.

Riolo, F. (2010). Trasformazioni in allucinosi. *Rivista di Psicoanalisi, 56*: 635–649.

Sand, S. (2007). Future considerations. *Psychoanalytic Review, 94*: 83–97.

Scharff, J. S. (2013). *Psychoanalysis Online*. London: Karnac.

Szekacs-Weisz, J. (2007). Mindless bodies-bodyless minds. *American Journal of Psychoanalysis, 67*: 291–298.

Turkle, S. (1997). *Life on the Screen*. New York: Touchstone.

Usuelli, A. (2008). Riflessioni sul terrorismo. *Rivista di Psicoanalisi, 54*: 683–706.

Winnicott, D. W. (1953). Transitional objects and transitional phenomena. In: *Playing and Reality* (pp. 1–25). London: Tavistock.

Winnicott, D. W. (1963). Communicating and not communicating leading to a study of certain opposites. In: *The Maturational Processes and the Facilitating Environment* (pp. 179–192). London: Hogarth, 1965.

Winnicott, D. W. (1967). The location of cultural experience. In: *Playing and Reality* (pp. 1–25). London: Tavistock.

Winnicott, D. W. (1971). The place where we live. In: *Playing and Reality* (pp. 104–110). London: Tavistock.

CHAPTER FOUR

Intimacy, sexuality, and pornography online

Jill Savege Scharff

Since the 1990s, as more people got computers, the Internet has been a fact of life, with more and more of us logging on to get information, do our shopping, communicate with friends and family, and conduct business online. Providing access to information and interaction—all of it free and without censorship—has been a guiding principle of the Internet. It has become a ready source of information (not all of it reliable), support, and temptation. It is easy to find whatever you want on the Internet, and that includes high-speed access to social interaction and unlimited sexual fantasy and activities. In 2012 there were 2.5 billion Internet users, and the number continues to grow: the proportion of users looking for sexual content is running at over eleven percent (Kraft, 2014). In 2008, 100 million men in the United States and Canada were accessing Internet pornography (Ogas & Gaddam, 2012).

Online dating

Many websites now offer online dating sites where people can post their photographs and personal attributes and can scroll through to find someone they want to communicate with and possibly schedule a date. The single person will go on a site such as Match.com; exchange may lead to a speedy conclusion of non-interest or may lead to further email, text, or phone conversation that ends there or proceeds to in-person meeting that may or may not lead to a relationship. Match.com reports that one in five couples now meet online. The Internet has offered a useful transitional space in which to assess the fit between two personalities looking for love. In this situation, the Internet expands the range of likely contacts, speeds the process for people who value efficiency, and reduces anxiety for those who feel competent at work but less skilled in a competitive social situation. The busy lawyer, traveling on cases and working late hours while building his career, finds Internet dating more convenient than going to bars to meet partners; the divorced or widowed woman in her sixties can find partners for companionship, dating, travel, and/or sex without relying on her couple friends to take her out or recommend dates with their friends, whom she might wish to reject.

General online activities include social networking on MySpace, Facebook, Friendster, video-sharing on YouTube or Instagram, instant messaging, texting, gaming, webcamming, and tweeting. These lead on to other activities such as social bookmarking on reddit, StumbleUpon, or Second Life, and teledildonics at HighJoy or RealTouch.com. There are many ways of attempting to cover one's tracks and hide online activity—file-shredding, renaming files, surfing and emailing anonymously, using workaround web pages, removable media, and remote storage. But as everyone now knows, once on the Internet, nothing goes away. When online activity moves into the sexual realm, the non-contact arenas—MySpace, Facebook, chat rooms, instant messaging emailing webcamming, and paraphilic activities of Internet voyeurism and exhibitionism—are less risky than the contact interactions—cruising or hook-up sites, and paraphilic activities with strangers, whether transvestite, BD/SM, or pedophilia.

Some analysts view the analysand's use of online sexuality as a flight to a new object. In my view it is more like a dream that reveals fantasy objects, fears and wishes in the transference. The Internet functions as a potential space for relating, in which defenses and anxieties are personified, and that can be useful in analytic treatment.

Computer mediated relating

Other people are not actively arranging in-person dating, but are living a fantasy life of dating though computer-mediated relationships. They prefer the anonymity of websites such as Second Life. The appeal of physical attributes is of less importance than the willingness to share and self-disclose. A person on Second Life can enhance physical characteristics and so inhabit an imaginary body and flirt with greater confidence. She can develop various personas and discover which one works best for her. "Acting as a persona that he or she usually does not take on, this may be considered an experiment or transitional functioning, whereas previously it may have been considered poor self-cohesion" (Kantrowitz, 2009). The Internet offers a transitional space for practicing role relationships, prior to moving out into the real world. But it is a pseudo-intimacy. Problems arise when the person stays stuck in virtual reality, never making any real, personal connection.

Computer-mediated relating and Internet infidelity

Computer-mediated relating is highly problematic when the person already has a real relationship that is being sidelined by a preoccupying online life. The real husband never gets the chance to respond to a confrontation because the wife has found comfort and understanding online instead. These affairs are often platonic, although some may involve the use of sexting (sending explicit pictures through text or twitter) and chatting online with or without a web camera. This goes on among adolescents in high school on Instagram because they think the image will disappear after thirty seconds and will only reach the intended recipient, but the images tend to be discovered when forwarded to jealous or outraged others. Intervention by parents and school staff may stop the behavior, but the loss of reputation can be devastating and lead to cyberbullying and the need to find a new school. For celebrities, the fall-out is severe. Anthony Weiner lost his seat in Congress in 2011 because of sexting, and yet in 2013 he was reported again for sexting. In couples where a partner is sexting or chatting online, the wife may not even know of the virtual affair, because of the ease with which her husband can maintain a hidden online relationship. In some respects, these interactional activities can be more problematic than the viewing of porn, when, for example, a man who uses porn believes that it is just for masturbation and is quite separate from the intercourse he has with his partner. From his point of view it does not threaten the relationship, whereas the man with a virtual confidante has, in his wife's view, replaced her as his intimate partner.

Clinical example: Rose and Andy had been together for twenty years and their twin sons were in senior year of high school. Rose's beautiful face was tense and sad, and her eyes stared sadly into the distance as she spoke of being on the point of leaving Andy. Andy smiled pleasantly in a practiced way and sat very still, looking anxiously at Rose. Andy said he had been oblivious to how unhappy Rose was, but in the last year it has been clear to him. Rose was unhappy that she had given up her own career and ambitions to raise the boys, fitting in occasional part-time jobs around the edges of her family life, while Andy worked a phenomenal amount of hours to secure their financial future, while maintaining a steady involvement in their community. Andy had become an automaton, praying for control and acceptance instead of sharing his feelings or resonating with Rose's feelings. Rose had become so lonely that she had an online affair with a man out of town and had fallen in love. She enjoyed the excitement and felt that the acceptance and appreciation she found with him justified the risk. Rose had frequent interactions with this man through email, texting, and webcam interactions, while never having met in person. Andy said, "When Rose told me about the online relationship, I was angry, but I didn't dare express it, I didn't want to destroy a marriage we might be able to save."

Rose said that she too was afraid to destroy the family by confronting her unhappiness and prodding Andy to react and respond. She married him because he is stable and offers security but now she can't stand his remaining so steady in the face of the affair and the threat of her leaving. She said that she is a passionate, opinionated person, and she wants him to join her in heated discussion of points of view and shared feelings. When he stays "flat line" she feels depressed and despairing. Andy said, "I love it that you are passionate and creative. I always loved you. But I didn't say it. I expressed it in acts of service. I need you, and I need to feel loved too." He paused, looking uncomfortable, holding back. Suddenly he spoke. "I'm just going to come right out and say it. We haven't had sex in months. Maybe once or twice in the last year, and that's it."

Sex had been good in the first years of the marriage but as Rose realized that there was no closeness, no emotional intimacy, she began to lose interest. She still had desire for sex, but not for sex with Andy. Affection between her and the boys filled her needs, but they would be leaving soon. Andy said that Rose had been occasionally affectionate, which he said he really needs, even if she doesn't want to have sex. Rose said, "The affair is over, and I now see it was a fantasy of finding someone to take care of me." Andy accepted the affair as his responsibility too. He had contributed to its occurrence by his obliviousness and his obsessive devotion to work. Rose had supported his work drive by enjoying the reassurance of her self-worth and the financial security that his success brought her.

Rose decided that she must be the one to open the door to sex. Andy responded, and from this there followed a feeling of intimacy and hope for the future. Rose said, "I'm trying to let go of anger and regret about how things were going, and look at what we have now. We've both been through a wake-up call. Look at what I could have lost and how close I came to it. I am here to ask questions about who I am and what I want." Andy said, "I want to focus on the emotional side of myself, on my relationships, and on communicating my thoughts and feelings." Rose said, "We are here to find a new intimacy. We have to look at this wall between us, because until we do I can't feel forgiven, and we can't really recapture what we have lost." In this case, Internet sexuality was a threat to the marriage but then served as a "wake-up call" to re-establish intimacy.

Online sexuality

The patient's values and morals may differ from those of the therapist, and this can lead to the pathologizing of the patient's behavior. There are three distinct profiles of online sex users: the recreational, the compulsive, and the at-risk user. The therapist needs to distinguish between what is developmental and part of a healthy sexual outlet and what is fixed behavior, what is harmfully compulsive to the individual. Thinking in terms of categories is useful to prevent therapists from over-pathologizing sexual behavior online.

Recreational users account for forty-seven percent of online users. They go online for less than one hour per week for sexual arousal, and report no negative consequences. Sometimes the recreational user searches for content to satisfy sexual curiosity or get specific sexual information. Galatzer-Levy and Cohler (2002) note that the Internet is especially useful for gay adolescent boys who can read about the struggles of other boys who are coming out and can find support for their developing gay identities.

At-risk users initially explore online sexuality in a non-problematic, recreational way. They have no history of sexual compulsivity, and no signs of problematic sexual behavior, but when a life problem crops up one way of emotionally handling it might be through escaping into spending increased amounts of time online, focusing on sexually arousing activities.

Compulsive users have sexually compulsive traits that have been in evidence before the Internet was accessed for sexual purposes. There may have been previous use of print, video, or DVD porn, or phone sex, visiting prostitutes, or having sex indiscriminately with strangers. They cannot stop accessing porn and they experience negative consequences as a result. They experience intense sexually arousing fantasies, urges, and associated sexual behaviors that are intrusive, driven, and repetitive. Lacking impulse control puts them in conflict with society, where they can encounter social and legal sanctions.

Pornography

The most frequently researched topic online is sex, with people looking for sexual websites that dispense information and advice, joining chat rooms and discussion groups, and so finding support for healthy sexual development. This is particularly useful for adolescents in search of sex education, when middle and high schools are failing to provide adequate information and support. Adolescent females are more likely to research questions about sexuality and males are more likely to seek out pornographic images for arousal and masturbation. In a less helpful way, some adolescent males use Internet pornography in a defensive way to disguise the meaning of their sexual fantasies and to obliterate the anxiety associated with conflict about them (Galatzer-Levy, 2013).

Whereas in the past the visibility of going to pornographic book stores or video shops discouraged mainstream users, now anonymity, accessibility, and affordability drive the ubiquity of Internet porn for many more users (Cooper, 1998). Most pornographic websites are free and easily assessable. Of contemporary users, more are men. Only ten percent of female Internet users access porn whereas seventy percent of male online users (mostly age eighteen to twenty-five) access sites such as Pornhub and Xhamster, where they watch three to eight videos per visit once or twice a week while they masturbate, and leave the site in less than ten minutes (Kraft, 2014). Young women prefer engaging in fan fiction and older women read romance novels. Taking figures collected by a method that the researchers call "scraping" (extracting data from numerous searches of the top five web sites for men and for women), Ogas and Gaddam (2012) reported fifty-one million male visitors to porn sites per month, only 0.3 million female visitors to the adult story and video sites per month, and 2.6 million women to the romance and fan fiction sites. This gender difference in viewing reflects men's preference for lust, with the visual stimulation of graphic sex, and women's preference for love, with written material that focuses on being courted, loved, and made special by the desired, financially successful, alpha male (Symons, 1979).

Clinical example: Azar was upset that her husband was staying on his computer late into the night, watching porn instead of having intimate conversations with her, which might have led to sex. She discovered that for him the arousing image was long legs in high heels, and it made her extremely jealous that he preferred looking at *those* long legs to caressing *her* long legs in the high heels she was happy to wear for his pleasure. She insisted that he come for therapy. He said that he had always had attention deficit disorder and that looking at the screen was one thing he could concentrate on. In addition, he had been addicted to marijuana as a teenager, and, although he was clean of substance use, he obviously had an addictive tendency. He was unable to look at any sources for his cued interest in long legs, but he was able to admit that he dreaded long conversations that always seemed to involve complaints about him; these made him feel that his wife did not want to be with him, and so he went off by himself to use porn. It is usually not easy for men to stop using porn, but in this case the man gave it up when he realized that his wife was eager to engage with him sexually. Interestingly, his wife was active on a fan fiction website but this did not alarm him. On the contrary, he was proud of her creativity.

Excessive or addicted sexual behavior on the Internet

There is a tendency to pathologize the use of porn, with dire predictions about it leading to ruin and becoming an uncontrollable habit. Certainly, there are some who cannot give up the habit easily, even though it threatens their livelihood.

Clinical example: Andrew, a promising associate earning a substantial salary at a law firm, was caught watching porn on the firm's computer on company time. He was fired immediately.

In shame, he withdrew socially, rejected his fiancée, and refused therapy, while continuing to use porn.

This is the type of case that might seem to suggest that Internet porn use fits the addiction model (Wilson, 2014). Wilson's argument is that porn produces repeated hits of dopamine that are highly rewarding in youths and which explain vulnerability to addiction, while in older people the reward cycle needs more and more of the stimulus to get the response. They continue to want more porn even though they do not like it. Wilson contends that watching porn has sensitized the user's brain to porn sex rather than real in-person sex, and that this has led to porn-induced brain-based erectile dysfunction. It follows from this way of thinking that the user can be treated only with a twelve-step model and with rehabilitation at an expensive treatment center focused on abstinence except for sex with the spouse. This approach may help some priests, for example, but cannot be effective for a married person when sex with the spouse is, for relational reasons, often not fully functional. In such a case, a behavioral-psychodynamic couple sex therapy approach is needed.

A Cambridge University study has been interpreted to support Wilson's point of view: comparing forty-four men who looked at porn when they felt like it to twenty-two who felt compelled to watch it, the researchers suggested that, compared to the healthy volunteers, the men with compulsive sexual behavior showed enhanced attentional bias to sexually explicit cues (Mechelmans et al., 2014). The researchers link this result to their more recent observation that sexually explicit videos are associated with a greater activity in a neural network, similar to that observed in drug-cue-reactivity studies, which connects to a user's feeling of increasing desire for porn in spite of not liking it. The researchers conclude that their studies provide support for an incentive motivation theory of addiction that underlies the compulsive users' aberrant response towards sexual cues. Laier, Pawlikowski, Pekal, Schulte, and Brand (2013) showed that indicators of levels of sexual arousal to, and craving for, pornographic Internet cues predicted tendencies towards cybersex addiction, but that real life sexual contact had no influence on the frequency of porn use.

Ley (2012) argues that the escalation hypothesis is not confirmed, the addiction model does not apply to Internet porn use, and there are no brain-related issues. Many studies that usefully look more deeply into the intrapsychic and interpersonal dimension broaden the dialogue beyond the addiction or gratification hypothesis, but they remain focused on the individual porn user (Dryer & Lijtmayer, 2007; Kalman, 2008; Miliner, 2008). Wood (2006, 2011) calls for a psychodynamic perspective on the impact of online sex on the unconscious and its fuelling of manic defense, flight from anxiety, and sadistic part-object relating. Internet porn use is usefully conceived of as a social and moral issue for couples. Cebulko (2007, 2013) finds the addiction model inadequate to explain how individual pathology arises or to address the couple relationship in which marital partners convert long-standing emotional intrapsychic and interpersonal problems into a concrete symptom.

To fill out Andrew's story: his fiancée had hoped he would attend couple therapy with her but when he would not do so, she decided on a temporary separation to see if it would motivate him to work on his issues. On the rebound, she developed a relationship with a married professor she was unable to resist. This illicit relationship brought her tremendous anxiety, and even greater shame when it was discovered. In therapy she was able to see that this unsuitable and personally harmful choice revealed her underlying propensity to resonate with a partner for whom sexuality was compulsive and associated with shame and negative consequences. She realized that Andrew's porn use was only one of many areas of mutual dissatisfaction with their relationship, and, without his co-operation in repairing trust and intimacy, they could not recover as a couple. In the end he lost her too, and she moved on, understanding her own concerns about sexuality and autonomy, and therefore becoming more confident in choosing her next partner.

Whether or not Internet porn use is damaging is a matter of debate. How are we to decide on the harm? How much is too much? Once a week, four times a week, eight times a day? There is no normative amount for how often a person has sex without porn. Couples tend to choose once or twice a week as the normative amount of sex for a couple, but some are more active than that and still feel normal, while one third of couples are not having sex at all, and they are not coming to therapy to change that (Kraft, 2014). So it is hard to say at what point porn use becomes harmful, either to self or to significant other. Which is the more damaging, extreme hard core porn or fetish porn? Multiple quick visits or surfing for hours? Heterosexual porn for men or women, gay porn for gays or heterosexual women, lesbian porn for lesbians or men, or shemale porn? Much Internet porn offers vanilla sexual content that is not particularly shocking. Porn does tend to objectify women, however, and extreme hard core and fetish porn makes many people uncomfortable because of the up-closeness of it, the violence, the peculiarity, and the degradation. There are predictions that aggressive porn will lead to actual violence against women, but no research study has shown such a correlation. A far greater concern is that access to porn will introduce the user to websites that offer live sex workers. These workers provide still photos, live photos delivered from the web camera in real time, sex-related merchandise, X-rated videos, streaming video, virtual meetings for sexual release, live sex shows, and sexual encounters in which to participate virtually on webcam. In this case, the Internet can offer a more sanitary and comfortable place in which to arrange an exchange of sex for money. Some websites offer exchange of sexual services, and at this point accessing the Internet for sexual interaction brings much more risk, especially if the sex worker is under the age of eighteen.

Escort services are flourishing because of the ease of making arrangements on the Internet for assignations. There may be no conflict for the single person, but for the person of stature or the person in a long-term relationship, the conflict over values and priorities, and the possibility of eventual discovery, create problems, whether the sex is erotic massage, oral sex, or intercourse, straight, gay, group, BD/SM, or whatever. The protection of anonymity that the Internet offers is now lost, as is that of no physical contact, and therefore no disease, offered by virtual reality. Accessibility is enhanced, anonymity is relinquished, and affordability is gone. Just as the porn user can find anything he can imagine on the web, the person (usually a man) with money can find an escort who will fulfil that fantasy at the right price. When the man is a celebrity, the risk is enormous, and many have lost careers or positions of power over the revelation of such meetings when on trips paid for by governments or corporations. Eliot Spitzer (Client-9) not only had to resign as Governor of New York in 2008 but he lost his run for Assistant Comptroller in 2013—and his resignation as Governor cost Hillary Clinton the support of his superdelegate vote. The National Science Foundation, the Securities Exchange Commission, and the Department of Defense have all had to investigate the use of government computers by male employees surfing for porn (Ogas & Gaddam, 2012). Prostitution is illegal in the United States, and yet it is easier than ever, as if it were merely a business arrangement rather than an infidelity or a crime.

Child pornography

Accessing child pornography is a significant problem of growing concern. "Teens" is the age category most frequently searched for by male Internet porn users. It is a short step from there to looking for child porn. There is an alarming proliferation of content featuring children as sex subjects and appealing to children as consumers. It has been noticed that sexually abusive adolescents in treatment are increasingly downloading child pornography (Horne, 2004). The U.S. Custom Service estimates that there are 100,000 child porn sites worldwide. Twenty thousand new ones come online each week (Kraft, 2014). Sometimes the content from a child porn site may be downloaded unintentionally, but lack of intent is hard to prove. Some sites use electronically created digital images that do not use real human beings, or they morph the image of an adult body onto the body of the child so that only the child's face is shown. In many sites, the age of the porn subjects is getting younger and younger, and they are shown in more and more abusive situations. Any visual depiction of sexually explicit material involving the display of the genitals, or the body in a sexually suggestive pose, of a person under the age of eighteen is illegal in the United States. The legal consequences are huge. The deliberate pedophile viewer may be content to merely look, but for some, sorting and collecting of the images is the main gratification (Taylor & Quayle, 2003). Even when searches are deleted, they can be recovered, or discovered, for instance, when the computer goes in for repair, because repair shops are mandated reporters. Pedophiles also tend to communicate with other pedophiles in order to share child pornography, and this electronic sharing is the place where pedophilic activity commonly gets exposed.

Therapeutic approaches

The diagnosis of compulsive sexual behavior names the behavior that is the presentation of co-morbid pathology. Treatment for compulsive sexual behavior involving the Internet includes psychotropic medication, environmental management, support, and psychotherapy.

Serotonergic antidepressants such as Prozac, Zoloft, and Paxil treat underlying depression and reduce the urgency and frequency of masturbation. Zoloft is additionally useful when attention deficit disorder complicates the presentation. Mood stabilizers such as Tegretol, Depakote, and Lithium carbonate can be helpful for dealing with a manic omnipotence that drives the behavior and interferes with reality testing.

Clinical example: Antonio, a gay male analysand in psychoanalysis, had been unable to control the impulse to interrupt his work as a foreign correspondent in favor of going to his preferred website looking for porn. His particular cued interest was trampling; in other words he wanted someone to step on him repeatedly. He would have liked his husband to participate in this but his partner refused because he found it unappealing to so degrade the man he loved. So, Antonio looked for it on the Internet. He understood the roots of his unhappiness in terms of his feeling unable to get recognition in his visibly successful family. Compared to them he felt weak and bossed around. But his understanding was not enough to help him control the obsessive use of Internet porn. He was compelled to masturbate many times a day, whether he had been sexually active with his husband or not. In this case, a consultation from a sexologist led to medication with Zoloft, which reduced the frequency of the urge to masturbate. After this, he felt vastly relieved and able to get on with his work, but his cued interest did not change, and it continued to create conflict in his relationship, as he tried to push his partner to be the way he wanted.

The therapist can suggest various manipulations of the environment to discourage problematic behavior. At the simplest level, it can be helpful to move the computer into a public space or install blocking and filtering software. The patient can develop an Internet health plan, setting a boundary around time of recreational use of the computer, such as an hour a day, devising ways to account for the time spent, delineating which sites may safely be visited, and privileging sites that offer information and peer support. The patient should find an accountability partner (a friend rather than the spouse or partner) to whom he or she accounts for time spent on the Internet. This person may be the sponsor if the patient enrolls in a twelve-step program, Sex Addicts Anonymous, or Sexual Compulsives Anonymous. The patient's spouse or partner may enroll in a support program for co-dependents of sexual addiction.

Psychotherapy for social and relational issues

Individual psychotherapy: The therapist reviews the co-morbid pathology and makes a treatment plan comprising medication as needed, environmental management, and psychotherapy. She negotiates an individual health plan with the patient who signs it as a contract basic to his continuing in treatment, and sets individual goals for treatment.

Group therapy: These groups are usually slow-open, some members leaving as their behavior comes under their control and others staying for longer-term benefit. Learning that he is not the only one experiencing these issues decreases the patient's sense of shame and alienation. Being in the group provides support from peers who know first hand what the patient, at the mercy of this symptom picture, has been going through. They also know about his denial and his wish to hide, and so they are in a better position to confront him than are his family members or therapist. He can learn from their experience of recovery and feel inspired. For the single patient, group psychotherapy is convenient and affordable.

Couple therapy: The first step is for the person with compulsive sexual behavior to take responsibility for the symptom picture, and agree to an individualized treatment plan, which may include individual therapy or group therapy. The couple needs time to re-establish trust and communication, and this will go much better if the user owns the problem. To the couple therapist, this smacks of scapegoating, creating an index patient, even though research has shown that the partner is in some ways complicit in the behavior, usually because of a trauma background or specific personality characteristics that favor not knowing. At this stage in the recovery process, however, it is better for the index patient to work on the problem and for the partner to learn to recognize and avoid co-dependent behavior from a twelve-step support program. While the treatment program is beginning, the couple should delay attempts to rebuild intimacy. Once the individualized treatment program is in effect, regular couple therapy meetings focus on the impact of the symptom and the quality of the relationship. These couples have been through a "cycle of discovery, confrontation, demands for change, ultimatums, extraction of promises of change, forgiveness, and return to relative peace. Husbands and wives maintain a state of denial, except when crises of compulsion, discovery and betrayal break through until reassurance and forgiveness re-establish the status quo and the cycle is reinforced" (Cebulko, 2013). Since discovery and the onset of treatment, have they been pulled apart by conflict over the symptom? Or were they growing apart anyway, and the symptom is just the tip of the iceberg? Do they want to repair and rebuild, or do they need to talk about separation and divorce? What is the nature of their sexual interaction? Is there conflict over frequency, sexual fantasy, and repertoire? Can they be helped to talk about and accept their differences and hidden similarities? Some improvement may come from the efforts being made, but the therapist must bear in mind the tendency to revert to the cycle of relapse and forgiveness. For lasting change in the quality of the couple relationship, the couple will need to look more deeply into their internal object relations and projective identification set that leads them to treat each other as disavowed parts of themselves (Dicks, 1967; Scharff, D., 1982; Scharff & Scharff, 1991).

Family therapy: Having designated Internet addiction as a disorder, China has established 400 in-patient treatment units with a multimodal approach including group and family therapy (Medalia & Shlam, 2015). The treatment approach is by confrontation, exhortation, and psychoeducation.

The intrapsychic dimension: findings from analytic treatment

Leonoff (2000) described a man who, in spending hours looking for the perfect soft bondage scene to masturbate to, was conducting an endless search that threatened to destroy him through utter depletion. In keeping with Cebulko's (2013) finding of a childhood sexual trauma in the predisposition to compulsive Internet porn use, Leonoff found that the man's compulsion stemmed from his need to release bodily anxiety, resulting from his mother's breaking of the incest barrier. In order to protect his narcissistic integrity he was creating a split in which he was excited by erotic porn images that were, ideally, as exciting as his mother but less overwhelming because kept at a manageable distance, while, at the same time, he felt frozen by his wife, the ideal opposite of his mother.

Corbett (2013) reports on the analytic treatment of two gay male patients accessing interaction online, one of them trying to deal with the guilt and emptiness of a complicated grief reaction and the other trying to overcome his shame-based repression of desire. Corbett found that the Internet offered these men and their analyst a potential space in which the men could create sexual experience, and, as the analyst listened, that potential space on the Internet opened to a productive relational field for the analysis of transference and countertransference.

Anderson (2007) told of a married man who did not have sex with his wife and who spent time online cruising websites. According to his religion and his self-concept, he should live in Christ and have intercourse only with his wife, but a disparate part of him wanted to have oral sex with a man, and the Internet was the most convenient way to arrange this. Explaining what drove him to the Internet to find a man, he said, "I get a sense of ecstasy and oneness that you're supposed to get when you worship God" (Anderson, p. 129). Bernstein (2010) describes preparatory work with a male patient who idled away his days watching pornography in order to fill a sense of internal deadness. Having found comfort in the relationship with his woman analyst, he reverted to searching online when she was absent. She saw his use of searches for pornography as stimulating attempts to soothe his sense of narcissistic depletion.

Wood (2014) describes compulsive child porn use as an addiction, in that it is a repetitive behavior—rather than because the pedophile shows greater activity in a neural network similar to that observed in drug-cue-reactivity studies. She believes the behavior becomes repetitive because the solution of Internet porn is temporary and fundamentally unsatisfying. The desire for the body of the child is filled with hate for, and envy of, the desirability and innocent perfection that the child embodies and that is so lacking in the self-concept of the pedophile. An attempt to connect with an idealized child object promises to fill the empty and lonely spaces in the mind of the socially isolated pedophile with excitement, but as soon as it is over the emptiness returns, and a further attempt is made to fill the terrifyingly, unmanageably lonely space of the absent and neglectful maternal object. Perhaps this is why some pedophiles store, hoard, and share so many images, as if the hoarded collection will fill the void and that sharing them will ensure connection to others who appreciate what they have to offer.

Clinical experience leads to the theory that the Internet provides a potential space in which to repeat and master childhood sexual trauma, find new objects, rejoin lost objects, and fuse with ideal objects to soothe the sense of narcissistic depletion and to deny castration anxiety. Internet porn use is an act of obedience to, and defiance of, a persecutory object, and it is an attempt to fill the void left by an absent maternal object. Experiences in the Internet zone occur in a virtual world. Objects found on the Internet can be transferred to the analytic space for constant revising in the light of new experience in the therapeutic relationship.

Conclusion

The Internet is a source of sexual information, a support of healthy sexual functioning, and a supply of erotica that, for some, stimulates, through recorded or live pornographic images, sexual pleasure and release: for others there is disquiet; and for some, offense. There is controversy over the use of pornography, whether it corresponds to an addiction model or not, and no agreement on what is a normative amount of viewing or choice of content. Therapists might usefully think of online sexual activity as a continuum from the healthy recreational to the compulsive. They must be aware of their personal bias in order to reach a value-free assessment of the needs of their patients. Therapy relies on medication, environmental management, and psychotherapy, always bearing in mind that out-of-control sexual online activity is a symptom, the final common pathway for the converging intrapsychic and interpersonal issues of index patients and their significant others.

References

Anderson, J. W. (2007). Harmful versus beneficial religion: A psychoanalytic perspective. *Annual of Psychoanalysis, 35*: 121–136.

Bernstein, S. (2010). Treatment preparatory to psychoanalysis: A reconsideration after twenty-five years. *Journal of the American Psychoanalytic Association, 58*: 27–57.

Cebulko, S. (2007). *The Impact of Internet Pornography on Married Women: a Psychodynamic Perspective.* New York: Cambria Press.

Cebulko, S. (2013). Internet pornography as a source of marital distress. In: J. S. Scharff (Ed.), *Psychoanalysis Online* (pp. 37–47). London: Karnac.

Cooper, A. (1998). Sexuality and the Internet: Surfing into the new Millenium. *Cyberpsychology and Behavior, 1*: 181–187.

Corbett, K. (2013). *Shifting sexual cultures, the potential space of online relations, and the promise of psychoanalytic listening. Journal of the American Psychoanalytic Association, 61*: 25–44.

Dicks, H. V. (1967). *Marital Tensions*. London: Routledge.

Dryer, J. A., & Lijtmayer, R. M. (2007). Cyber-sex as twilight zone between virtual reality and virtual fantasy. *Psychoanalytic Review, 94*: 39–61.

Galatzer-Levy, R., & Cohler, B. (2002). Making a gay identity: Coming out, social context, and psychodynamics. *Annual of Psychoanalysis, 30*: 255–286.

Galatzer-Levy, R. M. (2013). Obscuring desire: a special pattern of male adolescent masturbation, Internet pornography and the flight from meaning. *Psychoanalytic Inquiry, 32*: 480–495.

Horne, A. (2004). 'Gonnae No' Dae That!': the internal and external worlds of the delinquent adolescent. *Journal of Child Psychotherapy, 30*: 330–346.

Kalman, T. (2008). Clinical encounters with Internet pornography. *Journal of the American Academy of Psychoanalysis and Dynamic Psychiatry, 36*: 593–618.

Kantrowitz, J. (2009). Internet interaction: The effects on patients' lives and analytic process. *Journal of the American Psychoanalytic Association, 57*: 979–988.

Kraft, C. (2014). Problematic Internet sexuality. Lecture. The Foundations of Psychoanalytic Couple Therapy videoconference course. International Psychotherapy Institute, Chevy Chase, MD, November, 2014.

Laier, C., Pawlikowski, M., Pekal, J., Schulte, F. P., & Brand, M. (2013). Cybersex addition: Experienced sexual arousal when watching pornography and not real-life sexual contacts makes the difference. *Journal of Behavioral Addictions, 2*: 100–107.

Leonoff, A. (2000). The unlikely fate of the ideal. *Canadian Journal of Psychoanalysis, 8*: 153–166.

Ley, D. (2012). *The Myth of Sex Addiction*. Lanham, MD: Rowman & Littlefield.

Mechelmans, D., Irvine, M., Banca, P., Porter, L., Mitchell, S., Mole, T. B., Lapa, T. R., Harrison, N. A., Potenza, M. N., & Voon, V. (2014). Enhanced attentional bias towards sexually explicit cues in individuals with and without compulsive sexual behaviours. *PLoS ONE, 9*: e105476.

Medalia, H., & Shlam, S. (2015). *Webjunkies*. Doumentary film. Kino Lorber studio.

Miliner, V. (2008). Internet infidelity: a case of intimacy with detachment. *Family Journal, 16*: 78–82.

Ogas, O., & Gaddam, S. (2012). *A Billion Wicked Thoughts: What the Internet Tells Us About Sexual Relationships*. New York: Penguin Plume.

Scharff, D. (1982). *The Sexual Relationship*. London: Routledge.

Scharff, D., & Scharff, J. S. (1991). *Object Relations Couple Therapy*. Northvale, NJ: Jason Aronson.

Symons, D. (1979). *The Evolution of Human Sexuality*. New York: Oxford University Press.

Taylor, M. & Quayle, E. (2003). *Child Pornography: An Internet Crime*. Brighton: Routledge.

Wilson, G. (2014). *Your Brain on Porn: Internet Pornography and the Emerging Science of Addiction.* Kindle only. Commonwealth Publishing.

Wood, H. (2006). Compulsive use of Internet pornography. In: J. Hillere, H. Wood & W. Bolton (Eds), *Sex, Mind, and Emotion: Innovation in Psychological Theory and Practice* (pp. 65–86). London: Karnac.

Wood, H. (2011). The Internet and its role in the escalation of sexually compulsive behavior. *Psychoanalytic Psychotherapy, 25*: 127–142.

Wood, H. (2014). Internet offenders from a sense of guilt. In: A. Lemma & L. Ciaparotta (Eds.), *Psychoanalysis in the Technoculture Era* (pp. 114–128). London: Routledge.

CHAPTER FIVE

Transitional space: the role of Internet community for transgender and gender non-conforming patients

Andi Pilecki

Analytic writing has focused on the use of the Internet as a screen for projections of idealized self and other objects, the creation of pseudo-relationships, and the disruption to cognitive and emotional development. Little has been said about its potential as a transitional space where socially marginalized communities and individuals can find an uncommon venue in which to meet others with shared experience and perspectives. Among the most marginalized are transgender people, whose gender identity, expression, or behavior is different from that which is typically associated with the assigned birth sex. They may identify as trans women (male-to-female/MTF), trans men (female-to-male/FTM), gender queer (defying binary male/female categorization), or they may use other language to describe how they relate to the spectrum of gender (for a fuller description of trans terminology see transequality. org). Navigating through a sociocultural climate in which binary gender roles are explicitly and implicitly enforced, transgender/non-conforming (TGNC) people often learn to take cover, early in life, to protect themselves from rejection, alienation, discrimination, emotional abuse, physical violence, and, essentially, annihilation. I am particularly concerned with those who have experienced significant gender dissonance and are likely to seek hormonal and/or surgical treatments. The Internet provides an accessible space in which transgender people can develop and flourish. Internet community is frequently the first opportunity to express and explore true feelings and thoughts about gender and to find guidance, support, and validation. As such, it functions as a transitional space in which TGNC people can find themselves and move toward integration and wholeness.

Transgender identity development often begins on the Internet. Until then, constructing and maintaining a false self (Winnicott, 1956, 1965) has often become an essential survival strategy for TGNC people. Communicating with others on the Internet, they can gradually experiment with revealing various aspects of the self. As identity evolves, self-acceptance deepens, and social connections expand over a broader network. Such connections potentially mitigate the shame that can develop within the context of being an outsider to dominant culture, where your appearance, perspectives, social experiences, values, voice, and culture are hated or essentially invisible. This is particularly relevant within the LGBTQ (lesbian, gay, bisexual, transgender, queer, or questioning) community, where initial contact with peers is often made online. A study by the Gay, Lesbian, Straight Education Network published in 2013 found that LGBTQ youth are more likely than non-LGBTQ peers to forge meaningful relationships online. This was especially true for transgender youth who, reflecting both the risks and benefits of the Internet age, reported some of the highest levels of victimization online, but also frequently used the Internet as a vehicle for connecting with other LGBTQ people (GLSEN, CiPHR, & CCRC, 2013).

People in transgender identity evolution at the stage of "seeking information/reaching out" (Lev, 2004) often spend significant amounts of time online. Lev attributes the increased accessibility and visibility of transgender-relevant information and resources to both the transgender liberation movement and to the Internet. For TGNC people, this is often the first place where peers, mirroring, affirmation, support, and guidance can be found. As one patient said: "The Internet was a huge part of my life. It was crucial to cementing my identity and building relationships with other queer people." Another patient said that it was only after she discovered a transgender chat room started by the spouse of a trans woman that she realized it was possible to be transgender *and* have a life and family. Prior to this, she explained, her only exposure to transgender people was on salacious talk shows such as *Jerry Springer*, which left her feeling hopeless. It was only after finding, and building, relationships in this chat room community that she realized she could be loved as a transgender person.

In addition to chat rooms, common Internet resources for the TGNC community include blogs, email lists, Google and Yahoo groups, meet up groups, role-play games (RPGs), You Tube channels, and websites. These are cyber spaces where TGNC people, often for the first time, find each other, express previously safeguarded thoughts and feelings, and forge relationships in which they feel accepted and understood. As the blogger Halle (2014) explained, "Hers (blog) was one of those that helped me to understand I was not crazy for having the feelings and desires I did." The TGNC person's use of the Internet may appear to be almost obsessive at this stage, but must be understood in context. This is often the first step a TGNC person takes out of the desert of loneliness and isolation that is the binary gender system, into an ocean of gender diversity and possibility. Furthermore, Internet community provides a setting in which to express and explore previously hidden aspects of self in relative anonymity, a transitional space where TGNC people can experiment with identity and build relationships with minimal risk of being outed at school, work, and home. This anonymity allows for exploration, experience, and expression that would seem unsafe in life offline.

An important aspect of the "seeking information/reaching out" stage of transgender identity development, says Lev, involves reimagining the past. This involves transforming once shameful experience and memories into "acts of defiance and pride" (2004, p. 245). Again, TGNC people look for support within the Internet community. They can begin to relate around, and thereby transform, experiences of bullying, shame, alienation, and rejection into sources of connection with a larger community. In this alchemic process, such experiences are transmuted from alienating trauma to unifying identifications. As Ayme Michelle Kantz (1997) writes,

"Those of us with 2 spirits need to realize that the very thing that makes us misunderstood, reviled and hated by society is the very thing that is our source of strength and pride" (p. 210).

Internet, or analytic therapy?

It is a sad fact that so many TGNC people have had to find understanding on the Internet rather than in the safe and intimate setting of meeting with an empathic therapist. The importance of a sensitive, secure holding environment when working with TGNC patients cannot be overestimated. The therapist's ability to contain and metabolize the patient's shame, fear, and distrust is crucial. Perhaps the most useful therapeutic tool one can employ, particularly in the early stages of work with TGNC patients, is empathy, in which the therapist decenters from her own subjective experience and meets the TGNC patients where they are. As Stark (2000) articulates, the therapist must listen to her patient and "take her at face value, trust what she is saying is her truth" (p. 39). Such validation of where the patient is can open the space to engage more fully and deeply into what it is like to be there. This kind of space allows for previously repressed material regarding gender to rise to the surface. Many TGNC patients, having learned early on to hide signs of gender variance, will begin to recover and put together lost fragments of memory related to gender identity, or "subconscious sex" as Serano (2007) termed it (p. 78). This distinction clarifies that gender is felt rather than chosen. One patient described this process of repression in the following way: "It's like you wall stuff away in a room. Then you barricade the door. Then you cover it in tape and put something in front of it so that no one will even remember there's a door there."

Another point of distinction is recognizing that TGNC patients have not only *felt failed* but have actually *been failed* (Stark, 2000). These patients have survived and carry inside them the trauma of being gender non-conforming within a cissexist society. (Cisgender describes types of gender identity where experiences of gender match assigned sex at birth. Cissexism refers to the invisibility of, and discrimination against, TGNC people whose sex assignment does not match their gender). TGNC people have been bullied by peers, explicitly or implicitly shamed by family, alienated and ignored by dominant social institutions such as religion and media, and made invisible by stories and mythology woven into the cultural fabric, which generally say nothing of TGNC characters unless it is to mock or diminish them. While accounts of gender non-conforming expression can be found across cultures and throughout history (Rudacille, 2005; Serano, 2007), mainstream culture in the present era leaves little room for gender diversity other than in pathologizing and incriminating narratives. Many TGNC people have adapted to this climate by contorting themselves in order to blend in, avoid abuse, and maintain attachments. The therapist's acknowledgment of, and attunement with, these realities is key to facilitating an environment secure enough for trust and therapeutic alliance to develop. Otherwise patients may turn to the Internet as their only source of help.

Not all TGNC patients find empathic therapists, particularly if they want to transition but are scared of it. Some of them feel they are not allowed to express any doubt or uncertainty about transitioning for fear that therapists will use this to withhold referral letters for hormones or surgery. It should be noted that such a perception is not unfounded. Therapists and other clinicians have historically, and are often still, in the position of "gatekeepers" who assess TGNC patients and decide whether or not to refer them for hormonal and surgical procedures (Lev, 2004; Serano, 2007). One patient, when discussing an initial consultation for hormone therapy, explained that distrust toward medical practitioners evolved, in part, after reading so many stories (many of which were found online) of TGNC people whose access to hormones had been restricted by doctors and/or other clinicians. This patient explained: "It's really hard to express any doubts or questions I might have. I feel like I have to be extra vigilant because people could jump on that doubt and be like 'Maybe you're not really transgender, and this is just a phase'."

Fortunately, as transgender care becomes more integrated within the medical and mental health fields, TGNC patients have wider access to practitioners with greater levels of experience and competence. This is crucial because they need access to potentially life-saving medical treatment and therapy. Nevertheless, many TGNC people continue to experience discrimination within the healthcare field. In a reputable study published by the American Foundation for Suicide Prevention and the Williams Institute (2013) sixty percent of TGNC patients reported that a doctor or healthcare practitioner had refused to treat them. Clinicians who do offer TGNC- competent care pave a safe, informed road to transition and greater resolution of gender dissonance. Another patient, when describing her experience with a doctor during a hormone consultation said: "I had an appointment with the doctor and it was great. When I told her I was trans, she didn't even bat an eye. It was as though it was the most normal thing."

TGNC people pay close attention to how they are regarded by clinicians, and they post TGNC narratives describing negative medical/therapy experiences on the Internet. They also post recommendations for trans friendly therapists and doctors. "Susan's Place" and "Laura's Playground" are sites that list resources, including gender therapists and those providing web therapy, for the transgender community. Unfortunately, many LGBTQ people live in regions where they do not have access to therapists who are competent and experienced with regard to gender and sexuality-related issues. In response to this need, some therapists offer services using voice over Internet platforms. Open Path Collective, for example, is a website where LGBTQ people can search for both local therapists and those willing to work remotely.

Patients may avoid discussing gender altogether with therapists who seem intolerant or uncomfortable. A transgender psychiatrist (Anon, 2004) describing interactions with her analyst wrote, "I learned to keep the discussion within the bounds of what was comfortable for him … I had simply given up the discussion … he told me he knew better than to 'confront a delusion'" (pp. 21–22). The writer goes on to explain: "He may have just been unable to grasp the fact that thinking in terms of psychodynamics and conflict theory offered little understanding of transexualism, although those theories can be useful in understanding what is involved in being transsexual" (p. 24).

Therapists should always be aware of their impact on patients. It is especially important to monitor countertransference when working with TGNC patients, many of whom have experienced significant disruptions within attachment relationships and general social stigma. Therapists who have unexamined biases or rigid theoretical views regarding gender nonconforming expression could inadvertently create an atmosphere of unchecked, harmful enactments. While using theory to understand and explain the etiology of transgender identity can potentially interrupt empathy and, thereby, the therapeutic process, theory can greatly support understanding with regard to the experience of being TGNC.

The most illuminating analytic theory for understanding the internal and relational worlds of many TGNC patients is Winnicott's concept of true and false self (1956, 1965). The false self develops within a relational context that threatens the survival of the true self. The false self is based on compliance and adaptation to environmental failures. Winnicott (1965) asserts, "This is a defence whose success may provide a new threat to the core of the self though it is designed to hide and protect this core of the self" (p. 58). TGNC people, who often have a sense of being different early on, learn to modify gender expression in order to blend in, thereby avoiding threats to attachment and to the survival of true self. Many patients describe early experiences in which they learned to hide gender variance, such as receiving prohibitions against dancing in certain ways, playing with certain toys, wanting certain clothes, or having too many friendships with girls or boys (depending on assigned gender). Adaptations are made in an attempt to preserve some level of acceptance and of belonging at the expense of the true self. As one patient said, "It's like an act that you feel you can never stop. Or else … You don't know but you feel it will be something awful. Total ostracization. You could never possibly be accepted this way so you have to hide it." Again the Internet, accessed from the privacy of the home computer or hand held device, offers virtual space in which to feel more real.

TGNC patients enter therapy when the split between true and false self has become unbearable. The true self, having been buried deep beneath the surface, beyond the reach of harmful interpersonal contact, is cut off from the world of the living, leaving behind a deep impression of deadness and disconnection. This burial, according to Winnicott (1965) can "lead many people who seem to be doing really well eventually to end their lives, which have become false and unreal" (p. 102). Transgender people, in fact, have some of the highest rates of attempted suicide: forty-one percent in contrast to 4.6 percent in the overall U.S. population (Herman, Haas, & Rodgers, 2014). In an astute and sensitive observation of suicide, Winnicott (1965) explained that in cases where there seems to be no other option, suicide is used as the only defense against "betrayal of the true self" (p. 143). In other words, in the absence of any reasonable outlet for expression and contact, suicide may seem like the final and only opportunity to save any semblance of true self. From this perspective, access to information and community made available by the Internet can be literally life-saving.

TGNC people have valid reason to avoid revealing themselves. This same study reveals fifty-seven percent of research participants reported that family chose not to speak with them. High rates of victimization, discrimination, or violence were also reported at school, work, and when accessing health care. This creates a cruel double bind in which the TGNC person is forced to decide between a life lived in hiding, where relationships are conducted primarily by the false self, or a life out in the open, where the integrity of the true self is threatened with discrimination, alienation, and violence. One patient explained: "I have constructed a total puppet masculinity. My posture, eye contact, hand gestures, voice—it's all forced and phony to blend in and hide … I have to protect my self from the inside and the outside."

Many adult TGNC people have spouses or partners, children, established careers and life-long friendships all built around the projected, gender conforming self. As Winnicott (1965) said of the false self, "The defence is massive and may carry with it considerable social success" (p. 134). The decision to come out should not be taken lightly, as it may carry with it significant internal and external upheaval. One patient has discussed the Internet, specifically You Tube narratives, as a venue through which she has learned about other transgender peoples' positive and negative experiences of coming out and transitioning: "Some trans people on the web have thrown it all away because they rushed it. They've lost their families and everything. The young ones have more support. I'm going slow—this works for me."

Making the move toward revealing the true/TGNC self is often a terrifying experience because this is the point at which one emerges from the protective façade of the false, gender-conforming self into a potentially dangerous world. At this point the TGNC person enters the next stage in the developmental model of transgender emergence—"disclosure to significant others" (Lev, 2004). This is often the most difficult part of the process, as it brings up the most intense fears regarding social and relational security. As one patient put it: "I don't like the feeling of hiding but I do like the feeling of protecting my self from being ostracized."

Ready to disclose to significant others, TGNC people must have moved beyond seeking information and reaching out and have at least developed relationships and some support network online. It is prudent to have some support structure established before diving in to telling loved ones, who may have the most difficult time accepting the news. Another patient, when reflecting on the process of coming out as an opportunity to have "real" relationships for the first time, combined with the risk of losing relationships that reveal themselves as conditional, said: "I'm afraid to find out which relationships are real, and which are not real." This speaks to the belief many TGNC people have developed after years of living a fragmented life, namely that relationships are conditional and depend on continued performance of normative gender. As one patient described: "It often feels acceptance is contingent on what people expect. People expect me to be male. I'm trying to keep a foot in both worlds."

Furthermore, some patients have expressed the belief that relationships are essentially trans-actional, and that continued attachment is dependent on a kind of servitude. One patient said, "In the back of my mind I'm always thinking 'These people only like me because I'm doing things for them'. Love and friendship are conditional. When I'm not doing something I'm expected to do, anxiety peaks." This quote reveals an internal world where powerful associations have developed between service and love. Pleasing and doing for others, which includes performing gender in ways consistent with the perceived and actual expectations of attachment figures, has become the primary defense against severe attachment anxiety and the threat of abandonment. Furthermore, TGNC people may feel they have to give parts of themselves away in order to maintain precarious attachments. As one patient put it: "It felt like nothing about me was worth loving or respecting. I was giving away parts of myself because otherwise there wouldn't be any reason to love me."

Klein's analytic theories of splitting, projection, and introjection shed light on defenses often employed by TGNC people. Klein (1946) defines splitting as an early attempt to divide good (gratifying) from bad (frustrating) objects, and describes ways in which this division impacts the development of early object relations: "When persecutory fear is too strong, the flight to the idealized object becomes excessive, and this severely hampers ego-development and disturbs object relations. As a result the ego may be felt to be entirely subservient to and dependent on the internal object—only a shell for it. With an unassimilated idealized object there goes a feeling that the ego has no life and no value of its own" (p. 103).

Some TGNC patients, having learned early on to divide "good" and "bad" parts of self, in this case, gender conforming (good) and gender non-conforming (bad) parts, may describe significant feelings of worthlessness, and depend greatly on external affirmation to maintain a fragile self-system. Early awareness of gender variance and concurrent stigmatization can provoke that most basic human fear: loss of parental love. Because experiences of gender and sexuality bias are so intertwined, Downs's description of the early compromise solution many gay men make to hold on to the elusive love of their parents reflects the experiences of many TGNC people. Downs (2005) writes: "Along with the growing knowledge that we were different was an equally expanding fear that our 'different-ness' would cause us to lose the love and affection of our parents. This terror of being abandoned, alone, and unable to survive forced us to find a way—any way—to retain our parents' love. We couldn't change ourselves, but we could change the way we acted. We could hide our differences, ingratiate ourselves to our mothers, and distance ourselves from our fathers whom we somehow knew would destroy us if he discovered our true nature" (pp. 10–11).

Attachment theory and research also contributes to understanding the TGNC patient. John Bowlby (1981) explained that from "cradle to grave" (p. 247) we seek out responsive attachment figures as our primary means of security. Bowlby (1973), in discussing Bandura's social learning theory, explains, "Observational learning provides a powerful means for the cultural transmission of which situations are to be avoided and which can be regarded as safe" (p. 159). For TGNC people, receiving transmissions about gender conforming behavior is far from an innocuous experience. These transmissions can form the basis for dividing the self into internal/true, external/false parts, in order to avoid situations that could be unsafe.

Winnicott (1965) observed that the relationship between false and true self can evolve over time and that treatment can facilitate the process of reaching an optimal dynamic balance. In thinking of this as a continuum, we see at one end the fully emergent true self (rarely achieved but at least possible with access to Internet community and gender competent therapy); at the other end lies the extreme of the false self posing as the true self, all significant relationships with family, friends, and colleagues being constructed around the false self. When TGNC patients live at this end, they often describe feeling unreal, and believe that relationships are conditional and cannot survive the introduction of the true self, that is to say, the transgender identity. At the middle of the continuum, the "False self defends the True self; the True self is, however, acknowledged as a potential and is allowed a secret life" (p. 143). Here are the TGNC people who need time and space on the Internet.

At this point, TGNC patients may not be out to anyone in their actual lives, but they may have built up some degree of a virtual life. This is where the Internet can serve as a transitional space for the true self to emerge without risking the protection of false self and subsequent threats to attachment. In this transitional space, TGNC people can begin to build ego strength and develop hope that a better life is possible. Through reading the accounts of TGNC people on blogs, watching others transition on You Tube, reading weekly emails sent from trans activists, and engaging in transgender chat room discussions, they can broaden the landscape of their internal object relations set in which it is possible to be transgender and experience love, acceptance, and recognition. Growing up within a social context marred by transphobia (fear and hatred of TGNC people) and cissexism shapes early object relations in such a way that this union seems impossible.

The importance of being seen and recognized by those who share similar experience cannot be overerestimated, and this is where the Internet has been immensely helpful as mirror of the self. Devor (2004), who constructed a model of transsexual identity formation informed by Heinz Kohut's theory of witnessing and mirroring, wrote: "If one is only witnessed and never mirrored one can end up feeling profoundly alone in the world. One can feel as if they are the only one of their kind" (pp. 46–47). A patient, when describing her experience of isolation, said, "I'm afraid I'll never be seen for who I truly am."

Internet community often serves as the first place, the launching pad, from which TGNC people can begin to unearth awareness of gender variance and experience the kind of mirroring necessary to alleviate that sense of being the only one of their kind. As one patient described, "It was the first time I found out there were others like me, who felt like I felt." Over time, however, Internet community, in and of itself, cannot be enough to fulfill the TGNC person's relational, social, and self-actualization needs. To achieve an optimal balance between true and false self, it becomes necessary to cultivate relationships offline also. In this way, the Internet can serve as a transitional path to travel from one end of the false/true self continuum to the other. In describing the evolution of a person's transitional object to its eventual de-investment by the person, Winnicott (1953) explains: "It loses meaning, and this is because the transitional phenomena have become diffused, have become spread out over the whole intermediate territory between 'inner psychic reality' and 'the external world'" (p. 91).

Through the course of time and the maturational process, TGNC people will usually feel the need for further integration, to bring parts of their worlds together in order ease the tension cause by psychic and social divisions. As one patient put it when describing a desire to maintain important aspects of life *and* transition: "I want to be able to keep parts of my life and still be this … I'm getting tired of this whole separation business."

Prior to moving into this more integrated stage of identity development, in a sort of reversal of the splitting process described earlier, TGNC people may experience what some patients have referred to as "the pink fog". Historically, aspects of self that had been split off were those relating to gender non-conformity, because such expression threatened the availability of the good, gratifying object, based on the responsive attachment figure. In the pink fog, transition and all things trans may become idealized, while all representatives of life constructed around the gender-conforming role may be coded as frustrating objects. Lev (2004) describes this early stage in coming out as "akin to being 'over the rainbow'" (p. 244). During this period, transition may appear to be a panacea, offering the pot of gold at the end of that rainbow and a longed-for solution to a lifetime of suffocation under the armor of the false self.

TGNC patients may describe fantasies in which they move to another state, change their name and gender markers, and cut ties with anyone from their previous life and any aspect of life lived under the guise of the false self. In this fantasy, we see an understandable desire to have a life where one is finally known and seen by others in ways congruent with how one knows and sees oneself, and where the trauma of the past is finally over. Some therapists may see this as a manic denial, or a delusion, or some other kind of pathological defense, but it can be more accurately and empathically understood as an attempt to recover from the terrible way things were. To help in understanding, I borrow words from Alvarez (1997) concerning the defenses of an autistic adolescent patient: "I think now that these so-called defenses were desperate attempts to overcome and recover from states of despair and terror … a desperate need that things should be, or should have been, otherwise" (p. 754).

For many TGNC people, transition offers a path toward reconstructing things as they should be. It is important for therapists to recognize this as an understandable and rightful need, and to leave space for the longing and grief associated with not being able to change the way things have been. Some adult TGNC patients, who did not come out until later in life, have described feeling happy for, but also envious of, younger TGNC people who have so much more access to information and resources than they had when growing up, because access to the Internet was not available to many before the 1990s. There is often a need to grieve what was lost and cannot be—such as certain gender-specific rites of passage. Early in the transition process, many adult TGNC people experience a stage of development akin to a second adolescence. This is often brought on by the introduction of hormone therapy, but is also related to the social, relational, emotional, and identity experiences that accompany this period. Such experiences may include choosing one's name, experimenting with a sense of gender-specific style, dating for the first time in one's identified gender, individuation from family and friends, building a sense of group identification within LGBTQ community, and other such endeavors of self-discovery.

This can be a particularly difficult time for family and friends, who may suddenly find themselves on the outside of a process about which they know little and by which they feel threatened. Couples and family therapy is suggested at this point, as transition is something that involves the entire system, not just the individual. Individual therapy and/or support groups (such as those offered by PFLAG—Parents, Families, and Friends of Lesbians and Gays), may also be recommended for significant others and family members who are struggling, in order that they have their own space in which to process reactions. TGNC people may pull away from relationships, not because they do not want or need to maintain these attachments, but because it is so hard to believe that they could continue to be accepted and loved. As one patient described: "I realized I wasn't being a very good spouse because I really withdrew from my wife. I just started to feel hopeless, like there was no way things would work out." This fear is not unfounded for many TGNC people who report that their families no longer speak with or engage with them (Herman, Haas, & Rodgers, 2014). Despite this unfortunate trend there are also many family members who, while they may struggle, ultimately want to stay connected to TGNC loved ones. The Internet provides access to support and information for family members and significant others as they search for and discover websites for organizations such as PFLAG (community.pflag.org), TYFA—Trans Youth Family Allies (imatyfa.org), and COLAGE (colage.org).

At some point, as TGNC patients make their way through the developmental process, there is usually an emerging recognition that the past cannot be erased as though it never happened, along with a concurrent desire for a more integrated life. As one patient put it: "I was brought back down to earth when I realized there's really no option to wipe the slate clean. The only way I could do that would be if I left everyone I knew, moved to Australia, worked in a coffee shop and never talked to anyone. I don't want that!"

In the final stage of transgender identity development, which Lev (2004) terms "integration and pride", TGNC patients "ideally … do not deny their previous selves" (p. 266). At this point, a primary task is to reconcile the past with the present, and synthesize gender with other, equally important aspects of identity, such as that of parent, partner, musician, teacher, therapist, and so on. Some TGNC patients have had sex reassignment surgery (SRS) at this point, but not all have been able to (for financial reasons) or decided to (for myriad reasons, such as not seeing this as a necessary part of the process). Some TGNC patients will decide to make some physical changes, such as undergoing hormone therapy, but will not pursue surgery. Many trans men (or FTM—female-to-male), for example, will take hormones and have top surgery, but not bottom surgery, because these surgeries are commonly thought of as not very effective in terms of constructing desired genitalia. Some TGNC patients will want to live a stealth life, or one in which transgender status is relatively invisible, while some will want to be more visible and vocal about being transgender. There are many roads to integration, and the outcome may appear quite different depending on the road traveled. The common feature of this stage, however, is some degree of resolution with regard to gender dysphoria, and an increased sense of congruence between internal and external experience. Regardless of the language used to describe oneself, at this point, the TGNC person has succeeded in achieving a greater sense of comfort and self-acceptance. This, in the words of Winnicott (1965), is also a time in which a more optimal balance between true/false self has likely been achieved. "In health: the False Self is represented by the whole organization of the … social attitude, a 'not wearing of the heart on the sleeve' … the gain being the place in society which can never be attained or maintained by the True Self alone" (p. 143).

Once the gap between trans and non-trans worlds has been closed there is less reliance on Internet community. Through the process of integration, self-expression and needs for connection and support are more evenly dispersed throughout one's social network. Yet there may still be an online presence as a blogger or chat room participant to support other TGNC people who are earlier in their process. In a statement reposted by Halle (October 2014), a blogger, by the name of Caroline, describing her evolving relationship to online community throughout the course of her transition process, wrote: "This was my therapy, my support group and I have to say for a few years something of an obsessive life. Now it lies mostly idle, creaky with age and gathering dust. Today, my fingers already ache through lack of practice tapping the keys."

By this point, there has usually been space for not only the recognition, but also, as Alvarez (1997) describes, fulfillment of the TGNC patient's "rightful need of assurance, safety, protection, and even justice" (p. 758). The transition process can make this possible because the TGNC person finally has the assurance inherent in the experience of being witnessed and mirrored. Devor (2004) explains, "Transition allows [TGNC people] to make changes that enable others to witness them as they see themselves. Transexualism thus can allow severely and chronically unwitnessed people to survive and thrive" (p. 46). Transition can help TGNC people to not only *feel* but actually *be* safer from the violence and discrimination that are unfortunate aspects of a cissexist society. This process can make it possible for TGNC people to come out in their own time, on their own terms. As one patient described, "I want to have control over who I tell and how I tell them." TGNC people will hopefully also feel protected by their developing support system and community. They will experience the justice of finally feeling a fuller connection between mind and body, and between internal vision and external expression of self.

This rightful need for justice may also be transformed into activism. Situating oneself as a visible, accessible member of the online community establishes a position from which to help others all over the world achieve assurance, safety, protection, and justice. In this way, some TGNC people become advocates, educators, and mentors to peers who may be at earlier points in the process, or who are struggling with various issues that emerge when living as a "gender outlaw" (Bornstein & Bornstein, 1994). One patient described such an interaction: "Someone I knew from the network posted something on FB that worried me. I contacted her on FB and we opened up a chat window. She said it meant a lot to her that I reached out. She really needed someone right then."

Once there is less dependence on Internet community as a source of support, there may be more time spent in this advocacy/education/support role. One patient, in preparing for sex reassignment surgery, watched You Tube channels where transgender women discussed their experiences with and after surgery. This patient shared some of these clips in therapy, one in which a trans woman answered questions viewers submitted regarding surgery, and another where someone discussed the sensitive subject of post-surgery depression and regret. This is a perfect example of ways in which individuals who have actually been through this process can use the Internet as a venue to discuss the complexity of transitioning. This patient also mentioned receiving regular emails of affirmation, education, and support from TGNC people she follows on You Tube.

In addition to in-person social engagement and visibility, some leaders within the gender liberation movement, such as Kate Bornstein, maintain an active Internet presence. Bornstein (Kate Bornstein, 2008), who describes herself as an "author, performer, and advocate for teens, freaks & other outlaws", all of which, she says, make her a "queer and pleasant danger" has a blog, Twitter, and Facebook page where followers can stay connected to her work. Additionally, Bornstein (2010) contributed a video to the You Tube campaign "It Gets Better" (itgetsbetter. org), started by syndicated author and columnist Dan Savage and his partner, Terry Miller. Savage and Miller (It Gets Better Project, 2010) started this campaign after a string of LGBTQ teen suicides had received widespread media attention. "It Gets Better" features over 50,000 user-created videos of LGBTQ and allied people discussing their own experiences from adolescence on, providing a powerful message of hope and support to LGBTQ youth who are suffering now as a result of bullying.

Tumblr, the popular blogging source, includes blogs such as the "Transgender teen survival guide" (transgenderteensurvivalguide.tumblr.com), which is designed to be a safe, supportive space for young people who are questioning gender identity to share stories and concerns and receive support. This is a space where teens can find each other, ask questions, share resources, and offer support to others who are struggling. When one anonymous individual, for example, posted about cutting and feeling suicidal, other bloggers posted such responses as: "We love you, and we want you to stay with us. Please keep yourself safe, my friend (Ren)" and "You are not alone in this. We are here for you. We want to help you. Many of us have been there and know what it's like. So we are all, and I'm sure the followers will agree, sending you tons of cuddles (Chrissi)." Bloggers also share the addresses of crisis and counseling resources such as Trans Lifeline (translifeline.org), a crisis hotline run by and for transgender people and the Trevor Project (thetrevorproject.org), which provides crisis intervention and suicide prevention to LGBTQ youth ages twelve to twenty-four. Trans and questioning youth also ask for and receive recommendations for therapists via the Transgender Teen Survival Guide blog and others like it.

While the aforementioned blog caters to teens, Internet community represents and creates space for TGNC adults across the intersectional spectrum of identity. The site Laura's Playground (lauras-playground.com), for example, states that it is a space for "Transsexual, Transgender, Transgenderists, Crossdresser, Androgyne, Intersexed and Transvestites, (MTF) Male to Females, (FTM) Female to Males, Transwomen, Transmen, families, wives, husbands, partners and friends". Those who identify as gender queer can find chat rooms and blogs through reddit (redditt.com/r/genderqueer), the experience project (experienceproject.com/groups/Am-Genderqueer), and You Tube (youtube.com/user/Genderqueerchat). TGNC people of color can find Internet community in spaces such as Facebook (facebook.com/TransPOCC), Tumblr (tumblr.com/tagged/trans-poc), and through the website for TPOCC (Trans People of Color Coalition) (transpoc.org).

In addition to providing access to emotional and social support, the Internet can be a place to raise funds. TGNC people can garner financial support for hormonal and/or surgical treatments through the fundraising site gofundme.com. Through this site, TGNC people can set up a fundraising account that can be shared via email, Facebook, and other methods of online communication. A financial goal is set, and then family, friends, and other community members can contribute to reaching this goal. Most insurance plans do not cover transgender medical treatments, so this website has become a vital resource within the trans community.

Family members and significant others, who have traveled through their own developmental process, also have an active Internet presence, where they create spaces for education and support for loved ones. One such resource is transgenderchild.net, an online resource for parents and families of transgender youth. Here, parents and family members can find local support groups, as well as online support and information in the form of blogs written by parents and a private Google support group. Spouses and significant others have blogs and other kinds of Internet presence where they share their stories and offer peer support. One such example is the blog shewasthemanofmydreams.wordpress.com, a blog maintained by Diane Daniel (She Was the Man of My Dreams, 2010) where, as she describes on the home page, she discusses her "gender journey with (her) past husband and present wife".

The role that Internet community plays in the lives of TGNC people evolves in the process of identity formation. As has been discussed, this is often the first space in which other TGNC people are discovered, and where that deeply painful feeling of being the only one is finally alleviated. While there are risks as well as benefits, the advent of the Internet and concurrent accessibility of resources and community has been life-saving for many TGNC people. Within the context of Internet community, suicidal TGNC people find alternative ways to emerge from the confines of false self, thus preventing the annihilation of true self. As the process of self-actualization evolves, the Internet serves as a transitional space from which TGNC people can build a network of connections, find their own shape, and develop the confidence and self-acceptance necessary to move beyond Internet life alone, and toward a more complete synthesis of identity in dynamic connection with the world. Throughout this process, therapists meeting with the TGNC patient in analytic psychotherapy in person or in teletherapy can serve a vital role in the birth of true self.

References

Alvarez, A. (1997). Projective identification as a communication: Its grammar in Borderline Psychotic children. *Psychoanalytic Dialogues, 7*: 753–768.

Anonymous (2004*)*. The Psychoanalytic treatment of gender dysphoria: A personal reflection. In: Leli, U. & Drescher, J. (Eds.), *Transgender Subjectivities: A Clinician's Guide* (pp. 19–24). Binghamton, NY: Haworth Medical Press.

Because two options aren't enough for everyone • /r/genderqueer. (2014). Retrieved December 10, 2014, from http://www.reddit.com/r/genderqueer

Bornstein, K. & Bornstein, K. (1994). *Gender Outlaw: On Men, Women, and the Rest of Us.* New York: Routledge.

Bowlby, J. (1973). *Attachment and Loss: Volume II: Separation, Anxiety and Anger. The International Psycho-Analytical Library, 95*: 1–429. London: The Hogarth Press and the Institute of Psycho-Analysis.

Bowlby, J. (1981). Psychoanalysis as a natural science. *International Review of Psychoanalysis, 8*: 243–256.

Crowdfunding for Everyone! (2010). Retrieved December 10, 2014, from http://www.gofundme.com/

Devor, A. (2004). Witnessing and mirroring: A fourteen stage model of transsexual identity formation. In Leli, U. & Drescher, J. (Eds.), *Transgender Subjectivities: A Clinician's Guide* (pp. 41–67). Binghamton, NY: Haworth Medical Press.

Downs, A. (2005). *The Velvet Rage: Overcoming the Pain of Growing Up Gay in a Straight Man's World.* Cambridge, MA: Da Capo Lifelong.

For Parents. (2006). Retrieved December 9, 2014, from http://www.imatyfa.org/resources/parents/

GenderqueerChat. (n.d.). Retrieved December 10, 2014, from http://www.youtube.com/user/GenderqueerChat

GLSEN, CiPHR, & CCRC (2013). *Out Online: The Experiences of Lesbian, Gay, Bisexual and Transgender Youth on the Internet.* New York: GLSEN.

Halle (2014). *Trans thoughts and reflections—Caroline.* Retrieved December 9, 2014, from http://t-central.blogspot.com/2014_10_01_archive.html

Herman, J., Haas, A., & Rodgers, P. (2014). *Suicide attempts among transgender and gender non-conforming adults.* UCLA: The Williams Institute. Retrieved from: https://escholarship.org/uc/item/8xg8061f

I am gender queer. (n.d.). Retrieved December 10, 2014, from http://www.experienceproject.com/groups/Am-Genderqueer

In The News (2012). Retrieved December 10, 2014, from http://www.transpoc.org

It Gets Better Project | Give hope to LGBT youth. (2010). Retrieved December 10, 2014, from http://www.itgetsbetter.org/

It Gets Better, says Kate Bornstein. (2010). Retrieved December 10, 2014, from https://www.youtube.com/watch?v=JxhZJJAGjW0

Kantz, M. (1997). You are not alone: A personal quest for a support system. In: Israel, G. & Tarver, D. (Eds.), *Transgender Care Recommended Guidelines, Practical Information, and Personal Accounts* (pp. 208–210). Philadelphia: Temple University Press.

Kate Bornstein@katebornstein (2008). Retrieved December 10, 2014, from http://www.twitter.com/katebornstein

Kate Bornstein Is A Queer and Pleasant Danger-this is her blog (2006). Retrieved December 10, 2014, from http://www.katebornstein.typepad.com

Kate Bornstein: Public Figure (2013). Retrieved December 10, 2014, from http://www.facebook.com/KateBornsteinGenderOutlaw

Klein, M. (1946). Notes on some schizoid mechanisms. *International Journal of Psychoanalysis, 27*: 99–110.

Lev, A. (2004). *Transgender Emergence: Therapeutic Guidelines for Working With Gender-Variant People and Their Families*. New York: The Haworth Clinical Practice Press.

Open Path Psychotherapy Collective. (n.d.). Retrieved December 9, 2014, from http://openpathcollective.org/

PFLAG National (2014). Retrieved December 10, 2014, from http://community.pflag.org/

Rudacille, D. (2005). *The Riddle of Gender: Science, Activism, and Transgender Rights*. New York: Pantheon Books.

Serano, J. (2007). *Whipping Girl: A Transsexual Woman on Sexism and the Scapegoating of Femininity*. Emeryville, CA: Seal Press.

She Was the Man of My Dreams (2010). Retrieved December 10, 2014, from http://www.shewasthemanofmydreams.wordpress.com

Stark, M. (2000). *Modes of Therapeutic Action: Enhancement of Knowledge, Provision of Experience, and Engagement in Relationship*. Northvale, NJ: Jason Aronson.

Susan's Place Transgender Resources for Transsexual/Transgender Communities (n.d.). Retrieved December 9, 2014, from http://www.susans.org

The Transgender Teen's Survival Guide (n.d.). Retrieved December 10, 2014, from http://www.transgenderteensurvivalguide.tumblr.com

Transgender Child, information on Gender Variant Youth and Families (2014). Retrieved December 10, 2014, from http://www.transgenderchild.net/

Trans People of Color Coalition (2010). Retrieved December 10, 2014, from http://www.facebook.com/TransPOCC

Transgender Terminology (2014). Retrieved December 10, 2014, from http://transequality.org/Resources/TransTerminology_2014.pdf

Transsexual—transgender—crossdresser—gender dysphoria—transgendered chat—transgender forums. (n.d.). Retrieved December 9, 2014, from http://www.lauras-playground.com

Tumblr (n.d.). Retrieved December 10, 2014, from http://www.tumblr.com/tagged/Trans-people-of-color

Winnicott, D. W. (1953). Transitional objects and transitional phenomena—A study of the first not-me possession. *International Journal of Psychoanalysis, 34*: 89–97.

Winnicott, D. W. (1956). On transference. *International Journal of Psychoanalysis, 37*: 386–388.

Winnicott, D. W. (1965). *The Maturational Processes and the Facilitating Environment: Studies in the Theory of Emotional Development. The International Psycho-Analytical Library, 64*: 1–276. London: The Hogarth Press and the Institute of Psycho-Analysis.

CHAPTER SIX

Psychoanalysts facing new technologies in a world of liquid modernity

Adela Abella

I will develop some reflections on the interface between the individual and society in terms of the repercussions of technological innovations on human development and on the practice of psychoanalysis. I will describe some consequences of the frenetic lifestyle induced by the demands of the contemporary world, a world filled with quickly evolving and all-embracing communication technologies that reshape thinking and relating. My central idea is that this way of life has a profound impact on relationships, and on the therapeutic encounter in particular, where it gives rise to challenges that may be unsolvable. In particular I will consider the ways in which psychoanalysts react to, and try to understand, the effects of new technologies on the minds of adults and of children in contemporary society.

Throughout time, important innovations in communication tools have generated high expectations and, at the same time, powerful fears. Five centuries before the Common Era, Socrates expressed his concern that the development of writing would have a weakening impact on memory and, thus, pervasive consequences for the individual's capacity to think and to reach truth (Plato, 1997). In *Phaedrus,* Socrates conveys his fear that "this invention will produce forgetfulness in the souls of those who have learned it. They will not need to exercise their memories, being able to rely on what is written, calling things to mind no longer from within themselves by their own unaided powers, but under the stimulus of external marks that are alien to themselves". In fact, Socrates' reservations are based on the opposition between those "alien marks" (the writing) and "the living and animate speech of a man with true knowledge". Following the same path of thought, during the fifteenth century, Italian humanist Hieronimo Squarciafico worried about printing having similar effects. Thus, in 1477 he declared that "abundance of books makes men less studious … it destroys memory and enfeebles the mind by 'relieving it of too much work'" (in Gifford, 2011, p. 56).

Similar fears have been stirred up by the telephone, the television and, more recently, by mobile phones and the Internet (see Chapter Two). Serious concerns have been raised about their possible impact on the development of intelligence, emotional control, and interpersonal relationships. Over the past thirty years, large increases in IQ, of about twenty points, have been described, an increase which is supposedly linked to children being ever more exposed to, and stimulated by, new technologies. Nevertheless, there are good reasons to think that these technologies are also reshaping intelligence in ways difficult to identify and impossible to predict. The title of N. Carr's paper (2008)—"Is google making us stupid?"—sums up a widely shared preoccupation. Other major conflicting issues are the impact of violent TV movies and video-games upon fantasy and behaviour as well as the social retreat and isolating effect produced by these powerful and absorbing technologies.

Confronted with these profound and rapid transformations in communication technologies strong emotional reactions are the norm, ranging from apocalyptic predictions to idealizing and often manic hopes. It is quite understandable that innovations in communication might arouse high emotional reactions in society, given that they deeply alter our relationships to time, space, knowledge, and, in consequence, to self-representations and social interactions. Psychoanalysts also tend to react no less strongly.

Psychological and social changes brought by new technologies

Within this effervescent and widely shared concern, is it possible for us to reach some more carefully considered, although still tentative and provisional, conclusions? Psychologists, sociologists, teachers, therapists, political scientists, all strive to identify the major trends of individual and societal transformations. Some changes have been described in the way intelligence works in those generations who have grown up with the Internet. There is a reduction in the capacity to read a long text, and there is less depth in comprehension and knowledge, but there is more breadth. Links between different experiences and fields are emphasized. Drawing on the establishment of new connections between formerly separate phenomena may enhance some forms of creativity.

The risk of excessive and even addictive usages of the Internet has to be considered. There is some agreement that the prevalence of real addiction to the Internet is limited, whereas excessive use is widespread, especially among male adolescents and young adults. Given the interactive nature of the web, it has not caused the restriction of social interaction that was found after widespread engagement in watching television, but there is still concern about degradation in quality of interaction. Positive contributions of the Internet are also notable, especially an increase in freedom of access to information and knowledge, and freedom of expression for large portions of the population who were excluded from traditional cultural spaces and media.

Whether for better or worse, our world has deeply and definitively changed, and there is no way back. We must live with it, whether we like it or not. Given this necessity, there is a serious risk in idealizing the past to avoid confronting the real world of today, a world of acceleration and hyper-stimulation. The opposite risk must also be considered: the hollow idealization of every technological innovation and the trivialization of largely unpredictable, but probably profound, consequences of an intensive exposure to new communication technologies, especially in babies and young children.

Individual development

On a clinical and pragmatic level, many authors have addressed the importance of intimate interactions for health and confirmed the relational substrate for human development (Brazelton & Cramer, 1990; Emde, 1981; Golse, 2006; Manzano & Palacio Espasa, 2009; Stern, 1985; Trevarthen, 1979; Tronick, 1980). Their research on the minute-to-minute interactions of mother and baby has illustrated the health-promoting and disruptive effects of various types of encounters between the child and the outside world. A person develops inside and through a net of relationships with others. During the first years of life, these relationships are mostly confined to some highly significant others: parents, siblings, nannies, and extended family members, who convey their conscious and unconscious phantasies and conflicts to the baby.

On a theoretical and metapsychological level, Lacan made some important contributions on this issue (Evans, 1996). He found that the individual must escape the imprisonment inside an illusionary and self-centred ego in order to confront the other. He suggested that the unavoidable confrontation with alterity runs through language and speech. Mind is thus built under the influence of the outside, of the Other, this influence having a double effect. On the one hand, it is humanizing: thanks to language, the individual enters the cultural and social field, which allows him to move beyond the animal and become a man or a woman. On the other hand, it is alienating: decentred from himself, the individual is assigned to the position of a satellite forced to turn around the Other. Thus, the double-sided value of socialization is emphasized as simultaneously humanizing and alienating. Following this path of thinking, Laplanche (1986) has highlighted the structuring effects of the messages coming from the mother as well as their pathological consequences (Abella, 2014 in press).

The baby's limited initial network gradually expands to include a wider number of individuals, for example, teachers and schoolmates, whose internal world will also influence the growing child. That is not all. The child comes into contact with a variety of more abstract, depersonalized social institutions which carry sets of values, expectancies, and prohibitions. When the individual and society interact, individual genetic potentialities are activated in such a way that the biological dimension is shaped by cultural forces. We can recognize here the old philosophical debate between nature and culture. In the field of psychoanalysis, this interaction is understood mainly in two ways: as an organizing force and as an alienating, even pathogenic, influence.

Individual and culture

The preoccupation of psychoanalysts concerning the effects of the encounter between the needs of the individual and the requirements of society has a long history. In 1927, in *The Future of an Illusion*, and still more radically three years later, in *Civilization and its Discontents* (1930), Freud provides a general picture of the opposition between the interests of the individual and those of society. For the sake of maintaining social cohesion, Freud says, civilization must restrict the individual's sexual and aggressive drives. "It seems that every civilization must be built up on coercion and renunciation of instinct" (1927, p. 7). In order to counter the profound dissatisfaction that these social restrictions inevitably arouse, society offers some compensations to the individual, such as moral and cultural ideals expressed through science and art. Indeed, both morality and culture can provide narcissistic satisfactions and a certain degree of disguised and sublimated realisation of repressed instinctual wishes.

In fact, following Freud's views, sublimation appears as potentially the most effective defense mechanism. Its great usefulness draws from the fact that it allows both the individual and society to win on all fronts. On the one hand, sublimation provides some instinctual satisfaction to the individual. It is, of course, a partial and disguised satisfaction but it brings the important advantage of avoiding conflict both with the environment and with the superego. Thus, instead of being confronted with the fear of retaliation, the individual can consolidate his links to the society in which he lives: he gains a sense of belonging and therefore of safety. Further, insofar as sublimatory activities are socially valued, the subject's self-esteem is reinforced. On the other hand, society also wins, given that it is both stabilized and enriched by the sublimatory activities of its members, which supports evolution and transformation.

However, in Freud's view, these substitute satisfactions are rarely sufficient, and therefore frustration becomes overwhelming. Still more serious, he continues, the conflict between society and the individual is internalised and takes the form of a conflict between the superego (heir to social prohibitions and values) and the ego (seen as a manager trying to reach an agreement between opposite sides in order to offer some outlet to the individual's wishes while satisfying the superego's demands). This conflict brings about an unconscious feeling of guilt, which contributes to an increase in the individual's unhappiness. Guilt adds to, and aggravates, frustration. For Freud, the roots of discontent in civilization lie precisely in this unconscious feeling of guilt. Finally, Freud suggests that society's moral requirements are often excessive, they "impose great sacrifices" and "oppress the life": "What we call our civilization is largely responsible for our misery" (1930, p. 86). Thus, these immoderate constraints imposed by society give rise to revolt, neurosis, and self-destruction. This line of thinking leads Freud to a question filled with anxiety and pessimism: Will our society succeed in avoiding its self-destruction?

Our present society is, in a number of respects, very different from the one Freud described. There is broad agreement on certain features that characterize our present day world, such as: the endless rise of individualism, slackening of traditional family and social links, democratization of all relationships and increasing erosion of authority, practically unlimited sexual freedom, failure and abandonment of classical utopias and political ideals, alarming pessimism concerning the future of the planet, and submission to the unbridled seduction of the Internet.

Zygmut Bauman, an outstanding contemporary sociologist, has suggested the term " liquid modernity" for the description of contemporary society in contrast to the preceding one, which he qualifies as "solid modernity" (Bauman, 1999, 2005). Unlike solids, he explains, liquids cannot maintain their form when subjected to an external force, however light it might be. Links between particles are too weak to resist any pressure. For Bauman, this is precisely the characteristic of human relationships in a liquid society.

Solid modernity

Quickly summed up, the paradigm of the "solid modernity" that characterized the first half of the twentieth century is the factory, with its fixed structure in both spatial and temporal senses. This is the era of tools. Tasks are clearly defined, routine organizes life, relationships are predictable and clearly established. The central social imperative is order, and the major risk is that of totalitarianism. The individual knows what to expect, and settles on projects set for the duration of his life. All aspects of life (work, family, leisure) are framed by institutions that establish daily routines and give meaning to human actions and to their consequences. This society primarily provides security to the individual. In exchange, it subtracts freedom. Bauman recalls Freud's conclusions and agrees with him that discomfort in this type of civilization is due to a form of security that shows little tolerance for the pursuit of happiness by the individual (Bauman, 1999). In short, the individual gets security in exchange for freedom.

Liquid modernity

The typical scenario of "liquid modernity" is radically different. Its emblem is the Internet, characterized by decentralization, flexibility, and the sanctification of acceleration and change. Intangible networks replace hardware tools. The central social imperative is no longer order but flexibility, with a resulting expansion of the individual's freedom. Everything (or practically everything) is supposed to be possible and depends only on the individual's desire and ability. This has two major consequences. First: since everything is possible, one must avoid "missing anything". This leads to a frantic consumerism and a lack of commitment, whose goal is to avoid the risk of losing opportunities: indeed, someone who is already engaged with something risks losing new opportunities. (The desperate need to avoid loss of opportunity leads to frantic consumerism and lack of commitment.) Both work and intimate relationships become fragile; human links are most often fleeting and unstable. The second consequence of this "everything is possible" mindset is that autonomy and individual responsibility are emphasized: failures are considered the sole responsibility of the subject. He alone assumes responsibility. In summary, the key words of liquid society are: flexibility, instability, acceleration, frantic and endless change, lack of "signposts", including moral and ethical standards, sacralization of maximum productivity and consumerism, the mythology of individual responsibility (Rosa, 2010).

In short, Bauman agrees with Freud that discomfort in solid society is caused by a form of security that shows little tolerance for the pursuit of happiness by the individual (Bauman, 1997). In liquid society the case is quite different: here the terms are reversed. Now discomfort arises from a freedom that, in its quest for pleasure, shows very little respect for personal security (Bauman, 1999). According to Bauman, the consequences of gains in freedom coming at the cost of personal security are stress, workaholism, feelings of emptiness, and depression.

Treating patients in a liquid world

I will now illustrate some of the difficulties faced by psychoanalysts in treating patients who live in a world that fits, in a number of aspects, Bauman's description of liquid society.

Nina, forty-two years old, came to see me when her only child was four months old. She introduced herself as a brilliant and successful businesswoman who, at age thirty-eight, had hurried into having a baby out of fear of "losing this possibility". Having met a "quite appropriate father" and after a year of unbearable waiting, she rushed into a series of painful procedures for medically assisted procreation, and she finally had a boy whom she loved deeply. Everything was fine with this beautiful baby, who was "just perfect"—except that he didn't fit with her way of life. She was particularly mortified by the recent loss of a promotion she had been expecting for some time. In addition, though deeply loving her son, she was destabilized and terribly bored by the calm pace required in taking care of a baby. Thus, she fed him while checking and answering her emails, and had him watch a baby channel on television while she surfed Facebook for lengthy periods of time. Her relationship with her son's father was deteriorating. She was resentful of his being less disturbed in his professional life than she was. She felt he was critical about her way of managing their baby. His disapproval was extremely hurtful to her, given that she had always been recognized as fulfilling her tasks to perfection.

In her twenties, Nina had had some brief cognitive behavioural therapies that were successful in controlling a variety of symptoms, mainly anxiety. Now she thought the problem was deeper, so she decided to try psychoanalysis. She expected that I would solve her current problems quickly, given that she had to resume work in two weeks. As we talked she recalled her first therapy for vaginismus. She felt that this therapy had been fast and definitively effective, because from then on she could have intercourse and always had rapid and satisfactory orgasms. However, she was disgusted by any foreplay and felt dirty after intercourse, so much so that she had to immediately rush into the shower after having sex. She was unhappy with her partners' frustration at the lack of more leisurely pleasure in touch, but, she concluded: "That's the way it is, and I can't help it".

Throughout the first hour Nina spoke without any sign of concern or guilt. Her tone was factual and hyper-rational, as if she expected that I would entirely share her views. The only emotions she expressed were sheer discomfort and astonishment at the injustice she felt she was suffering, and impatience to be rid of the problem. Later on, we would see that this was not the whole picture and her feelings were much more complex. As for myself, during our first meeting, I had to fight with my personal feelings of irritation and helplessness while trying to counter the risk of judging her. I could feel her pain from profound narcissistic wounds and her need to rigidly stick to an idealized image of herself, but I found it difficult to reach those. All in all, it was hard to touch her or to be touched by her. It was as if I was meeting an extra-terrestrial being, devoid of all that I consider to be common humanity. This made me feel disconcerted, scarcely willing to engage with her, and, therefore, guilty. In retrospect, I wonder if I was taking upon myself not only my own guilt, resulting from my feelings of rejection towards a woman who was clearly suffering, but also *her* unconscious guilt which she could not yet bear.

We started to meet once a week. Nina warned me that she would need to make great efforts to maintain this, for her, very high frequency. She predicted that her commitment would probably only last a few months. She told me about her frenetic life, working long hours and frequently traveling, her mobile phone permanently in her hand. She had moved house several times, often changed friends and sexual partners, and, lacking free time, had a poor cultural life. She was a steady user of Facebook and Twitter, which gave her the feeling of being always up to date and on the move. The pleasures she allowed herself (some skiing in winter, exotic holidays in summer, fleeting sexual encounters at any time, and intense and constant consumption of high quality commodities) seemed to leave her with a feeling of emptiness and the need to rush into more of what had already proved to be disappointing and futile.

There was an addictive quality to all aspects of her life. Every need or frustration was felt as being urgent and unbearable, therefore demanding immediate and total resolution. Unfortunately, once she obtained satisfaction, it most often turned out to be partial and ephemeral, which pushed her to hurry into a new search for relief or pleasure. The circle was thus restarted in what looked to me like an endless and frantic whirlpool doomed to failure. All her links (family, professional, and social) seemed of the fragile and unstable quality described by Bauman. Moral and cultural ideals with their pleasurable and compensatory value were apparently absent from her life. Her frantic quest was reinforced by a social environment in which all her colleagues and friends seemed to function as she did. The immediate satisfactions offered by new communication technologies had an irresistible tempting quality and gave her the feeling that everything was within her grasp. She was persuaded that she not only had the right to have everything, but also that she could have it immediately. All she had to do was help herself.

Nina filled the hours of the first month of treatment with a relentless and detailed description of the story of her life. Sometimes she spoke as a serious professional, conscientiously fulfilling her part of our shared task. At other times I heard in her the plea of a little girl needing help. At the beginning of the fifth hour she stared at me expectantly. She had come to me thinking I was one of the best psychiatrists around. She had told me everything, and so now she was expecting me to give her the solution. I told her that I understood she was used to getting quick and effective solutions for every problem, so it would certainly be hard for her if a ready-made solution did not appear from outside, and that she had to look inside herself. I said that it must be unfamiliar for her to value her feelings, wishes, fears, and fantasies in such a way as to allow her to reach the personal solutions best suited for the particular person she is. She was astonished. I realised that she was honestly trying to understand my words but that, like her baby's needs, they were too alien to her world for her to comprehend them. I was suggesting a slow pace, an attitude of open questioning, some renunciation of certainty, and some tolerance for delay of satisfaction. I thought that the incentive for accepting such an effort-laden path might be the ability to get some pleasure in thinking about one's own internal world and one's relationships with others. This was absolutely strange to her. She was at a loss. She didn't know if I could help her at all: Was I really a good psychiatrist? Or had she been wrong in choosing me? Was I cheating her? As for myself, I was not sure I could really help her, and even wondered if I should suggest cognitive-behavioural therapy.

At the end of the second month Nina overpaid me. At the beginning of the next hour I gave her back the excess of 100 Swiss francs. She looked surprised, and asked, was I sure? She said that 100 francs was nothing for her, and that I might have kept them, since maybe I needed them more than she did. She tried to guess the reasons for my action, and seemed to see the refund as a despicable and inelegant sign of small-mindedness. Finally, she found an "excuse" for me. She decided that I was obliged to be honest. Otherwise my work would have no sense. She then spoke about her father. All his life, he had run a family business in the old patriarchal way— being honest, emphasizing good work over quick gains, taking care of his employees, finding pleasure in his modest gains, and combining his work with enough time for his family and his passions. She had loved him deeply while being mortified by what she judged a shameful lack of ambition. He had been a good man but also a weak man and a coward. Then she added, with a mixture of triumph and sadness, that she had earned in a year as much money as had passed through her father's hands in his entire life.

We came to understand that she saw me as similar to her father in a number of important ways, her father and I both being the opposite of her. I could better understand, now, her phantasy of me as one of the best psychiatrists around. It was painful for her to discover that I was just an ordinary physician after all, someone trying hard to do good work, not the owner of a private clinic, not even a worldwide renowned professor. She guessed I was ignorant of how business runs today. With a distinct shade of contempt in her words, she added, "It is not a child's game. You must be intelligent, quick and tough. It's a war for survival: if you don't devour the other, you will be devoured." By overpaying me she had laid a trap to test me: Was I honest and weak like her father, or quick and tough like her?

The problem was that since she had her baby, she couldn't be tough all the time. She was sometimes surprised to be taking so much pleasure in being tender and quiet with her little boy. In the following hours, some warm, appreciative, and nostalgic feelings towards her father came through. She started to get in touch with the complexity and the contradictions of her internal world for the very first time. She was altogether amazed, relieved, sad, hopeful, afraid, and lost.

After half a year Nina had to decrease the frequency of her treatment and, following some chaotic months, she decided to stop it. She had, however, made what she considered great progress which allowed her to discover a surprising new way of being in the world. Thus, she once expressed great pride for what she felt was an achievement: after doing her shopping, when leaving the store she realised that it was raining: "Instead of rushing under the rain so that I would not lose some minutes, which would have meant that I got home all wet and in a bad mood, I just stood there staring at the rain and waiting for it to stop. It was strange". Then, after a brief silence, she added: "It felt good". Nevertheless these blissful moments, when she could be calm with herself, were rare, and most of the time she felt exposed to discomfort and anxiety. One of her major difficulties in changing her way of life was her lack of solid sublimations that could provide substitute gratifying outlets. Each time that Nina tried to renounce or decrease her frantic consumerism and hyper-stimulation at any level, whether material, relational, or communicational, she found herself confronting a void. She recalled her father's interests in life, the pleasure he got from them, and the respect for his various activities which his family and social environment earned him. She loved her son, but she had no real interest in her life outside her work or her ephemeral sexual encounters, both of which were decreasing.

The problem is that the task of building and engaging in solid sublimation activities, sufficient to provide some deep pleasure and some narcissistic reassurance while reinforcing links to society, demands time and patience. The immediate and always available satisfactions provided by new technologies, even if fleeting and mostly illusory, are probably an irresistible temptation and a too-easy escape from psychic pain. It has been said that cognitive behavioural therapies, with their offer of quick, circumscribed, and well-delineated treatments, might be better suited to the consumerist demands of our accelerated world. However, the results of the treatment of Nina's vaginismus speak to the limited effectiveness of treatments that are too quick, too circumscribed, and too superficial.

It may well be that psychoanalysis has something precious to offer in terms of deepening our contact with ourselves and with others, and, thus, allowing a more authentic and satisfying life. I believe that psychoanalytic treatment provided Nina with some understanding and some true experiences, which opened up new avenues for her life. When thinking about her, I sometimes wonder if she will be able to move forward and develop these new avenues by herself while being immersed in her accelerated and consumerist world. Beyond this particular case, the difficult question remains as to how to make our psychoanalytical tools relevant for the ever-changing and hyper-stimulated patients in our times of liquid modernity. This may be one of the greatest challenges facing psychoanalysis.

The effects of technology on the mind of the psychoanalyst

I come thus to a central question: How do psychoanalysts react to, and how do we try to understand, the unavoidable effects of new technologies on the working of our minds? A first important fact to acknowledge is that as psychoanalysts we use technology daily and intensively. Some colleagues have their own blog or are frequent users of social media such as Facebook or Twitter and seem to find them useful or enjoyable. There may be many who do not, but I don't know of any active psychoanalysts who do not use their mobile phones and the Internet every day. Some usages of technology are helpful. They facilitate documentation, provided that there is some caution concerning the reliability of the broad and unequal variety of Internet sources. Technology allows easy contact with colleagues living on the other side of the world, and may allow treatment by telephone or by the Internet when patient and analyst are far away from each other. Certain usage of technology might facilitate the diffusion of psychoanalysis.

There is, however, also a dark side, which concerns, amongst other things, restrictions to privacy and hyper-stimulation. We find ourselves, along with everyone else, overtaken and often crushed by the overwhelming acceleration of the pace of life and the hyper-stimulation of a world in which, in trying to save time, everyone ends up not having enough. I was recently touched by a colleague's mail which said: "How are you? Very busy, I guess." In fact, she is right: we are all busy, and most of us are very busy. For some of us this "very busy" is too busy.

I am speaking not only of the private sphere, where we must deal with a mass of demands coming from our family, our friends, our cultural life, our sport and our pet, our associative engagements, our garden and our holidays. In our professional life also, there is an increasing number of conferences, meetings, committees, boards, task forces, lectures, telephone conferences … We may have a huge pile of reports, minutes, papers, and books to read and to write, to which must be added an ever increasing and daunting mountain of emails and instant messages, which must be answered as quickly as possible. This can have serious consequences for our work. A friend of mine told me recently: "If I read my mails in between two sessions, my listening is not the same." He then added: "But who would waste the chance of using a few minutes when we are so drastically short of time?" Another analyst confessed that he had to fight the urge to check his mobile phone during sessions "just to see if there is something urgent, while the patient is in silence".

This is for me a major issue. How can our thinking and our listening resist the acceleration and hyper-stimulation that the new technologies impose? The problem is that psychoanalysis requires a slow pace and enough time to think, with unfilled spaces and time to waste (Ogden, 2005). Moreover, creativity often demands a degree of silence and emptiness (Abella, 2012). The accelerated show-business-like activity that is often required of an active psychoanalyst today—unrelentingly writing papers and books, lecturing, participating in committees, frequently travelling, permanently consulting her computer—might be extenuating and sterilizing for some of us. Thus, the traditional image of a psychoanalyst as someone who thoughtfully reflects about her patients and about herself, taking the time for a second look, being patiently open to what is unapparent and needs to be unveiled, coexists alongside a new one: an efficient, busy, and hyperactive professional, a conqueror striving to take up the challenges that an increasingly accelerated world poses to psychoanalysis. The balance between the requirements of these two opposed stances is not an easy one. Moreover, it is already having important consequences, not always easy to manage, for the life of both psychoanalytical societies and individual psychoanalysts.

The effects of technology on the mind of the patient

Many psychoanalysts have expressed deep preoccupations concerning the effects of new technologies on their patients. I will refer here mainly to children and adolescents, although some of the comments can equally apply to adults. Many adverse consequences have been described. At the most trivial extreme we find a particular use of mobile phones that seems to promote the elimination of any feeling of separateness or loneliness. The child or the adolescent checks his mobile phone constantly, looking out for any incoming instant message and ready to immediately answer back. This allows the illusion of being in constant contact with others, irrespective of who these others might be, at the expense of compromising the relationship with those who are actually present. A young student aged twenty-one complained recently of how, when she goes to the restaurant with her friends, the first thing everybody does is to put his or her mobile phone on the table: "Everybody watches his/her mobile all the time, and answers at once. You feel everyone is half absent, as if those who are not there were more important than those who are actually on the spot". The question is: might this possibility of filling all one's free time with one's mobile or with videogames hinder the elaboration of a sense of separateness, the access to the pleasures of being with oneself and the acquisition of the capacity to wait and to postpone satisfaction? It could be said that in today's world, and still more in tomorrow's world, there will be no place, and therefore no need, for silence, emptiness, and loneliness. To my mind, this is a terrifying perspective, evoking George Orwell's *1984*.

At the other extreme, we are confronted by severe addiction, where we have the feeling that videogames are used as particularly pathological psychic retreats, sometimes with an almost delusional quality.

This is the case for Arthur, who is twenty-three years old. For several years, he has spent all his nights and almost all his days immersed in his computer. He has completely abandoned his studies, rarely sees his friends, and, when confronted with parental pressure and prohibition, turns violent. He lies, steals, threatens, and refuses all forms of treatment. He seems to be living in a strange, private world which seems so vital to him that he needs to fiercely defend it from any kind of intrusion, whilst his external life seems severely impoverished.

We need to consider the specific role of videogames in this pathology. Can they be considered as the main agent leading him to social retreat and personal inhibition? Is it because they are so easily available that Arthur has been seduced into such an extreme pathological usage?

Is it their particular characteristics, such as extremely strong sensory stimulation, that make them so tempting to him? Or might we speculate that, in the absence of Internet videogames, Arthur would have chosen another pathological refuge whose consequences would have been, not exactly the same, but similar? This is a point of discussion. I have treated young patients whose activities would be considered much more "highbrow" or intellectually rewarding, such as reading good literature or playing music, but they use these activities in equally pathological, addictive or retreat-like ways.

This is the case with Nadia, twenty years old, a brilliant student suffering from severe eating disorder and emotional withdrawal, who enjoys reading great literary masterpieces, but without this arousing any feeling in her: one could say she is denuding the piece and stripping, vomiting, any life out of it. Or, again, Thomas, nineteen years old, who has quit school and has no interest in life except his drum kit, which he plays for hours in complete isolation. Books and music are used by these young people in a way similar to Arthur's addiction to the Internet.

In other cases, playing videogames can be the tool that a given child or adolescent has chosen in order to solve some internal problems. Thus, some psychoanalysts suggest that videogames can work as a transitional object in a potential space in the sense of Winnicott (1953), or as a malleable environment, following Marion Milner (1952). From this point of view, videogames might offer what every game offers: the possibility of experiencing omnipotence, of living out and elaborating different fantasies, of exploring body changes and conflicted relationships in a safe and controlled way. In other words, videogames may offer the possibility of mental growth. This is probably the way most healthy children and adolescents use them, and so do some patients.

Nine-year-old Marc was brought to my office because he was always angry, dissatisfied, and complaining that everybody was luckier than him. The beginning of the treatment was difficult. Marc refused to speak, looked down on me, and seemed entirely absent. One day he spoke to me about a videogame he played at every opportunity. He had created an avatar, a heroic character who was often violent—"But life is like that" he explained—while, at the same time, this avatar was able to express pressing needs and longed-for goals. Hour after hour we explored the feelings and thoughts of his avatar. Through this work, Marc began to recognize himself in him. Indeed some working through took place through this videogame, both when he played alone at home and when he played beside me. Marc did not use this as a pathological retreat, at least not always, but as a manageable passage between his internal world and shared reality.

Nevertheless, despite a clear improvement, this therapy left me puzzled. Marc's difficulties in verbalization and symbolization remained important, with a strong trend towards action. He often seemed to expect instantaneous fulfilment of his wishes and expectations, as if he lived in a virtual world. I wondered if a more traditional verbal therapy, had it been possible, would have helped him to further develop his capacity to think and to postpone.

Finally, one of the fundamental features of the Internet is the fact that it allows and facilitates communication. Every day many of us enjoy the experience of improved communication with our loved ones and with our colleagues. However, this is still a double-edged sword. On the one hand, the risk is that children and adolescents (and even adults) use social networks or their mobile phones in order to maintain the illusion of never being alone, thus avoiding the experience and the working through of separation anxieties. On the other hand, another very annoying feature is the fact that relationships in cyberspace are limited and often superficial, devoid of all the richness and complexity contributed by nonverbal language. They are, in a certain sense, too easy. We can interrupt the contact at any moment when a conflict threatens to arise. Therefore, these digital relationships can hardly replace real interactions with fully and bodily-present people.

However, the possibility of limited, well controlled and carefully rationed relationships, even if they lack complexity or, better, *because* they lack complexity, makes the web useful for some patients at some moments.

Susie, a twelve-year-old I have seen since she was eight, has always had significant problems with her peers. One of her main difficulties was to imagine that others might think and feel differently from her, which provoked constant trouble with everyone around. During a session, she tells me she chats online every night. She explains that she changes her identity constantly, sometimes presenting herself as being older or younger than she is, at other times pretending to have a boyfriend, or to belong to a wealthy family, or to be so beautiful that all girls are envious of her. Realizing how astonished I am, she reassures me: "But everybody does that. It is fun!"

I do not know if everybody does indeed do that, but for Susie the faked personas she assumes are a way of exploring who she is and who she wants to be, and of confronting in a protected way the difficulties she fears most. Far from isolating her, these virtual and fantasised interactions have in fact prepared the way for real and more complex relationships.

Technology as pharmakon

To sum up, thinking about our reaction to new technologies and their consequences for our world and for our ways of thinking, relating, and understanding, calls to mind the ancient Greek word, *pharmakon*, used by Plato in *Phaedrus* (Plato, 1997), where Socrates discusses the harmful effects of writing on memory. *Pharmakon* has a double meaning: it can be a remedy or a poison. I think it is important that we psychoanalysts keep this ambiguity in mind as we confront the impact of technology, so that we can look at the reality as honestly as possible. Extremes should be avoided. There is the risk of a simplistic idealization, which underestimates or ignores the dangers and problems. But a greater risk is the defensive demonization of what is feared because it is new and unknown. This attitude leads our young patients—and the younger generation in general—to perceive us as haughty, ill-informed, and out-of-date. They then see us as being out of touch with them and their needs, and dismissive of their actual world. Between these extremes, we must find a more balanced and more difficult pathway—the one of trying to grasp, and accept, the troubling complexity of this new reality.

References

Abella, A. (2012). John Cage and W. R. Bion: an exercise in interdisciplinary dialogue. *International Journal of Psychoanalysis, 93*: 473–487.

Abella A. (in press). Conviction, suggestion, séduction: des points de vue divergents. In: A. Abella & and G. Dejussel (Eds.), *Conviction, Suggestion and Séduction*. Paris: PUF.

Bauman, Z. (1997). *Postmodernity and its Discontents*. New York: New York University Press.

Bauman, Z. (1999). *In Search of Politics*. Cambridge: Polity.

Bauman, Z. (2005). *Liquid Life*. Cambridge: Polity.

Brazelton, T. B., & Cramer, B. G. (1990). *The Earliest Relationship: Parents, Infants, and the Drama of Early Attachment*. New York: Perseus Books.

Carr, N. (2008). Is google making us stupid? *Journal of the American Psychoanalytic Association, 29*: 179–219.

Emde, R. N. (1981). Changing models of infancy and the nature of early development: Remodeling the foundation. *Journal of the American Psychoanalytic Association, 1*: 179–219.

Evans, D. (1996). *An Introductory Dictionary of Lacanian Psychoanalysis*. Hove, Sussex: Routledge.

Freud, S. (1927). *The Future of an Illusion. S. E., 21*: 1–56. London: Hogarth.

Freud, S. (1930). *Civilization and its Discontents. S. E., 21*: 57–151.

Gifford, D. (2011). *Zones of Remembering: Time, Memory and (Un)conscious*. Amsterdam & New York: Rodopi Press.

Golse, B. (2006). *L'être-bébé: les questions du bébé à la théorie de l'attachement, à la Psychanalyse et à la phénoménologie*. Paris: PUF.

Laplanche, J. (1986). De la théorie de la séduction restreinte à la théorie de la séduction généralisée. *Etudes Freudiennes, 27*.

Lemma A. (2014). An order of pure decision: Growing up in a virtual world and the adolescent's experience of the body, in A. Lemma & L. Caparrotta, eds, *Psychoanalysis in the Technoculture Era*. Hove, Sussex: Routledge.

Manzano, J., & Palacio Espasa, F. (2009). *Scénarios Narcissiques de la Parentalité*. Paris: PUF.

Milner, M. (1952). The role of illusion in symbol formation. In: M. Klein et al., *New Directions in Psychoanalysis*. London: Karnac, 1985.

Ogden, T. H. (2005). On psychoanalytic supervision. *International Journal of Psychoanalysis, 86*: 1265–1280. Plato: *Phaedrus*, trans. by Alexander Nehamas & Paul Woodruff. In: J. M. Cooper & D. S. Hutchison (Eds.), *Plato: Complete Works*. Indianapolis, In: Hackett, 1997.

Rosa, H. (2010). *Alienation and Acceleration: Towards a Critical Theory of Late-Modern Temporality*. Natchitoches, LA: NSU Press.

Stern, D. N. (1985). *The Interpersonal World of the Infant: A View from Psychoanalysis and Developmental Psychology*. New York: Basic Books.

Trevarthen, C. B. (1979). Communication and cooperation in early infancy: A description of primary intersubjectivity. In: M. Bullowa (Ed.), *Before Speech*. Cambridge: Cambridge University Press.

Tronick, E. (1980). *Babies as People*. New York: Collier Books.

Winnicott, D. W. (1953). Transitional objects and transitional phenomena, *International Journal of Psychoanalysis, 34*: 89–97.

PART II

CONCERNS ABOUT TELEANALYSIS: ETHICS, LEGALITIES, INTERFERENCE

CHAPTER SEVEN

Thinking ethically about beginning online work

Ernest Wallwork

This essay explores some of the ethical and technical challenges posed by shifting to the use of distance-shrinking communication technologies (principally the telephone and/or online with a web camera), for psychoanalysis and psychodynamic therapy. I will focus primarily on the challenge of talking honestly with patients about the values/disvalues and risks of using these technologies as well as the perennial problem of obtaining truly informed, voluntary consent. The difficulties presented by the unique situations of two very different patients about altering the frame to work at a distance illustrate some of the dilemmas many of us face, as the availability of online resources expands and, at the same time, alters the nature of our clinical practice. I will share how I thought about, and sometimes talked over, moral concerns about working from a distance with patients.

Because I see patients in two different private practice offices 350 miles apart—one in Washington, DC, where I live with my family, and the other in New York state, where I am a professor at Syracuse University—I have been conducting treatment using voice communication on the phone and audiovisual communication on the Internet for over two decades, to make up for missed appointments that could not have been made up otherwise, and to find time to meet analytic patients three or four times a week. This experience has convinced me that good enough psychodynamic therapy and psychoanalysis can be done from afar. But I also prefer in-person work, because, in my experience, both partners in the therapeutic dyad have greater access to non-verbal affective communications when meeting in person. Transference and countertransference meanings are richer, or at least their richness is easier for me to pick up, during in-person sessions, though I also know that working from a distance sometimes helps to elicit transference-countertransference dynamics that have not appeared in office meetings. One reason for this increased access to unconscious material is that psychic defenses are sometimes relaxed when the transferential Other is not physically proximate. With most long-term analytic patients, shifting the frame from the office to cyberspace from time to time seems to augment the work, if the dyad remains alert to the shifts in affect and meaning that the different venues—office, telephone line, and Internet—evoke.

The term "ethics" is not employed here in its usual connotations among mental health professionals. I have in mind a more complex, multifaceted reflective process than the rule-following paradigm commonly associated with adherence to professional codes of conduct, such as the "Principles and Standards of the American Psychoanalytic Association" (Dewald & Clark, 2001). Evaluating conduct by subsuming it under a moral rule or duty is one, but only one, aspect of good moral decision-making that functions primarily to guard against blatantly immoral conduct, for example, the injunction against sleeping with a patient. But rule-following is not an adequate approach to deciding the desirability or undesirability of those many clinical decisions that involve multiple conflicting values, rights, and responsibilities of differing degrees of significance. Consider, for example, the many disparate moral considerations that go into deciding how to protect a particular patient's confidentiality in a public presentation. The professional duty to protect the patient's privacy by a disguise and/or informed consent is too general and abstract to cover the complex moral and technical issues involved in balancing, for example: protecting the patient fully from being identified, even by intimates who know her analyst's name, with an iron-tight disguise; truthfully presenting clinical material to colleagues despite a thick disguise; protecting the patient from the various harms (such as betrayal) resulting from informing her of your desire to publish; shielding the patient from the range of negative affects aroused by reading your draft write-up; discussing alterations suggested by the patient; making sure the patient is truly informed of all relevant considerations, including the real risks of being identified; assuring the voluntariness of the patient's decision despite the multiple transferential meanings of the consent request; avoiding subtle forms of manipulation and coercion in discussing the pros and cons of publication; and making sure the patient knows that consent can be withdrawn at any time prior to publication or before a public announcement of the presentation. How one says what needs to be said ethically adds another level of ethical considerations that go to the analyst's tactfulness, respect, care, and concern for the patient in talking about the frame-changing and relationship-altering options involved in proposing to make a patient's confidential material public.

Despite our childlike human yearning for a single meta-principle or decision procedure that will always and everywhere provide the right moral answer, most of the clinical situations that call for ethical reflection and action, such as the matter of obtaining the patient's informed consent discussed above, are too complex and murky to be so easily resolved. Except in the most egregious situations, we seldom possess a single simple yardstick that determines which of several conflicting moral standards should trump others. What we need in order to arrive at a reasonably good moral decision in complex clinical contexts is not so much a set of *a priori* rules to be followed, but "wise judgment" (*phronesis*, in Aristotle), which involves the capacity to balance, while weighing, the significance of conflicting values and responsibilities in relation to the particular facts and relational dynamics of specific individuals in unique situations (Wallwork, 2012, 2013).

Clinical example: Brandon

Almost thirty years ago, in the dark ages before the Internet, and before I considered the possibly of conducting analyses by phone, my initial reaction to my patient Brandon's request that we continued his analysis on the telephone, after he was transferred out of state, was to refuse. I thought it would be unethical to assent to his request because I did not believe psychoanalysis could be done anywhere outside the privacy and safety of an office setting where patients arrived and left through different doors to minimize encounters that might compromise confidentiality. I was a newly minted psychoanalyst then, who could not imagine any of my teachers or supervisors approving of phone work. And it would be several years before I heard an analyst publically admit to working with psychoanalytic patients by phone.

My ethical objections to phone work would have ended with my initial adamant refusal if it had not been for my patient, who was just as certain that I was wrong. I heard him out, because it was the decent thing to do ethically and I was following subconsciously one of the most important moral injunctions in our field, which is to listen with what Ella Sharpe and Jane Hall call *benevolent curiosity* to what our patients have to say (Hall, 1998; Sharpe, 1950). My patient was a forty-five-year-old executive who was progressing nicely in the middle phase of his analysis. He was steadfast in his refusal to terminate a process that had been, and continued to be, so beneficial to him. Without the analysis, he argued, he would not have earned the promotion that led to his being transferred to the home office. He had spent a small fortune and struggled to squeeze out enough time for four-times-a-week sessions over the previous four years. He did not want to pick up with someone new. He doubted that he would be able to work as well with anyone else. I responded that he did not know that. The urban area to which he was moving had many fine psychoanalysts. Besides, working with a new analyst might be a good thing. Countless analysands had transferred to other analysts in midstream and successfully completed analyses with their new analysts. In fact, I had done it myself, so I felt confident that he would be able to build on his good beginning with someone else.

My patient countered that that might be true for other people, but "I'm not other people! I've told you about some really shameful things I've done that I've never told anyone about before and I'm not going to go down that road again. I can't start over. And, you know what, I won't." Yet, he did not want to terminate the analysis, either. He was worried, and I was too, about his becoming self-destructive again in his new position, and damaging both himself and his firm. We felt we had a good understanding of the unconscious motivations that had led him to become self-destructive at work and in school, but neither of us was confident we knew all there was to know about his penchant for self-destructiveness when he was successful. He was convinced that he needed me to keep himself from blowing this major career opportunity. And, he could not trust that a new analyst would be able to help him untangle a subtle self-sabotage shortly after they had started working together. My patient went on to plead with me to just "try" a "trial analysis" by phone to see if it could work for us. Otherwise, he would simply stop analytic work altogether.

An aversion in myself to talking by phone became clear to me as I mulled over my patient's arguments on behalf of the benefits of continuing and the risks of not. I had never liked talking by phone, to anyone, but especially with family members and close friends. I could not imagine how I could do an analysis by phone, even if other therapists could. But my patient's arguments gradually convinced me that I should try at least a short-term experiment, which would provide some evidence in support of or against my doubts.

After he moved and we started teleanalysis, I was pleased at how quickly we co-created a safe analytic space that enabled us to slip easily into our familiar roles, with their ever-changing transference-countertransference dynamic. I was also surprised when the new venue opened up fresh psychic territory that had been sequestered by Brandon's defenses during the entire four years we had worked together previously. The warm, cozy, affectionate tones Brandon adopted while talking to me evoked countertransference fantasies that our phone sessions were a kind of pillow talk between lovers. The phone helped Brandon see this too and trace its antecedents to erotic feelings for a high school chum. Exploring the homoerotic undercurrents of our "pillow talk" was difficult, but far easier for Brandon to do from the safe distance created by the telephone wires. When Brandon returned to my DC home office several weeks later, our physical proximity evoked a homoerotic panic that enabled me to appreciate just how powerful teleanalysis could be as a unique venue.

In retrospect, in light of what I learned subsequently from working with Brandon, my initial negotiations with him about whether we could continue by phone were ethically negligent. I think he did a good job of obtaining my informed consent to what he, not I, was proposing, in that he succeeded in bringing forth a number of the potential benefits of phone analysis that my preoccupation with the risks of failure discounted. But we failed to discuss how best to guard the privacy of phone sessions. It was several years before I learned that land-lines are more secure than wireless calls. I also did not talk with Brandon about how to maintain the frame during phone sessions, so it was a while before I discovered that he was distracted at times because he was reading the mail and business papers and walking around while "chatting" with me. Informalities commonly associated with talking on the phone crept into our sessions, eventually necessitating hitting a "reset" button to re-enforce the frame. Also, we did not discuss beforehand the importance of regularly scheduled in-person sessions at periodic intervals. Our different opinions about the value of in-person sessions created problems later when we disagreed on the frequency of return trips.

Brandon completed a very successful, if lengthy, analysis after fifteen years, eleven of them on the phone. If he had transferred to a new analyst, as I originally proposed, he would have to have quit within six months, because his new job description was revised to include extensive travel that had not been anticipated beforehand. Because we could continue regular sessions wherever Brandon was, working with me by phone not only meant he could continue his analysis, it meant he could complete it.

The unforeseen length of Brandon's analysis left me with two technical concerns, with ethical implications, about teleanalysis that deserve more attention from the analytic community. The first is whether teleanalysis proceeds more slowly than traditional in-person work. I suspect it does, in part because connecting with and disconnecting from the analyst usually happens so rapidly on the phone and online that the patient is deprived of the reverie beforehand and afterwards that occurs when patients drive or walk to and from their office appointments. This reverie seems to me to play a valuable role in the patient's processing, especially working-through fresh analytic insights.

My other concern is whether analyses using telephone or Internet-based communication tend to last longer than they would if conducted in-person. Again, I suspect that they do; because such sessions are so comparatively easy for an analysand to integrate into the rest of her daily life, there are fewer pressures to finish up. I suspect Brandon's analysis would have ended after about eight years (when we briefly considered terminating) if we had been able to continue meeting in person, because he could ill afford to spend so much time getting to and from my DC office. The fact that he could go into his office and close his door for our fifty-minute sessions meant he could indulge his fears that he was not yet ready to terminate. The advantage, however, was that Brandon did not terminate until he was really ready.

Clinical example: Carl

My patient Carl posed very different technical and ethical challenges when the possibility arose of working from afar. By the time Carl entered analysis, I was much more experienced with teleanalysis and prepared to address upfront the many ethical issues involved. But I had never tried teletherapy with a patient as severely disturbed as Carl. Before I explain how I handled the many issues raised about using the Internet with a web camera, I want to share what Carl said, several weeks after he had moved, about how well he thought I had succeeded.

Carl started our tenth distance analysis session this way: "I hate you. Really! … This whole fuckin setup stinks … I lie here, spilling my guts in my own living room miles away and you just sit there, silent or pontificating on a computer screen from fuckin' Washington, DC! You're like one of those talking-head dummies and about as much use to me right now as they are on fuckin Fox fuckin news …" "I think I'm getting worse," Carl continued despondently after a long pause. "I've opened some of my old escape hatches … I don't know that doing this bullshit analysis works online. It's controversial you know. I've read some of the garbage you guys write about tela-whatcha-call-it fucking online fuckin' therapy. It's inferior at best. Maybe it just doesn't work. I can't help but think I've being duped with your Koolaid … If I told anybody around this friggin' town what I'm doing with you online … Oh, My God! They'd think me loony!"

As I struggled to maintain my analytic equilibrium, Carl continued on with this rant, unleashing his pent-up fury at me for the distancing therapy we were doing, while looking directly at me on the screen, and I thought about how frightened, alone, and desperate he must be—as he had been often as a child. Carl had been traumatized repeatedly when very young by physical and sexual abuse during parental absences; here he was struggling once again to process the loss of the corporeal presence of the individual upon whom he had come to rely recently—"more than anyone else," he'd admitted begrudgingly before leaving DC. I had dissolved into a face on a laptop computer monitor and he was enraged with me, imagining I had left him. Although it was his job promotion (due in part to the success of the analysis) that had terminated our in-person sessions, he was right, I had left him in the sense that I was not as fully present any more. He was attacking me now, I reminded myself, as I wrestled with the disappointment and anxiety he evoked in me, because he was missing something in our relationship. The safe analytic space of my office had been lost. The Internet could not, or at least not yet, make up for our very real geographical separation that left him feeling on the cusp of fragmentation, dissolution, and annihilation. I thought again about how upset he had gotten a few days previously when my face abruptly disappeared—or, more precisely, fragmented, as computer images sometimes do when they break down into pixels. Carl had become panicky for a few moments before my image was restored. Afterwards, he had reverted defensively to verbally assaulting me to ward off anxiety evoked by finding himself on the edge of disintegrating along with my image. His sadism functioned, as it often does in sadomasochistic patients, to rid himself of unbearably toxic self-states by projecting them outward and blaming another, while simultaneously connecting to the other by making him or her real through pain.

The transition to teleanalysis was far more excruciatingly distressful for Carl than for any of my other patients who had continued their analyses from a distance, by audio using the telephone or by audiovisual communication using a web camera. For Carl, the rupture in our relationship following his move was another in a long series of abrupt traumatic abandonments. Anticipating some of Carl's difficulties in working at a distance I had tried to refer him to another psychodynamic therapist in his new location. Unlike Brandon, he was willing to see someone else. But, it turned out, that that was simply not possible. There were no analysts, or even psychodynamic therapists, anywhere near the rural setting to which Carl's firm had relocated him.

Should we terminate or continue online?

As soon as we learned of his impending transfer, a web of ethical issues arose as to whether Carl and I should continue the analysis remotely or terminate it before he left DC. I was dubious from the outset about our ability to work analytically from afar, largely because I was afraid Carl was too severely disturbed to do so. It is one thing to widen the scope of analysis, but it is quite another to treat severely disturbed, primitively organized patients at a distance within the constraints of the new technologies. For example, how would I be able to help Carl if he deteriorated and needed emergency care in a community I did not know?

I knew Carl, despite his tough exterior, to be a hyper-sensitive, tactile guy attuned to subtle noises, slight movements, barely discernable smells. I was afraid he would find the affect-thinning, flat screen visages on the computer monitor disconcerting at best, even before we tried it. I suspected Carl's hyper-vigilance to sensual clues would lead him to experience noises that had nothing to do with us as meaningful, such as online technological glitches. To what extent these constraints would disrupt Carl's analysis was impossible to predict.

I had doubts, too, about whether Carl and I could manage to create a safe therapeutic setting in cyberspace. Containing his violent affective storms had been a problem from the outset of his analysis in my office. Moreover, Carl had a penchant for challenging the frame repeatedly, and with such potentially harmful conduct that I had considered terminating his analysis several times, but on each occasion we had somehow managed to find some new way of making analytic sense of his egregious behavior that moved the work forward. I worried that online Carl might feel emboldened by the distance separating us to attack the frame with more effective destructive force and that I would have less affective leverage from a distance to help him to contain and to reflect on his conduct. We had had a hard time establishing a therapeutic alliance at the outset. I worried that the precarious mutual trust that we had built might break down online. And then, what? How bad might things get? Would some of the "anger management" issues that had brought Carl into analysis resurface in risky forms of acting out, such as road rage, excessive drinking, and barroom brawls.

I also worried about what might be lost in the intensity of transference-countertransference enactments that are so central to treating seriously disturbed patients. Carl's analysis had been a tumultuous ride from the outset. I must admit that part of me hoped for some diminution of Carl's vicious verbal attacks on me and the analysis, but I also knew that hope for him lay not in burying or muffling toxic affects but in surviving the ruptures they produced so that he could gradually understand better, and find psychic leverage to modify, what was happening unconsciously within him and with me.

On the other side of the risk/cost-benefit ethical calculation, the potential advantages to Carl of continuing his analysis were considerable, if we could manage to keep going. Clearly, he needed an analysis in order to suffer less and to feel better, but also to achieve his twin goals in life: to find a life partner and a successful career. He had tried several forms of psychotherapy and most psychopharmacological remedies before realizing they were insufficient and that he needed an analysis to acquire a handle on his deepest issues. He desperately wanted help. His career was in tatters, as a result of a pernicious self-destructive streak that ran deep in him. All his intimate relationships had ended poorly. Potential partners were often repelled quickly or, if they hung on for a short period, the relationship suddenly collapsed.

Another argument for continuing the analysis was Carl's innate resilience. Time and again, when continuing seemed futile or too dangerous, Carl somehow found untapped inner resources that, in tandem with his stubborn tenacity, saved the day. Carl might be severely troubled, and a cyberspace setting was scarcely ideal for either of us, I reasoned, but it was just possible he could find the psychological resources and commitment with which to persevere, even in adverse conditions.

In addition to a favorable risk/benefit calculation, continuing ethically required that Carl's autonomy be respected in the form of fully informed consent—not in the trivialized version of informed consent that reduces authentic consenting to signing a form, but the robust sense of a mature commitment made after honest discussion of all relevant sides of the issue, including non-dynamic treatment options and what we would do in an emergency or stalemate. During the months that Carl and I had to discuss our options, in conjunction with the information we were gathering about mental health services available in the community to which he was moving, we had ample opportunity to decide on the best initial course of action, which was to try to continue the analysis on the most secure site possible, as well as the one providing the most extensive access to verbal and nonverbal clues by using a web camera. We further agreed that if the analysis proved too difficult, we would consider other options, such as taking a break from the analysis or terminating the work temporarily with the prospect of resuming if Carl were to be transferred back to the DC area.

By the time Carl and I had decided to try to continue the analysis remotely, I felt it would have been unethical not to have tried at least to continue on a trial basis. The potential benefits outweighed the risk of various costs. Carl was knowledgeable about all known relevant information. We had agreed on how to handle crises, if they were to arise. And we had negotiated a mutually satisfactory set of arrangements regarding a new appointment schedule, a higher fee since he would be earning more, his use of the couch in his at-home setting, and his preference for audiovisual communication using the Internet with web camera rather than the purely auditory connection offered on the telephone.

Ethical aspects of negotiating

Treating Carl ethically, as an equal participant in these negotiations about our options regarding whether we would go on and for how we would reframe the setting, was absolutely essential for both therapeutic and ethical reasons. Carl was stuck in, and suffering from, a deep-seated, all-pervasive sadomasochistic paranoid-schizoid relational scenario, which Jessica Benjamin refers to colloquially, in language I sometimes used with Carl, as the "doing or done to" scenario. One of my main aims during our negotiations about if and how to proceed—which were occasionally conducted face-to-face sitting in armchairs and, more often, spontaneously, as Carl free associated on the couch—was to try to help Carl appreciate that two people can actually discuss conflicting opinions and interests, and negotiate a mutually satisfactory resolution of their differences. Carl had very little experience with mutuality and with genuine respect for another individual as a real person upon which to draw. Even as he and I were trying to talk about what we were going to do after his transfer, he kept slipping back into the role of either the sadistic bully or the abused victim. And, of course, he tried—and sometimes succeeded—in making me feel that I was abusing him or was a victim of his abuse.

I was not so naive as to believe that treating Carl with respect during our negotiations would do much to nudge him out of his entrenched S&M patterns. But I hoped the experience of being respected, while participating in a mutual give-and-take dialogue, would provide him with a glimpse of an ethical relational ethos beyond the "doing-done to" scenario that cost Carl and his partners so much pain and suffering.

Restrospective regrets

Despite my efforts to anticipate how Carl might react to shifting the frame to distance analysis using a web camera, I failed to appreciate fully how truly awful the transition would be for him. Removed from all his friends, familiar hangouts, athletic teams, coworkers, and bar buddies, Carl felt again the aching loneliness and desperation of his childhood and adolescence. And he regressed. Frantic for the dependable attachment that had eluded his grasp since infancy, Carl looked initially to our sessions over the Internet for consolation, but I seemed too far away. Our sessions became a fresh site for feelings of alienation, depersonalization, and despair. In polar contrast to those patients who feel as close or even closer to their analysts when face-to-face on screen (Kudiyarova, 2012; Richards, 2014), Carl experienced a profound loss of the secure connection we had found in my home office. The computer screen felt like "we're separated by a fuckin' glass wall," Carl complained bitterly. He had felt similarly shut out emotionally by his parents. They were absent far too much during his childhood and it was at those times that he had been abused. But even when he was with them, he felt as if they were not really there. Communicating over the Internet with my face on the computer monitor felt to Carl as if I was not really present either. And he reacted, as he had with his parents, by becoming a provocative bad boy, by retrieving destructive behaviors that had figured prominently during the first year of the analysis, in a desperate gambit to win my attention by making me pay.

Carl succeeded. His misery, rage, and potentially self-destructive conduct kept me keyed-up for weeks. I knew he wanted to punish me for abandoning him. In his view, I should not have let him go. If I loved him, I would have kept him close. His retrieval of self-sabotaging behavior was partly a form of self-punishment for bringing about his own abandonment, but partly, too, a way of getting to me. I could not help but worry about him. He was all alone and desperate, and he had a history of very bad choices. So, I suffered, too, as he intended, for being so far away.

I found myself regretting not having explored more thoroughly options that would have kept Carl from leaving in-person analysis, such as refusing the job promotion and transfer. The problem with that option at the time was that he very much wanted to accept the promotion. He wanted to believe he could do it. And I wanted to believe that about him, too. But, after he decided to go, we should have spent more time anticipating feelings of abandonment, helplessness, and destructive rage, and the possibility of his retrieving harmful patterns. At the time, I thought dwelling on these risks might undermine Carl's tenuous confidence about moving on. But more discussion might have prepared him better.

I knew that some of my regret for not having explored his likely reactions more thoroughly was counter transference guilt that Carl was projecting into me. But some of my regret was genuine moral remorse. I had tried to remain analytically neutral when Carl and I talked about his and our options, but I am sure Carl sensed my optimism about his ability to work productively over the Internet with the web camera. I had allowed my previous experiences with other, healthier patients to bias how I talked with him, and this bias drained away the real danger from our discussion of various risks. He wanted to please me. So, we had colluded.

Also, neither of us realized that seeing each other on screen would feel so distancing, even as it brought us together. Carl and I had tried it before he moved, to see how it went. We both concluded that we could do it. But our experimentation with using Internet communication and an image on the monitor from the web camera turned out to be misleading. It was conducted in the context of Carl's expectation of seeing me the next day, which was very different from the affective context of total abandonment that flooded Carl in his new locale.

For weeks, Carl seemed on the brink of a serious decompensation, as we soldiered on with the analysis, aware that there were few other options. I found some leverage with him by adopting meta-perspectives that explained what I thought we could understand, drawing on our previous work, about what was happening to him. To counter his destructive conduct, I also confronted him with the serious risks he was running and spelled out clearly for him why he had reasons, which seemed covered up right now, to be very concerned about his temporary retrieval of risky behaviors he had decided to give up. I tried to couch my assessments in language he used about himself, respecting his ability to see why he had reasons to work hard to keep himself safe. That concern, conveyed through my words and efforts to understand him, meant a lot to Carl as evidence of my care, and helped him realize that we were still connected, despite his anxieties to the contrary. Gradually, we found a way of reconstituting an analytic atmosphere online, though Carl always preferred in-person sessions. In time, we were able to make use of what had happened during the transition to distance analysis to advance Carl's analysis, which, like Brandon's, lasted longer than expected. I was relieved to find that we could, after all, continue analysis effectively at a distance, but the experience with Carl left me more cautious about the use of the new technologies, especially with seriously disturbed patients.

Conclusion

Brandon and Carl are typical of many teletherapy patients today, in that they would not have been able to benefit from continuing their analyses without the use of distance-shrinking technologies. There were costs to working online for both that suggest the importance of being reluctant to agree to such work if satisfactory arrangements can be made for in-person work. Brandon's case shows that well-functioning neurotic patients may not appear to suffer any losses from working at a distance, and may seem to enjoy fringe benefits from shifting to the phone or Internet, but there may be long-term costs, such as slower progress and longer analyses. Carl's deterioration highlights the importance of being cautious about shifting to online work with seriously disturbed patients. I hope that my work with Brandon and, especially, Carl has conveyed the value of covering as many ethical bases as possible before agreeing to distance analysis.

References

Dewald, P., & Clark, R. (Eds.) (2001). *Ethics Case Book of the American Psychoanalytic Association.* New York: American Psychoanalytic Association.

Hall, J. S. (1998). *Deepening the Treatment.* Northvale, NJ: Jason Aronson Inc.

Kudiyarova, A. (2012). Psychoanalysis using Skype. In: J. S. Scharff (Ed.), *Psychoanalysis Online: Mental Health, Teletherapy, and Training* (pp. 85–94). London: Karnac.

Richards, A. K. (2014). Book review of *Psychoanalysis Online. Journal of the American Psychoanalytic Association, 62*: 555–558.

Sharpe, E. (1950). *Collected Papers on Psychoanalysis.* London: Hogarth.

Wallwork, E. (2012). Ethics in psychoanalysis. In: G. Gabbard, B. Litowitz & P. Williams (Eds.), *Textbook of Psychoanalysis* (2nd edition) (pp. 349–366). Washington, DC: American Psychiatric Publishing.

Wallwork, E. (2013). Ethical aspects of teletherapy. In: J. S. Scharff (Ed.), *Psychoanalysis Online: Mental Health, Teletherapy, and Training.* (pp. 85–94). London: Karnac.

CHAPTER EIGHT

Legal aspects of teleanalysis in the United States

Donna Vanderpool

In this chapter I will address legal issues of teleanalysis and teletherapy in the United States. I present many examples of state law, but the examples are not exhaustive and they are given to illustrate points of law rather than to cover every state and its particular situation in relation to teletherapy. This area of law is developing very quickly, and so readers should not assume that the examples are still current. If there is no example discussed from particular states it does not mean that there are no examples. Situations crop up without precedent and new laws arise to deal with them. Much of what I say will apply in general to the policy of governments around the world, but the specifics will be quite different, designed to meet local needs. Nevertheless the discussion covers universal elements, and alerts therapists to various legal issues. It cannot be assumed that all that is reported here will apply to therapists working with patients in other countries, because other jurisdictions may have different legal issues that therapists must contend with. My main purpose is to give an overview that increases therapists' awareness of the shifting legal environment. My main point is that therapists need to familiarize themselves with the legal issues relevant to them and their patients in whichever states or countries they live.

I will first present some information on standard of care and its connection to HIPAA (the Health Insurance Portability and Accountability Act of 1996), the statute of major concern to health providers and therapists. Then I will focus on the legal aspects of technology, correcting many misconceptions about online privacy, with particular attention to Skype, the widely used consumer-grade platform. I will look at compliance with professional standards of practice, ethical guidelines, and insurance company policies. I will conclude with remarks on the standard of care and requirements of technology in telemental health.

The standard of care

Healthcare professionals already know that their care must meet what is called "the standard of care" and they are held responsible for ensuring that their care meets that standard. But do they know how it is defined clinically and legally? The standard of care includes, but is not defined as, optimal care. Rather, the standard of care is defined as a continuum of acceptable treatment options, with optimal care at one end of the continuum and barely acceptable care at the opposite end. For patient safety purposes, providers should strive to deliver patient care that is as close as possible to optimal care.

For legal purposes, providers' care needs to meet the minimally acceptable care standards. Providing care that does not meet the minimum standard of care is considered negligence. To prevail in a malpractice lawsuit, a plaintiff must prove four legal elements:

a. negligence (failure to meet the standard of care, or breach of the standard of care)
b. duty (to meet the standard of care)
c. damages (financial, physical, or emotional harm)
d. direct causation of the damages by the provider's negligence.

This makes it seem as if the health professional will not be at risk because the bar to prove negligence is so high and the acceptable standard of care so low, but that is not the whole story. To complicate the issue, there is no set standard of care for any treatment option, but various statutes, regulations, opinions, guidelines, and policies can be brought in as evidence of the applicable standard of care in any clinical care situation.

Statutes—state and federal

Statutes are enacted by legislatures at the state and federal level. An example of a federal statute relevant to telepsychiatry is the Health Insurance Portability and Accountability Act of 1996 (HIPAA) enacted by Congress to protect the confidentiality and security of health information. A subsequent law, the Health Information Technology for Economic and Clinical Health (HITECH), increased HIPAA's significance by:

- **Expanding coverage under HIPAA**: Business associates are now directly liable for HIPAA violations and subject to enforcement (civil and criminal penalties) under HIPAA. Prior to this law, business associates' liability was limited to that assumed via a business associate agreement; there was no applicable government enforcement.
- **Requiring breach notification**: Inappropriate use or disclosure of unsecured protected health information by covered entities or business associates must now be reported to HHS and to the patient.
- **Increasing the civil monetary penalties**: Civil penalties were increased; now each violation can result in penalties up to $50,000.
- **And providing additional HIPAA enforcement**: Various enforcement provisions were added, including requiring audits of covered entities and business associates, and enabling state attorneys general to enforce the federal HIPAA regulations. A whistleblower provision was also included, but has yet to be enacted. Once enacted via regulations, individuals who report HIPAA violations are able to share in monetary penalties and fines collected by the government.

An example of a state statute related to telemedicine concerns requiring informed consent specifically for telemedicine in addition to consent to treatment.

Regulations—state and federal

Regulations are promulgated by agencies. Federal regulations include the Privacy Rule and Security Rule, enacted by the U.S. Department of Health and Human Services (HHS) to implement HIPAA. State agencies include professional licensing boards, many of which have enacted regulations related to services delivered by telehealth, as detailed below.

Court opinions

There have not been many reported cases involving care delivered via telemedicine, but where they have come before the court, the courts have upheld licensing boards' discipline of professionals for the unauthorized practice of medicine, particularly related to prescribing over the internet. In the *Hageseth* case, a Colorado psychiatrist (with only a restricted Colorado license) was charged with a single felony count of practicing medicine without a valid California license. He had prescribed an antidepressant over the internet to a nineteen-year old college student in California who committed suicide. The psychiatrist argued that California had no jurisdiction, but the appellate court ruled that California did have jurisdiction. The psychiatrist pleaded no contest in 2009 and was sentenced to nine months in jail.

Other regulatory materials—federal and state

Regulators have issued guidelines and position statements on delivering care remotely. As an example, the New York Department of Health issued Statements on Telemedicine, explicitly stating that the standard of care for telemedicine services is the same as for services rendered to patients in the physical presence of the providers.

Authoritative clinical guidelines

Various professional associations have developed clinical guidelines related to telehealth. The American Psychological Association issued Guidelines for the Practice of Telepsychology (APA Guidelines). The American Academy of Child and Adolescent Psychiatry issued a Practice Parameter for Telepsychiatry with Children and Adolescents which applies to starting a telemedicine practice for patients of all ages.

Policies and other guidance documents from professional organizations, including ethical codes

In addition to general clinical practice guidelines, many professional organizations have developed policies and other guidance documents on telehealth. For example, the American Psychiatric Association has issued a Resource Document on Telepsychiatry and Related Technologies in Clinical Psychiatry (APA Resource Document).

Other factors

Other items could be used as factors evidencing the standard of care, including journal and research articles on telemedicine, as well as accreditation standards and policies and telemedicine service facilities' procedures for offering telemental health services.

Legal aspects of technology

Ensure compliance with federal law

HIPAA is relevant to all healthcare providers, but treating patients remotely adds an additional level of exposure for patients' protected health information. It is important to clarify a few of the many myths about this extensive law designed to ensure that health records are confidential.

MYTH: All healthcare providers must comply with HIPAA.

FALSE: Only those providers that are "covered entities" must comply with HIPAA. By the term "covered entities, HIPAA is referring to those health care providers that electronically transmit specific transactions with health plans, such as the electronic transmission of claims forms to insurance companies. Providers who bill electronically, or have a billing service that does so on their behalf, are covered entities, and must comply with HIPAA, or face significant civil and criminal penalties.

MYTH: HIPAA is not a big deal.

FALSE: Penalties for HIPAA violations are significant. Penalties for civil violations are up to $50,000 per violation. Criminal penalties can be up to ten years imprisonment and $250,000. In additional to federal enforcement, state attorneys general are now authorized to enforce the federal HIPAA law.

MYTH: HIPAA is not relevant to those not covered by the law.

FALSE: The only significance of not being covered by HIPAA is that the provider is not subject to HIPAA enforcement. However, the confidentiality and security protections under HIPAA represent the floor of protections. All mental health professionals—separate and apart from HIPAA—are held to higher confidentiality obligations under state law and professional ethical obligations. Recognizing that the HIPAA rules are floors of protection, several courts have allowed the HIPAA rules to be used as evidence of the standard of care, even in cases involving providers not required to comply with HIPAA.

Three main regulations under HIPAA

The three relevant regulations under HIPAA, promulgated to implement the HIPAA law, are a) the Privacy Rule, b) the Security Rule, and c) the Breach Notification Rule. For additional information on HIPAA, therapists should consult the HHS website.

a. **Privacy Rule**: Enforced since 2003, this regulation requires covered entities to protect the confidentially of all protected health information (medical and demographic patient-identifying information), in any form (paper, oral, and electronic). Among other confidentiality protections, covered providers who release patient information to third parties (called business associates) performing a function or service for them, must get written assurances from the third party, in the form of a Business Associate Agreement. Under this agreement, business associates promise to maintain the confidentiality of patient information to the same degree as covered entities. Under a subsequent regulation (the Omnibus Rule), business associates are directly regulated by the government for breaches of patient information. Misuse or inappropriate disclosure of patient information by a covered entity or business associate violates HIPAA and subjects the covered entity and/or business associate to civil and criminal penalties. There are other requirements under this regulation, including providing a Notice of Privacy Practices, appointing a Privacy Officer, and providing training to providers.

b. *Security Rule*: This regulation covers only electronic protected health information, and became enforceable in 2005. There are specific protections, policies, and procedures for electronic information that covered entities must enact to prevent the unauthorized use and disclosure of patient information. Examples include, but are not limited to, encryption, passwords, firewalls, backup, and audit trail of who accessed protected health information.

c. *Breach Notification Rule*: This regulation directs who is to be notified in the event of unauthorized disclosure or use (breach) of unsecured protected health information. Note that properly secured (encrypted) protected health information provides a safe harbor exception—unauthorized disclosure of secured protected health information is not a breach. In the event of a breach of health information, in addition to notifying the affected individual, covered entities must notify HHS either immediately (if 500 or more individuals are affected) or yearly (for breaches involving less than 500 individuals).

Ensure compliance with state law and licensing boards

States that have addressed telehealth typically require in general terms that patient information be kept confidential and secure. For example, regulations of the Delaware Board of Examiners of Psychologists require licensees to "whenever feasible, use secure communications with clients, such as encrypted text messages via email or secure websites." Other states have more extensive requirements related to technology. Florida regulation 64B8–9.0141, for example, requires that physicians providing healthcare by telemedicine are "responsible for the quality of the equipment and technology employed and are responsible for their safe use. Telemedicine equipment and technology must be able to provide, at a minimum, the same information to the physician which will enable them to meet or exceed the prevailing standard of care."

States that have addressed telehealth also require that patients consent to the use of technology after having been informed of the risks and limitations. States may have specific elements required in written consents. For instance, Delaware requires psychologists to obtain and document consent for the use of non-secure communications. These requirements may vary among professionals in the same state since each professional licensing board can develop and implement its own requirements.

Therapists who want to comply with the law for their own and their patient's protection need to be licensed both where they practice and where the patient resides. As the Louisiana State

Board of Social Work Examiners put it, professionals using electronic means to provide services must understand that "their practice may be subject to regulation in both the jurisdiction in which the client receives services and the jurisdiction in which the social worker provides those services." Accordingly, providers must comply with the laws, regulations, and expectations of licensing boards related to telehealth technology.

Ensure compliance with authoritative guidelines

As mentioned above, authoritative guidelines can be used to evidence the standard of care in malpractice litigation. Relevant to all teletherapy providers are the various standards and guidelines promulgated by the American Telemedicine Association (ATA) after discussion in its telemental health special interest group (to which any mental health professional may belong, not just the medical doctors). The ATA's Practice Guidelines for Video-Based Online Mental Health Services (2013) has technical guidelines including videoconferencing applications, device characteristics, connectivity (bandwidth and resolution), and privacy.

The American Psychological Association's (APA) Resource Document notes that "the use of the internet can increase the risk for a breach of confidentiality if practitioners (or patients) are not diligent in the application of security measures. Viruses, hackers, spyware, and other threats are continually evolving alongside the development of security measures." The Resource Document includes technological safeguards, such as firewalls, encryption, audit trails, networks and connection issues.

Guidelines 4 and 5 from the APA Guidelines address confidentiality of data and information. Guideline 4 mandates that, "Psychologists who provide telepsychology services make reasonable effort to protect and maintain the confidentiality of data and information relating to their clients/patients and inform them of the potentially increased risks to loss of confidentiality inherent in the use of telecommunication technologies, if any." Further under this guideline, "When necessary, psychologists obtain the appropriate consultation with technology experts … to apply security measures …" and that "Psychologists who provide telepsychology services take reasonable steps to ensure that security measures are in place to protect data and information related to their clients/patients from unintended access or disclosure." Under this guideline, psychologists "are cognizant of relevant jurisdictional and federal laws and regulations that govern electronic storage and transmission of client/patient data and information." Guideline 1 states "Psychologists who provide telepsychology services strive to take reasonable steps to ensure their competence with both the technologies used and the potential impact of the technologies on clients/patients, supervisees or other professionals."

To give another example in the field of psychology, the fourth item in the Ohio Psychological Association's Telepsychology Guidelines addresses secure communications as follows, "Psychologists, whenever feasible, use secure communications with clinical clients, such as … secure websites … Non-secure communications avoid using personal identifying information."

According to the Standards for Technology and Social Work Practice of the National Association of Social Workers (NASW) and Association of Social Work Boards (ASWB), "Social workers should adhere to the privacy and security standards of applicable laws such as HIPAA and other jurisdictional laws when performing services electronically."

Ensure compliance with ethical codes

The use of technology does not change the rules of ethics that apply in person. Mental health professionals are always ethically required to maintain patient confidentiality, regardless of the treatment medium. Various professional codes of ethics have addressed this. The introduction to the American Psychological Association's Code of Ethics (2010) states that the ethics code "applies to these activities across a variety of contexts, such as in person, postal, telephone, Internet, and other electronic transmissions." Section 4.01 of the Code states "Psychologists have a primary obligation and take reasonable precautions to protect confidential information obtained through or stored in any medium." Similarly, the NASW Code of Ethics (2008) states: "Social workers should take precautions to ensure and maintain the confidentiality of information transmitted to other parties through the use of computers, electronic mail … and other electronic or computer technology."

Ensure compliance with applicable health plans

Policy on reimbursement for services rendered via telehealth is inconsistent. Medicare will pay for limited remote services, provided the patients are in a facility in an underserved area. States are increasingly requiring state Medicaid programs to cover telemedicine visits.

Private payers are increasing their coverage for telemedicine services. Several organizations have released state telemedicine reimbursement surveys, including ATA, the National Conference of State Legislatures, and the Center for Connected Health Policy. Medicaid and private health plans can require that specific, approved technology be used for services to be covered.

And what about Skype?

The framework discussed above—ensuring compliance with the various factors that can evidence the standard of care—should be used to evaluate any specific technology being considered. Given the prevalence of Skype and other similar applications in telehealth, the following four factor examples are instructive, as therapists re-examine whether these consumer grade platforms can meet the requirement of compliance with security requirements.

American Psychological Association Task Force on Telepsychotherapy. Division 29 (Society for the Advancement of Psychotherapy) of the APA completed a task force report on telepsychotherapy. The report addresses Skype as follows: "The Internet is not regulated and not currently protected by privacy laws. Skype, for example, is not an encrypted site and is, therefore, not a confidential means of communication. Providing psychotherapy on unencrypted sites is ill advised."

West Virginia Board of Psychology Examiners Policy Statement "Telepsychology—Skype." The Board noted the APA task force comments about Skype—the lack of encryption means Skype is not a confidential means of communication. The Board also agreed with the task force comments that "providing telepsychology on unencrypted sites is ill advised." The Board goes on to say that to use Skype, the Board believes that psychologists would need to:

- check with their malpractice carrier to see if Skype is covered
- check with the patient's insurance to determine coverage
- use only with established patients
- avoid using with high risk patients
- ensure patients fully understand that Skype is not the same as conversation, and anything said on Skype can be published, used, broadcast, etc.
- obtain written consent before using Skpe.

APA Resource Document. After acknowledging that many providers use Skype and FaceTime for videoconferencing and that some of these services may say they are secure and private, providers must ensure full HIPAA compliance, including breach notification and providing audit trails if using these technologies. "Such entities, when they have access to [protected health information], may be defined as 'business associates' under HIPAA, thereby triggering the need for specific agreements and HIPAA compliance by the third party."

Oklahoma State Board of Medical Licensure and Supervision v. Trow (2013). This licensing board action was based on several complaints, including one filed by the state Medicaid program, alleging the physician used Skype with Medicaid patients despite Skype not being a Medicaid-approved telemedicine technology. The Board referenced its own policy statement on Telemedicine in Mental Health, which included the following under Telemedicine Network Standards: "an appropriate telemedicine network shall meet all technical and confidentiality standards as required by state and federal law in order to ensure the highest quality of care." The physician was found guilty of unprofessional conduct based largely on deficiencies in prescribing practices, without mention of his use of Skype. However, subsequently the Board enacted regulations requiring telemedicine to be a) sufficient to provide the same information to the provider as if the exam has been performed face-to-face, and b) HIPAA compliant.

Summary

When selecting a teletherapy technology, professionals should ensure compliance with:

1) HIPAA. It is the therapist's responsibility to ensure that the technology services company is HIPAA compliant.

- Under the *Privacy Rule*, the technology vender must provide a Business Associate Agreement if it stores (for any amount of time, no matter how short) or has access to protected health information, and must have confidentiality policies and procedures in place. The vendor's privacy policy should state if the information is stored or accessed.
- Under the *Security Rule*, the technology vendor that is a business associate must provide audit trails, documenting who has accessed protected health information, and must comply with all of the Security Rule's requirements.

- Under the **Breach Notification Rule**, the technology vendor that is a business associate must notify the covered provider of any breach of protected health information.
- PRACTICAL TIPS: To ensure the vendors you are considering will help you comply with HIPAA, you may want to look for those vendors that have HIPAA expertise and share that HIPAA expertise on their website. Specifically look for:
  - Acknowledgment of HIPAA
  - Statement about the vendor's status as a business associate. Most vendors are a business associate as they store (even if just for a very short time) patient information, even if they don't access it. Business associates should have language about the provision of a Business Associate Agreement
  - If a vendor claims not to be a business associate, therapists should get their written assurances that they do not store or access any patient information.

2) Licensing board requirements
3) Payer requirements
4) Professional association standards

(such as those from the ATA regarding clinical guidelines and technology standards, such as bandwidth, image resolution and other technical aspects, and the standards of national and state organizations).

Legal aspects of treatment

Standard of care considerations

To meet the standard of care when treating patients remotely, providers must meet all applicable requirements for in-person treatment, in addition to factors unique to telehealth.

States are increasingly enacting more statutes and state licensing boards are promulgating more regulations and policies related to treatment via telemedicine. They vary state by state. However, states are consistent in the following two positions:

1. Services are deemed to be rendered in the state where the patient is located; accordingly, providers must determine licensure requirements in the patient's state. Providers must also determine and comply with applicable law relevant to providing healthcare services in the patient's state.
2. The standard of care for remote healthcare services is the same as if both parties are in the physical presence of each other. Professional associations, including the American Psychological Association, assert this as well.

State licensing boards across specialties, are consistent in wanting some type of registration of the telemedicine provider in the patient's state. However, the type of registration can vary. For example, for physicians, according to a Federation of State Medical Boards survey:

- fifty-eight state medical and osteopathic boards require full licensure in the patient's state
- eleven state medical and osteopathic boards issue a special purpose license, telemedicine license or certificate, or license to practice telemedicine across state lines
- one state—Minnesota—requires telemedicine registration.

Penalty for non-compliance

The consequences of being found to be practicing without a license can be significant, and can include, as mentioned in the *Hageseth* case above, criminal penalties such as incarceration. Such penalties are not limited to physicians. New York is just one example of a state with criminal penalties for psychologists found to be practicing without a license which is a Class E felony with fines of up to $5,000 and/or imprisonment of up to four years. Moreover, professional liability insurance policies typically exclude coverage for unlicensed practice and criminal activities.

Various telehealth requirements to comply with

As mentioned above, providers must comply with the laws, regulations, and expectations of licensing boards in states where their patients are located as well as in the state where they are located. States vary in the extent to which telehealth is addressed. Those states that have addressed it are consistent in requiring confidentiality, security, and consent, as discussed above. Additional state requirements vary state by state; for example:

- Social workers in Louisiana providing distance therapy must have a website containing information proscribed by the licensing board.
- The Colorado Board of Psychologist Examiners issued a policy recommending an initial in-person visit prior to using telehealth.
- Psychiatrists in Florida must have a documented patient evaluation, including history and physical examination to establish the diagnosis before issuing a prescription.

Keep in mind that it is not only telehealth requirements that must be met, but also other relevant laws from both states, such as proper disclosure of mental health information and child abuse reporting.

Technology considerations

As mentioned above, consent to the use of technology must be obtained according to various states' law and professional organizations' guidelines. Additionally, providers must develop, and patients must agree to, contingency plans in the event of technology failures.

Patient considerations

Contingency planning is critical for patient safety.

> At the onset of the delivery of telepsychology services, psychologists make reasonable effort to identify and learn how to access relevant and appropriate emergency resources in the client's/patient's local area such as emergency response contacts (e.g., emergency telephone numbers, hospital admissions, local referral resources, clinical champion at a partner clinic where services are delivered, a support person in the client's/patient's life when available).
>
> (APA Guidelines)

The APA Resource Document also addresses emergency management in remote treatment as follows: "Psychiatrists … may not be familiar with local resources in the area of the patient. The internet is extremely limited when emergency intervention is required. In order to practice remotely, clinicians may need to make the effort to learn local resources or consult with services in that area."

Appropriate patient selection for treatment delivered via telemedicine is crucial. Providers need to thoroughly assess each potential patient to be treated remotely. As noted in the APA Resource Document, "most sources discourage the use of e-therapy for suicidal patients." Some states, such as Delaware, spell out patient-specific factors to be considered. The New York Office of Professions for Psychology takes a broader view and in its Guideline: Engaging in Telepractice, recommends that psychologists consider the particular impact of telepractice on dimensions of mental health practice, including, but not limited to:

- awareness and assessment of non-verbal behavior by the patient
- ensuring the privacy of patients and protection of confidential information through the transmission of information
- relational and transferential issues
- access issues such as distribution of computers and familiarity with technology
- temporal factors such as simultaneous communication, time between responses, and formalized "sessions"
- provisions for emergencies, and
- development of technological proficiencies and on-line culture/language.

References

American Academy of Child and Adolescent Psychiatry. Practice parameter for telepsychiatry with children and adolescents. Available from http://www.aacap.org

American Psychiatric Association. Resource Document on telepsychiatry and related technologies in clinical psychiatry (2014). Available from http://www.psychiatry.org/learn/library--archives/resource-documents

American Psychological Association. Ethical principles of psychologists and code of conduct (2010). Available from http://www.apa.org/ethics/code/index.aspx

American Psychological Association. Guidelines for the practice of telepsychology (2013). Available from http://www.apa.org/practice/guidelines/telepsychology.aspx

American Psychological Association. Telepsychology 50-state review (2013). Available from http://www.apapracticecentral.org/update/2013/10–24/telepsychology-review.aspx

American Psychological Association, Division 29 (Society for the Advancement of Psychotherapy). Report from the Society for the Advancement of Psychotherapy task force on telepsychotherapy. Available from http://societyforpsychotherapy.org/report-task-force-telepsychotherapy/

American Telemedicine Association. Practice guidelines for video-based online mental health services (2013). Available from http://www.americantelemed.org/resources/standards/ata-standards-guidelines/practice-guidelines-for-video-based-online-mental-health-services

American Telemedicine Association. State telemedicine gaps analysis—coverage & reimbursement (2014). Available from http://www.americantelemed.org/policy/state-telemedicine-policy#.VHoROZG0KSM

Center for Connected Health Policy. State telehealth laws and reimbursement policies. Available from http://www.cchpca.org/state-laws-and-reimbursement-policies

Federation of State Medical Boards. Telemedicine overview. Available from http://www.fsmb.org/Media/Default/PDF/FSMB/Advocacy/GRPOL_Telemedicine_Licensure.pdf

Hageseth v. Super. Ct. of San Mateo Co., 150 Cal. App. 4th 1399 (2007).

Louisiana State Board of Social Work Examiners. Distance therapy. Available from http://www.labswe.org/distherapy.html

National Association of Social Workers. Code of ethics (2008). Available from http://www.socialworkers.org/pubs/code/default.asp

National Association of Social Workers and Association of Social Work Boards. Standards for technology and social work practice (2005). Available from http://www.socialworkers.org/practice/standards/naswtechnologystandards.pdf

National Conference of State Legislatures. State coverage for telehealth services. Available from http://ncsl.org/research/health/state-coverage-for-telehealth-services.aspx

New York Department of Health. Statements on telemedicine. Available from http://www.health.ny.gov/professionals/doctors/conduct/telemedicine.htm

New York Office of Professions—Psychology. Guideline: Engaging in telepractice. Available from http://www.op.nysed.gov/prof/psych/psychtelepracticeguide.htm

Ohio Psychological Association. Telepsychology Guidelines (2009). Available from http://www.ohpsych.org/psychologists/files/2011/06/OPATelepsychologyGuidelines41710.pdf

Oklahoma State Board of Medical Licensure and Supervision v. Trow (2014). Available from http://melniklegal.com/av/2014_Oklahoma_Trow_Decision.pdf

US Department of Health and Human Services. HIPAA information and resources. Available from http://www.hhs.gov/ocr/privacy

West Virginia Board of Psychology Examiners. Policy statement: Telepsychology—Skype. Available from http://www.wvpsychbd.org/policy_statements.htm

CHAPTER NINE

Teleanalysis: problems, limitations, and opportunities

Lin Tao

In one of the most famous Chinese mythological novels, *Journey to the West*, two omnipotent figures in the heaven, *Thousand-Mile-Eye* and *Wind-Accompanying-Ear*, have supernormal powers of receiving information from far away. With the development of technology services offering voice over Internet connection with web camera, such as the widely used consumer platform Skype, we can communicate in word and image with family and friends at a distance, our words in synchrony with our facial expressions and body movements. Innumerable people now use the Internet to communicate with one another freely and inexpensively, as if erasing the boundaries and limitations of space and time. Technology has been changing our way of thinking, behavior, and life in general. How does technology affect the psychoanalytic situation in particular? Does a secure connection on the Internet offer a "good enough" setting for psychoanalysis, with enough oxygen in the atmosphere for the survival of the analytic couple and the analytic process? Or does it indulge an omnipotent fantasy of the analyst as both *Thousand-Mile-Eye* and *Wind-Accompanying-Ear*?

Addressing these questions stirs controversy. Some analysts find technology expedient and effective in supporting analytic communication. Others doubt that psychoanalysis is possible when communication is through cyberspace. Psychoanalysis in person requires a secure setting, with attention to many aspects such as agreed fees and manner of payment, regular time, length and frequency of appointments, and a physical and psychological space for meeting that supports an analytic process including transference, countertransference, interpretation, and working through. These elements together carry the weight of the analytic effort. Does Internet transmission of sound and image, in contrast to physical co-presence, throw analysis off balance? Will the practice of teleanalysis lead to the final collapse of psychoanalysis or will it lift psychoanalysis to a new point of balance in keeping with the goals of psychoanalysis?

We must assess the potential of Internet communication for supporting an effective analysis. We must not accept its use without careful examination and reflection on experience. In this chapter, I will explore the vulnerabilities, problems, and limitations of Internet communication in terms of its technical fragility and impact on analytic process, the virtual setting and the analytic frame, and the loss of access to the dynamics of slow entry into, as well as away from, the analytic session. I will address the risks of misperception, fragility of communication, and insecurity of the analytic setting and space, and illustrate them from clinical experience with patients in psychoanalysis and psychoanalytic psychotherapy. All the patients described began analysis in person, and after the analyst(s) had relocated, they continued with the analyst(s) through Internet communication using computer-to-computer voice over Internet protocol with web camera. I want to raise points of difficulty not to discredit the use of technology but to contribute to the current vigorous discussions of whether it can be useful in the psychoanalytic situation. Finally, I describe the criteria for selecting a patient for teleanalysis and I discuss the appropriate analytic stance.

Technical fragility and its influence on analytic process

Incomplete perception

In teleanalysis, since the patient and the analyst can communicate only by seeing and hearing each other, many important sources of information may be lost, including nonverbal and pre-verbal aspects. The patient will lose the chance to feel the atmosphere in the room offered by the analyst, which always has significant meaning to the patient. When I walk into my analyst's room for personal analysis, I will be impressed by the psychoanalytic smell and atmosphere in that room with my analyst physically inside that room. When I walk into a real space within which a person is there with me, and all the elements of real interaction are involved, I feel that it is a true, human relationship in which I can grow. I feel warm, safe, and held by the surrounding subtle atmosphere in that room. In comparison to that, I cannot imagine I will have the same feelings if, instead of walking into that analytic room, I open the computer at home or office, log into my software program, and see on my screen, sent by a camera, a mobile picture of the face and part of the body of my analyst and his room.

Although we are hard put to describe the analytic atmosphere in the analytic room, we perceive it with our whole body and mind, our sensory organs, and our intuitions. We can see, hear, smell, touch, and perceive intuitively, so that we can develop full nonverbal and preverbal communication. Technology-assisted psychoanalysis (even though it includes a moving image as well as sound) inevitably loses some important aspects of communication and perception. For instance, the patient cannot smell, cannot feel the vivid atmosphere in the presence of the analyst in the same room, and cannot feel the warmth of the room in which he would have been together with the analyst, all of which is important for the patient's unconscious infantile need to feel the security, constancy, stability, and intimacy of the mother's womb and her embrace. An experience of the container is essential to the development of the infant part of the patient. The analysand in the transference experiences not only an object but a total situation (Joseph, 1985; Klein, 1952). However, analysis that is not in person restricts the patient's experience of both the analyst and the situation, which, in different degrees, may make the patient feel the analyst and the analysis to be artificial, rigid, machine-like, cold, and distant. Since the setting prevents both sides from perceiving the other's information in full, the patient could be anxious that the analyst would miss some important information about her. For his part, the analyst faces the problem of incomplete perception. For instance, he loses the chance to observe the whole process of how the patient comes into the analytic room. He cannot smell and vividly feel the patient as a corporeal presence.

Example: the influence of restricted visual acuity on the analytic situation

Miss H, a university student in her twenties: In one session soon after shifting to teleanalysis, she asked her analyst, "Can you see my tears through the video?" She worried that her analyst would miss her sadness in the session. Although this worry could reflect distrust in her analyst's attunement, his interpreting that as a transference resistance circumvents acknowledging the reality underpinning her question about the format. The truth is that, due to the limitation of information transported by Internet, it is indeed very difficult to see tears clearly, unless the patient wipes them off her face or her voice shows some hint of crying, thus leading the analyst to become aware of the tears. This example poses the question: How does the patient feel in the analysis when silently shedding tears lying on a couch beside a computer with a picture of the analyst who cannot see the expression of sad feelings and who speaks to the patient as if there were no tearful sadness? Because of the actual limitation of view offered in the setting, the attentive and attuned analyst may not be able to connect fully with the patient at this moving and crucial moment.

On the other hand, perhaps the teleanalytic couple, lacking total sensory perception of co-presence, can gradually adapt to this situation of incomplete perception by withdrawing their mind energy from other channels of perception, such as acute vision and smell, to focus on hearing as the main channel for arriving at intuition. It is not difficult to find the evidence in nature, where animals privilege individual organs to perceive the world: when one organ develops, other organs are reduced in importance. In fact, any analyst and analysand who had to switch from working on screen to audio because of poor connection, will need to adapt.

After periods of in-person analysis, patients who must change to teleanalysis gradually settle down into the analytic process; though they tend to complain about the technology-assisted setting, their complaints can be understood not only as objective complaints but as having unconscious meaning. Discussing the problems arising from using technology generates useful material to explore the unconscious mind. The analysand becomes able to focus on hearing as the way of sensing the analyst and analytic situation. On one occasion, Miss H said to her analyst, "I like to hear you, as your voice makes me feel warm and safe, and I feel embraced by your voice holding me."

Meanwhile, with the ongoing adaptation, listening and looking at the screen, the analyst can find himself able to be fully engaged in a real and deep connection. The relationship between the analyst and the patient cannot simply be called a screen relationship: it is a human relationship through the medium of the Internet. The more both of them enter into an analytic process, the more real and human the relationship becomes. It seems that the screen is like a barrier, and both parties have to gradually get over it, and then can get into a relational field. Otherwise, all they see and feel is simply a screen. Once accustomed to working on screen, the analyst thinks of his patients as real analysands, not just as talking images, and vice versa. It is a subtle mental state, by which the analyst seems to see through the screen, and his mind seems to be with his patient in the same space: he sees her and hears her and seems to be with her, even though they are not in the same physical space. At that moment, there seems to be nothing stopping his intuitive perception and attunement and nothing in the way of detecting her hidden feelings of anxiety or anger. In the subtle atmosphere of teleanalysis, the analytic couple can develop a real connection as they adapt to the new external virtual space, and in their minds create an internal space where both parties are emotionally present. The question is to what extent it can contribute to analytic effectiveness.

Interruption or loss of connection in teleanalysis

Internet transmission of sound and image operates on software and depends on adequate bandwidth, both of which are easily disturbed by unknown and uncontrollable forces related to the Internet. These unseen factors cause loss of vocal clarity, irritating intermittent metallic sound, or even the complete interruption of connection. These irritations are fewer with improved Internet speed and quality of computer, but they do still happen from time to time. Distortion and sudden loss of analytic contact influence the analytic frame and process in different ways. Since we cannot know when and why it happens, we cannot predict the moment of disturbance, but if and when it happens, it seriously disturbs the emotional connection. Then, patient and analyst may both develop a conscious or latent anxiety about it happening again to interrupt their connection—particularly likely for the patient, who cannot see the analyst and may not realize the interruption has occurred.

Example: sudden loss of analytic contact by unknown causes

Mrs. K, an accountant in her forties, felt that her sense of security was much threatened, and the natural process of the analysis negatively influenced, when the analytic couple began teleanalysis. She often asked her analyst whether he was still there if he remained silent when she was talking or thinking, because she worried that their connection might have been disrupted without her noticing it and that her analyst might therefore have missed what she was talking about. For some time, she would still ask him whether he was there and whether he could hear her, so as to confirm the good Internet connection between them, before telling her analyst something particularly significant for her. The anticipatory anxiety related to potential technology problems restricted the patient's free association and sense of security in the analytic process. With the analyst's voice arriving through her earphone to her ears being the only evidence of his existence, the absence of his voice predicted the possibility of his *complete* absence, which aroused strong anxiety in the patient when she was in deep regression. The analyst sometimes had to answer her by saying "I am here" or "I can hear you" when she asked him for confirmation. The patient in teleanalysis may need the analyst to answer her so as to differentiate fantasy and reality, but such a deliberate action on the part of the analyst can disturb his freely associative mind and even sacrifice his neutrality and abstinence. The analyst's silence is an essential part of his being there with the analysand, in keeping with his ideal of being a secure container ready to receive whatever she might convey verbally or nonverbally by means of a projective, communicative process (Bion, 1970). But at these times the analyst's silence destroys the container, and breaking the silence also destroys the container.

In Chinese Taoism, the natural process is stressed, because there lies the real path to the truth. When we deliberately do something to complete some aim, we, at the same time and to some extent, disturb or even break the natural balance in the system. In psychoanalysis, when the analyst has to speak so as to counteract the patient's sense of insecurity due to the constraints of technology, he has to sacrifice part of his mind and his energy to think about which sound to make or what to say and when to make the intervention, which is distracting for him and complicates the already complex analytic process. The analyst who intends to confirm the stable connection and prove his presence may unwittingly convey affirmation or disapproval. Certainly, this response could be colored by the patient's fantasy, but could also be triggered by the analyst's inappropriate timing of his response to the patient's expression of anxiety, even though it may have been the right timing for breaking the silence to prove the analyst's presence. It is hard for the analyst to satisfy both sides at once. What's more, sometimes the analysand may seduce the analyst to utter a sound to prove he is there, or answer the question as if to make up for the limitations of the teleanalytic setting.

Once, when Mrs. K asked her analyst whether he could still hear her, her analyst replied by uttering "Hmmm." If he kept quiet, she would really believe they had a problem with the connection, and would stand up to check it, and indeed the connection was, at times, broken. When she smiled and said, "I love to hear you say something," her analyst realized he had been manipulated by her at that moment, even though he did not deny the need to demonstrate his presence and check the connection. My point is that the Internet connection really makes the analytic process much more complex and brings about problematic processes that are hard to deal with. The uttering of non-specific sounds, or having to answer the analysand's question, in teleanalysis could be a fruitful topic for further research.

Having discussed some problems and limitations due to the technical fragility of the teleanalysis setting and its influence on the analytic process, I will turn my attention to discussion of the space for the setting, because it is so different from that in analysis in person.

The teleanalysis setting and the analytic frame

Concerns about the analytic frame

Classical analysis conducted in person requires a reliable, confidential setting in which patients can reveal their primitive wishes and fears. It is the analyst's responsibility to provide this setting and to maintain a firm frame within which patients can safely express themselves. Bleger (1967) eloquently addresses the importance of the frame and its symbolic meaning.

> We may say that a patient's frame is his most primitive fusion with the mother's body and that the psycho-analyst's frame must help to re-establish the original symbiosis in order to be able to change it. The disruption of the frame, as well as its ideal or normal maintenance, are

technical and theoretical problems, but what basically blocks off any possibility of a profound treatment is the disruption the analyst himself introduces or admits in the frame. The frame can only be analysed within the frame, or, in other words, the patient's most primitive depend-ence and psychological organization can only be analysed within the analyst's frame, which should be neither ambiguous, nor changeable, nor altered. (Bleger, 1967, p. 518)

Bleger sees the frame as the receiver of the symbiosis. How is this replica of the intrapsychic inheritor of the infant–mother relationship to be received in the teleanalytic frame? The develop-ment of a person needs a space—from the mother's womb for the fetus to the mother's embrace for the baby after birth, to the family environment, the home, and beyond. All of these spaces function as a holding environment. The interaction between baby and mother occurs in a space that contains the baby and the mother's presence, a space that is the prerequisite for their rela-tionship to develop and without which deep anxiety is the result. This deep anxiety is delivered into the analytic situation, where it needs to be addressed and understood. In a technology-supported space in which patient and analyst are physically in different rooms, both lose the common physical space that holds them and their relationship. The patient loses the ideal of the physical holding environment of the analytic room with the analyst physically in it. To such a patient, technology offers an inadequate setting, in which it may not be possible to create the necessary degree of security and confidence in the setting which is essential for moving on to interpretive elaboration (Carpelan, 1981; Meltzer, 1967).

Winnicott (1947) said, "For the neurotic, the couch and warmth and comfort can be symboli-cal of the mother's love; for the psychotic it would be more true to say that these things are the analyst's physical expression of love. The couch is the analyst's lap or womb, and the warmth is the live warmth of the analyst's body" (p. 72). In teleanalysis, no matter whether the patient is neurotic or psychotic, he or she can only see the analyst and parts of the analyst's space through the virtual space which is like a window; the patient is outside the window and is not physically in the analyst's space, which can, to various degrees, result in the feelings of being excluded, of not being together, and of being separated.

Limitations of virtual space

When comparing teleanalysis with in-person analysis, the significance of the room chosen for analysis is one of the most important elements. Unlike in-person analysis, where patient and analyst inhabit the same room for the duration of the session, in teleanalysis patient and analyst are separated physically in different rooms, or to be more precise, analyst and patient are not in the analyst's room. Instead, the patient is in a room selected without the analyst's input. The patient from the patient's room and the analyst from his consulting room enter a third space, the virtual space provided by software through the Internet. When patient and analyst are con-nected, the mobile picture of the patient moving to lie down, and then lying on the couch in the room, appears in this virtual space while the analyst appears as a face and shoulders against the backdrop of the consulting room. These three spaces in teleanalysis, compared to the one space in in-person analysis, complicate the work. (Here, I am talking about external space, not the internal space.)

In in-person analysis, the analyst offers the patient a reliable physical space, a room with a couch and other carefully selected furniture, books, and objects. That room with its strong walls, floors, and ceilings made of cement and steel is solid, symbolically experienced by the patient as the analyst's strong mind and embrace. Neither patient nor analyst need ever worry that this space will suddenly disappear due to unknown reasons. For teleanalysis, the two physical spaces and the one virtual space must be united so that they can form the required space for analysis. The survival of the three spaces for teleanalysis is totally dependent on the Internet, and this makes them inevitably less stable than that of in-person analysis.

Examples: the change from in-person analysis to teleanalysis

Even though the analytic relationship has been well established, after the analyst leaves, it will be as if the patient is connected to the analyst by a long and possibly unstable umbilical cord. The patient never, particularly at the beginning of teleanalysis, gives up the feeling that the analyst is far away from them, although they could, to some extent at some times, feel warm and moved in the analysis.

Miss Y, a twenty-year-old saleswoman in Internet technology, agreed to continue analysis before her analyst left for another city, but after the teleanalysis started, she firmly reduced her frequency from four sessions a week, refused to lie on the couch, and shortly afterwards, cancelled sessions with no warning, and finally dropped out. She told her analyst, "I feel you are like a picture projected onto the wall, when I want to reach you with my hands. I suddenly find it is an unreal image, and what I can touch is only the empty air." She could not tolerate the new teleanalysis setting after their separation. Mr. M, a postgraduate in his thirties, once said to his analyst, "Your leaving is like a broken kite. And I am the kite. You lost interest in me. You will go away, leaving me alone floating."

These patients' reactions to the analyst departing and switching to teleanalysis seem to indicate that teleanalysis may not have been strong enough to make them feel the analyst's presence and have a sense of their being together as securely as in-person analysis does. Even though the analyst could offer them regular teleanalysis sessions, the virtual space did not seem able to take the place of his previous analytic room. The patients felt to some extent distant and insecure. When patients regress deeply, they urgently need the analyst's physical presence. For instance, in one session, Mrs. K suddenly regressed to physical expression of her anxiety and fear by rapid breathing and muscle tension, as well as a little trembling of her limbs. She said, "Where are you? I want to grasp you! I need to locate your exact position." In this case, where the physical space was replaced by a virtual one, the analyst's mental space for the patient was seemingly not enough to maintain her sense of security and warmth. Once teleanalysis was established and ongoing, anxieties appeared much less frequently. However, appearances may be deceptive. The anxieties may not have been dealt with once and for all, but may have gone underground, as the patient succumbs to the features of the virtual space so as to survive the analytic process. In that case, the frame of teleanalysis has led to a psychic retreat (Steiner, 1993) and loss of opportunity for the emergence of the true self (Winnicott, 1960). This is a real obstacle to psychoanalysis. In clinical practice, we need to look out for a gradual reduction of complaint about the virtual space of teleanalysis, so as to identify whether this implies adaptation or psychic retreat in need of analysis.

Misperception of information

As I have pointed out, in teleanalysis the patient on the couch can only perceive the analyst through sound. This limitation not only will result in incomplete perception, as I have discussed above, but also in misperceiving sounds that are heard. In one session, Mr. M suddenly asked his analyst, "Is there someone else in your room when you are analysing me? I wonder because I heard footsteps in your room just now." This was not necessarily a paranoid transference, since he had no other clues to test his perceptions. The analyst noticed some knocking sounds outside the window, which he thought might have been misperceived by the patient as footsteps in the analyst's room. The analyst clarified what had happened and tried to explore whether there was some transference element in his doubts. Mr. M did not express that sort of idea again about the analyst and his office security but it is suspected that this paranoid anxiety had penetrated into the depth of the patient's mind, and was lurking there silently.

At the beginning stage of teleanalysis, it was difficult for the analyst to choose how to respond to his patient at this moment. The analyst could be silent, or give an explanation of what really happened around him, or give an interpretation of the patient's fantasy based on the misperception, but none of these responses seemed good enough, because the analyst and the patient, at that moment, were not in the same real objective world. They did not share a common physical reality. As a result, the analyst's response might be ineffective or even be experienced by the patient as a disguised comment, if the patient was in a paranoid state. It may be better not to interpret the patient's fantasy as the analyst might do in in-person analysis, but to acknowledge the difficulties they both are facing. The analyst could say, "This is a difficult moment for both of us due to the constraints of the virtual setting. We are in different physical spaces, and have different perceptions of sound." In this way, the analyst would not deny the patient's perception of the sound but leave open the possibility of exploring the element of fantasy that led her to attribute that sound to the presence of another person.

The journey to the analyst

Psychoanalysis requires of the patient motivation (suffering, curiosity, the wish to understand, and the willingness to be a patient), traits of personality and character, and capacities (Greenson, 1968). Here, I want to talk about another possible essential element that qualifies the patient for analysis, but I find it difficult to define, and so I will try by using a story.

There are some Chinese expressions related to Buddhism, such as: "Devote the pure mind to Buddha" (Yi Xin Xiang Fo) and "Your wishes will be realized if you are sincere" (Xin Cheng Ze Ling). Both expressions embody not only the disciple's sincerity, but also the ideal, sacred, reliable, and powerful figure of Buddha, who, the disciple believes, can bring good luck and change of destiny, all of which are actually in the mental attitude of the disciple. I am not trying to suggest psychoanalysis is a religion, but I do think that the patient's sincerity and belief in psychoanalysis is important. In the famous Chinese mythological novel, *Journey to the West*, Ts Tang Seng sets out on the journey to the West to search for Buddhist scriptures with the help of his three assistants, one of whom is the Monkey Sun Wukong. The Monkey Sun possesses numerous magic powers. However, although he is so powerful, the West Ru Lai (the most powerful

Buddha) does not allow him to fly with Ts Tang Seng on his back, directly to the West. They must walk to the West, experiencing eighty-one dangerous difficulties, which is the precondition for seeking the Buddhist scriptures. It is not an overbearing torture, but a way of testing and tempering the mind for sincerity and belief, without which Ts Tang Seng will not understand the truth of Buddhist scriptures. By analogy, in in-person analysis the analyst resides in the analytic room and the patient is on a journey to the analyst, and analyst and patient must believe that pains, conflicts, wishes, and fears should be expressed and experienced in order to achieve a final working-through in the journey of psychoanalysis. Like Ts Tang Seng undergoing tests of his mental sincerity and faith, the patient on the journey to the analyst has in mind some essential elements to be confronted.

In this ritual procedure, sincerity and belief are interdependent and interactive. Of course, the patient may sometimes have resistance on the journey to the analyst, but the most important thing is that the patient has the chance to experience it and overcome it and continue the journey to the analyst. I suggest this makes the analysis deeper and the patient's mind for analysis much richer. The journey to the analyst is a subtle, overlooked but important part of psychoanalysis, which cannot be ignored. However, teleanalysis, born of modern technology, condenses this journey to just one click of the computer mouse. It is just as if the Monkey Sun directly flies to the West with Ts Tang Seng on his back, which the West Buddha will not allow them to do, because, although they could get the Buddhist scriptures by this short cut, it is not considered the road to the truth of the Buddhist scriptures. To be able to find the analyst just by clicking the mouse is more like a magic game than making a real, serious connection. This mouse-clicking connection probably deprives the patient of elements of the journey that are important to experience. In my view, in teleanalysis something essential may be lost.

For those in in-person analysis, the journey to the analyst functions as a kind of buffer zone against too strong an intrusion of real life into the analytic session. So, the journey is like a path around a transitional zone protecting the analytic field from the direct interference of real life. In teleanalysis this protection zone is lacking. By mouse clicking, patients can get directly in time and space from daily life to analytic field. Several minutes before the session, the patient may be having dinner, talking or quarrelling with someone, sleeping, watching television or working, and then jumps into the analytic field through the Internet. This sudden "jumping into" has repercussions on the analytic state of mind in the patient.

Klein (1952) thought that external incidents and actions in daily life that might seem to refer only to external reality turn out to be meaningful in analysis because they connect to and represent accessible unconscious fantasies. Similarly we might think that what is happening just before a teleanalytic session could have unconscious underpinnings useful for analysis. That is interesting, but I am focusing on something different. On the journey to the analyst's room, the patient's mind has been preparing for the coming session, consciously and unconsciously. The patient could bring any external event that happened outside the analytic room before the session and use it for in-person analysis. All the external events reported in the session can be considered as scenery on the way to the analysis. Upon analysis we find that they have been seamlessly combined with unconscious fantasy that can then be analysed.

If you want to cook dinner, on the way home you buy anything you need for the meal. Similarly, as you head towards a traditional analytic session, you sort your thoughts and feelings, to prepare your mind and open it to the analytic task. But attending a session of teleanalysis is a switch-on and- off event, as if you suddenly jumped into the kitchen from your work office without any transition. Much is lost. For instance, teleanalysis patients can often present themselves in a similar way, no matter whether they are late or not. In in-person analysis, if the patient were late, the analyst would hear footsteps hurrying or unconcerned, different ways of knocking at the door, of entering the room, with sweat on the face or not, out of breath or not. In short, the analyst can see the immediate impact of all these external experiences that are so real before the session. The patient cannot hide them. The instant arrival of the patient on the screen, always the same no matter what has happened, cannot reflect the patient's state of mind. The advantage of convenience and connection across a distance carries within it a disadvantage in terms of foreshortening the journey to the analyst and all that it brings into the session.

The ending of the session also contributes material for analysis. In in-person analysis, when the analyst says that it is time to finish, patient and analyst stand, the patient sees the analyst in person, walks to the door, possibly saying goodbye, crosses the waiting room, opens the door, and goes out to the street. During this process, the elements of reality are gradually re-established in mind, even though some residue of regression may still hover. We can consider the departure from the session as another journey, a transition to everyday life. The patient who suddenly gets a phone call on this journey may feel that the transition has been interrupted, strongly or mildly. The phone call, intrusive and sharp, drags the patient away too quickly from the natural transition back to reality. Teleanalysis condenses the journey away from the session to just one click of the computer mouse.

In in-person analysis, it is the analyst who is left in the analytic room, and it is the patient who leaves that room for the journey away from the session, meaning that regressions may be left there, protected in the safe space of that room with the analyst in it until the patient's return. This makes for a feeling of being "held", not only when the patient is in the session, but also outside it. By comparison, when patient and analyst close the connection in teleanalysis, the patient's experience is of being the one left in the room, while the analyst is the one who leaves. Facing the sudden loss of the analyst and being left alone in front of a machine, the patient may feel abandoned.

What happens externally will surely influence what happens internally. The holding environment in teleanalysis may be good enough in some respects, and better than nothing for those who cannot have in-person analysis, but it may lose out on the precious moments so rich with information just before and after sessions. In teleanalysis the analytic couple replaces the physical entry and exit with a routine of beginning and ending the session.

In order to reduce the influence on analytic process by the problems discussed above, the analyst might like to establish with each analysand a rite of saying goodbye as a special setting for the ending of the session in teleanalysis. After letting the patient know it is the time for ending the session, the analyst waits for the patient to click off the connection. Concluding the session in this way leaves a fantasy that the analyst is still there in the virtual space, as he would be felt to be in in-person analysis.

However, there is another aspect of this problem: The patient may use the clicking on and clicking off to satisfy an omnipotent phantasy. Miss L, a business woman in her thirties, in psychoanalytic psychotherapy twice a week, insisted on her clicking on to start the session and her clicking off when the session was going to end. When the analyst addressed this phenomenon, she explained that her clicking on and off made her feel safe, as she had captured the analyst's image and stored it in her laptop. With a click, she could make the analyst appear on her laptop and she still had him in her laptop after the session ended. The analyst was like a little magic man magically stored in her laptop that made it seem as if she possessed him, rather than coming to him for help.

In summary, the journey to the analyst, as well as the journey away from the session, should be part of what Bleger (1967) called the frame of the analysis. The manner of clicking and its timing in relation to the beginning and ending of sessions is a complex feature of teleanalysis and cannot be simply compared to the knock at the door or closing of the door in in-person analysis.

Patients' power over the setting

Even if the Internet connection were perfect, the virtual setting would still have limitations. In in-person analysis it is the analyst who offers the setting, the room, the couch, and the rules. It is the analyst who holds firm against any attack by the patient on the setting so as to create the necessary, safe analytic environment for the patient. However, the maintenance of the teleanalysis setting is done equally by analyst and patient. For instance, both of them have to provide a reliable computer, a fast-enough Internet connection, a good quality headset, microphone, and web camera, and a private room. The patient's power over the setting can subvert the analyst's power of maintaining it. For instance, the resistant patient can influence the setting and the analytic process by choosing a slow Internet speed that breaks up the screen image and interrupts the communication, or a poor quality microphone that distorts the analyst's perception of sound and interferes with the ability to make sense of what is said. These choices reduce the security, constancy, and consistency of the teleanalysis setting and attack the analyst's linking and thinking.

Example: interruption in communication by the patient

In the middle of one session, Mrs. K suddenly sat up and checked her computer. When the analyst commented on the sudden interruption, she explained to him that she had become unsure about whether the battery of her computer would last the whole session. Her unconscious had taken advantage of her power to influence the setting for reasons that they could explore. But even if she could understand her motivation for the attack on the setting, she had experienced, consciously or unconsciously, that she had the power to influence or even damage the working space. In another treatment, as the analyst began saying that it was time to finish the session, Mr. M immediately took off his earphone and lay on the couch quietly, not getting up as usual. The only way the analyst could reach Mr. M, by his voice, had been removed by Mr. M, and so the analyst found himself put into a position where he was powerless to communicate with Mr. M.

Carpelan (1981) held that the analyst, unless absolutely obligated, should not change the external frame of the analysis. Thus he should not let himself be manipulated and controlled by the patient. To a degree quite different from in-person analysis, the patient in teleanalysis really can manipulate and control the setting, in a way beyond the analyst's ability to establish a firm frame. When this leads to an image of the analyst as weak and unreliable, the patient cannot develop the basic trust and necessary dependence in the transference. In in-person analysis, the patient would lose trust in the analyst who failed to maintain the setting under the patient's attack. This would strengthen the conviction that the analyst is an unreliable object that cannot meet the patient's fundamental need for security. If we imagine the patient's primitive infantile conflict as a monster imprisoned by defense, the monster will be let out only when it feels safe enough, only when the analytic environment is strong enough to bring the monster under control. How can patients dare to let out their imprisoned and threatening monsters if they might destroy the analyst, the analytic environment, and the objects in it? How can patients dare to let out their primitive unconscious infantile conflicts if their unconscious fantasy might destroy the analytic space and the analyst?

When connecting with the analyst on the Internet, an adolescent patient, Q, in twice-a-week therapy, usually moved his webcam to and fro, or let it turn over on his computer desk and then suddenly drop, making it as if the analyst had fallen and was lying on the ground looking up at him. The analyst associated to what one would see through the videographer's camcorder if he were shot and the camcorder were to fall on the ground in the battle field. The analyst felt that the young man had a wish to make him dizzy or shoot him. In fact, in one session, he actually pretended to have a gun in his hand and directed it at the analyst. In later exploration, he acknowledged his wish to "kill" the analyst's analytic mind, which might be too threatening to him. Finally, he dropped out. One would wonder whether he felt he owned the power to really kill the analyst's mind and felt unsafe in the virtual setting.

This leads to a consideration of which patients are suitable for teleanalysis. We have to assess the developmental level of the patient, the capacity for object constancy and the ability to distinguish fantasy and reality. Borderline and psychotic patients may not be suitable if they are unable to make the distinction. Patients who act out their destructive wishes on the frame make it impossible to work in teleanalysis. Patients who do not want to try the novel frame, do not feel able to explore and work in the virtual environment, cannot bear the actual distance, or try but cannot get over their discomfort, are not going to get what they need from teleanalysis.

For teleanalysis to have a chance of being effective, patient and analyst must both fully and honestly acknowledge the problems and limitations of the frame, accept that it is the only choice open to them, and decide to work together within its limitations as best they can. Neither analysts who completely distrust teleanalysis nor those who boast of its value without acknowledging its problems, may really help the patient in teleanalysis. Both members of the analytic couple need to have sincerity, a firm wish to survive the difficulty from the beginning, the hope of making a good enough connection, and the courage to travel together on the road to their common destination.

The patient's resistance: acting in

Teleanalysis can function as a kind of space where both members of the analytic couple are able to find each other. When the patient and the analyst are connected on the Internet they come into the same virtual computer space, one in which they can see each other while they are in their own rooms. Then something interesting happens: patient and analyst are connected even though in separate rooms. The analyst observes how the patient is behaving on screen, which makes the patient appear small and far away, and presumably the same is true of the analyst's appearance to the patient. This weakness of the analyst's power over the frame encourages the patient towards acting in and acting out. The patient has the power to decide when and how to connect to the analyst, and he or she also has the potential to close the connection and so close the door on the analyst. Patients in their own rooms can wear whatever they want, even pajamas. They can make tea beside the computer and drink it in the session without any explanation. They can change the position of the furniture, add or remove something from the room, and change the décor, all of which reduces the firmness of the frame.

Before his analysis changed to teleanalysis, Mr. M had always wanted to wear slippers into the analytic room, take them off, and put his naked feet on the couch. He never actually did that, so there was enough time and space to explore the meaning of that impulse. However, when the frame was changed to teleanalysis, he really did put his naked feet playfully on the couch in his own room during sessions, without any interest in thinking about its meaning.

At the beginning of one session, the analyst was surprised to find that Mr. M did not lie on his couch but on a mat on the floor. Mr. M explained that it was a mat that he used for meditation, and on which he felt relaxed. The analyst was aware that Mr. M. had expressed anxious and unsure feelings in recent sessions regarding something that was unclear but that would be fearful for him to talk about, if only he could figure out what it was. Lying on the mat, Mr. M told the analyst that he felt relaxed, and he was able to say what the fearful "something" was. By exchanging the couch for the mat, he projected his anxiety into the discarded couch, and then he could tell the analyst the fearful "something". But he told the analyst only what the something was, not what he felt about it, or how he felt about telling it to the analyst. The analyst lost the most important and valuable element, the patient's feelings, combined with his thoughts and their inhibition in relation to the analyst, represented by the use of the couch.

Reflecting on Bion's (1970) container function, based on Klein's (1952) concept of psychoanalysis as a total situation, Carpelan (1989) writes: "The internal object which by projective identification is transferred into the analyst is linked with various kinds of psychic phenomena, and it is the totality of all this which the analyst has to receive. Thus, the transferred becomes the contained. The analyst's task is then to find the meaning of the transferred and of the whole situation" (p. 148). Mr. M adjusted the setting to suit himself and meet his needs, and the analyst could do nothing but watch it happening. This left the analyst feeling that he could not engage with the total situation, because it had not *been* a total situation. There was a hole in it, through which important feelings leaked. Here, we again see how fragile the teleanalysis setting is. This kind of acting in is very different from that in in-person analysis, which is a more solid setting, while in teleanalysis the patient has more potential to damage the setting. Even if the analyst gave the patient some interpretation of the meaning of his moving from couch to relaxation mat, it would not be effective because the feelings have disappeared. As Joseph (1985) said, "Interpretations dealing only with the individual associations would touch only the more adult part of the personality" (p. 448). In that session, although the patient could tell the analyst about his anxiety, he gave a highly intellectual narrative. The analyst thought he was being perceived as a potentially critical but also significant figure, and that Mr. M was afraid of exposing himself to the analyst, suspecting that this might result in the analyst's contempt and criticism, although, on the other hand, he also wanted to be dependent on the analyst and to trust him. These conflicts, related anxieties, fantasies, and defenses associated with his attachment to the analyst might have been more contained in solid and stable in-person analytic space and therefore potentially easier to explore and analyse. The analyst was left wondering to what extent Mr. M had left the couch altogether because of the limitation and problems of teleanalysis.

Discussion

I have referred to early anxiety and insecurity that are conveyed by technical insecurities. I have shown that the process of analysis can be influenced. I have compared teleanalysis to in-person analysis, and shown how the problems and limitations of the virtual space could present obstacles to the required functioning of the analytic frame. In teleanalysis, the maintenance of the frame is not the sole purview of the analyst: the patient can disrupt or even damage the frame quite beyond the analyst's control. In my view the teleanalysis setting is to some extent not as safe, stable, constant, and consistent as that of in-person analysis. For instance, I think it is doubtful that the setting of teleanalysis can allow the patient to experience fantasy states of primitive fusion with the mother's body. As Belger stresses, the frame which receives the infant–mother symbiosis and the patient's most primitive dependence and psychological organization can only be analysed within the analyst's frame, which must therefore be neither ambiguous, nor changeable, nor altered. But in teleanalysis the patient can alter the frame. The problems, limitations, and fragility of the teleanalysis frame, which I have discussed in detail, may threaten or even damage the function of the frame as a stable projection screen for the patient's mental state. Despite these limitations teleanalysis has been a boon for many patients who would not otherwise have access to psychoanalysis, but enthusiasm and gratitude should not block our critical assessment of what works and what does not. Applying technology in the conduct of analysis is still a new and controversial path in the psychoanalytic field, and there are still many facets which need to be explored in the light of theory and clinical experience. We need further research to address the various weaknesses.

By facing the problems and limitations of the frame in teleanalysis, compared to the in-person analytic frame, I do not aim to sentence teleanalysis to death, but to argue for an appropriate attitude towards teleanalysis. New technology proposes many questions which psychoanalysts have not previously had to address. They could not have imagined psychoanalysis occurring when patient and analyst were not in the same physical space. If the analyst or the patient in an established in-person psychoanalysis temporarily moves to another place but can have access to the Internet, is it reasonable to maintain continuity of care or should that be considered an enactment, fulfilling the patient's infantile wishes or alleviating both parties' separation anxiety? As we seem to be attracted by the "convenience" or "better than nothing" aspect of teleanalysis, we must constantly dedicate our analytic minds to understanding all the questions raised by this new technology.

By exploring the advantages and problems and limitation of teleanalysis, we see that it has much in common with in-person analysis, but also has its own new aspects. Teleanalysis in the twenty-first century can provoke excitement, interest, curiosity, and enthusiasm, but at the same time doubt, sense of betrayal, hatred of the unknown, and threat to the established protocol, as did Freud's introduction of psychoanalysis itself in the late nineteenth century. As in analytic work, the appropriate attitude towards teleanalysis should be non-judgmental and exploratory. We face the positive and the negative aspects equally without judging teleanalysis to be right or wrong. We approach it with trust and hope and a degree of constructive doubt, as we explore it, get to know it, and understand it. An extreme positive or negative preconception damages the open, exploratory analytic process to some extent. If the enthusiastic analyst denies the problems and limitations and their unconscious meaning for the analytic relationship, he will not be successful in teleanalysis. If the skeptical analyst is too doubtful of teleanalysis, he will blame the frame and lose confidence in his analytic work. Appropriate levels of trust, curiosity, and doubt facilitate analytic exploration.

Another aspect requires attention. As Feldman (2009) said of in-person analysis, "In addition to the inevitable and appropriate doubts about his understanding and his work, the analyst is subjected to conscious and unconscious pressures from the patient, the aim of which seems to be to fill him with uncertainty, confusion and doubt" (p. 217). In teleanalysis, the pressures on the analyst are more complex. When the patient complains frequently about the teleanalysis situation, the patient's dissatisfaction amplifies any uncertainty, confusion, and doubt in the analyst. The analyst struggles with how much this complaint is coming from reality, and how much is coming from the patient's projection. When the patient complains that the analyst is distant, cold, and indifferent, the analyst wonders if he is being constrained by the virtual space or if the patient is using the problems of the frame to meet her unconscious needs. When the analyst accepts the patient's complaint and then analyses it, he can see how the patient "contributes to the creation and maintenance of internal objects whose qualities are ambiguous, and whose motives doubtful, with which the patient is engaged" (Feldman, 2009, p. 217).

Summary

In this paper, I have discussed the limitations and problems of teleanalysis. I presented my reflections on clinical practice in this relatively new area of psychoanalysis, and illustrated my ideas with clinical examples. I concluded by arguing for a balanced, open-minded, profoundly analytic approach to teleanalysis.

References

Bion, W. R. (1970). *Attention and Interpretation*. London: Tavistock.

Bleger, J. (1967). Psycho-analysis of the psycho-analytic frame. *International Journal of Psychoanalysis*, 48: 511–519.

Carpelan, H. (1981). On the importance of the setting in the psychoanalytic situation. *Scandinavian Psychoanalytic Review, 4*: 151–160.

Carpelan, H. (1989). Reflections on Bion's container function and its pathology. *Scandinavian Psychoanalytic Review, 12*: 145–161.

Feldman, M. (2009). *Doubt, Conviction and the Analytic Process: Selected Papers of Michael Feldman*. Hove: Routledge.

Greenson, R. R. (1968). *The Technique and Practice of Psychoanalysis*. Madison, CT: International Universities Press.

Joseph, B. (1985). Transference: the total situation. *International Journal of Psychoanalysis, 66*: 447–454.

Klein, M. (1952). The origins of transference. In: *Envy and Gratitude and Other Works* (pp. 49–56). London: Hogarth Press 1980.

Meltzer, D. (1967). *The Psycho-analytical Process*. London: Heinemann.

Steiner, J. (1993). *Psychic Retreats: Pathological Organizations in Psychotic, Neurotic and Borderline Patients*. London: Routledge.

Winnicott, D. W. (1947). Hate in the countertransference. In: Through Pediatrics to Psychoanalysis: *Collected Papers*. London: Tavistock, 1958.

Winnicott, D. W. (1960). Ego distortion in terms of true self and false self. In *The Maturational Processes and the Facilitating Environment*. New York: International Universities Press, 1965.

PART III

TECHNOLOGY IN TRAINING

CHAPTER TEN

The use of technology in clinical supervision and consultation

Janine Wanlass

As mental health practitioners, we clearly recognize the value of ongoing clinical supervision and consultation in the provision of ethical and clinically competent service delivery (Bernard & Goodyear, 2009; Watkins, 2010). This stance is reflected in our licensing standards, which require substantial supervised clinical hours for emerging clinicians, and in our research findings that support consultation as a protective factor in preventing ethical missteps and promoting job satisfaction (Kanz, 2001). The explosion of advances in technology with worldwide reach has implications for the provision of supervision and consultation, offering new alternatives to the traditional face-to-face, in-person delivery method. As with most innovations, such advances in technology offer new possibilities and new concerns about efficacy, ethics, best practice standards, and method-specific practice considerations.

Although telemental health services have existed in the United States since 1959 (Godleski, Nieves, Darkins, & Lehmann, 2008), the manic pace of technological change within the last decade has outpaced our nascent efforts to consider, research, and regulate current telemental health practice. Maheu, Pulier, McMenamin, and Posen (2012) propose a call to action, noting that individual service providers, regulatory boards, graduate training programs, insurance companies, clinical researchers, and professional associations need to act quickly and thoughtfully to establish ethical guidelines, training options, and practice standards for all aspects of telemental health practice. This chapter discusses one aspect of telemental health services, that is, technology-assisted supervision and consultation (TASC), and offers case examples to illustrate practical and dynamic issues in its implementation. For the purposes of this discussion, TASC refers to any clinical supervision or consultation conducted either regularly or intermittently via telephone, tablet, desktop computer technology, or videoconferencing system. Email, blogs, chat groups, and social media such as Facebook and LinkedIn are not included in this category, since they generally do not replace in-person supervision and consultation sessions.

Rationale for use Research on TASC typically offers three primary reasons for its implementation (Kanz, 2001; Maheu, Pulier, McMenamin, & Posen, 2012; McAdams & Wyatt, 2010; Sorlie, Gammon, Bergvik, & Sexton, 1999; Wanlass, 2013; Wood, Miller, & Hargrove, 2005). First, TASC provides access to supervision and consultation to practitioners who are isolated in remote geographic areas. Second, TASC allows practitioners to benefit from clinical expertise not available in their local area. Third, TASC is convenient and cost saving, as practitioners avoid travel costs and hassles, making it easier to pursue consultation. Although not widely discussed in the clinical literature, a fourth benefit might be the increased confidentiality in discussing clinical cases with a consultant outside one's geographic practice area, particularly when the patients involved are practicing clinicians themselves.

Providing mental health services in rural areas presents many unique challenges, including the pressure to effectively treat a wide range of problems, since nearby referral sources are often non-existent (Stamm, 2003). As Wood, Miller and Hargrove (2005) note, "Through its ability to negate many of the obstacles that frequently hinder supervision of interns and new practitioners in rural areas, the use of telecommunication technology to deliver supervisory services can provide supervisees with a knowledge base and experiential alternatives previously deemed inaccessible" (pp. 173–174). For example, a newly licensed practitioner in a small town approximately five hours away contacted me about a child involved in a traumatic car accident in which her mother was killed. Although this practitioner had experience treating children, this three-year-old patient was younger than the practitioner's typical treatment population. Grieving and economically challenged, the family could not afford to transport the child for treatment in another community. The practitioner could not leave her practice for a day a week to obtain in-person consultation on this case. TASC provided this practitioner with an option for ongoing consultation, offering the support and expertise needed for her to effectively treat this young child.

Practitioners in rural communities or geographically isolated locations are one group in need of consultation; however, sometimes practitioners in larger communities struggle to find expert consultation for a particular issue or treatment modality. TASC allows the practitioner to obtain consultation from an expert of her choosing. For instance, a practitioner in a metropolitan area had five years' experience treating patients with eating disorders. As she furthered her training, she shifted from a cognitive-behavioral perspective to a psychodynamic perspective. Wanting consultation on a case with an anorexic patient, she contacted a psychodynamic practitioner in a distant locale who had written extensively on the subject. TASC allowed her to obtain valued input from a practitioner with a similar orientation. A relatively experienced practitioner treating a transgendered patient provides us with another example. Despite the practitioner's inexperience with this area of practice, the patient had seen this practitioner for a number of months and did not wish to switch providers when this issue emerged. The practitioner dutifully searched for a consultant in his area, but he could not meet with this person due to an ethical conflict. He obtained additional training by attending workshops, participating in a list serve, and seeking ongoing consultation from an expert in another state.

While some critics of TASC would allow exception for geographically isolated practitioners or those seeking expert help, there is more resistance to convenience as justification for TASC. Using technology to replace in-person visits to avoid traffic or travel time and expense seems a questionable trade-off to those who value the in-person experience. Advocates for the "convenience" rationale suggest that anything that increases flexibility and accessibility enhances potential use. Therefore, practitioners who might be unwilling to sacrifice three clinical hours to participate in a one-hour in-person consultation might agree to devote one clinical hour to consultation via technology. Clearly, these options would need to be fully discussed, including tackling the practitioner's potential resistance to the supervisory process. Additionally, most researchers and some licensing boards agree that TASC is not desirable or preferred for unlicensed clinicians in ordinary circumstances (Rousmaniere, Abbass, Frederickson, Henning, & Taubner, 2014).

In some instances, TASC may afford more confidentiality protection than in-person consultation. Although practitioners make every effort to disguise the identity of their patients, certain facts in a case may make some patients more identifiable than others. When the patient is a practicing mental health therapist, the treating practitioner may better protect the patient's confidentiality by seeking consultation from someone outside his immediate clinical community. For example, when I first began practicing psychoanalysis, there was one other analyst working in the area. Few people were in analysis locally, making any disclosure of that fact a potentially identifiable characteristic. Seeking consultation from an analyst in a different geographic location provided me with an added layer of protection for the analysand, who was also a practicing clinician. In another instance, I was treating the victim of a very public crime. The patient already felt victimized by the media and by people learning about what happened in a way she could not control. Needing a consult, I asked my patient's permission, who was relieved at the idea of consultation from an expert in another location where her identity could remain unknown.

Ethical and regulatory considerations. Much of the criticism of TASC and the anxiety surrounding its use falls into the area of ethical concerns and regulatory matters. Since ethical codes are discipline specific, each practitioner must investigate the ethics surrounding telemental health practice in her discipline. Additionally, licensing boards differ from state to state in their regulatory restrictions or guidelines for telemental health practice, and supervisory regulations often differ from regulations regarding counseling or psychotherapy. A comprehensive discussion of state-to-state specifics is beyond the scope of this chapter; however, readers are referred to the American Counseling Association 2014 Code of Ethics (www.counseling.org), the American Psychological Association 2013 Guidelines for the Practice of Telepsychology (http://www.apa.org/practice/guidelines/telepsychology.aspx), and the official state licensing board websites in your home state and in any states where you intend to practice.

In McAdams and Wyatt's (2010) investigation into state regulatory practices, they found existing regulations for TASC in just thirteen percent of states, with thirty percent of states reporting ongoing discussions about potential regulatory actions. Few boards forbade the use of TASC or mandated specialized training to conduct TASC, but most suggested specialized informed consent procedures, restricted the use of TASC for unlicensed professionals, promoted the development of graduate coursework in ethical and competent telemental health practice, supported the careful selection of HIPAA (Health Insurance Portability and Accountability Act) compliant technology for service delivery, advised encryption of any case material transmitted electronically, cautioned about necessary review of malpractice insurance policies, and recommended the identification of local supervisors to assist in crisis situations (Maheu, Pulier, McMenamin, & Posen., 2012; McAdams & Wyatt, 2010; Rousmaniere, Abbass, Frederickson, Henning, & Taubner, 2014; Wanlass, 2013). Additionally, telemental health practitioners intending to offer TASC across state boundaries might wish to obtain permission from the licensing board in the state where they reside and from the licensing board for the state where the supervisee practices prior to beginning an ongoing consulting relationship.

Practical issues with TASC implementation. In many ways, providers of TASC are engaged in a familiar activity, providing supervision and consultation about clinical matters. Most have experience establishing expectations for supervision, forming a supervisory alliance, attending to moments of parallel process where patient/therapist dynamics are replicated in the supervisory interactions, evaluating and providing feedback on the supervisee's strengths and vulnerabilities, and maintaining adequate records of their supervisory work. Couched in the familiarity of this experience, however, is the unfamiliar. TASC providers, themselves, must become comfortable with technology and be able to assess the feasibility of technology use for their supervisees.

What does comfort with technology involve at a practical level? Technology becomes an aspect of the supervisory setting; therefore, TASC providers set up the technology situation much as they would a clinical office. Arranging a reliable, stable Internet connection, finding a private and confidential place to work, adjusting lighting, camera distance, and focus, testing sound volume and clarity, agreeing on who contacts whom to start the supervisory hour, and setting time parameters—all become part of the supervisory frame. If the TASC provider requires process notes or videotaped materials, tutorials about methods of encryption, clarification about when and how clinical materials will arrive (e.g., by email, fax, shared computer screen, or regular mail), and discussion about how confidential materials will be stored or discarded become part of the introductory supervisory consultation. Fees and billing practices are established, which often include electronic payments or credit card charge authorization forms.

A common source of anxiety for TASC participants involves security concerns, since confidential health information is being disclosed, placing the TASC exchange under regulations of HIPAA, which were modified in 2009 by the Health Information Technology for Economic and Clinical Health Act (HITECH). TASC providers need to carefully investigate videoconferencing options, as some imply they are HIPAA compliant but do not meet the necessary standards. Supervisees should be adequately educated about the risks to confidentiality and guided to use complicated, unique passwords for accounts (more than eight characters, mixture of upper/lower case, inclusion of numbers or symbols). Protection against common computer hacking can be increased if users avoid downloading attachments or opening email from unfamiliar users (Rousmaniere, Abbass, Frederickson, Henning, & Taubner, 2014). TASC providers employed at universities, hospitals, clinics, or agencies need to trace who has access to their computer account, such as instructional technology personnel, and make certain any confidential material is completely deleted from easy access accounts or safely stored in a separate, password protected database.

One of the most important and often neglected aspects of setting up a workable TASC arrangement involves anticipating technology glitches and designing a back-up plan should technology fail. For example, the supervisor and supervisee exchange phone numbers where each can be reached in the event of an emergency, a technology failure when initiating the session, or when the technology cannot sustain the session. For instance, I tell my supervisees that after the second drop or disconnect during a videoconferencing session, they automatically switch to phone. I offer a landline phone number, which tends to be more secure and stable, helping to restore a sense of containment after unintended drops and disconnects. In providing TASC internationally, I practice having the supervisee switch off the video portion of the connection while maintaining the audio, which often helps stabilize the line when the Internet connection is shaky. In terms of group supervision, I do a trial run of the technology with all participants prior to starting supervision, and I provide the plan for disconnect and reconnect in an electronically circulated written document, which I review verbally on a periodic basis.

Clinical process considerations. How does the use of TASC influence the clinical process of supervision? What is the relative efficacy of TASC compared to in-person supervision? What aspects of the supervisory process require greater attention, adaptation, interpretation, or discussion when TASC is employed? What are the clinical contraindications for using TASC, and how are they assessed in both supervisor and supervisee? How is TASC introduced, and can it be effectively combined with in-person supervision?

Although these are excellent questions, we do not have an established body of empirical research findings to guide our understanding and implementation of TASC. Much like the recent ethical guidelines, emerging practice standards, and growing technical options for telemental health services, discussion of these issues is just beginning, mostly drawing from anecdotal experience via case reports and qualitative interview data. Preliminary empirical research findings do support the effective use of TASC for individual supervision, group supervision, and clinical teaching, both within the United States and abroad (Rousmaniere, Abbass, Frederickson, Henning, & Taubner, 2014). Cummings (2002) found that supervisees using TASC were less guarded in their self-disclosure, and Sorlie, Gammon, Bergvik, and Sexton (1999) concluded that an effective supervisory relationship could be established and maintained. Certainly, more research about the clinical experience of TASC is forthcoming and will help illuminate areas of common ground with in-person supervision and areas of difference.

There are many areas of controversy in conducting TASC, such as establishing a supervisory relationship, encouraging self-disclosure, creating containment, utilizing non-verbal cues, detecting shifts in states of mind, and experiencing parallel process moments. I will address these through the use of clinical examples.

Vivian

Vivian is a forty-year-old clinician who has practiced in the field for the past ten years. She requested ongoing consultation with me after hearing a presentation at a national conference. In response to her inquiry, I had a preliminary consultation with Vivian by telephone, establishing parameters such as fee, methods of communication, and supervisory goals and expectations. Informed consent paperwork was electronically distributed for completion, and verification of Vivian's license to practice confirmed. State licensure laws did not prohibit such an arrangement, and a tentative plan for consultation was established.

Vivian and I agreed that it would be best to initiate the supervisory process in person, in part because we would both be in the same locale within the next month. This decision was influenced by four factors. First, an in-person meeting was easily arranged within a month's time, and there were no pressing clinical issues. Second, the supervisor and supervisee were strangers to each other, without a prior collegial acquaintance to build from in establishing a supervisory alliance. Third, the supervisee disclosed that she was not currently in any form of treatment, raising concerns for me about adequate containment. Last, I prefer to begin a supervisory or consultation arrangement in person whenever possible. After in-person meetings, the supervisory pair has a visual image of each other to carry in mind and an experience of feeling connected to draw upon across the geographic distance.

In the first in-person meeting, Vivian commented on how much easier it was to talk in supervision by phone. She seemed surprised that she was more anxious and had difficulty finding words when engaged in face-to-face contact with me. She found my voice more comforting and containing than my gaze, experienced as penetrating and a bit persecutory. Vivian's remarks about self-disclosure were consistent with Cummings's (2002) observations that for some supervisees, distance makes disclosure easier, perhaps mitigating some of the vulnerability experienced in an in-person encounter.

Vivian's comments about orientating to my voice as a source of containment continued throughout our consultation arrangement. Other supervisees have made similar comments, suggesting that when the telephone is the medium of communication, the auditory sensory connection dominates the interpersonal interaction. This seems similar to a mother's early exchanges with an infant, where auditory channels are more developed than visual ones. It also parallels the experience of an analysand on the couch, out of visual contact but connected by the sound and feel of the analyst's presence. Vivian's choice of a phone as the vehicle for connection rather than a videoconferencing system was explained as a matter of convenience but also seemed to capture her need to manage the level of closeness within the relationship. Such practical choices need to be explored for their dynamic underpinnings, helping the supervisor understand the conflicts and challenges of the supervisee.

The use of TASC does present some unique containment issues. An in-person encounter in the supervisor's office offers a distinct space with physical boundaries that, along with the supervisor's presence, help promote an experience of holding, attentiveness, and containment. The supervisee directly observes the supervisor's focused attention on the supervisee and the clinical material. In TASC, both supervisor and supervisee create the "office," linked in Vivian's case by an invisible phone line. As a supervisory pair we discussed where each of us would sit for the sessions, describing our surroundings verbally to provide a sense of grounding. Nevertheless, Vivian often wondered aloud what I was doing during the phone encounters— was I taking notes, distracted by external stimuli such as email, bored and falling asleep? Vivian helpfully described these moments for processing, which reflected the critical, condemning voice she carried inside about her clinical work. Additionally, Vivian's struggles in supervision helped her decide to return to therapy, something she felt strongly should be "in-person."

Vivian's willingness and ability to articulate her nonverbal responses highlights a common challenge in TASC, particularly when conducted by phone. How are nonverbal experiences conveyed? In part, both supervisor and supervisee describe in words what cannot be directly visually observed. Vivian tells me when she feels agitated, and it is also conveyed in her tone of voice, the pace of her speech, and the way she loses her place as she reads the patient session material. In concert with Vivian, I feel agitation in my countertransference. I find myself fidgeting in my chair and talking in hushed tones to contain the upset.

Critics of TASC wonder if this lack of visual non-verbal cues compromises the supervisory process (McAdams & Wyatt, 2010). Certainly, vigilance is required by the supervisor. She needs to listen very carefully for changes in affect conveyed in tone of voice or pace of breathing, to ask about silences that could be observed without questioning in an office setting, to more often verbalize countertransference experiences that capture the nonverbal component in the interaction. In my experience, fatigue sets in more quickly with TASC than in-person, perhaps illustrating the cost of such careful attentiveness in the absence of certain sensory cues.

Was TASC an effective form of consultation for Vivian? She reported benefitting from this arrangement, and improvement in her clinical work was apparent. She exhibited a strong, somewhat reactive transference to me, intensified by the distance and a perception of a tenuous holding environment. Of course, it is impossible to know whether this supervisee would have had a similar experience if she were meeting with me weekly in person. I did periodically discuss whether in-person consultation with a local clinician might be more helpful, but Vivian replied that her difficulties likely would have been similar given her dynamic make-up.

Anna

The issues of nonverbal cuing, discerning states of mind, parallel process, and cultural challenges are further illustrated by my consultation experience with Anna. Anna practices in a foreign region where knowledge of couple and family treatments is limited. Following an extended in-person clinical training experience with me, Anna approached me about the possibility of consultation via videoconferencing, and the supervisory arrangement commenced some six months later. The logistics of this situation were complex, given the supervisory pair's minimal experience with the technology selected, the substantial differences in time zones between the pair, my limited cultural experience with Anna's native country, and Anna's caseload of children and families residing in her country but originating from many different parts of the world.

Prior to beginning the consultation process, Anna and I tried two different videoconferencing systems, selecting the one with the best security and most stable connection. Anna had to guide me through the installation process, as the instructions were not in English. This created an unusual power reversal right at the onset of supervision, which was noted and discussed. Additionally, the time difference required me to start work very early and Anna to work very late. These time differences were represented in our visual fields, as the windows in our offices were captured by our computer webcams. Additionally, unlike an in-person visit where the supervisee comes to the supervisor's office, I had a view of Anna's place of work. Thus, I stepped into Anna's experience with a kind of intimacy and sensory flooding absent in an in-person arrangement.

Anna's face occupied my computer screen, as mine did hers, offering each of us easy access to visual nonverbal cues such as changes in facial expression. Similarly, the audio connection was excellent, allowing for perception of subtle changes in vocal tone, sighs, tapping of fingers, and magnification of noises within and outside our offices. Thus, our encounters carried an immediacy, intensity, and level of intimacy that exceeded that of an in-person visit, where the supervisee sits some three feet away from the supervisor. Both parties were more exposed, creating an unspoken shared vulnerability in the supervisory dyad.

An experience with Anna about a year into the consultation process helps illuminate some of the common parallels in TASC and in-person work, perhaps addressing some common skepticism about TASC. Anna presented a case where a young infant was hospitalized in an area somewhat distant from his home. Anna worked with both infant and mother around a failure to thrive issue, which the hospital treatment team viewed as emotional in origin. As Anna told me about her encounters, she became tearful, connecting emotionally both to the vulnerability of this young mother who felt desperate and helpless in her inability to feed her child and to the primitive anxieties of the infant himself. Embarrassed by her tears and atypical lack of containment, Anna unconsciously backed away from the camera and microphone, making it difficult for me to understand her words, also choked with emotion.

Much like the mother–infant dyad Anna was discussing, a heightened level of anxiety and desperate sense of longing fell between the supervisory pair. I felt an impulse to reach through the computer screen to soothe my distressed supervisee. Anna alternated between wishing to terminate the video connection altogether, protecting her from feeling so exposed, and grasping for my words as a means of anchoring herself during an emotional free fall. Clearly, this was a moment of parallel process, where the dynamics of the mother–infant pair were replicated in the supervisory dyad. The experience was mainly conveyed nonverbally, perhaps amplified by the visual access to subtle and overt facial expressions captured by our cameras. The supervisory pair was living out the case dynamics, helping to understand the emotional world of this mother and her baby.

Another example from work with Anna highlights how technical problems experienced in supervisory sessions often carry emotional significance. For a short period of time, Anna's Internet connection was less stable, creating frequent drops requiring reconnections. Additionally, my travel schedule necessitated a missed supervisory appointment once each month for three months running. Anna was presenting sessions of a couple fighting about the wife's recent affair. This couple originated from a country Anna had never visited, and the couple had trouble understanding Anna's English.

Listening to Anna's report of the couple sessions, I noticed an odd flatness to Anna's voice, a disconnected and choppy feel to her sentences, a drop in her eye contact with me, and her repeated need to focus the camera and adjust the volume. The intermittent loss of contact altogether, resulting from drops in the Internet connection, added further chaos to the session experience. Both Anna and I expressed frustration with the technology. Only in retrospect could we discuss how the drops mirrored the disconnects in the couple relationship that predated the wife's affair, the inadequately processed absences of the supervisor that "chopped up" the work, the cultural disconnects between the couple of supervisee and supervisor, and the chaotic internal worlds of the husband and wife pursuing treatment. We could see how we had attributed too much of our frustration to the technology, minimizing the projective process we were experiencing in relation to this couple. In a way, this was like spouses locating all their difficulty in the affair, unable to acknowledge the rifts and trauma that predated this sexual acting out.

These clinical vignettes suggest that TASC mirrors much of the ordinary process of in-person supervision, such as establishing a supervisory frame, cultivating a working supervisory alliance, identifying and exploring points of resistance, recognizing moments of parallel process, and making use of the transference/countertransference dynamics (Watkins, 2010). In these examples, technology is just another dimension of the supervisory experience to examine and understand. Readers might assume that TASC could be regarded routinely as another option for those seeking expert help.

But when is TASC problematic or contraindicated? Again, we must visit both practical and dynamic factors in making this judgment. From a practical standpoint, if the technological connection is unstable, is difficult to use, lacks adequate security, or is cost prohibitive, proceeding with TASC seems unwise. Similarly, if state licensing laws prohibit TASC or if the supervisee is unlicensed, the TASC practitioner absorbs too much risk in implementing this arrangement. Even if the TASC practitioner agreed to assume such risk, heightened anxiety and the potential for acting out frustration within the supervisory pairing could be problematic.

Dynamic issues in either the supervisor or supervisee may also serve as contraindications for TASC. In my experience, supervisees with histories of parental deprivation may be unable to tolerate the inherent distance in TASC (Wanlass, 2013), particularly if they are not pursuing concurrent treatment. The lack of face-to-face contact may trigger unbearable feelings of deprivation and abandonment. Supervisees or supervisors who carry high levels of anxiety may be unable to manage the strain on the containment function generated by TASC. Supervisors with a more reserved manner or who speak infrequently in the consultation hour may find the use of the telephone aversive, as it requires the narration of non-verbal experiences more than in-person work. Additionally, generational issues may play into comfort levels, as younger clinicians raised with technology are often more comfortable with its use than senior clinicians who privilege in-person work.

The rapid changes in form and use of technology suggest that TASC is here to stay. Even state licensing boards that currently prohibit TASC report that this is just a stop-gap measure, giving them time to develop standards and address regulatory challenges (McAdams & Wyatt, 2010; Rousmanier, Abbass, Frederickson, Henning, & Taubner, 2014). We know something about the benefits and challenges of TASC, but further narratives describing its use and empirical research on its dimensions are needed to guide effective practice and establish training protocols. TASC does have the potential to make supervision and consultation more widely available to the clinical community, provided we fully understand the impact of technology on supervisory practice.

References

Bernard, J. M., & Goodyear, R. K. (2009). *Fundamentals of Clinical Supervision*. Upper Saddle River, NJ: Pearson Education.

Cummings, P. (2002). Cybervision: Virtual peer group counseling supervision—hindrance or help? *Counseling Psychotherapy & Research*, 2: 223–229.

Godleski, L., Nieves, J. E., Darkins, A., & Lehmann, L. (2008). VA telemental health: Suicide assessment. *Behavioral Sciences and the Law*, 26: 271–286.

Kanz, J. E. (2001). Clinical-supervision.com: Issues in the provision of online supervision. *Professional Psychology: Research and Practice, 32*: 415–420.

Maheu, M. M., Pulier, M. L., McMenamin, J. P., & Posen, L. (2012). Future of telepsychology, tele-health, and various technologies in psychological research and practice. *Professional Psychology: Research and Practice, 43*: 613–621.

McAdams, C. R., & Wyatt, K. L. (2010). The regulation of technology-assisted distance counseling and supervision in the United States: An analysis of current extent, trends, and implications. *Counselor Education & Supervision, 49*: 179–192.

Rousmaniere, T., Abbass, A., Frederickson, J., Henning, I., & Taubner, S. (2014). Videoconference for psychotherapy training and supervision: Two case examples. *American Journal of Psychotherapy, 68*: 231–250.

Sorlie, T., Gammon, D., Bergvik, S., & Sexton, H. (1999). Psychotherapy supervision face-to-face and by videoconferencing: A comparative study. *British Journal of Psychotherapy, 15*: 452–462.

Stamm, B. H. (Ed.) (2003). *Rural Behavioral Health Care: An Interdisciplinary Guide.* Washington, DC: American Psychological Association.

Wanlass, J. (2013). Technology assisted supervision and consultation. In: J. S. Scharff (Ed.), *Psychoanalysis Online: Mental Health, Teletherapy, and Training* (pp. 215–225). London: Karnac.

Watkins, C. E. (2010). Psychoanalytic constructs in psychotherapy supervision. *American Journal of Psychotherapy, 64*: 393–416.

Wood, A. V. J., Miller, T. W., & Hargrove, D. S. (2005). Clinical supervision in rural settings: A tele-health model. *Professional Psychology: Research and Practice, 36*: 173–179.

CHAPTER ELEVEN

Teaching psychoanalytic psychotherapy and infant observation by video link

David E. Scharff

T his chapter reports on beginning, maintaining, and developing a distance learning project for teaching mature students in psychoanalytic psychotherapy, and later candidates in psychoanalytic training. The members of the group were at a significant geographic remove from one another and from the teachers from whom they wished to learn. I report on the use of videoconference capacity in four centers and its expansion through adopting a central bridge with enhanced connectivity. I discuss briefly some of the technical challenges the equipment and technology pose, the opportunities and challenges to in-depth communication, and some of the dynamics that have emerged in our early experience with the technology. Examples illustrate some dynamics of teaching through this medium to overcome the barriers of geographic separation in large and small group seminars, and in long-term group supervision.

Many students want to learn psychoanalysis and psychoanalytic psychotherapy but live and work at a prohibitive distance from the centers of training. The barrier of geographic space has historically posed a major obstacle to the teaching and learning of psychoanalytic theory and therapy for those areas without analysts. Students in such areas have either been precluded from training, or have only been able to train by dint of great personal sacrifice. In addition, some of the teachers or schools of analysis, and some specialized analytic skills, exist only in certain centers, making access to those teachers difficult and available only by special, often expensive, arrangement. Modern technology offers to change many aspects of this situation, and perhaps ultimately to alter the landscape of training. There have already been reports of psychoanalyses and psychotherapies conducted by telephone, and by video link (Aronson 2000; see also Zalusky Blum, Chapter Seventeen, Commentary; J. Scharff, 2012). There are also reports of supervision by video link (Arlene Richards, personal communication) and of online discussion groups and courses that offer a chance for students to communicate with teachers and other students at great distance (Sebek, 2001). Perhaps none of this is surprising in our era of information technology and of rapidly expanding communication. However, to my knowledge, there are few reports of training in psychoanalysis or psychoanalytic psychotherapy that experiments with the use of the most advanced methodologies in face-to-face communication in real time across large distances (Fishkin & Fishkin, 2014; Fishkin, Fishkin, Leli, Katz, & Snyder, 2011).

Part of the wonder of using the technology of live point-to-point video communication is how rapidly it allows participants to feel that they know each other even when they have never been in the room together. Many of us have now had the experience of meeting for the first time after participating in videoconference seminars, and have discovered that we feel we do know each other in a way that holds up over time. If anything, the video link seems to heighten and intensify experience in the way that a special and highly anticipated learning experience can also do. For many of us, such conditions serve to hone attention and amplify ordinary situations, serving perhaps to idealize opportunities that might seem ordinary in ordinary circumstances. With time and experience, the situation tends to normalize, but has so far retained a special residue that helps participants to tolerate the technical complications and occasional disappointments that attend the process.

Establishing the videoconference technology

It took two years of assessing the available technology, deliberating on the costs and benefits, and making pilot tests to learn how to use the technology, before the faculty and board of the International Psychotherapy Institute agreed to invest in equipment that would let us make regular contact with our satellite programs in Salt Lake City, Long Island, and Panama City, Republic of Panama. This lead time was important for dealing with resistance to innovation and building consensus to support moving forward. As co-director of the institute, I had also been in negotiation with the Tavistock Clinic in London, where the chief executive officer had already bought video equipment to support the clinic's role as an international training institution. The early work reported below is taken principally from varying uses of these sites, supported by working partnerships with faculty of the International Psychotherapy Institute and of the Tavistock Clinic.

I do not want to suggest that one can walk into using this medium without any difficulty. There are technical difficulties and adjustments in the use of this equipment. We had early frustrations requiring tolerance and help from faculty, students, and staff. A running-in period allowed us to become comfortable with the equipment, and we needed initial adjustments that were made fairly easily by the training provided in live-time by the vendor, and by the help desk that was always available. In undertaking this kind of venture, the technical difficulties should not be ignored. In our experience they can be dealt and lived with, but participants should be forewarned and ready to put up with some degree of difficulty, more during the early adjustment phase than later. The intrinsic value of the project needs to be sufficient to compensate for initial annoyances and interruptions. Our students' strong support of this way of working has gotten us through.

The first illustration comes from a seminar in infant observation run by an experienced child psychotherapist at the Tavistock Clinic in London, Jeanne Magagna. This method of observing infants in their families has been a mainstay of psychoanalytic and analytic psychotherapy training in Britain for many years (Miller, Rustin, & Shuttleworth, 1989). Let me give two vignettes from this seminar with the lessons we have learned from early in the process.

The first comes from the initial meeting of the seminar, in which Ms. Magagna introduced the methods of infant observation as developed in London and especially at the Tavistock Clinic. In this method of studying infant development, the student makes weekly hour-long natural-istic observations of an infant at home, after which the student writes up the observation from memory, including personal reactions to the baby, the family, and the experience. There is no intervention, except in cases of extreme need, neglect, or abuse. This exercise in observation and reflection without action provides first-hand data for learning about child development, including the influence of parents and family. It also focuses on the use of the self as an observ-ing and experiencing instrument in the presence of the infant mental state, a valuable prepara-tion for working with countertransference in the conduct of psychotherapy and psychoanalysis.

In this first meeting of the seminar, Ms. Magagna reviewed the methodology of conducting infant observation that the students had already read about (Miller, Rustin, & Shuttleworth, 1989), and then surveyed the anxieties of students as they contemplated recruiting and inter-viewing families. In order to detoxify anticipatory anxiety, she used role-play to rehearse the first interview with the family. She had often done this before in small seminars, but this was her first experience at using it to overcome the barriers of spatial separation between seminar participants. She made time for hearing the participants' worries and ambivalence about ask-ing families to let observers view their babies—babies that have usually not yet been born at the time the student approaches the mother. In order to get used to communicating across a distance of five thousand miles, the teacher in a room in London suggested that the student who would role-play the potential observer should be in Washington, and those playing the potential parents be in Salt Lake. Then she asked the other seminar members to report on their impression of the feelings of each role-playing participant, rather like the "double" in psycho-drama who speaks for the inner thoughts of a participant. While this method may seem con-trived to the psychoanalytic therapist, on this occasion it served two purposes admirably. First, it let the group members put themselves in the shoes of all participants of an observation, the observer and the parents. (In this case, the baby had not been born yet. Presumably, in another case, someone could have also role-played a baby.) But more importantly for our purposes in convening a seminar by video link, it placed students at sites that were geographically remote from each other in an intimate exchange as they conjectured about the psychology of the unfa-miliar infant observation situation. The role-play was helpful practice for the new venture, to be sure, but it was even more effective in providing a bond for the learning project between students not in the same room. They found they were able to talk across the distance, use each other's empathy, correct each other's perceptions that seemed inaccurate, and enjoy the relief of finding shared anxieties.

In the next meeting, one student reported her first observation, as she would have done in an ordinary infant observation seminar with all students in the same room. Other students had not yet found babies to observe. This focus on one infant let that group also secure their bond, and learn about beginnings together. Each week, before that first student in Washington reported, Ms. Magagna asked a student in Salt Lake to be ready to review the observations from the prior meeting of the seminar and give her own understanding of issues. This innovation provided for active participation at both sites. From this point, Ms. Magagna worked with the students in Salt Lake to support their recruitment of families for observation, and when they soon found a first one, they felt a new sense of balance between the two sites. Soon there were infants being observed in both sites, and the two subgroups came to feel like equal participants in the shared project.

At this point, the story of the seminar becomes more or less the story of an ordinary seminar teaching this particular psychoanalytic method, including any usual use of group dynamic interpretation to facilitate the study task. My second vignette concerns the study of that first baby, a girl I'll call Michele, who was born into a family where her mother's attention was at first distracted because of the rivalrous importunities of the two-year-old brother. The seminar participants in both sites experienced the drama of Michele's fight for room to come to life in a family that was ambivalent about giving her space. It was difficult for the group to tolerate hearing reports of the inattention of a mother preoccupied with her demanding older boy, who at times seemed to them to be the villain of the piece. Nevertheless, the liveliness of the entire family, and of the student who conducted the observation, infused the group with energy and carried their hopes not only for the infant's development, but for their own progress and learning as well. This led to some idealization of the process. Soon baby Michele settled in to secure her place with her mother by competing quietly but competently with her brother, who then seemed less like a giant and imposing ogre, and more like a healthy and slightly anxious two-year-old.

In a parallel way, the Salt Lake seminar group felt like a second child who did not have her own space. At first they did not have a baby of their own to observe, and so they had to fight for space to relate to Jeanne Magagna. There were more students in Washington, and I was there with my own previous experience of infant observation, while the faculty member in Salt Lake, although skilled and enthusiastic, was inexperienced in the teaching of infant observation. Even though Ms. Magagna adroitly gave Salt Lake its turn and paid kind and dutiful attention to students there, they were younger and lesser sibs. It was only as they began to present their own observations that they came into their own. I could see the parallel to the way baby Michele claimed a space with her mother, and the relief and pleasure the mother took in making a more secure bond with the infant, just as Ms. Magagna and the Salt Lake students now made a more robust working bond for which, I could now see, the entire group had been saving space.

In many ways, the dynamics of this seminar, divided by 5000, miles closely resembled the dynamics of any group containing subgroups, of any such seminar teaching psychoanalytic concepts and method. The difference is that the use of the videoconference technology and the existence of two subgroups amplify certain aspects both of the group's dynamics and of the case or situation being examined. These can be understood and worked with using the same internal monitoring processes that an experienced teacher uses in ordinary teaching of a seminar.

Using videoconference for a seminar in four cities

The next example of the use of videoconference equipment to teach psychoanalysis and analytic psychotherapy comes from a lecture/workshop given in February, 2001, by Anne Alvarez, a renowned teacher at the Tavistock Clinic, on her work with autistic, developmentally delayed and severely disturbed children, as described in her classic books, *Live Company* (1993) and, more recently, *The Thinking Heart* (2012). Teaching from London she was linked by video with approximately thirty students gathered in Washington, DC, Salt Lake City, Utah, and Panama City, Panama. It began at 2 p.m. in London, which was 9 a.m. in Washington and Panama, and 7 a.m. in Salt Lake City.

For the first hour, Dr. Alvarez gave a lecture on a conceptual scheme for differentiating levels of interpretive intervention in patients with differing levels of illness. Drawn from her work with autistic and developmentally delayed children, this lecture sketched an innovative framework for kinds of interventions that promote self-observation, psychic integration, transferential interpretation, and genetic reconstruction. During and after the lecture, students interacted with her through questions and comments. In the second hour, a student presented a case of a mildly autistic boy in analytic therapy. The student had the case in weekly supervision with Dr. Alvarez by telephone, but they had never met face-to-face. Their way of working in the video group supervision demonstrated the rapport they had already established, and their pleasure in seeing each other for the first time was obvious. The boy was articulate with that brand of exaggerated and awkward insight not unusual in some mildly autistic children who arrive at ordinary insight with an intelligence that astounds their therapists. The therapist's process notes therefore provided moments of high entertainment. For instance, at one point the boy, who had come into the session with his fly open, talked about his father's pride in his twenty-two-foot-long car, exclaiming that there was no way that car could be that long. The therapist said to him that perhaps he was thinking of other things that might be longer than someone would expect. The boy agreed, astonished that she would know that, but was unable to bring himself to say the word. After waiting, the therapist said, "Like penises?" "That's it!" said the boy. "But don't worry. I won't tell anyone you said that word."

When the therapist read this part, the group at her site in Washington immediately burst into laughter, and on the screen, one could see the other sites begin laughing a split second later. The pleasure and responsiveness over all four sites was obvious on the screen. At the end of the session, after the therapist had made another interpretation that met with the boy's approval, she announced it was time to stop. "OK," he said. "I'll see you next time. And I want to congratulate you on your psychic powers today." Again the three groups and the teacher burst into laughter a split second apart, and the mood of delight sparked by a wonderful session, the kind that brightens a child therapist's heart, was palpable across the vast space—5000 miles of live communication. Then discussion of the case resumed, and Dr. Alvarez discussed the boy's situation and the therapist's handling of his internal issues and particularly his transference to her.

In this situation, we were able to demonstrate that intense learning and sharing can take place across sites, producing a teaching experience that is in many ways indistinguishable from ordinary analytic case conferences. Students can communicate the intricacies of analytic process, carry on discussion that is rich in affect as well as intellectual understanding, and can profit from a teacher who would otherwise be unavailable to them. While this particular group supervision was entertaining, what is most notable about it for our interest here is the ordinary aspects—the ease of students' communication with each other and the teacher, and the satisfaction the teacher felt with the teaching and learning situation.

Teaching about videoconferencing across geographic separation

Soon after the session I just reported, we had occasion to travel to the Tavistock Clinic to present this work. While the Tavistock had the equipment, few staff had so far been able to bring themselves to use it. To dramatize the live quality of the medium, we asked some of our students in Washington, DC to join us live. Sitting in our conference room in Washington beginning at 6:30 in the morning, they joined us live throughout the presentation in London that began at 11:30 am there. The Washington students were able to see for the first time the edited video we showed in London at the same time the group in London saw it, a video that showed the examples I described above. The London group expressed some interest and enthusiasm, commented on their own resistance as being typically British and in the nature of an analytic conservatism. They also spoke helpfully of an idealization of the process that seems to energize it in ways that analytic process can also be idealized, and that should be taken into account in its use. The most dramatic moment occurred when a member of the London audience said that she felt there was a kind of unreality to the medium, a way in which people on the video screen felt to her as if they weren't quite there. "I think I resent that!" one of the Washington students protested. "I feel very much that I'm here!" The suddenness of the response caught the woman in London and the entire group off guard. People on both sides of the Atlantic laughed together as the encounter made the point that real people experienced themselves in direct communication as immediately as if in the room together.

An example from group supervision

For two years, a group of six therapists from one our institute's satellite programs in a geographically distant city had been meeting with me for twice-monthly supervision by video link. Each meeting was two and a half hours. Each participant had an hour for the group to discuss his or her case once every six weeks, and that left thirty minutes of general group discussion, which usually included time for the group to work with their own process in the mode of the affective learning groups developed at our institute (Scharff & Scharff, 2000). The colleagues in the distant city were professionally close before the supervision, and so from the beginning they had been able to share relevant personal material in the group in order to explore the resonance of such material with the supervised cases. Such events were shared occasionally during the case presentations, or in the group affective process usually held during the last part of the meetings.

On this day the presenter was a woman I will call Sherry. She began by telling a dream she thought pertained to supervision. "I was sitting with you (DES) on the patio of a restaurant with your wife and seven-year-old granddaughter. You had stitches on your face and forehead, and your wife also had stitches and obvious recent scars on her face. I wondered if I should bring it up with you. Finally I asked, and you said, 'A month ago there was a terrible accident, but we're recovering.' It seemed OK to discuss, but I felt badly as we went on. Behind me someone leaned over a balcony, smiling at me, like 'Have a nice dinner.' I thought that person was you too, but it couldn't have been. Then I was awakened by thunder."

Sherry said she has a patient who was hit by a train. The accident had scarred her face. She also thought the dream pertained to the fact that because she had missed the previous supervision, she had gone a month without meeting with me and the group. She missed the group, and thought that it had been also a longer time since all members of the group were present at the same time. One of the members, Julia, had had twins recently, and she had paid her a visit, but worried that this new mother wouldn't have time to continue the group supervision. Another member said he also wondered if Julia would rejoin the group, and Julia acknowledged the internal debate she had experienced about rejoining. Her life had changed altogether—dramatically, like the train wreck connected to Sherry's dream, only in a positive way. Sherry said the dream also made her aware of wanting grandchildren herself, but, she said, with humor, "My own children aren't ready to oblige me just yet." Another member, Kathy, said that this group supervision is where we discuss scars, and where she often also wonders about the safety of revealing herself. Sherry agreed that she also shared the quandary about whether to present a case that had not gone particularly well, exposing her own scars to the group and to me. She said, "I felt I needed the help with that patient and I didn't know how to get it safely."

This discussion had taken about fifteen minutes, when Sherry proceeded to present her continuing case. He is a man with significant trauma history, much improved. The wife has areas of difficulty, too, but generally hides behind the husband and acts as though all the problems are his. Sherry sees the man individually weekly and meets with him and his wife every other week. We have discussed this arrangement, which the group and I support, given the needs of the case. Sherry apologized profusely for not having prepared an individual session. She said, "All I have is a rather ordinary, not very interesting couple session. Nothing earth-shattering."

The session opened with the patient saying he felt deflated because he had been unable to surprise his wife as he had wished. He had ordered a satellite dish for her, hoping it would be installed in time for a special annual program not carried on regular channels, but this week he had to tell her about the surprise as she was making plans to watch the program at her mother's house. The wife said, "I really like that program and want to watch it every year. We haven't had cable installed in our new house, but once he told me about his gift, I was fine planning to watch it at home." The man said he did have an ulterior motive. He also wanted to help his wife be less bound to her mother and be with him more. She said that was fine with her.

Sherry paused in her presentation for group discussion. Members of the group noted the positive change in quality of this couple's work, from a time when the couple's material was shot through with effects of the husband's early trauma. This so-called ordinary material seemed to them to reflect both the individual's and the couple's progress. In this material, he had expected her to be disappointed and angry, while she had been able gently to hold him psychologically. The scars had faded for him and for them, like the scars in Sherry's own opening dream. They noted the resonance of Sherry's dream with the treatment. The couple is expecting their own first child, a kind of therapeutic grandchild for Sherry, when she is still attuned to their scars. They liked the way this "ordinary" material from the opening of the session demonstrated individual, couple, and family growth, a fading of the scars on every level.

Sherry resumed. In the session, the man now began to reflect on his wife's TV watching. She will watch anything, when much of the time he would like her to do things with him. He feels defeated when she seems to disappear into the TV. The wife is a bit defensive, saying she thought her TV-watching had been better lately. The husband started to cry when Sherry asked if he would be able to negotiate with his wife about watching TV. Sherry reported asking,

"Are you afraid the relationship won't survive if you ask her to watch less TV, that she won't love you enough to give it up?" The man said that was true, that he didn't feel he could negotiate at all about TV. The wife now said, "Of course you can ask me, and I'll turn it off. There's only one show a week that's important to me. I can give up all the others. But I know there are other things you do for me that are about your fear that I won't love you. Like when we're out for dinner, you save the last good bite of your food for me, or push dessert on me even if I don't want it."

A member of the supervision group interrupted Sherry here to remember the wife's eating disorder, noting that the husband was doing a mild version of what the wife's mother had done to her chronically, pushing unwanted food on her. Sherry hadn't noticed that echo, and thanked him for calling her attention to the link. After brief discussion, she returned to the session. "I asked the husband why he offered his wife the 'best food' in that way. He said, 'I want her to feel that she loves me.' The wife answered, 'You're very generous with me. I want to do things for you, too.' The couple went on to discuss the way his mother was so awful to both of them, that they could see this would lead to his worry that the wife would treat him badly. The wife said, 'Your mother dismisses you and me, too.' The man grew openly sad and wiped tears from his eyes. The session was almost over. He began to write me a check, noting he had not paid me in some time, and said, 'This isn't much, but there's more coming soon.'" Sherry said to us in summary, "It felt good! They talked about the core of his fear, and she was gentle and responsive."

The group noted the continuation of the trusting feeling in the session leading to the linking of the husband's fear of loss of love and the relationship with his mother. This session was calmer than earlier ones, even though it moved rather smoothly into the core issue for the couple of the husband's fear that the wife would not love him if he asked her to give anything up, and the way the wife took care of this fearful residue of his trauma in a loving way. They then turned to a more extensive discussion of the wife's way of turning attention away from her own issues, and that this brief mention of his pushing food on her was a small inroad to the struggle over food with her own intrusive mother, which she avoids discussing. She has turned down Sherry's suggestion for individual therapy several times, so the only therapy she can allow is these couple sessions. Then a member of the group said, "Well, the satellite dish he wants to give her is unconsciously related to food too, so his gift is a displaced, symbolic offer of food that comes from him instead of her mother. He's afraid she won't take it from him. In a hidden way, he's dealing with her eating disorder and the way it has tied her to her mother." The group discussed the way the husband tries to get her to accept his care of her, and how she vigorously avoids an awareness of her own needs and fears by solicitous discussion of his situation instead of her own buried hurts.

As the group carried on the discussion, I noticed how well they were working as a group, making thematic discoveries with much less input from me than usual. I felt a little left out, superfluous, in resonance perhaps with the husband's feeling left out by his wife's connection to her mother rather than to him. In a way, I wanted them to connect to my video conference "satellite TV", to be fed more by my "satellite dish". It was getting close to the end of the time for discussing Sherry's case, when Kathy said, "I just thought: David is watching our only channel. It's like he's on the balcony, watching and smiling at us." The group now began to discuss the way they felt I was tuned into them and providing a holding environment, one in which they could face their patients' scars. I said, "As I now think about Sherry's dream, I see the way the group often sees the reflection of their own scars in me, like the way your patients often feel their scars reflected by your face in the therapy—painful but also holding out hope for change. Sherry's hope for grandchildren is a countertransference to the couple's expectation of a child, the fertility of the treatment, and, at the same time, your own hopes for growth of yourselves as therapists. In resonance with the case, you use TV at a 'satellite' location, ergo 'a satellite dish' to get professional feeding and repair, for opportunities to lessen your connection to old ways of doing things through a strengthened connection to me across this geographic separation." I also now felt better about the "dish" I could provide in standing by as they were able to feed themselves. In later reflection, I also realized that Sherry's dream contained some residue from reactions to face surgery I had about the time the group began meeting with me, and to my wife's previous surgery. The dream resonated with the cascade of transference feeling of need for repair at all levels, for individual patients, couple, therapist, and in the supervisory relationship with me.

The dynamic resonance of this session of group supervision demonstrates the parallel processes found in ordinary group supervision. These were unimpeded by the use of the distance-learning video technology. In fact, careful attention to the transference elements of the video conference frame actually lets us use that dimension as part of our learning. This is similar to the way that the treatment frame is subject to transference and countertransference elements in face-to-face therapy encounters. In this particular session, the group was able to identify ways that the video technology itself became part of the theme that tied together experience, echoing up and down the line among patient couple, therapist supervisor. The technology, far from interfering in the process, instead became part of it.

Recent developments

In the decade since the experiences I have just described, advances in technology have allowed us to expand distance learning in two ways: teleconference and videoconference.

Teleconference

Since 2004 we have used inexpensive conference telephone services to offer weekly seminars in two programs, one of them a two-year program for psychotherapy trainees and the other a four-year program for candidates in psychoanalytic training. The participants come in person four or five times a year to attend immersions in theory and technique, and then meet weekly on teleconference call to continue the learning process. The weekly seminars on conference call offer continuity of training, coupled with regular individual and group supervision, which is often also given via video connection or telephone. The classes consist of four to ten people, each at a different office, in various locations with variable access to high speed Internet, which compromises the quality of the sound and picture for the class. In this circumstance, teleconference has often been better than free videoconference. These group members, having had plenty of time together in person in immersion blocks, and continuing to work together weekly over three or four years, know one another other well enough that face-to-face contact is not essential. We have found that candidates trained in this way become effective analysts and psychotherapists with skills comparable to those who graduate from traditional programs in which all the classes are in person. Nevertheless, as videoconference technology continues to improve in capacity, quality, reliability, and affordability, seminars currently held on the original teleconference service will no doubt move to videoconference format.

Videoconference

New bridging equipment, purchased and run in partnership with Westminster College in Salt Lake City, Utah, allows for fifteen sites in visual contact, along with an unlimited number of individuals and groups who participate through the use of video streaming and conference telephone. Individuals can install the software for connecting onto their personal computers and iPads, while groups can gather to connect by purchasing similar equipment at a relatively reasonable price. This technology currently supports two regular seminars. The first centers on psychoanalytic theory and clinical application, and is available to all our psychotherapy and psychoanalytic trainees, as well as to many other participants nationally and overseas. The second course focuses on psychoanalytic couple therapy, and currently enrolls approximately sixty participants in live contact, listening to clinical and theoretical presentations, and then discussing them in live time with one another and with the presenter. The couple therapy program was originally organized in collaboration with the Tavistock Centre for Couple Relationships, an institutional partnership made possible by both institutions having videoconference equipment. With this expanded capacity, the presenter and members participating can be virtually anywhere in the world. We have had participants from six continents and many countries, including Great Britain, Argentina, Honduras, Panama, South Africa, Spain, Poland, Lithuania, Turkey, Taiwan, and Hong Kong, among others. Both these programs serve several aims: They have value to some participants as the only program they take with IPI. In this way, they show the teaching philosophy in action in a limited time frame, and offer a trial of participation that allows participants to see if they wish to make a greater commitment to ongoing training. They offer continuity of teaching to those students and faculty who come to our in-person trainings, adding consistent regular contact and further diversity of programming.

So far I have spoken of technology's role in taking ideas to participants around the globe. Another aspect of the use of technology is to enable them to find us. An advanced student I had met some years earlier when teaching a course that occurs twice year in person over three years in China, requested group supervision for himself and a group of colleagues. He proposed a way of doing this effectively: The members of the group would share the cost of subscription to a reliable videoconference service, pay a fee for the teaching, which would be in English, agree on a time (evening in China, early morning for me), and find a competent translator. He selected a Chinese program called "Seegle Team" which allows for up to thirteen people to connect from their own computers without the necessity of expensive bridging equipment of the kind needed for courses with multiple participants. Working in this way calls for patience and willingness to tolerate uncertainty in connecting. I had to rely on the Chinese group leader to help me navigate the software because it shows up on my screen in Chinese. I needed the translator to help me understand the material and discussion. Sharing responsibility in this way, we co-created the learning setting. An additional group has formed with one of the colleagues with whom I teach that course in China (see Chapter Nine). Thus a student-led initiative using technology has brought continuity and depth to the in-person course for those who sought supervision. This supervision is crucial to the development of clinical skills among the most advanced students, who are thereby empowered as leaders, supporting the overall growth of skills in the entire group of participants in the China program. It has recently seemed quite remarkable to me that at the moment of writing this, the Chinese government has imposed much tighter censorship on the internal use of Google and other forms of Internet communication, but that this professional communication has been able to carry on nevertheless.

I have also had the opportunity to offer group supervision to a private group of couple therapists in Russia, who have chosen to connect by Skype, when they are all in a room together with their translator. Skype is sometimes unreliable, at which point we have to reconnect because the call has dropped, or there is junk on the line, and we hope for a different connection with better quality. In China, even with a paid service, there can be glitches. The server company occasionally imposes changes in the connections without properly notifying users, and the connectivity can be imperfect or can drop one of the members of the call. Meeting these challenges requires patience, acceptance of constraints, and collaboration between the overseas leader and the teacher who is based in another country and in a different time zone. We work together to set the frame, find a time that works, work with translation, manage the technology, and set up a learning situation that fosters the teaching and learning task.

For the groups in China and in Russia, we work with serial translation, that is, the translator speaks after the supervisor speaks and after the presenter or other members speak, a slow but effective process. In Russia, the translator is in the room with the group, but in China, the translator is in a separate location, and, in one of the groups, is actually in Taiwan while the group members are in different cities on the mainland. The situation for China is particularly complex, and yet technology makes the work possible. What is remarkable is that we get the work done, despite the inevitable technical problems that mark these endeavors from time to time. This is work that we could not have imagined in earlier years, so in spite of these occasional frustrations, we soldier on, grateful that technology has made this kind of international communication, and teaching and learning, possible.

Conclusion

The use of the free teleconference call service and the new videoconference technologies enables us to link groups that would otherwise not be able to join in the study of psychoanalysis and psychotherapy, nor receive supervision of clinical technique. With improving technology and decreasing cost, it is now feasible to join colleagues, students, and teachers at many sites across any distance in real-time teaching, learning, and supervision. In our experience, the technical and personal adjustments to the use of this technology are surmountable. Then opportunities open that allow the sharing of analytic ideas and clinical experience in a way that we are only beginning to explore.

References

Alvarez, A. (1993). *Live Company: Psychoanalytic Psychotherapy with Autistic, Borderline, and Deprived and Abused Children*. London: Routledge.

Alvarez, A. (2012). *The Thinking Heart*. Hove: Routledge.

Aronson, J. (Ed.) (2000). *Use of the Telephone in Psychotherapy*. Northvale, NJ: Jason Aronson.

Fishkin, R., & Fishkin, L. (2014). Introducing psychoanalytic therapy into China: The CAPA experience. In: D. E. Scharff & S. Varvin (Eds.), *Psychoanalysis in China* (pp. 205–215). London: Karnac.

Fishkin, R., Fishkin, L., Leli, U., Katz, B., & Snyder, E. (2011). Psychodynamic treatment, training, and supervision using Internet-based technologies. *Journal of the American Academy of Psychoanalysis and Dynamic Psychiatry, 39*: 155–168.

Miller, L., Rustin, M., & Shuttleworth, J. (1989). *Closely Observed Infants*. London: Duckworth.

Scharff, J. S., & Scharff, D. E. (2000). *Tuning the Therapeutic Instrument: The Affective Learning of Psychotherapy*. Northvale, NJ: Jason Aronson.

Scharff, J. S. (Ed.) (2012). *Psychoanalysis Online: Mental Health, Teletherapy, and Training*. London: Karnac.

Sebek, M. (2001). Internet discussion review: Varieties of long-term outcome among patients in psychoanalysis and psychotherapy: A review of findings on the Stockholm outcome of psychoanalysis and psychotherapy project (STOPP), by Rolf Sandell et al. *International Journal of Psychoanalysis, 82*: 205–210.

CHAPTER TWELVE

Emergency SMS-based intervention in chronic suicidality: a research project using conversation analysis

Michael B. Buchholz and Horst Kächele

Until now, no therapeutic conversation conducted over a month only by text messaging has been analyzed. For the first time, we present the analysis of a Short Message Service (SMS) conversation subjected to the research technique of microanalytical conversation analysis. The spare aspect of text messaging condenses affect. Using the research technique of conversation analysis, we show the presence of a working alliance, the mode of operation of psychoanalytic interpretation, and gradations of empathy. However, we caution against promoting the new electronic media as a new mode of therapy, because we must await the results of more research on further individual case studies of text-based interventions.

In acute psychosocial distress, exploratory psychotherapy usually is not the first response. We do not subscribe to emergency psychotherapy, as described by Bellak and Siegel (1987). Instead, we recommend admission to a psychiatric inpatient treatment, because being removed from the triggering situation rapidly relieves intrapsychic pressure, and because outpatient psychotherapy loses value with chronically suicidal patients when they are in crisis. Whether admission is suggested by the psychotherapist or initiated by the patient, the disruption threatens the therapeutic relationship and challenges the therapist's flexibility. Admissions to inpatient settings may support outpatient treatment but the outpatient treatment may be burdened by too many such accommodations.

Now we are working in an age of new media. What if therapists were to consider the use of email, Skype, or SMS text messaging? What changes might they then make to the design of useful therapeutic processes with the chronically suicidal patient? There is already a growing literature proselytizing the use of technology in therapy and analysis, but it is based on clinical narrative or anecdote. What is lacking is a study of detailed transcripts from clinical practice that will allow us to learn new things and to justify our position on the use of new media in clinical practice.

The material

We will present and examine text-based clinical material provided by a media-savvy colleague with the consent of the patient. This sequence of SMS messages occurred in the context of the patient's work-related absence at the same time as her therapist's vacation. The patient is a thirty-year-old woman who became suicidal after the death of her mother and sought out-patient psychotherapy. During two years of treatment, dissociative symptoms emerged and pointed to a possible history of traumatic experiences with her father.

The patient planned a stay of several weeks on travel for work in South America, while the therapist would be on annual leave in northern Russia. Until then, during disruptions in the treatment, they had communicated relatively reliably via email. On this occasion, they had to resort to text messaging, a medium that has been the subject of few empirical studies. The Stuttgart working group had tested the efficacy of text-messaging in relapse prevention (Bauer, Okon, & Sea, 2008); in this study, the functionality of the text-messaging was limited to mere data-exchange. Real possibilities of a text-messaging in clinical situations are still under-reported.

Imagine the situation confronting patient and therapist. On July 27, the patient is about to depart, and a text conversation begins and continues until a month later, when it ends on September 7. Their text conversation is relatively fully documented here. However, we cannot completely exclude the possibility that shorter responses of the therapists were not recorded. We follow with an analysis of the text-message conversation. We use the symbol P to indicate message coming from or signed by the patient. We use the symbol T for the therapist, and we show his contributions in italics. In brackets we give the actual day followed by the month of the SMS, but we have eliminated the year for reasons of confidentiality. The usually cryptic and fragmented nature of SMS communications is somewhat exaggerated by literal translation from the German and by leaving misplaced punctuation to preserve authenticity.

1. P (27.7.): Thank you, think a lot of you, get along, much uncertainty, many open questions. Greetings, P
2. P (7.8.): Dear T just in time—now I can clean up and pack. Couldn´t do it before. Thank you. Greetings, P
3. P (8.8.): Thank you, now I have to keep moving and must continue, again extremely lonely. P
4. P (9.8.): Dear T, I checked in. It was okay with him [her father]. He has to leave me. I am strengthened. And he has become suddenly old, weakened. Thank you. Greetings, P +
5. P (11.8.): Dear T both, well received and accepted. How are you doing, I shall mail this evening? It is a lot. Thank you + Greetings, P
6. P (12.8.): I am missing you, P
7. P (12.8.): Do I cling too much to you? So far I am getting along well, but still. Greetings, P
8. P (15.8.): Dear T, new number does not seem to reach you—then I keep going. Interior difficult, outside ok. No right to live. Today, many thoughts of you. Greetings P
9. T (15.8.): *"No right to live"? What has she done?*
10. P (16.8.): Now in clear distance I see everything clear ahead of me, like the story of another. I hate this person
11. T (16.8.): *How are you? T*

12. P (16.8.): She is bad + will never lose it. The efforts are pointless. She is tormenting herself+other

13. T (16.8.): *Dear P, the other who is she and what has she done. Our number-one issue. T*

14. P (16.8.): I cannot do anything against the feeling: I'm bad and worthless + without rights. It is ingrained + physically, not susceptible by logical reasoning

15. T (17.8.): *I understand that*

16. P (17.8.): Look, I want to be allowed to live

17. T (17.8.): *Who gives permission to do so? What can I contribute? T*

18. P (17.8.): Who? That's a good question: it is not the father, not only, it is superior, to what you can help—the mere questioning feels good

19. T (17.8.): *I am convinced that the experience of a good relationship underpins this right. Greetings Your T*

20. P (17.8.): Can you call me at times when you are back in XX? Since yesterday I work, that's good, it's too much what comes up when I'm free, I hope you are well, and thank you P

21. T (17.8.): *I'll call you then at times, number via email. Work certainly helps. T*

22. P (17.8.): Thank you, I hope time and again. There are moments where I feel liveliness, but it is strenuous. P

23. P (17.8.): Thank you, go crisper in the day as without you. P

24. P (18.8.): Good morning! For you it is evening. The support of yesterday is sufficient for the start of the day. Greetings P

25. T (23.8.): *Back in mobile phone country. T*

26. P (23.8.): I am pleased. I'm okay. Somehow I am relaxed what concerns the next few weeks. The states are changing again, here too I am so lonely, fears only at night in a dream

27. T (23.8.): *This pleases me to read. T*

28. P: (25.8.): Dear T, others are homesick or have fears of diseases; a German woman is therefore flown home 4 days ago. I have no home anyway but I'm okay so far. P

29. T (26.8.): *Dear P, thanks for the news. How is HOME generated? Greetings T*

30. P (26.8.): There I feel sure there I am allowed to exist—my heart is weary of life, there's no good and it does not matter

31. T (26.8.): *Ubi bene, ibi patria—so say the Romans. Your inner self cannot be destroyed. T*

32. P (26.8.): He might call, but he does not. He could come and visit me, but he does not. I lie here and it is hot and humid, falling apart. I crumble, dissolve me

33. T (26.8.): *A longing for redemption, an end. At its best, it would be like not to be alone*

34. T (26.8.): *It is a love that is not reciprocated. Let it go. T*

35. P (26.8.): Yeah, cry, it hurts so much. Also the fact that you are so far away

36. T (26.8.): *Crying is necessary, grieving process means detaching oneself. And I'm very connected with you. Greeting Yours T*

37. P (26.8.): That's true, but why. My life, my mind, my body, all in vain, in vain. Be killed on the spot, so bad it is

38. T (26.8.): *You had reasons to give him much—only these don't apply anymore. This is grim. T*

39. P (26.8.): You understand me, my life is over

40. P (26.8.): I imagine that I can be with you, up close and that you can stand me until I'm dead

41. P (27.08.): Dear T it is better now, and I'm sorry, but it was terrible. I just wanted it to stop. P

42. T (27.8.): *This idea also contains a seed of a desire to be close to me and that's a good thing. T*

43. P (27.8.): I imagined that I would be in your arm, to tell you how bad it was and stop breathing

44. T (27.8.): *Dear P, this is okay like that. T*

45. P (27.8.): I'm doing better now, but I do not take this anymore, again forever.

46. P (27.8.): I would now like to talk

47. T (27.8.): *Why not call right now! T*

48. P (27.8.): So I try

49. P (27.8.): Does not work with German chip and also not with local chip, but thank you—you see, here many things are easier for me, less stress, more space, but I still cannot get rid of it

50. P (27.8.): She inflicts pain on herself, but nothing is enough and something holds her back, ripped, torn apart, bind tightly, rape

51. P (27.8.): Everything in her is dirty and bad, the shell is deceiving and lying, punishments come quickly and bend me down that I know again that life does not apply to me

52. T (27.8.): *She is identified with the perpetrator—the father?—But what was her share? T*

53. P (27.8.): She should not feel live, enjoy, she does not have the rights that others have, now it would be time for another beating, I hardly can stand it

54. T (27.8.): *Yes, she may, because what happened is over. T*

55. P (27.8.): I am worth nothing

56. P (27.8.): Wretched, she is despicable. She deserves the utmost bad, abasement, humiliation. For this she is there, one must misuse her, she has no rights

57. P (27.8.): I do not know what I can do, run against the wall

58. T (28.8.): *For me she is valuable precisely because of her experiences. T*

59. P (28.8.): Do not be mad at me once it just does not work anymore. Think not bad, then it is good

60. T (28.8.): *I think not bad. You suffer yourself. T*

61. T (28.8.): *Is it better again T*

62. T (30.8.): *How are you? Do I have to worry? This is my third inquiry. T*

63. P (30.8.): Dear T in a bad state these days I was traveling alone. Cannot say what I did. I hate that. And to start again and again is robbing the energy for anything else what I should do or could. You do not have much vacation time left, despite Time is running out. P

64. T (31.8.): *Good that you are back from the PENAL COLONY. Was the trigger a current tension with a colleague?*

65. T (1.9.): *I'm in a hotel with email connection T*

66. P (1.9., 10.32am): Dear T, I'm feeling better, many greetings P

67. T (1.9.): *Thank you. Do you have time for email? Greetings T*

68. P (1.9., 6:59pm): Yes, no problem, thought that you do not go to the Internet

69. P (1.9., 7:06pm): I wrote to you, but received no reply from you, therefore I will rather wait. I'm so glad that the state of my misery is better now. How are you? P

70. T (1.9.): *Dear P, I will read the mail today at Lunch time. T*

71. T (1.9.): *Did not receive any mail. Send it again. T*

72. P (2.9.): Dear T would you consider to visit me? In all seriousness. P

73. T (2.9.): *This is a question that I cannot just answer from here; how can I reach you by phone from XX from? Greetings T*

74. P (2.9.): This is easy. We need to make contact only via SMS. Until 9/15. I live here and can be called. Will you think about it?

75. T (2.9.): *I will think about it, certainly. T*

76. P (3.9.): Dear T I have just e-mailed to you, it goes like this. Outside I shall not get quite old. Inside I am already old. When and how the end will come and what is it? Greetings P

77. T (3.9.): *Let's see if this time I find your mail. Greetings T*

78. P (3.9.): Dear T, thanks for the mail, I have replied. Went very well today

79. T (3.9.): *Dependency be according to John Bowlby, is a basal motivation, an ability for times of need. Your independence was a protective armor. T*

80. P (3.9): Dear T, the day was good, but my soul is weak and helpless. I'm on duty at the weekend, it will be right. Drink now wine on the balcony and go to bed. It is hot

81. T (3.9.): *Yes, we have to do some more working through. T*

82. P (3.9.): Maybe, now. It's too late. A vacuum that hurts

83. P (4.9.): I bodily feel the parts. Children, adolescents, and adults with bad intentions then, bondage pain shame shame contempt of myself

84. P (4.9.): She also has security and strength, indeed, but the other things are often so strong and overwhelming. I'm too heavy, too dirty, too bad

85. T (4.9.): *In due time we will clarify the events that are troublesome—clarify differentiate what when who has done it to her! Greetings T*

86. P (4.9.): Thank you for your reply. I wake up and get a sign from an important human being for me. That's good. How are you doing?

87. T: (4.9.): *I'm fine, thank you, again today conference. Greetings T*

88. P (4.9.): And I thought you are on vacation. Is it very difficult for you that I am so fixated on you? For me it is difficult. P

89. T (4.9.): *Holidays for most of the time—Your fixation: for me it is desirable T*

90. P (4.9., 10.47 am): And it is good for me if I allow it? As long as our relationship is good yes, but if not, it torments. It tears me at the moment

91. T (4.9.): *That is true. Now I go away, until later T*

92. P (4.9.): Dear T, I believe I cannot stand through this. I absolutely cannot imagine to come back and I do not know any other place for me. Slowly drifting out of the world

93. P (4.9., 2.58pm): to go. I'm desperate. lonely

94. P (4. 9., 11.40pm): That's nice that you write, I'm so heavy, so heavy

95. T (5.9., 7.35am): *a loneliness arises in you, but you are not alone. T*

96. T (5.9., 7.45am): *you need this echo. T*

97. P (5.9., 11.32am): Dear T, you said that the dependence is desirable. I cannot see the point. I think so often of you

98. P (5.9., 1.30pm): I cannot anymore. I always think that I am something I kidding myself with this connection. I do not know what I should do

99. T (5.9., 9.30pm): *In times of distress dependency is useful. T*

100. T (5.9., 9.35pm): *A therapeutic connection may be a help. Can, should express that you are not deserted. T*

101. P (5.9.): But I feel deserted; I know that what you do for me, is something special, but I cannot really feel and believe it. I leave you now

102. T (5.9.): *How are these fluctuation come about? As quickly? T*

103. P (5.9.): Both hurts so much. The waiting and hoping and giving up. Thanks anyway. To immerse, to sink, be gone

104. T (5.9.): *This was known to the little prince, as he felt his feelings for the fox. T*

105. P (6.9.): I do not know what to think, what can I believe in, what I can keep myself

106. P (6.9.): It is distressing this feeling I may—I may not. Tomorrow we can talk

107. T (6.9.): *what time—tonight, what number? T*

108. P (6.9.): I may come to you, but I may not actually touch. You give me your hand, but do not hold me. I sometimes bounce off. This torments me

109. T (6.9.): *I would be sorry for that. T*

110. P (6.9.): May I or may I not, yes that is the mother, not father. Have a good return home.

111. T (6.9.): *I'm on my way home. T*

112. P (6.9.): Thank you for this information. Greetings P

113. P (6.9.): Dear T! Thanks God, have again some ground under my feet. What I experience in the jobs, makes me helpless. But it has also helped me, where are you? P

114. P (6.9.): Dear T, I hope you have arrived well. Let me know if you have time, these days or send me an email. Thanks and greetings P

115. P (7.9.): Thank you. What is it that makes me cling to you like that. It hurts, maybe more than it does good. Come home well. P

Commentary

Overcoming a polarized debate

Dealing with the new electronic media to exploit their potential and usefulness for psychotherapy leads quickly to a polarization between supporters and opponents, both set in their positions. Trying to analyze concrete material for each camp to review can build bridges.

You may recall that psychotherapy and counselling have been conducted on the telephone for many years. Harvey Sacks (1992) had developed his method of analysis of conversation in such telephone-based counselling sessions. Conversation over electronic media is more than encoding and decoding between "sender" and "receiver" (Peräykylä, 2004). As they "see" and "read" the minimal words, people add to the objective message the symbolic meaning and affective tone, according to their own perceptions and subjectivity. This resonates with newer psychoanalytic approaches that speak of the "field" (Baranger, 2012; Ferro, 2003) and relational perspectives (Altmeyer, 2011; Buchholz, 2005; Mitchell, 2000).

Text-based therapy in crisis conditions

Here it is important not to perseverate on the difference between text-based therapy and a "normal" variant of psychotherapy and not to regard it as "deficient" just because the rhythm and inflection of speech, tone of voice, and gesture are missing, but rather to focus on what problems can this kind of conversation address and resolve? Text messaging allows relatively short communications and wherever communication has to be concise, each and every word carries a charged meaning. Informal language, abbreviations, and greetings and signing off are often missing, unlike an email and vastly unlike a written letter. How are such shortcuts used? How are we to understand them? Does the concise nature of the communication carry within it a special, unusual complexity?

The "scene of conversation" and the "scene of reference"

It is useful to distinguish between two levels. Tomasello (1999) identifies the "scene of the conversation" and the "scene of reference".

In this SMS material, the scene of the conversation is characterized by shortage of words. Attention turns to the way the participants operate under these reduced conditions. This may sound strange, but is not so unusual. We illustrate it with an example: The English word "flirt" comes from the French; it is derived from *fleureter*, the art of flirting. If a gentleman (as one might find in Balzac) is invited to visit a lady, he carries a bouquet for her in one hand. We might think narrowly that he is making a simple, conventional expression of courtesy. On the other hand, he could express the feelings in his heart for this hostess by the choice of flowers, the size of the bouquet, small variations in what he says as he presents the bouquet, and how long he keeps it in his hand, perhaps for a fraction of a second longer than necessary. Bystanders might not notice the flirting intent behind these gestures, but the hostess might. This is the scene of the conversation. The apparent nothingness of the interaction allows the parties an elegant measure of control. They can approach an intimate moment and withdraw with no loss of face if the flirting is not reciprocated. In case of failure, "nothing" happened. The scene of the conversation is similarly colored. This model of a social scene is illustrative of the model of text-based therapy, not in terms of the word content ("the bouquet") but in terms of the various aspects of control of the conversation and the conditions of constraint. Who answers and who remains silent? Is the one or the other in demand? What rights are granted or denied?

The scene of reference, however, is that which relates to the content of the communication: What are the writers saying in their communications? How do they know what is meant? How do they cope when the utterances are ambiguous because of the concise nature of texting? With regard of content, psychotherapists often set their sole attention. But they would lose out. The combination of both levels offers a delightful game of revelation and obfuscation, from which deeper meaning and emotional resonance can be drawn. In the momentary encounter, we need to attend to both "scenes" to relate to the patient's mood regulation and arrive at the moment for interpretation (Argelander, 1979). We will use the two "scenes" as complementary perspectives on the material.

Analysis of the material

An interesting point arises immediately upon observing that the text conversation starts with a "thank you" [1]. This implies that the therapist already had done something for which P thanks him. In everyday conversation a response would be expected, such as "You're welcome" or "Sure." But in the text stream there is nothing. Silence. Omissions are significant. P does not take this as rejection, but thinks of it as a waiting. She reacts by writing another eight messages

("Dear T") about how the way they think together and get along should not subside. She refers to a "him", by which her therapist knows she means her father. Patient and therapist must therefore already have a shared knowledge so huge that the reference to "him" is enough and the other knows who is meant. The scene of the conversation generates meaning: it does away with formats of reciprocity such as please and thank you. This is interpreted as familiarity, not as "infraction", by the participants. No one complains about lack of courtesy. The agreed-upon minimal nature of the texts encourages the tendency for an informal style. Our observation of the scene of the reference indicates "shared knowledge" from which only we are excluded.

The patient writes eight messages unilaterally. How her phrase "it's a lot" [5] on 11.8. came about, we do not know. Even as P writes: "You are missing, P" [6]. "Dear T" does not respond. This statement by P is ambiguous in terms of how to classify it. It could be continued in very different ways. For example, she might have continued, "You are missing, so write me!" or "You are missing, I miss you", or "You are missing, I need you", or it can stand for itself in terms of simply locating where she is and where her therapist is not. We are unable to assign P's comment as it is intended. If the therapist would react, then his answer based on his reading of the comment, would drive our decision on the category and thus assign to this small, tight phrase a meaning that the patient may or may not yet have. T is silent, as in any good analytic hour. P writes [7] at the same day a question: "Do I hang too much on you?" This, too, is an ambiguous conversational format. The question in the quantitative "too much" calls for a "quantitative" determination by T, which could be given only as an evaluation. At the same time, the question can only be answered by the questioner herself. She seems to have an implicit knowledge of it, as the second part suggests: "… but anyway". What this means and what it opens up is not clear. From the perspective of the scene of reference we might consider that the phrase connects to her well-being, "here so far along well". From the perspective of the scene of the conversation "but still" could mean that they question whether they really like each other in theory, although they got along well.

The construction of two scenes brings out the complexity when you imagine another sequel, "Come here so far along well, but still (even if you do not reply)." We cannot decide what was meant. This uncertainty for the participants, arising from the structure of texting, drives the affective density. It shows how parsimony and compression of expression is used by both parties to the conversation so that the therapist is obliged to speak with P. This is what the patient is trying to achieve. There is far more than encoding and decoding a message going on. We see blurring of communication and a complex mixing of the two scenes.

Therapeutic strategy: scarcity of utterance and putting down bait

Let's look at three days' later. In [8] P now evokes a reaction from T by the sentence, "No right to live" in response to a message about her condition—"internal hard, outside ok". "Almost" kept missing the words "I …", or even "He has …". Again, shortage of words and pronouns creates an indiscriminate response that therefore shows affective density. In the scene of reference, lack of subjectivity is implied by the phrase without a pronoun. In the scene of conversation the subject is missed, too. However, emotionality is quite involved by just the same means. The phrases condense both scenes into an intensified emotionally stimulating impact. This influences T to respond.

Look at [9] where T responds in quotes, on to which he hangs a question mark. Again, use of quotation marks and question mark transform a statement into a question, condenses the scenes of conversation and reference. We would now expect the message "What do you mean?" but, instead, we find a second question that refers to something within the conversational format, something that has already been discussed between the two: "What has she done?" could imply that there is another person who denied P's right to live. The conversation format is again of great importance because T reacts with his first answer in more than two weeks, so P now knows how to motivate him to respond. But he does not respond with a statement of concern, but the question format "What has she done?" This is a call for information! To manage the task of answering this question she must stay alive! It remains unclear how the therapist arrived at his question: "What has she done?" Where does that come from? Perhaps a simple spelling mistake or lack of capitalization which often happens in SMS-conversation. (In German „Was hat sie getan?" and „Was haben Sie getan?" are distinguished by capitals. So "What has she done" might be understood instead as "What have you done?") Perhaps even more likely, it stems from the psychoanalytic notion of suicidality as being due to the introjection of a malignant introject in the self. Is P addressed in the third person? In any case, the question itself unfolds enormous impact.

To characterize the therapist's overall strategy, we might use the phrase "to put down bait." The therapist does not answer for a long time. He shortens the "feeding conditions" in addition to the given shortage of text messaging, and when he sends his first utterance, it unavoidably carries greater charge. It *must* be downright ambiguous in order to tighten emotional bonds and to attach P.

The therapist's strategy seems counter-intuitive. Under conditions of extreme scarcity of conversation by text, one would expect the therapist to send a long message from time to time, or short texts at least once per day. The opposite is the case here. Has something constructive been achieved thereby? Undoubtedly, the answer is yes! We see a high degree of affective complexity and focus of attention—both very good conditions for therapeutic work. With surgical precision, as it were, the surgical field is uncovered and work can begin. How can empathy be possible under these circumstances?

Beginning to work

The therapist's question—"What has she done?" [9]—is answered in an important dimension the same day. "You" is "like the story of another" [10]. In this compressed and enigmatic way, the patient is told that "she" is the patient herself. "She" hates "herself", we learn from the text of the same day ("I hate this person"). The therapist responds with a question in everyday format: "How are you". But the context of the conversation converts the everyday meaning of this greeting to an update of the patient's self. The patient responds [12] in a bizarre narrative of cruel tormenting referring to "she" and "herself—the other". T's everyday question can be read with an accent on "you" ("How are *you*") and she then reminds P how bad she is and who she pesters.

Now the therapist chooses a different format: He's talking to his patient, "Dear P" [13]. This address, which we have not seen before, has a conversational meaning. It falls in the category of "pre-announcement", a well-studied conversational format. Doctors use such "pre-announcements" when they have to deliver bad news from diagnostic findings (Maynard, 2004) or narrators when they are about to tell a story (Goodwin, 1984; Jefferson, 1978; Mandelbaum, 2013; Stivers, 2008). Such "pre-announcements" advertise the kind of conversation that follows, they cancel out distractions, and indicate a special need for attention. They also indicate which response is expected ("Do you know what great/sad/awesome/funny thing happened to me today?") What is interesting is that conversation analysis (Heritage, 2011) shows that such "pre-announcements" co-organize the type of the following "empathic moments". The doctor, who prepares his patient for a bad diagnosis, uses other twists than a speaker who is going to tell a "great story". Words and tone of the "pre-announcement" are informed both by the speaker's intention and the listener's expected reaction. The patient, so the doctor knows beforehand, could be shaken or distressed. The audience for a great story will marvel, friends being told a joke will—hopefully—laugh.

Look at "Dear P" [13]. Here we see the greeting phrase as usually found in a letter format. Because it was omitted in the previous texts, it will now have the effect of a "pre-announcement". The scene of the conversation could therefore be "translated" as "Look out! Here's an important message and I am easing you into it". After this gentle "pre-announcement" the therapist can follow with the main question: "the other who is she and what she has done? That is our number-one issue T."

The soft, familiar form of the letter format together with the visually evocative expression "number-one issue" is an active attempt to build a working alliance even under the minimal conditions of text messaging. This is crowned with success. Whereas the patient previously had "the other" and the "I" dramatically mixed together in the scene of reference, now she makes [14] a clear differentiation: "I cannot do anything against the feeling …" This is constructive, succinct and limit-setting ("I" against "the other") against what comes from the other side of the border: "against the feeling: I'm bad and worthless + without rights." Self and introject are set against each other for a moment, can be formulated in their difference, are thus also felt. This differentiation is the counterpart of a therapeutically risky regression that would always be associated with dedifferentiation. The therapist then in his response [15] "understands" that the patient suffers. The differentiation-work underway is continued in the next message that P wants to be "allowed to live" and immediately the therapist responds, questioning: "Who gives permission to do so?" [17] The effect is amazing: What had been a diffused, irresistible impulse is inserted into a new frame of prohibition and permission. What the patient experienced as distressing, is now a matter of allowance and forbidding. A diffuse, physically almost unbearable feeling has become a solvable problem by therapeutic intervention, the steps of which we can track right here

The therapist's second question—"What can I contribute?"—inserts the frame of prohibition/permission into another frame, called transference in psychoanalysis. To both questions, the patient responds separately. She works with "what you can help—the mere questioning feels good" [19]. T's question is reformatted in a statement. It responds to the unspoken but clearly audible intent of the therapist to be helpful.

Frame, format, schema—notes on the working mode of the interpretation

We have just used the concept of frame and framing and want to take the opportunity to seek further differentiation. Frames are seen in cognition research as dynamic social constructs

(Altheide, 2002). They are not stable regardless of the activities of the parties in the frame, but dynamic and flexible and adaptable to given changing situations.

The concept of framing (as conversational activity) is useful for understanding how an interpretation can be successful by providing different frames for one and the same experience—and so transforming their meaning. Such framing is connected to the success of interpretation in positively changing cognitions—and, therefore emotions. The interpretation works, if you will, "via the head". It goes "top-down" and not "bottom-up". The same experience is suddenly "seen" in a different frame and this metaphor of "seeing" articulates the experience of cognitive-affective transformation (see Buchholz, 1996).

Conversational framing activities must be distinguished from relatively stable frame-formats of a message that are independent from a particular interaction. The most common formats are report or story, question and answer, representation or information. Formats have a "recipient-design"; they are recipient-oriented. You tell a story to children in a different way, you do not deliver a "report". The story is told for them in a different fashion than it is to an adult. You do not "know" this, but you do it. Formats use unconsciously acquired cultural tools of cognitive representation of "others" and social integration. Framing processes and supports cognitive-emotional experience. Formats, however, are ways of communicating and describing these experiences. In the example discussed here, T attacks the modal verb "allow" in [16] and makes the frame visible, within which P had been caught in her gloomy experience. T echoes "allow" in "permission" [17] using a question format that nevertheless makes a statement at the same time. Adults, like children, can be suffering or determined in the face of prohibition or permission.

In addition to frame sizes, conversation analysis and cognition research alike know the meta-concept of schema. Schemas represent different types of knowledge, from simple shape formats (four-legged animal) to complex knowledge. Schemas can link with one another. The activation of schemata affects memory and visualization of certain stocks of knowledge and experience.

In the example here we find an interplay of question format and schema. The question format [17] directly implies that P is seen by T as a "child" seeking permission or having to depend on prohibition. The schema of prohibition and permission is linked with corresponding, unspoken anger-experiences from childhood scenes. At the same time the question format has an appealing value; P is called upon to bear witness to her adult personality. The question format has thus, psychoanalytically speaking, multiple valences: it looks like an "information search", but it actually articulates a statement about regression and obedience. P responds to these multiple valences directly [18]—"That's a good question"—and confirms that just the question "feels good".

Let us analyze these ideas in two further examples of how an interpretation works to secure these findings. Consider the expressions [54] to [56]. Again we see a ban on enjoyment: "she" has no right, it was even time for a "beating"—and speaking in the first person P adds that she "hardly can stand it". The response of T: "Yes, she may because what happened is over" evokes the temporal dimension of P's entitlement now. P is no longer a child, which "hardly" stands being beaten, but an adult that has grown far out from this experience, but again and again staggers back into this schema of experience. The format of T's utterance is not a question, but a statement. T issues the permission. T takes over the role of the mighty, who opposes the ban exerted by the inner power of P, and fights on the side of growth and life in the schema.

In [78], P represents a direct question: "Why am I so dependent on you?!" a question format with question marks and exclamation marks to be read as a statement. To ask the question makes perceivable the frame of negative self-evaluation and against this framing the therapist works with "Dependency is … a basal motivation" with the implication that being dependent is a positive ability. The format used by T: "x = y" is typical for an interpretation. And he adds a new metaphor: "Your independence was a protective armor". This metaphor operates as a framework for a past which is opposed to the perceived dependence and can be framed positively now. P's response "my soul is weak and helpless" [80] alludes to this armor imagery.

The methodological concepts of frame/framing, format and schema seem to us to provide valuable information to investigate the operation mode of an interpretation, and could be useful in accurately investigating the mode of operation of other statements in the future.

Empathy is possible in text-based counselling

We would like to conclude with some reflection that empathy is indeed "articulated" in text-based therapy. Empathy is a somewhat ominous term for most therapists, but deeply appreciated in most schools. Like the word "love" it is hard to define. In many circumstances, you can rely on love and empathy as unassailable forces. Conversation analysis does not ask what empathy *is*. Rather, CA translates such an ontology into a procedural question: "How and by what means in the conversation is empathy *done*?" That sounds technically awkward. However, using that formulation opens the path to study empathy as a joint production of both sides. Patients contribute; they *do something* so that therapists can be empathic. Empathy is no "one-way conception".

How are we doing this when we are empathic? In everyday situations we can articulate formats that describe empathy. It was Goffman (1978) who described the empathic "Response cries" such as the "Oh!", "hmm", and "aah" of sighing compassion, silent participation, or evanescent excitement. We find hardly any of these in this text-message material, but for many people these are the clearest articulations of another's empathic participation. You may use these utterances yourself, if you get to hear of someone's experience of a tooth being removed, a first kiss, or news of a death.

Conversation analysis yields other empathic formats and different levels of empathy on a spectrum (Heritage, 2011; Heritage & Lindström, 2012). We sometimes use an "ancillary question" instead of a "response cry". This observation of conversation analysis is important because such a question can be omitted and conversation can be brought to a stop. Here T asks the ancillary question of who "she" is and what "she" has done—an example of utterance of ancillary questions.

Heritage refers to a second level called "parallel assessments". For instance, if a person tells how painful it was to fall on her knees, and the listener says: "Yes I know full well", that listener has responded in "parallel" with an analogue of his own experiences. We have seen a therapeutic example in the conversation analysis: "I understand that" [15], which comes as if out of one's own experience. Apart from empathic responses, there are other forms of empathic articulation. The practical dilemma to be solved is how to avoid being superficial, shallow, conventional, or downright indifferent and at the same time not be too exaggerated, possessive of the affect, or so "richly attentive" that the experience of the other is overshadowed and attention to other topics is removed.

Heritage cites forms of "subjunctive assessment", by which he is referring to expressions that are not in the indicative but in the subjunctive. Again, a common example: Someone describes a kitchen recipe and then mentions an ingredient which he has not yet tried adding, and then the listener says, "Oh wonderful, fantastic", as if he has already tasted it. Both go through an empathic moment with an experience they have in the subjunctive only.

We see a "subjunctive assessment" in the messages analyzed above, as the therapist says: "I am convinced that the experience of a good relationship underpins that right" [19]. This is, grammatically, formulated in the indicative; but it points to a not yet occurred future to come, assured of the right to live. The impressive expression [31]: "Your inner self cannot be destroyed", is a "subjunctive assessment", too. This sentence defies the logic of falsification: it cannot be rebutted, it cannot be confirmed. He focuses on the future of P's own experience and draws strength from there for the present moment of living.

Finally Heritage also mentions "observer responses" in which a listener responds in the role of an imaginary witness. This response manifests itself in such a way that the speaker is clear that the empathic listener follows the speaker's experience and then responds in a way that shows he actively imagines the scene being reported. The listener has been given access to the event without having experienced it. He positions himself as "observer" by the response he makes. Several points in the material argue for this particular position. Here it will suffice to cite the example [36]: "And I'm much obliged to you."

We can apply Heritage's ideas to psychoanalytical interpretation as an exposition of a further stage of empathy. For this you can cite such therapeutic phrases as "It's a love that is not reciprocated" [34] or "You had reasons to give him many things—only these don't apply anymore" [38].

The format is in two parts. It adds new details to the experience of what is already known and links them together. That P feels "love" is one detail; that it is not reciprocated by the other is the other detail. Now a connection is made, as in the second example: There were reasons to give him much—and then the link to the time that has run by, and so the reasons no longer apply.

In the second part of the transcript, the therapist repeatedly closes with evaluatory statements: "She had reasons to give him a lot" is followed by the statement: "This is grim". This evaluation is not a moralistic but an empathic opinion, a "parallel assessment". The same interpretation format can be found in the therapeutic expression [42]: "This idea also contains the seed of a desire to be close to me and that's a good thing." Again, an evaluation follows from empathic "parallel assessment". This format obviously protects the patient from being terrorized and attacked by her introject in the future.

Concluding remarks

We have presented for the first time a continuous sequence of text-based messaging in a clinical setting. We might call this therapeutic intervention another example of "secular pastoral care" (*weltliche Seelsorge*) after Freud (1913, 1927). As far as we know, this is the first time such material has been subjected to conversation analysis. Conversational analysis differentiates types of intervention in terms of therapeutic strategy and empathy. We have explained the technique and have tried to formulate the results in order for them to be of relevance to clinicians.

Our research raises some questions. Can this observation and analysis of text-based intervention lead to some new methodology of crisis intervention?

When indicated in a particular situation, such a text-based conversation is obviously less limited than it seems at first glance. We want to pose further questions and try some answers.

Can this type of text-based conversation be of help only in an already established relationship? Even when not dictated by the patient's work travel, or the analyst's absence, or the specific diagnosis of suicidality, can a dose of text-based conversation be helpful in any therapy or situation of human need?

The means of therapeutic talk-in-interaction can be reconstructed—belatedly from an *ex-post-facto* point of view. We think it would be an error to believe that these practices of talk could be *applied* in advance, in a forward direction.

We have reconstructed a text-based conversation and our analysis of it. This kind of professional help can be delivered only in the context of a pre-established therapeutic relationship by a therapist who in his own professional development no longer clings to the schematic of "diagnosis" and "intervention". The therapist should be able to use the peculiar opportunities of "conversation under restricted conditions" in a manner that allows the patient to participate in his own humanity.

We cannot say that our analysis establishes an art of text-messaging negotiation in all clinical situations, that "basic SMS-communication competencies" can be taught, and that it could take the place of established forms of psychotherapy. It would be an error to suppose that everyone could now conduct such a conversation. Any application to practice is for the future.

Our main intention is to demonstrate that therapists need not demonize text-based therapy, but that they can take a chance on using it when patients are in circumstances like those described above, when communication cannot be achieved otherwise. There is a historical precedent for text-based therapy in telephone therapy. To go to the other extreme, to be euphoric about text-based therapy, would be at least as great a mistake as to demonize it. We need to wait for further careful studies on process and outcome of such conversation formats in therapy and counseling.

References

Altheide, D. L. (2002). Tracking discourse. In: K. A. Cerulo (Ed.), *Culture in Mind: Toward a Sociology of Culture and Cognition* (pp. 172–187). London: Routledge.

Altmeyer, M. (2011). Social network psyche. Essay on the state of modern psychoanalysis. *International Forum of Psychoanalysis, 27*: 107–128.

Argelander, H. (1979). *The Cognitive Organization of Mental Functioning. An Attempt to Systematize the Cognitive Organization in Psychoanalysis*. Stuttgart: Klett-Cotta.

Baranger, M. (2012). The intrapsychic and the intersubjective in contemporary psychoanalysis. *International Forum of Psychoanalysis, 21*: 130–135.

Bauer, S., Okon, E., & Sea, R. (2008). Follow-up via SMS. In: S. Bauer & H. Kordy (Eds.), *E-Mental Health: New Media in Mental Health Care* (pp. 207–217). Heidelberg: Springer Medizin Verlag.

Bellak, L., & Siegel, H. (1987). *Manual for Intensive Brief and Emergency Psychotherapy (B.E.P)*. Larchmont, NY: C.P.S.

Buchholz, M. B. (1996). *Metaphors of "Cure": Qualitative Studies on the Therapeutic-Process* (2nd edition 2003). Giessen: Psychosozial-Verlag.

Buchholz, M. B. (2005). The body of the language: encounters between psychoanalysis and cognitive linguistics. In: H. R. Fischer (Ed.), *A Rose is a Rose: The Role and Function of Metaphors in Science and Therapy* (pp. 167–198). Weilerswist: Velbrück.

Ferro, A. (2003). *The Bipersonal Field: Constructivism and Field Theory in Child Analysis*. Giessen: Psychosozial-Verlag.

Freud, Sigmund (1913). On beginning the treatment (Further recommendations on the technique of psychoanalysis). *S. E., 12*: 123–144. London: Hogarth.

Freud, S. (1927). Postscript to "The question of lay analysis: conversations with an impartial person." *S. E., 20*: 251–258. London: Hogarth.

Goffman, E. (1978). Response cries. *Language, 54*: 787–815.

Goodwin, C. (1984): Notes on story structure and the organization of participation. In: J. M. Atkinson & J. C. Heritage (Eds.), *Structures of Social Action*. Cambridge, UK: Cambridge University Press, 1992.

Heritage, J. C. (2011). Territories of knowledge, territories of experience: empathic moments in interaction. In: T. Stivers, L. Mondada & J. Steensig (Eds.), *The Morality of Knowledge in Conversation* (pp. 159–183). Cambridge, UK: Cambridge University Press.

Heritage, J. C., & Lindström, A. (2012). Knowledge, empathy, and emotion in a medical encounter. In: A. Peräkylä & M. -L. Sorjonen (Eds.), *Emotion in Interaction* (pp. 256–273). New York: Oxford University Press.

Jefferson, G. (1978). Sequential aspects of storytelling in conversation. In: J. Schenkein (Ed.), *Studies in the Organization of Conversational Interaction* (pp. 219–248). London: Academic Press.

Mandelbaum, J. (2013). Storytelling in conversation. In: J. Sidnell & T. Stivers (Eds.), *The Handbook of Conversation Analysis* (pp. 492–508). Chichester, West Sussex, UK: Wiley-Blackwell.

Maynard, D. W. (2004). On predicating a diagnosis as to attribute of a person. *Discourse Studies, 6*: 53–76.

Mitchell, S. A. (2000). *Relationality: From Attachment to Intersubjectivity*. Hillsdale, NJ: The Analytic Press.

Sacks, H. (1992). *Lectures on Conversation* (edited by G. Jefferson, with an introduction by E. A. Schegloff). Oxford: Basil Blackwell.

Stivers, T. (2008). Stance, alignment, and affiliation during story telling: when nodding is a token of affiliation. *Research on Language and Social Interaction, 41*: 2272–2281.

Tomasello, M. (1999): *The Cultural Origins of Human Cognition*. Cambridge, MA: Harvard University Press.

PART IV

TECHNOLOGY IN TREATMENT

CHAPTER THIRTEEN

Occasional telephone sessions in ongoing in-person psychoanalysis

David E. Scharff

This chapter concerns the place of occasional remote analytic sessions in an ongoing, four times weekly, in-person analysis. To introduce the topic, I will first present a single session from the mid-phase of the analysis of a male architect, who had to travel occasionally to meet with his clients on the West coast. On the one hand, this session strikes me as unremarkable. If I were to read it in sequence among transcripts of his in-person sessions I would not be able to tell that this one was a phone session. This supports my point of view that the intermittent use of telephone communication for analytic sessions at a distance maintains the integrity and continuity of the analysis. On the other hand, this session is not typical of this patient's usual analytic work. It has more of a sense of alliance and pulling together than in other sessions during this phase, and it features a shared acknowledgement that his aggressive mood is off-putting to his colleagues and to his wife. This takes me to my second point, that a session of teleanalysis may *at times* be more effective than a session in person for some patients. In this session, the man admitted, essentially for the first time, the value of a more questioning stance about his misanthropic attitude. I felt that this session, unusual during the analysis because of being conducted on the phone, was also unusual in being a turning point. To provide further illustration, I then present Herbert's next session, in which he (who rarely dreamt or had dreams to tell me) reported two dreams, both of which addressed the transference directly. These successive sessions presented me with the curious question of why a patient might be able to work more effectively at a distance of 2500 miles, on the telephone, in a strange hotel than in my familiar office, a few feet away from me on the couch.

Herbert is a fifty-six-year-old architect, married to Eleanor. His former individual therapist referred Herbert and his wife for couple therapy. Herbert had experienced little sexual desire at any time during their ten-year marriage, the first marriage for each. There are no children and no conscious wish for any. Herbert was an only child in a large extended immigrant Jewish family in which many siblings of his parents lived in the same apartment building in Chicago. When the treatment directed at the marriage and the couple's sexual adjustment had achieved a degree of success, Herbert recognized that difficulties in maintaining intimacy lay with him. We all agreed that he needed individual therapy, and at a more intense frequency than he had had previously. His former therapist had died, and so I agreed to offer individual psychoanalysis. The blocks to further progress in his capacity to relate to his wife and colleagues lay chiefly in his unconscious resentment of women, stemming from anger at his dominating mother and from longing for and uneasy identification with his passive and underachieving father. I knew when we began analysis that Herbert's position at a national architectural firm would require him to travel around the country and occasionally overseas to meet with clients and monitor construction. He knew that I would be willing to offer teleanalysis at his regular appointment time when he had to travel. His current project is to design an office building for an IT company in Seattle.

Herbert attends faithfully in person, traveling for business only occasionally. When he leaves he always elects to keep the telephone appointments. But mainly we meet in person. He talks easily but he usually stays on the surface. Although he has dreams, they are an infrequent feature of the analysis. It has been difficult to awaken an interest in the deeper layers of experience whether by inquiring about the roots of his feelings or by interpreting resistance and transference. He takes what I have to say often with an attitude of, "If you say so!" He feels generally that analytic understanding is futile because it does not improve his pessimistic attitude or change his hopeless situation.

The first session I am going to report is the third session of the week. Keeping his 9.30am East coast time appointment, Herbert called at 6.30am West coast time from Seattle before going to work. He began by referring to the in-person session of the previous day in which the theme was his presumption that he is allowed to be generally grumpy if he wants to. It's an attitude he is entitled to, and if others do not like it, that's too bad for them.

He said, "I begin the day by being grumpy and then it gets worse. If I'm not contrarian, there's a danger I'll go back to living two lives. There is the side of me I let others see. There were years people only saw anger and sarcasm. It is only in the past few years that I've talked about it. The positive thing is that I let you and Eleanor see what it's like for me, maybe why I have to do this. That's the difference. I used to just feel bottled up and angry."

What he is saying about the "two sides of himself" is not clear. The word "contrarian" suggests that there is a side of him that is the opposite of grumpy. What is clear is that what he lets others see is the grumpy, angry, sarcastic side. So what is the true side of himself that this side covers? Then it seems that when he is grumpy, he has been hiding his anger and bottling it up inside, but now he lets his wife and me see that he starts out grumpy, and it gets worse. I conclude that he is saying that behind the grumpy, disagreeable side, there is a secret really angry side. And I am wondering whether we will ever get beyond the anger to a part of him that is full of hurt and longing.

After a pause he continued, "I know it's time for me to say, 'The world has had enough of the truth. It's time to rationalize and filter.' The walls are down. It's counterproductive to say, 'You're not ready for the whole truth.' There's this instinctive knee-jerk 'don't-go-there' feeling."

I said, "That's your construction of the world as a place that's against you."

He said, "That's my default position. The insight is that it's *me*! *I've* been doing it. It's where I go. Not doing it would take work. It's a big effort because it's not natural for me to change that. Even the thought of possibly doing that is something new."

Grumpiness is his first order defense.

I said, "It's been the best you could do, the only way you could do things. The idea now is to find out why it was all you could do, and then to see what other options you could have. But all of that seems foreign to you."

He said, "Five or six years ago was the first time I realized that I was empowered with the notion that 'when you're confronted with a challenge, I wasn't compelled to answer immediately.'"

I noticed his switch from "I" to "you" in his sentence: "I was empowered … you were confronted … I wasn't compelled." He meant to say that he had realized that, when confronted, he doesn't have to respond grumpily or impulsively, and instead can take his time to consider his answer: for instance, if I, as the analyst, confront him with an interpretation, he can take his time to respond. But the switch alerts me to his confronting me with a challenge instead of confronting himself. I must be aligned with an internal object that he himself switches into at times.

He continued, "I hadn't realized I could take control. I find lately, I can say, 'That's a hard question. I want to take time and get back to you.' That's behavior and programming that has just started to change."

He was assigning a history to this notion, so it must have been in development, but for him to speak of it or act differently was quite new. This turn of events has happened in a session on the telephone. I wonder what it is that gives him this new capacity to reflect, and wonder if it is the distance generated by not *being in the office.*

Agreeing that this was an advance, I said, "Yes."

He said, "It's a turning point in my professional life especially—No! In my whole life! Dr. G used to guide me. [Dr. G is his former therapist whom he idealized, and who was overtly supportive to him in ways I am not.] It felt like I was on a game show with three seconds to give the answer, and if I let it go, the opportunity was lost and I'd fail. I'd look terrible. My mother's idea was, 'Look sharp! Be quick!' I got points for it from her. As an adult I just knew it was always good to be quick. I always thought, 'Talk fast! Think fast'. Taking more control, taking time to think, has been an achievement.

"A few years ago, there was a woman client. She was high strung. She called me one day and rattled on about a problem regarding a building she and I were working on, and she said at the end, 'What do you think? What should we do?' I wasn't even a partner yet, and she wanted my advice. She'd blurted out a lot and she wanted an answer on the spot. So I said that what she thought was fine. I said, 'It's okay'. She said, 'Exactly!' and hung up. I had a rush, which lasted for about two seconds. Then I started worrying that I hadn't really thought it through, and so I began to panic and ran into the senior architect's office. He explained that there was a much more complicated context. He took it over, and said he would take care of it. Two weeks later we're on a conference call, and she quotes me and says, 'Herbert said such and such.' I was sitting on the phone and I wanted to say, 'I gave you that advice but you didn't tell me the full context.' But all I said was, 'Yes, it's true. I gave you that advice.' Since then I have a little bottle on my desk which says on it, 'Go away, Evil!' to remind me not to give into the wish to rush to say something before I think it through. In the end, the senior guy fixed it, but he had to back-track on what I had said. So now I give advice to the younger guys. 'The clients won't respect you any less if you take the time to think and talk to colleagues.' Can you appreciate what a change that is for me, to take control of myself? To not act like a trained seal?"

Of course I could appreciate the relief of making that change. But I was also tracking his reference to the telephone. On the phone he had been tricked into giving a quick answer. He hadn't been given the context, the time to reflect. Is he worried that I will use whatever he says against him today because he feels safer on the phone and not on guard as he is in person? But if I were to say this to him, he would respond with puzzlement, or say something like his usual "If you say so". So I simply drew on his analogy and got back to the analytic situation.

I said, "It's a good analogy. She seduced you into a quick response, and you rushed in without thinking."

He said, "If I act more reasonably, I feel a fraud". This kind of affirmative intervention would only act like a façade against my being really angry.

"Here, in analysis, it seems to me you take both roles. You give yourself the data about yourself, and you react reflexively. Reacting thoughtfully would feel like you were being a fraud." I added, "Except you've been working for months to get here."

He said, "I didn't know this was a destination."

I said, "Sometimes when you wander around, you don't know exactly what destination you're going to get to."

I think about how so much of Herbert's early family life was spent with parents and relatives angrily reacting to each other. For instance, he was often angry and dismissive with his mother as he tried to fend off her efforts to be close to him. The "fraud" must be that being a reasonable, friendly person wouldn't be true to his real self, the culture of that early family, and their expectations of him.

Here he had returned to his earlier point, and to ward off my own disappointment at his momentary retreat, I emphasized how he has worked in analysis to arrive at this insight. I was being like the old supportive therapist, but he fends me off as he fended off his mother. So instead we are drawn into a brief sparring dialogue, both of us in retreat from the moment.

He said, "OK, another thing. Maybe it's related. I was reflecting on a phone call I had with Eleanor this morning. I thought it was ungodly early, but then I realized that room service was coming anyway, so I said, 'Have a go!' So I called. But then I was grumpy and sharp with her, without any regard for her feelings. There could be an opportunity there. I could exercise more care for her feelings, and I just don't take the trouble to say words of any concern. I wonder why?"

I was surprised and pleased that he had brought this in, something that he usually does reluctantly and only with some prodding. I connect his reference to phoning his wife to phoning me—so early in the morning for him, the usual convenient time for me—but before I could say anything he made the link himself.

He said, "I think I do the same thing with you here. I just think, 'He's making me talk to him at this ungodly early hour, so I'll have a go at him!'"

I was interested in his repetition of the phrase "have a go". At first it meant, try to make a connection to the object of attachment (his wife) and then it meant, hit out at the object who is experienced as needing him to attach to me (the analyst). The offer of the telephone session is also felt to be a demand, a convenience for me, not him. He reverses the object that has the need. This connects for me with my earlier observation that in switching from "I" to "you" he was reversing the experience of being confronted so that I was the one facing the challenge. Now I am the one with the need that must be attacked.

I said, "So let's think about what's in the way of you being more considerate at times like this."

He said, "Well, it's my mother. I didn't want to indulge her by giving into her wish that I'd be polite or kiss up to her when she made me do things. It wasn't my job to make her feel better. She should have gotten that from her husband, not from me."

I said, "But now you *are* Eleanor's husband."

He said, "But when I hear her wanting something from me, I just hear 'Needy Person'. All needy people look alike. So they all get a cold reception, a stiff arm. They're on their own! Well, everyone is! My cousin in Israel said, 'The world is unfair.' Eleanor and you are saying you want more. And I say, 'I'm sorry! I gave at the office!'"

I thought to myself: But you've told me over and over that you don't give at the office either. He obliterates awareness of need in himself and in anyone else.

I said, "So how does it feel when *you* want something from *them*?"

He said, "Funny! I always think, 'I don't ask for much.' All I want is the ability to unload. At this moment, I can see that maybe that's asking a lot, but I'm generally not aware that I ask for much. I feel I take care of others, that I give all day long. I respond to my clients. It's like, 'Garbage in, garbage out! I schlep to you.'"

I heard him say, "I schlep to you" as being about him and me.

I said, "I feel that today you're telling me that you schlep to me by phone for my sake and then we have a 'garbage-in-garbage-out' kind of conversation."

He said, "Right. It's a burden on me. It's a pain. It puts pressure on my day. It's the anticipation of stuff. Once I'm here, I'm less resentful, but I come in resentfully. I'm looking to the schedule of the whole week, and when I do that, it makes me anxious. So it's annoying."

At first he was talking about the annoyance of phoning in from there to here. But the comment quickly generalizes to include his whole regular week of sessions.

Herbert continued, "You know what? Being forced to stare at myself here is a pain in the neck."

I remembered that he also hates feeling forced into sex. The anticipation is dreadful, but when he gets into it, it goes well. I felt that he had perceived me as a controlling internal object exerting force over his will, and I wondered what else he might say about it.

I said, "So who do you do it for?"

He said, "I think I do it for you. Instinctively, it's you! I know it's for Eleanor and me, but it's like going to the dentist: It's good for me, but I've got to go, so I don't have the option of not going."

He stayed directly in the transference. I wanted to accept the projection and connect it to its antecedents and to the affect that causes him so much trouble.

I said, "So I'm in the same boat as your mother and Eleanor. You do it for me like you did for your mother, and now feel you have to do for Eleanor. And you resent it from the beginning to the end of the day."

Suddenly I felt that Herbert took a side step. He seemed to change the subject, but I soon found that he was right on point.

He said, "I had a peek in that book you wrote. So, I can see it was a good thing that I felt this about you."

I said, "Go on."

He said, "I got the idea that the object of analysis is to recreate the relationships in your life in analysis."

I said, "Well, here it is. And we have to stop for today."

He laughed, and said, "I'll call you tomorrow."

In this session, Herbert had finally brought to conscious admission that he mistreated and alienated the primary people in his life, using grumpiness to push them away, while guarding against even more destructive anger. He experienced it directly in the transference and acknowledged its roots in his rebellion against his mother in order to protect himself from her controlling him and making him passive like his father. The resulting seething resentment had become a daily feature of his personality, souring his professional relationships and his marriage, and now available in the transference for work in analysis. In the session, I felt he had managed to say something himself that I had never felt I could say to him directly, because he would have experienced me concretely as being like his controlling, misunderstanding mother. I had felt that the resentment would have been beyond words. I began to see that this countertransference was a lead into how he had felt. And now, finally, here it was out in the open.

In the next session, also on the phone from Seattle, Herbert began by saying that he had had two dreams. This was a most unusual occurrence in this analysis, and led me to think of the two dreams as representing the two analytic sessions that were unusual in being conducted on the phone. He told the two dreams:

"In the first dream I'm in Washington and I see a colleague from the Chicago design firm I worked with in the eighties. He's with his wife shopping for real estate. At first we walk past each other, and then we recognize each other. I ask him what he's doing, and he says he's thinking of moving to DC. He didn't know I was here. The dream closes.

"In the second dream, I'm with my mother in Marshall Fields in Chicago. It's a store we went to often, and we were browsing. I see four young black women guards being given guns and training. Their supervisor is telling them how to use the guns. As the training is coming to a close, I get a hold of one of the guns and shoot all four of the women.

"I escape from the store in the chaos. I slip the gun into my trousers. There are crowds outside the store. I walk along a dark street and then get to a backyard. I don't know how, but it looks like your office. I'm prone on the sofa. You ask me what's going on. What do I see? I say that I see planes in the sky doing tricks, zooming and dipping. People are lurking outside of your windows. You're upset by that, so you go outside and chase all the people away. You are gone quite a while. You come back in, telling me there are no planes, that what I see isn't there, and that you won't stand for this. You say that someone was playing tricks on me but you weren't successful at finding out who it was."

Herbert said that he had just awakened a few minutes ago. "I am still in bed without time to reflect on it. It's very fresh."

Our agreement for when he was on travel was that he would recline on a couch or chair to approximate the setting in my office, but this time doing analysis on the telephone he had created a virtual scenario of intimacy (that is uncomfortable for me) and of unconscious communication (that is welcome). Because the session was on the phone, he did not have the regular driving time before seeing me, no time in which to forget the dream. Today the teleanalytic session had the unusual advantage of giving us access to raw dream material, in this case including undisguised transference material.

Herbert continued, "This is the first time I've dreamt about therapy. That was at the tail end of the dream. I was remembering comments about replicating real life experience in therapy, and there it is. You were in the dream in an active role. That's unusual. You were angry. That was very unusual."

The word unusual had come to my mind, and now Herbert used that word twice concerning my appearance and behavior in his dream. Here he was in bed, and here I was at the tail end of his dream. Through the session being on the phone, Herbert found freedom in the lack of in-person contact, and at the same time he pulled me close to his bed and his dreaming self.

Herbert continued to associate. "I don't know about the four black women security guards, unless racial diversity was on my mind because we had to put a black woman partner on our team to satisfy the client even though she has no relevant experience. We had to give her something to do so she would appear on the bill, but I had no idea how to do that." He paused and then continued, "There has to be some connection with that and shooting her in the dream."

He referred to killing one woman although in the dream he had shot four women. I thought of this as a condensation of various female figures into one through whom he directed his rage at all of them. Or did the number four refer to his four weekly sessions? Did he wonder what I had done to deserve to appear on his bill? And was the image of four women a reversal and condensation of his rage at me? He saw me as the angry one in the dream, but perhaps that was a reversal as well as a displacement of a wish to "have a go" at me with his gun.

Herbert continued, "I don't know what my mother was doing in there, in Chicago, in the department store."

I said, "What about your mother and Chicago coming in to the story with the women with the guns?"

He said, "The only thing I'm speaking to is race, the security guards, the authority. I'm not a violent person."

I said, "We were talking yesterday about you being angry and letting people know about it."

He said, "Right, my newfound free access to feeling. Friday at 5 pm, you can imagine the airport—the lines were long and people were delayed, anxious, pissed off. We were all missing flights because some security guy has to be trained. I thought, 'If there were guns around, this would be a good time to use them because of the incompetence of our government. I could wipe out the TSA.'"

I said, "Hmm. Seems there's *some* violence in you."

He said, "Only in my thoughts. True, I'm not without rage. Violence, of course not!"

I said, "There were four black women with guns. The blackness might represent the women your rage is aimed at—and there was your mother in the dream."

He said, "That's interesting. It does tie in with my mother. Her creed was, 'women are evil.' I operated in the shadow of her safety, and here's an opportunity to take out four evil women."

Herbert seems to be disagreeing with my idea that he was aiming his rage at his mother. He appears to suggest that he killed the evil women at his mother's behest.

He went on, "I left Chicago to come to DC and your couch to escape my mother's vice-grip."

Herbert prefers to think of me in positive terms and denies any similarity between me and his early object.

I said, "Tell me about that phrase, 'vice-grip.'"

He said, "An emotional vice-grip. My mother's dead and she's still affecting my life."

I said, "OK. So in the dream you killed the women but kept the gun for a future purpose."

He said, "I was just hiding it in my pocket. I slunk away, and then it doesn't show up at all in the rest of the dream."

I said, "The gun didn't come up in the part of the dream with me. It's as though it never happened."

He said, "Right. The third part of the dream, the part with you in it, was gone when I woke up. It was only in telling you the dream now that I was reminded of the tail end of it. I can still see what I dreamt about. It was night. I saw the planes doing tricks in the sky. There was a person on the lawn lurking, and you got uneasy, so you went outside and chased him away, and disabused me of the idea that I'd seen even a plane in the sky. That's back to TSA. One of the planes looked like a boat flying in the sky doing loops. For me planes and boats are associated with pleasant travel for escapism, not business, things I'd rather be doing instead of therapy. You try to chase away these distractions."

I said, "You see loops and dips, many distractions, but you don't see the rage and violence in yourself. That's like what happens here. There has been rage outside, but here you keep the gun hidden in your pants."

I am thinking that the "gun in his pants" also refers to the way his hidden rage is expressed in his sexual refusal, but that part of it is not here with us today. What is here is the rage he hides from me by hardly ever being annoyed or angry with me, and reporting on his anger at the world as being all out there, not in here.

He said, "I must admit that I am carrying a gun. I wonder who is the shadowy figure in the background? Yesterday I said I wasn't aware of the burden or the drag I am on others. Maybe this is the sign I see the shadow of the dark side."

I said, "Thanks to this dream, we've located an image in which you're murderous. You're in a murderous state of mind."

He laughed, "It's scary. It undermines my view that I'm not a bad guy. It indicates I'm capable of doing scary things, a very unsettling thought. I was hoping it was just a symbol."

I hear some noise in the background and ask what it is. He explained, "I'm trying to assemble tea while we talk, because I'm short on time after we hang up. Sorry."

This sort of intrusion is unique to an analytic session that occurs in a setting outside the analyst's control. I wondered if Herbert needed the tea to calm him, but even if it was indeed an attempt to lower anxiety, it didn't get in the way of his continuing to think.

He said, "It ties into yesterday, connecting you with what's going on in my unconscious mind. That's a first. It's like you're onboard and you're protecting me."

I said, "But I'm also telling you that you're not seeing what you do see."

He protested, "But it's a benign take on your role in protecting me, chasing away the person in the shadows. You got out of your chair and left the room, no big deal. You've assumed my mother's responsibility. She protects me from all evil. She tries to anyway."

I asked, "So how does it happen it's your mother and the four women that you shoot?"

He disagreed. "I didn't shoot my mother. I tried to put distance between us. Being given her protection felt good. It was from my primary caregiver, and in the dream you assumed that protector role."

Herbert seemed determined to keep seeing me as a good object despite the evidence in the dream.

I said. "I'm not sure about that. I'm the one saying there's something angry and painful inside you."

He said, "That fantasy isn't there. You chase away the demon, and then you say someone put phony thoughts in my head. It felt like you were protecting me. It's funny: while you were outside I looked at the clock. I thought you'd been away a long time before you came back. I thought you had looked into things carefully."

I said, "I entered your dream life and your inner world."

He said, "Well welcome to it! It's not a happy place. I thought yesterday's conversation cautioned me to be circumspect. I shouldn't be so, 'open', not so grumpy. I haven't told Eleanor yet because we spoke so briefly, but I guess I have to tell her I'll try to improve. It's a lifetime of programming I'm trying to change."

I said, "I was thinking about chasing the demons away. You do like to see me that way."

He said, "Yes. I've said that you try to get me to focus on the 600-pound gorilla in the room, and I'd rather daydream. But maybe the 600-pound gorilla is my slaying the black women. I didn't bring it to you in the office, and we didn't discuss it in the dream."

I said, "The main thing that I noticed was that you didn't bring the shooting to me at all. And today when you do bring it to us, you actually aren't in my office."

He said, "Yes. I casually walked into your office and talked about things in the sky, and I had the feeling that I was getting away with murder, walking away and nobody knows."

Thinking of how justified he has felt in being nasty to his wife who does nothing to stop him, I said, "That really helps me. I do feel that you're getting away with murder, in general. And with me, you 'get away with murder' because you keep the gun hidden in your pants."

He said, "I've been indulged and I have nothing to show for it, nothing but a trail of wounded people in my life. Where's the booty? It's very unrewarding crime if that's what I'm doing."

I said, "You get away with murder and you have nothing to show for it."

He said, "So when I listen to you or Eleanor confront me about my behavior and say it's calculated, I want to say, 'What are you talking about? Don't you see I'm unhappy about it, that I want to change it? I'm not in control of it. These are not my calculated moves. This is not the result I'm looking for.' In fact, in the dream, I played things down. I didn't know why I killed the women. It was dispassionate, as if my mother had trained a monkey to kill women. As a child I felt brainwashed, taught that there was no one good enough for me. The dream was like going to an amusement park and killing women. There was no repulsion or fear of guilt. They were a threat—so you take them out! In the dream, I'm telling you this, and you're horrified. But I was detached. 'It's no big deal. I didn't do it. She did it.' Well that's going to be my defense at my trial!"

Despite the dream's raw expression of murderous hatred, I did not feel horrified. I mainly felt relief that the aggression was "in the room". On the other hand, I realized it was not actually in my room: It was in his room across a continent. That distance, across which we were joined by the telephone, seemed to me to be part of why Herbert had been able to have and report a direct transference dream that delivered his violent self and his transference relationship to me as the mother who protected him from the world and from his own anger. I felt mainly relief that we had this new perspective.

Discussion

The point of presenting these sessions in the context of working across the distance of miles, and of needing to invoke technology—in this case the hundred-year-old technology of the telephone—is to show that ordinary analytic work is possible in distance analytic sessions. In fact, in this case, the spatial distance and the very fact of the lack of in-person contact, with its ostensible richness of bodily clues to reading unconscious communication, seemed to facilitate a quality of work not possible in our everyday in-person setting.

Although I did comment on the fact that he was not in my office as a feature of the day on which he "brought the gun to me", I did not really focus attention on this point during the sessions, so as not to disturb the flow of his associations merely to meet my own needs for inquiry into the practice of teleanalysis. I had the idea during the hour that the distance had let him bring something up that he could not raise in person because of the threat I would be intrusive like his mother, but this was not confirmed either in the session or later. So, beyond that, I can only speculate about why, with this particular analyzand and at this particular moment in the analysis, this was true. It seems to me that his defense of running away from his family, his need to get so much distance from them to avoid being like them, to avoid what he felt to be his mother's efforts at keeping him overly close, and in order to exceed their educational and economic situation, was echoed symbolically in getting a distance from me. Then, over this distance, he could reach back to me, reach into himself without feeling quite so much threat of impingement, and could find there a place from which to observe and discover a generosity towards others that ordinarily was too dangerous to deploy. Not surprisingly, when he returned to in-person sessions, he resumed grousing, perhaps because it was easier to be his aggressive self when I was physically present, and because it was less easy to step back and reflect on it with the threat posed by my physical closeness. He slid back into a narcissistic position from time to time. But in the telephone sessions he had acknowledged his grumpiness, his cold entitlement, his need for protection by "a primary caregiver", and his murderousness. He had imagined relating from a position of concern. In succeeding sessions he could no longer insist on inhabiting his "grumpy side" as his best option for screening his "really angry side", because he had revealed the underlying unconscious murderous rage on behalf of his mother and himself, and so it was now available for work. In this way, this pair of teleanalysis sessions in that time and place formed a turning point in the course of his predominantly in-person analysis.

CHAPTER FOURTEEN

Is there a difference between telephone and in-person sessions?

Lea S. de Setton

In today's world, technology defies our ability to comprehend it fully, but we have to make a start because its importance and impact are increasing exponentially. At the personal level, the use of media has become an identity symbol, proof of connectedness, and the most vivid expression of contemporary culture (Ermann, 2004). Online experience can have as much influence on everyday life as real life experience, especially for young people. At the professional level, technology has impacted global communication in every field, such as science, medicine, education, and business. By eliminating physical barriers to communication, interactive tools and media facilitate free interaction in a global scale. So technology has revolutionized human communication and lifestyle. It can make our lives simpler and more organized by providing us with tools and resources that help us control and adapt to our environment. Technology, however, is equally likely to introduce chaos by shifting boundaries, changing concepts of identity, and perceptions of time and space (Brendler, Pour-Aryan, Rieger, & Rothermel, 2013). Thanks to the speedy transmission of information, communication across huge distances and cultures, and the breaking up of old patterns and rhythms of response, our society is changing, and so are our relationships and the architecture of our brains.

As psychoanalysts we must contemplate the effects of technology on human experience and come to terms with it. Otherwise we would be left behind, unable to help, irrelevant to today's needs, and our patients would suffer from lack of understanding. We must recognize the significance of technology in our patients' lives if we are to adapt to the reality of this modern world. To be more specific, we must consider and test out its usefulness in providing treatment when in-person meetings are not possible, for instance, when patient or analyst is immobilized by injury or illness, commuting between two homes, traveling for work, or unable to travel through traffic to get to in-person appointments regularly for intensive treatment. But there are many individual and institutional obstacles to accepting change (Scharff, 2013).

Pichon-Rivière (1971), a leading figure in Argentinian psychoanalysis, observed from the history of science that the truth must always surmount great obstacles in order to prevail (Setton, Losso, & Scharff, in press). Every new idea disrupts an established order that struggles for survival, and hence must succeed by the power of logic, persistence, and patience to confront and overcome powerful internal resistances. Freud's experience of introducing the theory of the dynamic unconscious, of infantile sexuality, and eventually of psychoanalysis itself, is a vivid example from the nineteenth and early twentieth century. Now in the twenty-first century, practitioners using modern technology in psychotherapy and psychoanalysis are struggling for its benefits to be recognized.

The aim of psychoanalysis is to understand patients in order to help them transform their lives. Psychoanalysis unfolds in a psychic space where analyst and patient can meet and work. The patient reclines on a couch undisturbed by noise, intrusion, and the analyst's own concerns. Learning to trust the guarantees of confidentiality, attentiveness, attunement, and non-judgmental concern, the patient begins to express hitherto unacceptable thoughts and feelings in words, gestures, images, and bodily experience. Perceptions and misperceptions of the analyst occur in the light of early experience. As the patient talks and the analyst listens and responds, a relationship develops with the analyst to support the treatment process. This is the therapeutic alliance. Paraphrasing Meissner (1996), Dewald wrote: "The therapeutic alliance maintains a metaphorical space between analyst and analysand and allows the analyst to be used as a transitional object. The analytic space is perceived as a field of illusion in which distinctions between transference and countertransference with all their implications and vicissitudes take root and flourish" (Dewald, 1998, p. 191). According to Bollas (1998), analysis works as long as analysands submit to an experience whereby they are supported as they associate freely. They become subjects through a process guided by the intelligence of another. It is a transforming situation that recurrently changes one's self-experience. In my view, it is the development of the therapeutic alliance as a support for free association that allows the analysand to explore connections between past and present, engage with the analyst in transference and countertransference experience, and begin the process of transformation.

In the days of Freud and Pichon-Rivière, this special space could only be created in the psychoanalyst's office, where the psychoanalyst was responsible for the setting. In our times, thanks to technology, we have other options. The patient can create the setting, lie on a couch, and use technology to allow the analyst to observe, listen, and respond. The metaphorical space can be virtual, jointly created in cybernetic space, if that is what patients need under certain circumstances. The alliance can be built across a distance, and analytic process can occur. If the alliance is in place, the analytic process will progress, whether in person, over the telephone, or on Skype. In order to speak and associate freely, patients must forget the presence of the analyst (Bollas, 1998). Analysis using the telephone or Internet communication fulfills that requirement in the same way that the couch does. As Winnicott (1958) puts it, patients must reach their essential aloneness. The key issue is the therapeutic alliance, and that is what allows the analysand to go deep into her intensely personal experience of the past and the present, and what supports the analytic process as it unfolds in the intersubjective space.

Clinical illustration

Rosie is a twenty-five-year-old woman with a history of repeated sexual abuse by more than one person. When she came to see me, she had already been in treatment since her childhood with various psychologists and psychiatrists. She had tried to commit suicide several times. Her therapists complained that Rosie remained silent during the session and then expressed herself in action outside the session, and so they terminated the therapies. She had felt abandoned by every one of them.

Now an adult, she started psychotherapy twice a week at my office. In the first year of therapy, she was mainly silent, as she had been as a child. She was depressed, overweight, and emotionally paralyzed. During her long silences, I would let countertransference guide me. I would talk to her about her pain, her sadness, her wish to hurt herself and die. In her second year of psychotherapy she began to talk more, and decided to find a job, but she often skipped both work and therapy because she was very depressed and could not get out of bed. It was then that I decided to suggest phone sessions. My primary goals were to ensure the continuity of the treatment, understand her in her worst moments of depression, and be there for her so that she would not feel abandoned, as she had in the past. I knew she needed to feel that I was there to listen and contain her painful feelings.

Rosie talked about her eating disorder and how she would vomit every time she ate. She discussed her relationship with her intrusive mother. She brought in many dreams, associated to them, and was curious about them. In the transference she expressed anger toward me for not understanding her and tormenting her, just like her mother did. She was afraid of her sado-masochistic father, but she did not complain to anyone because exposure might "ruin the family structure". Despite some improvement in her ability to communicate, Rosie was still depressed and suicidal. She felt that her struggle between life and death was worse than any perverse behavior she had experienced. Since she did not want to cause ruin, and could not transform her life, she would rather kill herself.

After two and a half years of preparatory therapy, I offered her psychoanalysis three times a week. To ensure the continuity of the process, I agreed that she could have her regular appointment time by telephone when she felt too depressed to drive to my office. During the first few months of analysis, while lying on the couch in my office, she would leave her left leg on the floor, as if ready to run away and avoid confronting her own mind. Her pathological organization worked against her. She always felt she did not deserve to feel well because she was not good at her job and did not have a love relationship. She felt that time was running out.

During her second year of analysis, Rosie was able to finish her Bachelor's degree. She also tidied her room, a significant symbolic act. It was as though she wanted to clean her insides. She felt liberated. She began her first love relationship, but it was complicated by her boyfriend's mistreatment of her, and after two years she decided to leave him. She met another man who mistreated her and she fell victim to a stalker. She began studying for another Bachelor's degree but later dropped it. Nevertheless, in this phase of her analysis Rosie could talk openly, express her aggression toward the analyst, and analyze her dreams. She became able to work steadily, and started a healthy relationship. Now in her fifth year of analysis, Rosie has become engaged to a decent man. Her masochistic traits affect this relationship too, but at a much healthier level.

She is dealing with protest about her boyfriend's subsuming her, ambivalence about her family ties, anxieties about her commitment to her future as a wife and mother, and awareness of her tendency to complain and spoil things for herself.

Had it not been for the provision of sessions on the phone, this treatment would have terminated long ago. The use of the phone was important in undoing the damage done by abandonment in the past. It was also an accommodation to her depression-induced inactivity in the first few years, and to her current reality as a full-time employee. It has been important in supporting continuity of care and in enabling analytic process to continue as much as if the sessions had been in person. The main point I want to make is that, in my experience, sessions on the telephone are not particularly different from in-person sessions. So I will now present three sessions from one week in the fifth year of Rosie's analysis, so that readers can see for themselves whether there is any difference in the therapeutic alliance and analytic process across the sessions.

Session one

ROSIE: I've been fine. I had a quarrel with my fiancé. He's been writing to me; I don't feel like speaking to him. Last night we were going to a friend's birthday party at 8 pm. At 4.00 he tells me that his cousin from Ecuador is here and she's coming to the party with us. At 7.00 he tells me that we're going for dinner with his parents at 7:30. I told him we had another engagement. We wouldn't be able to get to the party till 10:30. He said he'd already told his father. I didn't like that he didn't take me into account and that he didn't care that we already had plans. We argued over the phone. He arrived at my place a few minutes later. I was so angry I didn't want to go out. I got dressed and went downstairs. I told him that we are two people and he has to take me into account. We went out to eat, and while we were eating his mother called to ask him to buy her some Coke. [Silence.]

DR. SETTON: [I can sense that she is very angry. I was thinking of her own mother whose intrusiveness made her angry for years.]
You felt she was very intrusive.

ROSIE: Yes … [Silence.] We had talked about making some changes in the apartment but hadn't made up our minds. He made the decision by himself and hired someone to do the job. It's his apartment, but we're getting married soon. He said it was a surprise. I told him I wanted to participate.

DR. SETTON: I wonder what this interaction reminds you of.

ROSIE: My mother. She chooses things for me. The last time I remodeled my bedroom, I would come home in the evening and she had been buying things without me.

DR. SETTON: I know this has been an issue for you, especially lately. You were upset because she wanted to make decisions about the wedding.

ROSIE: I know … [Silence.]
Last night Enrique ordered wine at dinner. His credit card didn't go through, so I had to use mine. Then they charged both cards. He doesn't even thank me when

I help him. I told him and he apologized. But I'd rather he took me more into account.

That day he called me at work and I couldn't talk right then. I called him afterward and apologized. Then he said he had deposited the money into my account.

DR. SETTON: I understand that you get very angry because you feel he doesn't ask for your opinion, but you don't talk about it to clarify things and find a solution. You keep the anger inside you.

ROSIE: [Silence] The other day we had a big fight over money. This week there is a concert that we both want to go to. We're going with a group, and I bought the tickets. They all paid me back except him. I have to keep reminding him to deposit the money into my account. He gets angry and says it's horrible to owe me money. He made a scene and said he would pay me back on the fifteenth. He didn't. It was incredible. I couldn't understand.

DR. SETTON: You want him to be honest with you.

ROSIE: Yes, the problem is not the money. [Silence]
I've had some strange dreams. In one I was chatting with friends, and all of a sudden I looked up and saw an image of Jesus staring at me, as if it were pointing to me. I tried to tell my friends he was there but my voice didn't come out; I couldn't speak. I woke up and couldn't go back to sleep. I don't know what it means.

DR. SETTON: You were with friends, and Jesus was angry.

ROSIE: Yes, he looked stern.

DR. SETTON: To be able to understand this, I would like to ask you, when you are angry with Enrique, what comes to your mind?

ROSIE: I think that I don't want to get married. What will our relationship be like when we're married?

DR. SETTON: And sometimes you feel you don't want to marry him?

ROSIE: When I'm super angry, I wonder what living together is going to be like.

DR. SETTON: It occurs to me that maybe sometimes you think it's better to stay with your friends. And Jesus, who represents your parents and grandparents, would get angry.

ROSIE: Maybe … Could be … Sometimes I feel I don't do what I should do.

DR. SETTON: Time is up.

ROSIE: Bye

Session two

ROSIE: [Silence]. I'm trying to remember something I thought this morning when I was brushing my teeth, and I can't. I'm worried; I feel that right now … I never expected … this … that I was going to get married.

I had such a bad year, 2012, and in September I met Enrique. Everything has gone so fast. We got engaged in August 2013. I'm getting married, but when I go to wedding-related appointments I'm like, out of it, wondering if this is really happening to me. All we talk about is the wedding; it's the only topic. I like talking about it, but not all the time. The wedding will pass, the honeymoon also … And then what happens?

DR. SETTON: And what is your fantasy of what will happen?

ROSIE: I will have to confront reality. I will be living with Enrique—a new life, different things, managing a house, a home. I'm scared that I won't be able to do it.

DR. SETTON: You fear failure—in what sense?

ROSIE: Managing the budget, the house has to be cleaned. Enrique has a cleaning lady who comes twice a week. We'll make dinner. I have to get used to it. Now we go to the grocery store together. He loves to cook. I'm worried about doing laundry.

DR. SETTON: I think you're afraid of not being a good wife and failing to meet your expectations for yourself. You have been very dependent so far, and it's scary to separate.

ROSIE: Yes. I'm too insecure. I had paid for part of my wedding dress. Then I went back in November and saw another dress I liked, and couldn't make up my mind. In the end I chose the second one. It's more traditional. [Silence.]

I had a dream I couldn't tell you yesterday; it was difficult to talk about it. I was at my place with Enrique and we thought someone was banging on the walls. When I looked out the window, there was a black man in the garden. There were some men on the stairs. I got the sense that they wanted to put a handkerchief on my nose. In the morning when I woke up I realized I was lying on the bed in my parents' room, and there were all these men. I was scared. One wanted me to call my parents, and the other one came and put a handkerchief on my nose, and I fell asleep. Then I really woke up.

DR. SETTON: Maybe you're feeling that Enrique and I are kidnapping you.

ROSIE: Ha ha … I don't know what it is.

DR. SETTON: Do you think it relates to other men in your history—the stalker and your old boyfriend, who mistreated you?

ROSIE: Now that you say that I remember that in December [a month earlier] I dreamed with Roberto [the sadistic ex-boyfriend] several times.

DR. SETTON: [I see she is still attached to excitement and pain.] You're scared of your own mind, of your bad thoughts about bad things that happened to you. And these thoughts are banging your mind/wall when you're alone with Enrique.

ROSIE: Yes, the bad things of the past … I don't know why I have the bad habit of asking Enrique about his ex-girlfriends. I met one he had dated for about six years. I've wondered whether he bought this ring for me or for her, because he had also given one to her. He said he sold that one. She already got married.

DR. SETTON: You doubt whether he really loves you.

ROSIE: Yes … He says he really loves me and he's never loved like this before.

DR. SETTON: Since you're so hard on yourself, you can't believe that someone can love you so much.

ROSIE: He doesn't like it when I talk to him about his ex-girlfriends and says I shouldn't mention them anymore or he'll get angry.

DR. SETTON: Maybe you bring up all these ghosts to spoil the moment and prevent yourself from being happy.

ROSIE: [She is silent for three minutes.]

DR. SETTON: Time is up.

Session three

ROSIE: I'm at home, tired; I'm not sleeping well.

DR. SETTON: What do you think about at night?

ROSIE: I'm tired and I fall asleep. Then I wake up at 1 am, I can't sleep and I play Candy Crush in the iPad.

DR. SETTON: [I feel disappointed that she is wasting her time on this instead of completing her second degree, but I don't say anything. I wonder if she feels she is wasting her time.]

ROSIE: Last night I had a dream. I woke up scared. I was in this neighborhood but in a different school, not the one where I work. It was my elementary school. I looked at myself in the bathroom mirror, and my teeth had fallen; I was pulling my teeth. I was traumatized that my teeth wouldn't grow again. Blood was running. I was driving, I got to the school, I was full of blood, the kids were there but I couldn't speak because I didn't have any teeth. I went to see my boss … [Silence]

DR. SETTON: What are you thinking about?

ROSIE: I don't know. I associate it a little bit with yesterday. When I left your office I went downstairs to the lab to pick up my test results. When I got there they said they didn't have them yet, that they had sent the blood to the U.S. When they gave me the results I went to see a doctor, he was going to write me a note because my hemoglobin was low. I was really stressed out. Then my aunt called and found out that the results were wrong.

DR. SETTON: You thought you were sick? [I thought she might be thinking the results of the analysis were not good, but I didn't say it, perhaps because I am worrying about it too, noticing her spoiling her relationship with her fiancé and using her engagement to avoid her education.]

ROSIE: I felt that Enrique was going to reject me.

DR. SETTON: The word rejection reminds me that you felt very rejected in elementary school.

ROSIE: Yes … I thought about my aggressive way of talking. When I want to say something, to complain, it's difficult for me to restrain my aggression. I remember in first grade I was a big fan of the little mermaid. There was a girl in my class, we competed with each other on who owned more things with the little mermaid image. One day we were arguing about the names of the characters and we started fighting, pulling each other's hair. In third grade I got into a fight again; I also pulled the hair of a girl who was bothering me. I cried when she pulled my hair and then I went and pulled hers.

DR. SETTON: She was making fun of you.

ROSIE: Yes.

DR. SETTON: I think that in elementary school you felt rejected and bullied. Maybe the dream represents your fear of talking, of being aggressive. Your teeth will fall out, you'll bleed, you'll scare others and drive Enrique away.

ROSIE: Yes, and mainly because of all the lies I've said since I was a child and in analysis.

DR. SETTON: What do you make of the lies?

ROSIE: It's a way of hiding and creating a world of my own. I don't know why I told the lies. I had fantasies about sex with my father and I made them real to justify being so crazy. Sometimes I think my relationship with my mother has been so enmeshed, as if we were glued together ... top to bottom ....

DR. SETTON: Symbiotic. It's been very difficult for you. Your fantasies about sexuality allowed you to take revenge.

ROSIE: Yes, maybe I didn't have any kind of relationship with my father. My friends have good relationships with their fathers. I love him ... But I run away from him.

DR. SETTON: What do you think happened? Did your mother criticize him?

ROSIE: Sometimes she talks about things that make her angry; she says he never sends her flowers. So I go and tell him and I get in the middle. Sometimes I make the mistake of telling Enrique that he's not thoughtful enough.

DR. SETTON: And you repeat aspects of your parents' relationship in your own relationship.

ROSIE: Aha ... [Silence]

I transfer onto Enrique the anger I feel toward my mother or my grandmother ...

DR. SETTON: Perhaps that's why you feel you're so aggressive.

ROSIE: Yes.

DR. SETTON: Time is up.

Discussion

The sessions presented above were part of a regular week of work in the fifth year of analysis. It is very difficult to determine which sessions took place over the phone and which in person. The telephone has allowed this patient to have an uninterrupted therapy. She often prefers to talk on the phone for a variety of reasons. She is too depressed to get dressed and drive; or she goes home after work and has her phone session, and then goes on to do other activities. There are also practical issues. She tries to do in-person sessions at least once or twice a week.

Of these three sessions, the first and the third were conducted over the phone. Is there actually any difference between the work carried out in those sessions and in-person work? I had to go back to my notes to remember which was which. Rosie prefers the sessions in person. She likes to see me and she feels that I like her. She feels appreciated by my attention to her. Nevertheless, she feels very comfortable having sessions on the phone. My experience of being in the session on the telephone is different from being in person. I find that working over the phone or on Skype requires more concentration. Analysts have to pay careful attention to the sound of patients' voices. We listen more closely to their breathing so as to gauge anxiety levels. At the same time, I find that the work on their dreams flows as smoothly as in person.

I believe that the quality of analytic work depends primarily on the therapeutic alliance, which stems from patients' early object relations experience (Etchegoyen, 1991). We create a psychological space with our patients. I feel that this is as possible on the telephone as it is in person. We need to work on their perception of their own reality with whatever resources we have at our disposal. We acknowledge patients' conditions and circumstances and incorporate them into the therapeutic process. If they are too ill to come to sessions in person, resorting to other means in order to reach them is a humane decision. Technology allows us to extend the experience of in-person sessions and preserve continuity. Continuity is very important to me, because I experienced it in my own analysis. Attending sessions twice a day in periods of immersion was forced and less helpful than ongoing teleanalysis, which was much more natural, more a part of everyday life, and properly adjusted to my situation. It allowed me to develop a reflective stance on my life every day. This personal experience has led to my belief in the value of analysis conducted using the telephone, but only for those who want to and for whom it is not contraindicated. Without the use of the telephone, in Rosie's case, there would have been no analysis.

Commentary

Lynn Stormon

This thoughtful analysis has clearly benefited the patient. I very much appreciate the analyst's patience and attunement in building a therapeutic alliance and providing continuity through the use of the telephone. I do agree that teleanalysis is important and that it makes analysis possible when it otherwise might not be. I appreciate Dr. Setton's sharing her reflections on her experience in her own teleanalysis. However, I think it's problematic to conclude that what was good for one patient will be good for another patient. I agree that analysts must weigh the patients' needs carefully before engaging in teleanalysis.

I guessed, correctly, which sessions had been in person and which on the phone. The choice of having sessions on the phone has been left with the patient by negotiated agreement. Since the patient decides how to meet, then her decision not to meet in person might be understood not as a simple matter of convenience, but rather in terms of acting on the frame in relation to transference/countertransference dynamics. I think there is more aggression expressed in the phone sessions than in the in-person session. Thinking in terms of how and when aggression gets expressed, I wonder if it feels safer for the patient to be angry at a distance. What are her fantasies about what she is doing to Dr. Setton by staying away?

Session one: The patient refers to three phone calls: (1) arguing with her fiancé on the phone about his father intruding into their plans, (2) his mother calling while they were eating, intruding into the couple space, and (3) her fiancé calling her at work, intruding into a space where she cannot talk. Because of the frequency of references to phone calls, I inferred that the session had been on the phone. The phone calls the patient reports had common themes of anger and intrusion. I wondered whether the patient phoned in because she felt angry that the analyst's investment in the results of the analysis, like getting a degree or getting married, seemed like an intrusive pressure to get healthy. The analyst interprets that Jesus is with the parents and grandparents, on the side of promoting marriage over being with friends. Does Jesus also represent the analyst in the patient's dream and in that way the patient expresses concern that the analyst/Jesus is angry at her for not wanting to get married?

Session two: In person, the patient expresses more insecurity and fear of failure than anger about getting married. Is the patient expressing a wish to stay with the analyst and not move on into more adult activities, such as getting married?

Session three: The patient reports that she doesn't feel well, can't sleep, and plays a game at night. The analyst reports unspoken negative countertransference about how the patient is spending her time. The analyst thinks about bad analytic results in relation to the blood test, but I am wondering whether the patient feels anxious about the good results of the analysis happening too fast and being hurried into getting better. Dr. Setton's interpretation about being rejected in elementary school pulls her patient away from what's going on between analyst and analysand in the here and now, and moves the focus into the past. Even there, though, there are signs of a conflict between analyst and analysand, displaced into the fight between the patient and a girlfriend Although thematic differences may be detected between phone sessions and in-person sessions, the work across sessions reflects the investment of both analyst and analysand in an ongoing analytic process. The analyst's flexibility in accommodating to the patient's difficulties in getting to the office allows this much needed work to go forward.

Commentary

Caroline Sehon

The session transcripts show how the analytic pair attends to the joint task of analyzing the patient's dreams, working in the transference-countertransference, and dynamically understanding the patient's resistance. The in-person session is sandwiched between two phone sessions during the fifth year of analysis. When the work in each setting is examined closely, no significant differences appear in terms of the number of exchanges between patient and analyst, the frequency of silences, the relative occurrence of dreams, the extent of interpretative versus non-interpretative interventions by the analyst, or an adherence to the primary task of analyzing the patient. The analytic couple seems quite familiar working analytically in either context, and the phone sessions proceed without any apparent interruption due to faulty connections, poor sound quality, or any other technological interference.

There is a stated agreement between analyst and patient that the sessions can occur by phone when the patient feels incapacitated to travel due to her depressed mood states. In the first phone session, Ms. Rosie did not reveal why she had chosen to meet by phone, on that particular day, and it is not possible to deduce the specific reason from the surface content alone. She also did not tell her analyst what shifted internally to allow her to drive to Dr. Setton's office for her next analytic session. In the third session, Ms. Rosie made an explicit reference to the setting, saying, "I'm at home, tired; I'm not sleeping well." Later in the session, she revealed that she met in person on the prior session, stating, "When I left your office, I went downstairs to the lab to pick up my test results."

In all three sessions, there is evidence for analytic process. In the first session by phone, Dr. Setton invited Ms. Rosie to consider how she internalizes her anger instead of confronting her fiancé who treats her with disdain. Soon after Dr. Setton confronted her patient's passive avoidance—"You don't talk about it to clarify things," Ms. Rosie followed with a dream in which her "voice didn't come out." Analyst and patient worked collaboratively on Ms. Rosie's dream, deepening the analytic process by examining the patient's ambivalent feelings of marrying her fiancé. As the session was about to conclude, Ms. Rosie reflected on her self-sabotaging tendencies, stating "Maybe … Could be … Sometimes I feel I don't do what I should do." New insights seemed to be pushing for awareness, as it would in good analytic work traditionally conducted in person.

On the second day, the analytic couple met in Dr. Setton's office. The thematic content built upon the prior day's work, revealing the patient's capacity for linking between sessions, regardless of the shift in the setting where the work took place. She produced a dream that she "couldn't tell [her analyst] yesterday; it was difficult to talk about it." It is unclear what was in the way of Ms. Rosie unveiling her dream on the previous day. No data was given to suggest that the telephone medium itself, partially or fully, accounted for her resistance. Dr. Setton explored the meaning of the dream by making a transference interpretation, "Maybe you're feeling that Enrique and I are kidnapping you." Although it seemed as if Dr. Setton made more interpretations during the middle session of the week, there is no data to attribute this phenomenon to the in-person setting as the causal factor. It could just as easily relate to Dr. Setton regarding the field as ripe to intervene more actively, midway, through the week of sessions.

By the third session of the week, Ms. Rosie drifted easily and fluidly back to the previous in-person session of the week. This material lends support to the idea that the functional setting is one held by the patient, by the analyst, and by the analyst-patient couple as an internal setting, not defined intrinsically by the external reality where they meet. In that session, Ms. Rosie managed to speak about "all the lies [she'd] said since [she] was a child and in analysis … It's a way of hiding and creating a world of [her] own." The analytic process continued uninterrupted, with the patient feeling safe enough not only to reveal her tendency to lie, but also to join with her analyst to investigate the unconscious meanings that accounted for such lies.

The analyst reports on sessions conducted during the fifth year of analysis, when the analytic process is well underway. It would be interesting to compare the analytic process between phone and in-office sessions at different phases of the analysis, to gather data as to whether there have always been similar process experiences independent of the external parameters, or whether there was a difference earlier on when the analytic couple was comparatively unfamiliar with the context of working together by phone. In addition, this inquiry could be complemented by studying the content and process material of a week's sessions in which the first and third sessions took place in person, with the middle session occurring by phone. Equally, other combinations of sessions, in-person or by phone, could be compared and contrasted to study the durability of analytic process between session contexts for Ms. Rosie and Dr. Setton.

Systematic and well designed studies are needed to examine the effectiveness of teletherapy and teleanalysis. In the meantime, patients like Ms. Rosie are fortunate when an analyst judiciously utilizes this experimental approach to treatment. In this situation, Ms. Rosie had already endured multiple failed therapeutic trials. As Dr. Setton asserts poignantly, "Without the use of the telephone, in Ms. Rosie's case, there would have been no analysis."

References

Bollas, C. (1998). Origins of the therapeutic alliance. *Scandinavian Psychoanalytic Review, 21*: 24–36.

Brendler, C., Pour-Aryan, N., Rieger, V., & Rothermel, A. (2013). Resistorless BiCMOS voltage reference with isolated substrate potential for biomedical implants. 20th IEEE International Conference on Electronics, Circuits and Systems (ICECS), Abu Dhabi, UAE.

Dewald, P. H. (1998). Book review. *The Therapeutic Alliance* by W. W. Meissner. *International Journal of Psychoanalysis, 79*: 190–192.

Ermann, M. (2004). On medical identity. *International Forum of Psychoanalysis, 13*: 275–283.

Etchegoyen, R. H. (1991). *Fundamentals of Psychoanalytic Technique.* London: Karnac.

Pichon-Rivière, E. (1971). *Del Psicoanálisis a la Psicología Social. Vol. II.* Buenos Aires: Editorial Galerna.

Scharff, J. S. (Ed.) (2013). *Psychoanalysis Online.* London: Karnac.

Setton, L., Losso, R., & Scharff, D. (Eds.) (in press). *Enrique Pichon-Rivière: A Pioneer in Psychoanalysis.* Lanham, MD: Rowman & Littlefield.

Winnicott, D. W. (1958). The capacity to be alone. *International Journal of Psychoanalysis, 39*: 416–420.

CHAPTER FIFTEEN

Technology-stirred projective processes in couple teletherapy

Carl Bagnini

The current situation regarding teletherapy is uncertain. We do not know for sure how secure teletherapy is or how supported therapists are to conduct it. The technology may or may not meet HIPAA requirements, and therapists' licensure may or may not allow then to practice telecommunication-assisted psychotherapy in a particular state. Some disciplines have issued best practice guidelines for continued discussion and there is a website featuring the Telemental Health Guide (2012), webinars, and certificate education for therapists who want to do teletherapy responsibly. Nevertheless, there is not yet a consensus between national and global authorities and professional associations on the legal and ethical basis for the conduct of psychotherapy and psychoanalysis conducted in cyberspace. Until the interested parties get together, relatively unregulated teletherapy places those who use it at risk. Therapists motivated by an ethical duty to serve have ventured into uncharted territory to bring help to patients who need it because of their circumstances, such as living in a remote area, having to travel for work, being immobilized at home, or leaving home for college (Carlino, 2011; J., Scharff, 2013; Lemma & Caparrotta, 2014).

Couples in need, who are geographically unable to attend sessions in person, or can attend only infrequently across long distances, and couples who have no access to qualified local couple therapists, have requested couple therapy using telecommunication, such as telephone, WebEx, and Skype. Therapists want to provide them with continuity of care. In some cases they feel that it would be unwise. For instance, they usually avoid teletherapy with deeply regressed or suicidal patients—arranging back-up psychiatric support for a suicidal patient in South Africa can be problematic. Yet there are some patients who simply cannot transfer. Therapists have to assess risk factors, network across state lines and internationally to find support, and be prepared for emergencies in many different environments, if they are to provide themselves with enough security to do what is needed.

How secure was Freud in Vienna when his radical notions exposed man's intense surplus of uncontained feelings and dangerous desires? His rational case for the irrational was akin to committing a crime against the status quo. He suffered anxiety and persecution when he left the established field of neurology to invent psychoanalysis. Then psychoanalysis spawned psychoanalytic psychotherapy, and now teletherapy. When the established mode of psychoanalytically oriented practice shifts from the office setting into cyberspace, the unexpected becomes usual. That psychoanalysis and psychotherapy can be practiced outside the office is chilling to traditional clinicians for whom a difference in settings feels immediately unacceptable.

Before video technology became available to psychotherapists it was widely used in business, politics, medicine, and commerce. At one institute where I teach, we have linked our psychoanalytic and psychotherapy distance learning programs with others in international locations in order to access skilled teachers and new candidates wanting to learn (D., Scharff, 2005). We have used video-conferencing in training for at least twelve years. We find that, in general, it works very well and is more intimate than participants expect at the outset. The training is less expensive for participants who do not travel long distances and do not have to pay for hotels. The initial outlay for the institute hardware was expensive but was well worth it in attracting a large number of participants who could then have training that they would not otherwise have received and for a fee that is quite affordable. An average weekly or monthly videoconference seminar has a class size of twenty-five to seventy participants.

For years, telephone treatment has been utilized in crisis situations, during periods of travel, or when patients moved but wanted to continue treatment. Hotlines or other helpline services began in the 1950s for vulnerable populations (Vincent, 2013). In the monograph "On Call" (1980) Warren Colman, a psychoanalyst in Great Britain, reported on a telephone help line staffed by volunteers in response to an increase in the problem of child abuse. There were problems at first. The anonymity and inexperience of the telephone volunteers combined with the inadequacies and helplessness of the victim. As they gained experience, and as they learned from their consultants about the power of unconscious projective processes delivered from the victim to the responder, they became more adept at containing anxiety and offering effective help.

So, teletherapy is not the first expansion of psychoanalysis. Community mental health approaches since the 1960s successfully expanded out-of-office treatment and intervention models across the lifespan, delivering meaningful direct and preventive mental health services to populations in need, at least until reduced US federal funding for mental health reversed that direction. I recall early in my career I made many home visits and treated families in their natural environment, often reaching family members who would not visit an office or clinic. I think of my teletherapy with couples as an extension of that domiciliary practice.

Teletherapy with couples

A few surprises accompany the new journey into teletherapy with couples. We have long been familiar with the various objects of concern in the couple session—the spouses, the therapist, the triangle connecting them in the treatment relationship (Bagnini, 2012; Scharff & Scharff, 1991). Now we have to incorporate into the treatment experience a "fourth object", technology.

We think about the effects of the technology in referral and treatment, the setting for the session, distance in space and sometimes time between us, and privacy and security.

We continue to explore this new setting and its stimulation of projective process; we have to address the format, and to differentiate aspects that are located within the central or core couple dynamics, and which emanate from the technology. Depending on the skills and maturity of the couple and of the therapist, the dimensions of the distance-therapy setting can blend relatively well into the treatment or they can set off primitive unconscious process. Awareness that the setting has human and non-human effects on projective process increases our knowledge of how technology promotes predictable and unpredictable results.

The setting: an example

In teletherapy the setting chosen by the couple shows us their personal possessions, choice of art work, sounds of domestic life, and presence of pets, all of them *in vivo* grist for the teletherapeutic mill. I had been working in teletherapy with a couple who experienced many deprivations in their marriage. In one session they brought their Rottweiler puppy into the room because they were caring for him after an operation. Discussion turned to care of the dog. Visibly caring for the puppy offered them a safe haven in which to demonstrate love and receive appreciation. They could give to the puppy, and the puppy could receive all the love and nurturing that the marriage did not provide. By bringing the puppy into the session the couple was conveying a hope that the therapy might distribute nurturing supplies throughout the family system.

I am interested in the unconscious dynamics conveyed in the domestic setting. I am also interested in unconscious dynamics conveyed across the distance between the couple and me by projective processes as alive as any in person in my office. In fact, I have found that teletherapy with couples using video-teleconference technology actually enhances projective processes and brings them out for our understanding of transference and countertransference, the engine of therapeutic action. I want to think first about technology as the route for referral and for the revelation of unconscious dynamics.

Referral

Prospective patient couples in the thirty-five to forty-five-year-old demographic tend to find their therapists on the Internet. They find therapists in group practices advertising teletherapy on a global level, with choices of various in-house therapists. Technology has shifted the traditional referral process from word of mouth to Googling and online exploration when searching for therapists. Google, Yahoo, and other search engines constructed by anonymous techies link prospective patients to lists of providers, the professional information about them, and recommendations from patients. Prospective couples rely on what they read without fact checking if information is up to date, accurate or not. Some of them actually prefer their therapy to be anonymous, possibly conducted on email or chat. Others choose teletherapy as a convenience for their lifestyle or to accommodate the partner who cannot attend the couple session. The trend is towards teletherapy squeezed in between business travel, the gym, work, and social engagements. This trend does not ensure an easy working environment for the psychoanalytically oriented therapist, and yet, with dedicated couples, it can work if we attend to the vagaries of the setting and their reflection of unconscious dynamic factors.

Projective processes in finding a therapist: an example

Ida and Greg (aged twenty-six and twenty-seven) sought couple teletherapy for their two-year marriage after two unsuccessful attempts at in-person couple therapy in office settings in their home town. During the telephone intake Greg, with Ida participating on their extension phone, explained that both therapists, the first a female, the second a male, had taken sides. Ida and Gregg each refused to continue treatment after a few sessions. As a couple they agreed that Ida liked the female therapist who saw things her way, and that Greg preferred the male therapist who joined with him, but they both knew it would be better to be with a therapist who did not take sides, except that in their town there were few choices. They found me by researching couple and family therapy training institute web sites that described teaching faculties. I was on faculty at several they had Googled.

Ida and Gregg had found me by using two online sources neither of which required personal contact with anyone that either knew me through professional circles or had been a former patient of mine to vouch for my capabilities. The couple stated they were comfortable enough with what they read, and were ready to proceed. I suspected they had to be befuddled, as many of my published clinical papers had odd titles and my presentations used professional language that the public would have difficulty translating. They were impressed, I later learned, by my publications and international teaching experiences. They had idealized my intellect, and they knew nothing about whether I had the emotional stamina or flexibility to refrain from taking sides, the original lament that had stalemated two prior couple therapies.

Technology had assisted the prospective couple in a selection process, for better or worse, and they had found me satisfactory for questionable reasons, but at least they had not been given access to details about my private life. Given the information highway, finding therapists may expose prospective patients to professional and personal information about us. The traditional idea about beginning treatment was that the therapist's personal life was private in order to preserve therapeutic neutrality. Nowadays a voyeuristic motive is promoted in prospective patients by their accessing the therapist's family information, such as his age, names of children, grandchildren, wife's affiliations, and so forth. Facts about training, specializations, and years of experience seem useful and necessary in guiding choices, but the additional exposure to therapists' private information produces conscious and unconscious reactions.

Every piece of information has the potential to elicit a projective process. This couple's initial projective process was onto my intellect, and it occurred before we met. I took their initial positive regard into account once therapy got underway. I anticipated that disappointment would ensue once I did not have immediate "right" answers for the considerable difficulties in the marriage. For example, Ida and Gregg were overly differentiated and took separate positions on every significant aspect of relating. My position as representing a couple state of mind was difficult for them to tolerate, as each of them demanded individualized attention. A dyadic holding was needed for a while with one-on-one contact with me in the company of the partner who eventually bore witness to tragic experiences of the other in their backgrounds in which each of them had suffered from neglect in rather large family groups. Fortunately I was able to do this turn-taking without appearing to take sides, perhaps because I met with them twice per week in order to increase their capacity to share me. During the nine-month couple teletherapy with Ida and Gregg, the major challenge was sorting out the basic unconscious assumptions that impeded safety and trust in intimate relating.

The effect of distance

The intensity of the wish for and fear of side-taking had been there in my work with Ida and Gregg from the start, as indicated by their failed attempts at two in-office therapies previously. The distance between them and me helped them sublimate their longings for the wished-for dyadic ideal. It might have inflamed their feelings about me, but in this instance distance and session frequency were sufficient to hold their longings until our time online. I kept in mind that they were fearful of getting close to me while desperately wanting to be close. In one session I wondered had I lived in their small town would they have been more frustrated by being closer to me geographically. They were actually relieved by the distance, even though fearful at times when a crisis occurred. As in office-based therapy we added sessions at times of increased conflicts, which tended to happen when they became hopeful about emotional closeness.

Technical problems, dynamic factors

Breaks in the lines can evoke abandonment anxieties and attachment traumas. Poor or interrupted connection can call out the history of inconsistent mothering and trigger awareness of unconscious processes that account for difficulties in maintaining a consistent communication between the couple and the therapist on line. Couple and therapist are sensitive to the added burden of depending on an environmental "technology mother" that gives so much opportunity but can also let the threesome down.

Poor connection stirs anxiety all around. The therapist's initial reaction is that poor connectivity will doom treatment. The sound may be good but the picture from the web camera is distorted on my screen. The picture may be good but the sound is garbled. Unlike in-office therapy, where the therapist is responsible for the conditions in the setting, in technology-assisted treatment, the couple and the therapist are equally responsible for setting up their connection. I have found that in early sessions couples are anxious about beginning, and this anxiety is compounded by having to get the technical set-up right. My set-up may be great, because I have guided the camera placement and my seating to maximize the viewing situation many times before, while the couple may have their camera aimed at the ceiling or the seating set up so far apart that the camera cannot provide adequate coverage of both partners. Couples respond in a variety of ways to my requests for adjustment, some with initial embarrassment, some with attention to my input, some with apologies, and others with outright indignation as though I am a voyeur looking in on a bedroom scene. From there, we go on to explore anticipatory worries about exposure. If we are vigilant to signs of unconscious factors beneath difficulties with technology, we will find that resistance to treatment comes into view and can be addressed.

The break-down in technology stops the *in vivo* communication (hopefully temporarily) but I know that out of sight is not out of mind. I think of the breakdown as a temporary dissociative state in which the therapist is present but incommunicado, and the couple is together but unable to connect to the therapeutic third. The couple can see and talk together but the therapist is blocked from hearing, observing, and verbalizing for a few moments and sometimes longer. When computers work we are so grateful that they and the access to the Internet that they provide support our work with couples at a distance. When they fail, we criticize them. Any transferences are displaced onto the machine. We may have to reboot, and if not successful we reschedule the appointment. During the interruption I am mindful that the couple is still communicating but not with me, and I reflect on the silence and on being left out while the couple experiences my absence. When we are reconnected I ask for feelings about our disconnection and associations to being separated. If I find a relevant connection, I link the content to the process of the marital situation and the treatment process.

I point out these troublesome aspects of teletherapy in anticipation of naysayers who justify staying with in-office treatment exclusively, given the unreliability of technology. I want to show them that the break-down in technology can provide opportunities for therapeutic movement when we enlarge the field of observation and analysis to include attention to the technological failures and their fall-out in the context of the couple and therapist transference relationships.

Seeing ourselves in relation to others and dealing with intimacy

Other aspects of teletherapy require adjustment in the therapist's sense of confidence. We see ourselves in a small box alongside the larger couple image. The couple sees us in a large picture, and they see themselves in a small box, which seems even smaller, there being two people in it. I may feel small seeing my own smaller image on my screen near the large couple image, or self-conscious knowing that a larger version of me fills the screen at their location. We are visually close and "on display" on screen. I feel more exposed and sometimes scrutinized in this more immediate, complex visual array than in the office setting where I feel protected by a prudently arranged seating distance. The conventional webcam forces a couple to sit closer, as on a small sofa. For some couples the psychological distance they prefer to maintain is interfered with by webcam limitations. Spatial arrangements symbolize intimacy concerns.

It is no surprise that when assessing the couple's sexual relationship there may be a range of reactions, from relative comfort if the couple feels safe with the therapist and the technology to embarrassment, physical squirming, expressions of anxious affection, pulling away, or looking away from the camera. While any of these reactions may occur in the office setting, the teletherapy space brings them out vividly and presses the observed behavior into conversation, especially during discussion of sexual material. We notice much glancing between partners and towards the therapist while tentatively exposing the underbelly of the couple's intimacy. When containment is favorable the therapist functions as the guardian of the couple's smaller space and the partners make good use of the opportunity. An underlying fear of voyeuristic motives or intrusions on the part of the therapist can reduce spontaneity and openness. Couples that continue to fear exploring sexual material react differently with frequent silences, awkwardness, worries about "being seen". The therapist is especially sensitive to the effects of the teletherapy format en route to exploring potential dynamics that inhibit the free expression of intimate life. The addition of teletherapy technology to the practice of couple therapy challenges our theories of transference and countertransference, anonymity, and psychological space.

Email communication: an example

Therapists who use technology in therapy may face requests to receive and respond to emails. Some patients find it natural or convenient to send us narratives and other communications in advance of meeting, or instead of bringing these to the teletherapy session. A policy has to be both flexible and comfortable for all concerned.

In a couple teletherapy session with Martha (twenty-seven) and Bill (twenty-six), I mentioned the value of dreams in couple work. Martha and Bill wanted to send me dream material in advance of scheduled sessions. The spontaneity necessary for working deeply with couple dreams had little cache for them. They thought they would save time by sending me their material ahead so that I could read them and be ready with my interpretation. They thought they could immediately start sessions with my responses to their dreams. In this instance I had to firmly and gently explain the importance of inviting dreams into the sessions without prior written correspondence. I realized that they had tried to comply with my wish for dreams to gain access to the unconscious, but this was exactly the opposite aim of dream work with couples. In my countertransference I experienced resentment. Having to spend my time reading emails without being paid for the time also brought a sense of being exploited, a dynamic that they experienced in their marriage. Projective identifications are ripe in couple dynamics and readily transmitted in changes to the frame that result from the apparent flexibility of the offer of teletherapy. When working with the availability of instant communication an immediate challenge to the frame is likely. We must be diligent and ready to set limits with explanations that help the partners set limits for themselves. Otherwise a manic saturation of the therapist's online space will occur, especially with younger technologically savvy couples.

Welcoming the unexpected: an example

Gwen and Steve (aged fifty and forty-eight), married for three years, have been in once per week teletherapy for five months. A major issue is their passivity about addressing conflict. Two teenaged children (a boy fourteen, a girl fifteen) from Gwen's first marriage have become problematic, coming home late on week nights, not getting to school on time, and procrastinating with homework. Gwen is unable to set limits and Steve, as stepparent, avoids both dealing with them directly and assisting Gwen with her sadness and frustration when the children act up.

In their twentieth session of teletherapy, Gwen and Steve hit an impasse. There was much sighing, looking at each other in frustrated silence, and looking to me to break the impasse. We had encountered this dynamic before, and I offered an observation. I said, "The frustration about the children continues to stifle you. Have you any thoughts about parallels between the children's procrastination and yours?" Steve pouted and proudly explained that he was a very responsible teen, and never had to be told his responsibilities. His parents took his good behavior for granted and did not praise him for being capable. Gwen responded that she had a nagging mother who was never satisfied with her and an older brother was her mother's golden child. As the couple quietly discussed their different scenarios I was thinking silently that they cannot get together because Steve insulates himself from his disappointment that adults ignore his accomplishments while Gwen is angry and disappointed with her mother and jealous of an older brother.

I was feeling inclined to provide an interpretation to loosen up the log jam. I wanted to say that Gwen was split off from setting limits with her children in case it felt like nagging them, so as not to resurrect her child-based anger at her mother; but that like her mother she is neglecting them because there are no consequences when they don't follow through. And I wanted to say that Steve is on his own, staying good and quiet, but unappreciated as he was in his family, not wanting to take on the teens without Gwen's cooperation, isolating himself from the group. I hesitated. Somehow this interpretation felt too intellectualized, paralleling the lack of affect in the couple.

As I wait, two poodles push open the door to the family room and enter. One, a miniature, and the other a medium-sized dog, enter the space behind the couple who are seated on a loveseat facing the monitor. As the couple and I become aware of their presence, the dogs go at it! Snarling they begin play fighting with a rubber doggy toy that each wants for its own. Sibling rivalry? I wonder. At first the couple pretends not to notice the dogs' melée, staring at the screen and at me. The dogs respond to being ignored by going at it more aggressively, as though demanding intervention from the couple, much in the way I suspect the teens do. This *in vivo* event shakes up the couple's detachment. I am preparing to ask that they remove the dogs as the play fighting is disrupting the session, but I wait because it occurs to me that the dogs are adding the necessary missing affect we are hard-pressed to release in the couple relationship. They are loud, and physically tugging at the shared toy, the little one holding its own with the larger doggy sibling. Gwen leaves her seat and yells at the two dogs to stop. She has their attention and they drop the toy, looking surprised. Steve gets up and opens the door and shoos them out of the room. Mission accomplished.

We used the *in vivo* situation to open up a space for comparing Gwen and Steve's slow response to the dogs' aggression to their reluctance to team up on behalf of protecting their relationship from attack by the teenagers. In subsequent sessions, the spouses' jealousy, rivalry, and fears of retaliation emerged and could be worked with. I silently admitted I wanted to send the couple a box of treats to thank the dogs for their unexpected consultation.

Concluding remarks

These thoughts and vignettes pertain to different aspects of projective process stimulated by communication technology in couple teletherapy and delivered in terms of choice of setting, alteration to the frame, and perception colored by transference. Teletherapy challenges us to expect the unexpected and deal with it analytically. Teletherapy may be a boon for some and a bizarre object for others. We proceed with caution and prepare for surprises.

References

Bagnini, C. (2012). *Keeping Couples in Treatment: Working from Surface to Depth*. Lanham, MD: Jason Aronson.

Carlino, R. (2011). *Distance Analysis*. London: Karnac.

Colman, W. (1980). *On Call*. Monograph of the British Health Services.

Lemma, A., & Caparotta, L. (2014). *Psychoanalysis in the Technoculture Era*. London: Routledge.

Scharff, D. (2005). Teaching infant observation by video-link. In: J. Magagna, N. Bakalar, H. Cooper, J. Levy, C. Norman & C. Shank (Eds.), *Intimate Transformations: Babies with their Families* (pp. 189–197). London: Karnac.

Scharff, D., & Scharff, J. (1991). *Object Relations Couple Therapy*. Northvale, NJ: Jason Aronson.

Scharff, J. (2013). *Psychoanalysis Online: Mental Health, Teletherapy and Training*. London: Karnac.

Telemental Health Guide (2012). www.tmhguide.org/clinicians-administrators/. Last accessed October 14, 2014.

Vincent, C. (2013). Internet therapy with couples. Video conference presentation at The International Psychotherapy Institute Couple Therapy Seminar.

CHAPTER SIXTEEN

A baby saved: a mother made

Nancy L. Bakalar

T his chapter is an account of a treatment in which I kept adapting both frame and focus when a patient's needs and mine were changing over the eleven years we worked together in psychotherapy and psychoanalysis. The therapeutic relationship with the patient, a woman I will call Mary, had begun as a referral for medication evaluation and quickly became a twice-weekly psychoanalytic psychotherapy, first in person, then by telephone, later by videoconference (VTC). When the dynamic movement stagnated over a two-year period, I offered, and Mary accepted, a four-times-weekly psychoanalysis. After four years of psychotherapy with her, I was contemplating a move from the East coast to a Western state in a year's time. I explained to all my patients that I would travel back to my practice on the East coast for several days four or five times per year to see them in person. For those taking medications I secured a local psychiatrist; and for those who wanted continuity of care, I would offer the choice of sessions using the telephone or videoconferencing (VTC) for the months when I could not see them in person. A year later the move was completed. As for Mary, she became pregnant unexpectedly and experienced great stress about her mothering capability. In response to her changing needs, I had to allow the analysis to evolve, guided by my training in infant observation (Magagna et al., 2005) and my reading of Winnicott (1960). "Dr. Winnicott adapted his technique to the needs of each particular case. If full psychoanalysis was needed and was possible, he would do analysis. If not, he varied his technique from regular sessions to sessions 'on demand' or to single or extended therapeutic consultations" (C. Winnicott & Shepard, 1977). One of my colleagues put it this way: "Sometimes I do psychoanalysis, and the rest of the time, I do whatever I can" (Dennett, 2013). In this case, "doing whatever I can" meant that we had to use the telephone and video-teleconferencing (VTC) to bridge distance between us and later we had to include the patient's baby daughter in the treatment.

Background

Since Freud (1909b) reported the case of Little Hans, psychoanalytic theorists, scientists, and clinicians have written voluminously about the psychodynamics of the mother–infant relationship and its treatment. Winnicott (1960) emphasized the importance of "the holding environment as a total situation", which includes not just the mother physically holding and caring for the baby, but also her provision of a safe, secure, reliable environment which protects the infant physically and promotes his growth. When done in a good enough fashion, it is unobtrusive; it can be taken for granted, and within that security the infant experiences the pleasure of "going on being". Joseph (1948), Pruett and Leonard (1978), Loewald (1985), Glucksman (1987), Arons (2005), and Lyons-Ruth (2006) describe working with mothers who form pathological relationships with their infants, who then suffer from psychological vulnerabilities and physical ailments. Fraiberg (1982) documented pathological behaviors in infants and toddlers who were neglected or abused. I knew the risks to my patient and her child, and I wanted to adapt my technique to meet her needs without losing my analytic perspective. Kris (1981) discussed the ethical challenges presented by patients in analysis whose children may be in peril and for whom intervening with advice is necessary. Norman (2001, 2004) developed a technique of talking directly to newborns, verbalizing what he observed so as to give the infants a feeling of being understood and contained. Salomonsson (1998, 2006, 2007a, 2007b, 2009, 2014) worked similarly, emphasizing the importance of communicating authentically with congruency between the therapist's vocal tones, facial expressions, and body movements. In a recent issue of the Journal of the American Psychoanalytic Association, Stuart (2012), Kite (2012), Blum (2012), Zeavin (2012), and Stuart and Ayeni (2012) shared their experiences of mothers asking to bring their newborns to analytic sessions. The authors were taken aback by the requests, but all agreed to it and reported that to have the babies present for a limited time supported and, in some cases, catalyzed the analyses. Reading this literature, I felt encouraged and authorized to proceed as the case required.

Case history

Mary was a twenty-eight-year-old, single preschool teacher when we met. Diagnosed by the referring psychiatrist as manic-depressive, Mary was taking six psychotropic medications, but was still miserable. At age two Mary had been left in the care of her father when her mother returned to university. Mary's father was an anxious man, given to strong emotional outbursts, thrusting his anxiety into Mary. He was also sexually inappropriate, taking two-year-old Mary and her brother into the shower with him, introducing her to pornographic materials by the time she was five, and, when she was a prepubescent girl, making sexually derogatory remarks to her. She was a shy, awkward little girl who had difficulty making friends, but proved to be a good student. Mary's difficulties lay in having tremendous anxiety and being unable to think her thoughts and to symbolize her feelings with words.

In the early sessions, Mary's mind swirled with unnameable thoughts and feelings. She often bent over from the waist, holding her head between her hands, shaking her head from side to side saying, "Bees are buzzing in my head!" I thought of this internal noise as beta elements—shards of not-yet-describable, raw, emotional pain (Bion, 1962b). Any movement I made, and most things I said, were experienced as intrusive, and further agitated her. She wanted me to be a statue, to not move or breathe. Mary's agitated response to my ordinary movements demonstrated a fragile mental structure, an insufficiently sturdy contact barrier (Bion, 1962b). I developed the hypothesis that Mary's parents had experienced her infantile anxieties as intrusive and thus could not contain them, nor soothe Mary.

The task of the first years of treatment was to use words to label feelings and to help Mary learn to think. She hated to experience her feelings, make links, and develop understanding about her internal life and how she operated in the world with others. In Bion's terms, she hated alpha function (Bion, 1962a, 1962b) but she did develop it through psychotherapy. Her thinking became less psychotic, life became more manageable, and she was able to taper and discontinue all medications.

Transition to telephone therapy and telephone psychoanalysis

A year before I anticipated moving across country, Mary had made appreciable gains in her twice-weekly psychotherapy and was able to get married, but was not yet finished with her therapeutic work. She had a secure attachment to me and a psychotherapeutic process was in place. I offered to continue our twice-weekly psychotherapy sessions by telephone. Mary accepted, and the transition went well. Mary mourned the loss of being with me in person in the familiar office. For the next two years Mary made progress internally and interpersonally, but over the following two years her treatment stalled. She reported still having serious arguments with her husband and feeling enraged by the toddlers for whom she cared. The sorrow I felt for the toddlers and for the damage I believed she was doing to them, and therefore to herself, led me to recommend increasing the intensity of her treatment to four-times-weekly psychoanalysis by telephone.

The recommendation for psychoanalysis induced a feeling in Mary that she was "really sick", that she couldn't "do things right", and that I was her critical, intrusive father who made demands. Many times over the first few months of analysis I gently explained that I was not her father, that I was a different person, and that I had no reason to hurt her. The anxious, bitter feelings of this negative transference resolved over several months. She then moved quickly towards self-understanding, partnering with me, and, at times, taking on the analytic function by making dynamic links herself. I felt optimistic that her analysis would be effective and relatively short, given that we had already worked together for nine years.

Pregnancy

The treatment seemed to be going well. Four years after my move to the West, I took a two-week vacation (longer than I usually take, and which I had not done since I made the move four years earlier). I knew that this would be a significant break for Mary and that it would recreate a sense of infantile abandonment in her, and we had worked on that. While I was away, Mary became pregnant. This came as a surprise to me, really a shock. As she approached forty years of age, we had talked in general terms about her feelings about pregnancy and she had always eschewed motherhood, having seen how it burdened her friends and family. In the analysis it became apparent that she had not consciously made a decision to become pregnant. She had allowed it to happen casually one night after more than twenty years of protecting herself from conceiving. We referred to this as an "actively passive" decision to get pregnant. She took pride in the grown-up, womanly role of being pregnant, and she wanted the attention pregnant women get, but she did not want a baby. Analysis revealed that the deprivation of my absence had stimulated her unconscious desire to return to a dependent role made manifest in the form of an actual baby. In identification with her baby, Mary's own infantile longing of being understood and cared for could be more easily worked on in her analysis.

Regression

The pregnancy and birth threw Mary into a profound regression, with negation of the fetus. She was unable to think about and plan for the baby. Eventually, severe anxiety awakened unconscious murderous wishes and dreams. Mary's husband, Dan, also denied the reality of impending parenthood. With little space in their minds for the baby, it was difficult to make space for the baby in their two-bedroom apartment, filled with stacks of books and unsorted papers. Three days before the birth, they had not purchased the usual baby furniture and supplies, such as a bassinet, changing table, and back-up baby bottles. A friend had given Mary a port-a-crib and hand-me-down baby clothes but Mary was "too tired" to open up the port-a-crib or wash the clothes, a task her friend eventually did for her. When she finally opened the crib, it was moldy and had to be discarded. In angst Mary cried to me, "But I don't know what to buy! I have never had a baby! How would I know?" Mary had limited creative capacity to envision what she might need to care for her baby. Through my clinical experience, and linking to what others have described (Bion, 1962b, and Bick, 1968, 1986), I knew that this failure to contain the infant leaves the child unable to think, symbolize, fantasize, learn, and be creative in an anticipatory way. In analysis we traced Mary's difficulty back at first to her own mother's inability to contain and help metabolize Mary's infantile anxieties, and, later, to the need for a shield against her father's anxious, raging attacks and her mother's inability to protect her. As Mary repressed her own anxieties, frustration, and rage linked to her internalized parental objects, she also constrained the development of her ability to learn, plan, create, and take in constructive feedback. This furthered our understanding of why in her early treatment she experienced me as a statue, and became agitated if I moved or spoke. In the transference I was experienced as an intrusive bad object that, once repressed, left her experiencing me as a statue. Effective treatment of patients like Mary is then not so much in the realm of making interpretations, but through being trustworthy and providing containment so that symbolizing and thinking can develop.

Birth of the baby and early post-partum period

Mary was tired and weak from lacerations during the delivery, surgical repair, and blood transfusions. Mary's mother[1] had come to help, but when Mary came home from the hospital with baby Therese, there was no food for the grown-ups and no bottles or formula for the baby. When we resumed sessions five days after the birth, Mary reassured me that the baby was fine, but the grown-ups were not.

Mary said, "I don't feel well and I can't drive and we need food and bottles and formula. Dan couldn't get himself to the store. Neither could my mother. We came home Monday night and I couldn't sleep because I was afraid the baby would stop breathing. Today I don't feel like I can give her what she needs. She screams and roots, and I don't want to feed her. She bites the nipple, so I just play with her. And I am angry at her because it was because of her that I got torn, lost all that blood, and was afraid that I was going to die … I knew I wouldn't, but I was very scared and shaking, and then I got angry at myself for being so scared."

In the countertransference, I became anxious about the situation in the home, about how Mary blamed the baby for the birth injury and experienced her as a bad object. I was even more concerned because I had no sense of where the infant was and how she was doing.

Meeting the baby

I first met baby Therese in person when she was twelve days old. Mary knocked softly on the door of my East coast office, and rolled in a heavy-duty stroller with Therese strapped inside. She removed all the coverings to reveal a beautiful baby. Therese had a lovely, clear, rosy complexion, round cheeks and was simply sweet. Who couldn't fall in love with such a beautiful baby, I thought.

Mary took a chair across from me. Her feet were flat on the floor, knees and thighs close together. She placed Therese on her lap, unswaddled, on her back. Then Mary began an anxious discourse, talking with both hands and crying. The baby lay there, arms and legs outstretched. There was no bodily support, no holding or cuddling, no checking to see how she was doing, even when she whimpered. She was simply out of Mary's awareness. I was unnerved, drew Mary's attention to her baby, and advised that Therese would feel more comfortable and safer if she were held close. Mary took this as a new idea. Anderson (1995) described a similar reaction with her patient P who brought her infant son to a session.

When Mary got ready to leave, she placed Therese in the car seat and pulled the straps so tight that I feared the baby would not be able to breathe. I commented that the straps looked a little too tight. Mary replied that she was terrified of harming the baby, so she wanted to ensure that she was safely bound. This vignette is consistent with many other aspects of Mary's care where she was so anxious about harming Therese that what she did to protect her often appeared potentially harmful.

Summary of first six weeks post-partum

After my return to the West, telephone sessions continued four times weekly, Mary sitting up in bed holding Therese on her chest. The pattern continued of Mary anxiously telling about experiences with Therese that she felt to be catastrophic, while simultaneously showing no apparent awareness of Therese in the moment. From time to time, I drew Mary's attention to Therese. I saw this as part of the treatment to help Mary learn to move back and forth more flexibly with her thinking, to keep several things in mind at once, or at least to alternate her attention between Therese and what was on her mind.

During these early weeks there were lapses in care. Mary was ambivalent about breast feeding, but never really decided to stop, another "actively passive" decision. As the hour of each feed approached, Mary decided that she would not nurse Therese that time. She supplemented with formula, and her breast milk dried up. But then bottle feeding created great anxiety for Mary. She had not purchased baby bottles and had only the disposable bottles brought home from the hospital. She agonized whether or not she could adequately clean the nipples and rings and whether or not the nipple would release milk at the right rate. Her unconscious fears were of poisoning and starving the baby. The parents eventually purchased a co-sleeper for nights, but during the day the baby lay on the living room floor unswaddled, flailing about. Mary said her husband laughed at the sight of Therese flailing. Mary told me that Therese stank. When I inquired, Mary replied that she had not yet bathed the baby who was now six weeks old. Mary was terrified of dropping and harming a wet, soapy baby. Mary also suffered anxiety and guilt in response to the baby's genitals because they aroused her. Mary became overwhelmed by ordinary infant care: the baby pooping felt catastrophic, as if the baby had defecated on her. The baby's physically leaking out linked to her own feeling of emotionally leaking out when distressed as a child in response to her father's leaking out his sexuality, rage, and anxiety. Mary didn't know how to clean Therese. She tried to do it on the mat in the living room without water. Mary asked me how to clean Therese's eyes to "get the 'gunk' out of them." I recommended that she use cotton balls with warm water. She said, "Oh, I've just been digging that stuff out with my fingernail."

Mother–infant therapy by video-teleconference (VTC)

I was concerned about how Mary was suffering in trying to care for her newborn. I was distressed by what I understood was happening between Mary and Therese and was worried about Therese's early experiences of not being contained (Bion, 1963, 1970), not being held (Winnicott, 1960), and experiencing the terror of her body contents leaking out (Bick, 1968, 1986) as she flailed, unswaddled. I recommended that Mary's analytic sessions include Therese. I thought of it as analytic mother–infant couple therapy in which I would pay analytic attention to them jointly, just as we do in marital couple therapy. I would give guidance as needed. Happily Mary agreed and was able to meet using VTC, which we have been doing now for over two and one-half years.

Using VTC I was able to see and hear the mother–infant couple in the natural setting of their home. This frame allows for the mother to be much more comfortable than she might be if she had to travel to an office four times per week for in-person sessions. The medium of VTC allows the analyst to see much more than she would see in person, and at the same time she can be a less intrusive presence because she is present only on the laptop screen. Jeanne Magagna (2013) and I believe that no one has conducted a long-term mother–infant intervention in this way.

Images using VTC

I saw that Mary was still having difficulty holding the baby in such a way that Therese would feel secure. Mary did not support Therese's head and it seemed that she repositioned her too often, handling her roughly by the chest, leaving me feeling that Therese's chest would be sore. Her neck was hyperextended during bottle feeds, making it difficult for her to swallow. Often the bottle was held down towards the baby's chest, not straight on in her mouth. Therese often coughed or slightly choked during feeds, spit up, drooled a lot, and suffered from frequent hiccups, symptoms of "leaking out" (Bick, 1986). Mary did not understand why Therese fussed. She repositioned her, or tried to burp her, patting her arrhythmically and with too much force. Sometimes Therese turned away or arched her back and neck in protest. As she got older, Therese pulled her hair, rubbed the sides of her head causing bald spots, and gouged her face making it bleed.

An observation of feeding at four months

Mary positions herself and baby Therese in the usual, large, over-stuffed comfortable living room chair. Mary offers the bottle rather tentatively. After a few seconds Therese latches on and closes her eyes. Before she begins to settle into rhythmic suckling, Therese grabs the fleshy part of her cheek and twists it clockwise and counter-clockwise four or five times. She pokes her eye, pulls her hair above her ear, and finally, still with eyes closed, places her forearm over her eyes, doubly blocking out the view of her mother's face. Therese's behavior seems to be an early version of avoidance as described by Fraiberg (1982). Mary holds her in a gently cradled position, cupping Therese's arm and forearm in her own hand but Therese's other hand, legs, and feet are not touching her mother.

During other sessions when Therese slept, Mary spoke in a more usual freely associative way. She often talked about her resentment that Therese got better mothering than she had, and resented all the hard work in caring for her baby. Mary especially suffered when unconscious fears and wishes of doing harm to Therese spontaneously became conscious, experienced as a fear that she would drop Therese or that the baby would suffocate in her crib. Mary experienced the needy baby as her intrusive father. Mary had "blocked him out" when she was a child to protect herself, and this had resulted in Mary often blocking out Therese. This left Mary blind to her daughter's needs.

Early interventions

My interventions were variable in approach and technique. Sometimes I called Mary's attention to Therese, and wondered aloud how she was doing, when it seemed as though Mary had "forgotten" she was in the room with us. Sometimes I addressed Therese directly and asked her how she was doing, or made sympathetic comments on her behalf, similar to the techniques that Norman (2001, 2004) and Salomonsson (2006, 2007a, 2007b, 2009) described, although they treated their infant patients in person and could speak more directly to the babies because they were nearby. I did this to help Mary begin to think of Therese as a person, separate from herself. I talked about the importance of keeping Therese swaddled and about positioning the bottle and the baby's head so that Therese could feed more comfortably. We talked about soothing the baby by holding her or swaying from side to side, and patting her gently and rhythmically. Amazed to discover something good, Mary said, "You know, when I soothe her, it soothes me!"

Most of the time these interventions were difficult for Mary to hear because she felt criticized, but she also understood that she did not know how to mother naturally and needed help.

She lacked implicit memory of good care from her own infancy. Because we had already worked together for nine years and because of her overall positive attachment to me, Mary was able to bear interpretations even though they felt critical to her. As she progressed in analysis, she experienced my help as different from her old experiences of her father as attacking. As much as I could, I used a soft, gentle, quiet voice and spoke slowly so that Mary would feel contained as much as possible while we worked on painful experiences. I told her that there was no shame in not knowing how to care for a baby, that everyone has to learn from experience (Bion, 1962b), and that it was more difficult for her because her parents had had a difficult time caring for her empathically when she was a baby. Learning that both her parents had had moderately traumatizing childhoods helped Mary assuage her anger and feel more empathic towards them and towards herself, as well. Mary usually responded with a grateful, but ambivalent, smile, tears streaming down her cheeks. She often tells me that she thinks she is getting the mothering from me that she always needed. One time, as we were signing off, she had a "slip-of-the-body" gesture and blew me a loving kiss.

Analytic thinking and interpretations

Interwoven with the mother–infant couple therapy my analytic thinking continued, albeit in a less continuous way than I normally work. Here is a vignette: Mary started a session telling me it had been a very stressful morning because Therese threw up. She said it in a tone of alarm and disgust as if unlimited vomit were all over her. To clean up after a baby has thrown up is not fun, but it puzzled me that Mary felt that her baby's vomiting was catastrophic.

The next day, the incident of Therese vomiting came up again. It reminded Mary of when she was nine years old. She and her family lived in a flat where her father had an office off the main hallway just inside the front door. As she passed her father's office where he was seeing someone, she vomited. She was terrified. She felt as though she had done something horrible and was a bad child. One might interpret Mary's vomiting outside his office simply as an aggressive attack on the father. Rather, this was a story about Mary and her inability to contain her bodily contents due to anxiety and anger in relation to her parents. As a nine-year-old, unconsciously her aim was to put her father in a situation in which he had to contain her upset and clean up her mess, putting her before his client. It then became clear why all her baby's poops, urine, vomit, and tears felt catastrophic, because, in projective and introjective identification with Therese, Mary relives the catastrophic feeling of leaking out and falling apart that she did as an infant, and in identification with her father as parent, Mary is overwrought when her daughter's bodily substances leak out. She uses projective and introjective identification as a defense against feeling needy and overwhelmed but ends up feeling more confused by identifying with the feelings she attributes to her daughter and her father. G. R. di Ceglie (1987) and Balsam (2000) describe such introjective and projective processes between mothers and their babies. It took Mary a while to realize that in the childhood scene outside her father's office door, in fact her father did hear her, came to the door, assessed the situation, and cleaned up. Mary added, "He didn't even get mad at me!" The analytic work focused on helping Mary make a distinction between what she and her father felt, and especially between what she feels and what Therese needs or feels. These discussions helped Mary pull back her projections and allow Therese to have her own feeling states.

Progress of the case

Within eight to ten weeks of seeing Mary and Therese using VTC, their relationship greatly improved. Mary developed the skill of talking with me and turning her attention to Therese as soon as she whimpered or coughed. As Mary and the couple were contained by the analysis (Bion, 1963, 1970), Mary developed the capacity to contain her daughter's affective upset.

Mary handled Therese more gently and supported her head. She kept her face at a bit more distance during feeds so as not to be intrusive. At the height of Therese's pulling away and showing painful, masochistic behaviors, I advised Mary to offer Therese her finger to hold or for Mary to stroke Therese's arm gently and speak to her softly as a way to pull Therese's gaze (and attachment) toward her. Within weeks Therese stopped pulling her hair, twisting the skin of her cheeks and labia, scratching herself, and poking her own eye. The hiccups lessened and eventually all but vanished. Mutual gaze remained difficult for Therese, but she stopped arching her back and turning away from her mother. As Mary relaxed with the support of the analysis, Therese became a calmer baby, which relieved Mary and allowed her to take gratification in being a better mother. During this phase Mary was able to move more solidly into the depressive position in that she was able to mourn the loss of her former adult childless life, unburdened by the work of parenthood.

Therese's early oedipal dynamics emerged by eight or nine months. When Therese began to babble, she made it clear that she wanted to be part of our conversation, getting fussy if Mary and I talked too much without including her. When we talked to her she became calm. Not surprisingly, I became a familiar person to Therese over the VTC. When still a lap baby, she smiled and waved, and imitated my gestures and I imitated hers. We played peek-a-boo over the airwaves and she laughed. At around one year of age, Therese was not quite able to walk, still at the cruising stage. During one session, Mary was on the floor with Therese. Therese took her first full solo step towards me, or rather, towards my image on the laptop screen. I could hardly believe my eyes, but said nothing, thinking maybe I was mistaken. Soon, Mary exclaimed, "Did you see that?! That was her first real step and it was towards you!" These vignettes show that even infants are able to develop attachments to the therapist using the medium of VTC.

Therese is about two years, six months at the time of writing. As new developmental stages came to the fore, Mary continued to need guidance. For example, it had not occurred to Mary that she needed to make meals for Therese. She was simply feeding her bits of bread from sandwiches. Mary felt overwhelmed with the thought of having to prepare meals; she had never really done so before, simply making a peanut butter and jelly sandwich or roasting a chicken when needed. Mary told me, "My mother never taught me anything!" Around this time Mary's mother visited. To my surprise, Mary reported that her mother coached her on how to make a dinner by preparing meat, vegetable, and pasta. Mary was incredulous that she never knew this! Since it was now apparent that her mother cooked for the family when Mary was a child, I wondered why Mary had not observed that, and taken it in. Through the analysis, I realized that Mary's defense of blocking out painful experiences linked to her parents, described by Fairbairn (1944) as repressing the bad object, had resulted in Mary blocking all that she could have learned from them as well. In a more global way, this defensive maneuver left Mary with little creativity and an inability to plan. As a mother she could not imagine what her daughter would need at each developmental phase, as a wife she could not plan her finances, and as a preschool teacher she did not have a concept of needing to make lesson plans.

Adapting the analytic frame

After Therese became a toddler and appeared to be doing pretty well, Mary suggested resuming individual psychoanalysis, using VTC. I too had been thinking it was time to do so. It had become problematic for Mary to talk about her disturbing feelings in relation to her daughter with her daughter present. Nevertheless, Mary said that having over a year of sessions with Therese present helped her to contain her sad, anxious, and mean thoughts and to speak carefully so as not to hurt Therese's feelings. On rare occasions when Mary was desperate to tell me a disturbing dream or thought when Therese was present, and yet not wanting to expose her daughter to her emotionally laden words, Mary emailed a few lines to me in real time. This allowed me to understand what Mary was suffering, to be containing and empathic, and also supported an appropriate affective boundary between Mary and Therese.

On friendly terms with her neighbors, Mary arranged for babysitting so that she could have her analytic sessions alone three days per week, leaving one day per week for conjoint therapy with Therese. This allowed Mary private space to speak openly about not just the ordinary frustrations of taking care of a toddler, but also about her fears that stimulated sexual and murderous thoughts in relation to her daughter, and about the understandable guilt which followed. Through the analysis, Mary was able to separate her love and ordinary frustration with her daughter from the resentment she felt because of the hard work, fatigue, and emotional distress in caring for the child.

In individual sessions, Mary spoke about her sexual arousal in relation to her daughter and in the transference. Mary uses a lot of emotional effort to avoid becoming overwhelmed when bathing and cleaning her daughter. I said to Mary that the mother's task of caring for her baby's body is an act of love, unlike the parent's misuse of the child's body for sexual pleasure. A man is to enjoy the intimacy of physical contact and sexual love with his wife, not his child, indirectly referring to her father. To symbolize these differences with language helped Mary understand and to form internal boundaries and strengthen her contact barrier (Bion, 1962).

Now in individual psychoanalysis again, Mary is aroused in almost every session. If the sensation is extremely strong or when it occurs at a certain moment, Mary tells me about it. Sometimes it is just there, and she does not mention it. When I make an interpretation that Mary experiences as being what she calls "on target", she feels aroused. This is a repetition of arousal in relation to her intrusive, sexually provocative father. When this occurs during a session, the contracting vaginal muscles may signify blocking the interpretation from getting in, or clamping down to hold onto the analyst/exciting father and what she gives.

During a recent session when Mary felt aroused, she said, "It makes me wonder if you are aroused too?" This was asked somewhat as a rhetorical question, but also in a tone of wanting and half-expecting me to answer. To maintain an interpersonal boundary and to fortify her intrapsychic boundary, I did not respond directly, but rather linked her arousal to its original source—her arousal as a child when she was with her father in intimate situations, and her wish and fear that he, too, were aroused then. In her individual sessions, she acknowledged that she was titillated by the sexual experiences with her father and had initiated some of the contact. As a young child, she "sensed" that this was "bad" or "wrong" which left her feeling guilty. These feelings then got activated in relation to her daughter and to me. That we are working together using VTC likely makes it easier for Mary to admit to these feelings and to feel safer in the transference too, since I am not in the same physical space as she when she experiences arousal.

Throughout the time that I have treated Mary I have never felt that she would do physical harm. She often reports, "I was thinking about you and what we talked about and what you would do in this situation." Now Mary has internalized her long experience with me as her analyst, a relationship in which she feels safe and contained, and where language (the symbolic order) has been brought to bear on frightening feelings and experiences so that they are more manageable. Mary seems to have largely resolved the anxiety fueled by seeing her daughter's genitals.

Discussion

I faced an ethical and moral dilemma with regard to changing the frame of Mary's analysis to one of mother–infant conjoint analytically informed therapy. I had to free myself from fears of disapproval from colleagues and supervisors. I decided to change the frame because I wanted to have the vivid presence of the baby to help me address Mary's regression following the birth, and I wanted to help her attend to the baby's needs as early as possible in the hope of avoiding or minimizing long-term adverse developmental effects. I also wanted Mary to have a good experience of mothering her baby, knowing that creating a good mother–infant relationship could be healing for her too.

After seven years of twice-weekly psychodynamic therapy, a successful transition into four-times-a-week analysis, the early resolution of the rapid eruption of the negative transference, and the achievement of the depressive position, Mary was able to think symbolically, and made her own dynamic links. However, on a deeper unconscious level, Mary understood that attachments to her original objects, her parents, were fraught with anxiety, frustration, and anger, and that the shadow of those attachments caused ongoing emotional suffering and created problems in forming sturdy, loving, trusting attachments to others in her adult life. Her resulting endopsychic situation also left her suffering in relation to herself.

Mary's pregnancy gave these issues immediacy as she both identified with her needy daughter and experienced her as an intrusive bad object. Helping Mary sort out her complicated feelings in relation to her daughter as a real, separate other, as opposed to an object of transference, allowed Mary to pull back her projections from the baby, her parents, and from me, and to understand and work through her internal dynamics. Now able to separate her anger and resentment of childcare from the person of her baby, Mary developed a deeply gratifying, loving attachment to Therese. Poignantly she said that before her relationship with her daughter, she never really knew what love was, and that now she is able to love and to feel loved by her daughter.

Classically, getting pregnant during an analysis might have been seen as resistance, but in Mary's case, her pregnancy and relationship with her daughter became the catalyst for strengthening her psychic structure. The finding that the infant can catalyze the treatment is consistent with what other analysts have found in working with young mothers. Benedek (1959) described parenthood as a developmental phase in which the mother introjects the care-taking experience and it further organizes her intrapsychically; that is, it continues to fortify current psychic structure. Loewald (1982) and Bibring (Bibring, 1959; Bibring, Dwyer, Huntington, & Valenstein, 1961) had similar findings. As Kite (2012) said, "In this way the *baby* becomes the demand made on the mind to work." Mary's unconscious drive to have a baby was fueled because she unconsciously felt she had infantile trauma and conflicts that she longed to understand. She also sensed the need to develop appropriate psychological boundaries between herself and others, which was worked on in relation to her daughter and in relation to me in the transference.

Mary's analysis has helped her to sort out and label her feelings, reclaim projections, and acknowledge and suffer reality. The analytic relationship and setting function together as a safe external container which, when internalized, strengthens the internal sense of containment, and strengthens the contact barrier (Bion, 1962). Over the course of treatment, Mary's ability to think and dream (Ogden, 2003, 2004) became unblocked and then evolved. Through treatment she developed alpha function, the ability to mentally convert raw psychic sensory experiences into thinkable, useable thoughts consciously and unconsciously, when awake and asleep. Continued analysis will strengthen this so that her thinking is more reliable and efficient. Although Mary still struggles occasionally with confusion between herself and Therese, sometimes attributing her anxieties to Therese, now she can sort it out more quickly and empathize with Therese's authentic feelings. This improvement in differentiation translates to her other close relationships as well.

Therese is growing well and meets all her physical milestones. Most of the baby's symptoms abated within the first few months of mother–infant treatment, consistent with the findings of Fraiberg (1982) and Beebe and Sloate (1982). Therese enjoys being cuddled and separates easily to go with baby sitters. Her play reflects symbolic thinking as shown recently when she used an ice cube tray as a toy guitar. She constructs towers and train tracks and easily completes toddler puzzles. Of some concern is that Therese drools excessively when she is tired or distressed and may have some speech difficulty. She understands well, and responds with appropriate words, but the words are garbled, not sufficiently articulated for a two-and-a-half-year-old. I recommended, and Mary has pursued, evaluation of Therese's speech development. Therese is a fairly strong-willed two-year-old, but she has not developed outright aggression as described by Fraiberg (1982) in disturbed mother–infant pairs whose treatment began when the child was older.

Summary

In this chapter I describe a long-term treatment of a woman which started as a twice-weekly psychodynamic psychotherapy and transitioned to a telephone therapy, telephone psychoanalysis, and finally a four times weekly analytic conjoint mother–infant treatment with a psychoanalytic perspective following the birth of her daughter. The frame was altered when the patient regressed and was unable to care for her daughter appropriately and after the infant developed disturbing defensive masochistic behaviors. The medium of the VTC supported frequent sessions in the natural setting of the patient's home and allowed the analyst to better understand the relationship between the mother and the baby and how the baby was developing. At the same time the presence of the analyst in the home by VTC was less intrusive to the mother than the physical analyst's presence, which was of significant dynamic importance because of the patient's early life experience of inappropriate boundary violations by her father. Within eight weeks the infant's masochistic behaviors largely resolved and a predominantly positive mother–infant bond developed. The mother made considerable progress in understanding herself and her baby and developed the capacity to care for her daughter in a loving way.

Note

1. To provide disguise in a previous description of an earlier phase of this treatment (Bakalar, 2013), I reported the mother had died, but I can now say that it was Mary's father who died.

References

Anderson, M. K. (1995). "May I bring my baby to my analytic hour?": One analyst's experience with this request. *Psychoanalytic Inquiry, 15*: 358–368.

Arons, J. (2005). "In a black hole": The (negative) space between longing and dread: home-based psychotherapy with a traumatized mother and her infant son. *Psychoanalytic Study of the Child, 60*: 101–127.

Bakalar, N. (2013). Transition from in-person psychotherapy to telephone psychoanalysis. In: J. S. Scharff (Ed.), *Psychoanalysis Online: Mental Health, Teletherapy and Training* (pp. 103–118). London: Karnac.

Balsam, R. H. (2000). The mother within the mother. *Psychoanalytic Quarterly, 69*: 465–492.

Beebe, B., & Sloate, P. (1982). Assessment and treatment of difficulties in mother–infant attunement in the first three years of life: A case history. *Psychoanalytic Inquiry, 1*: 601–623.

Benedek, T. (1959). Parenthood as a developmental stage: A contribution to the libido theory. *Journal of the American Psychoanalytic Association, 7*: 389–417.

Bibring, G. L. (1959). Some considerations of the psychological processes in pregnancy. *Psychoanalytic Study of the Child, 14*: 113–121.

Bibring, G. L., Dwyer, F., Huntington, S., & Valenstein, A. (1961). A study of the psychological processes in pregnancy and of the earliest mother–child relationship—1. Some propositions and comments. *Psychoanalytic Study of the Child, 16*: 9–24.

Bick, E. (1968). The experience of the skin in early object relations. *International Journal of Psychoanalysis, 49*: 484–486.

Bick, E. (1986). Further considerations on the function of the skin in early object relations. *British Journal of Psychotherapy, 2*: 292–299.

Bion, W. R. (1962a). The psychoanalytic study of thinking. *International Journal of Psychoanalysis, 43*: 306–310.

Bion, W. R. (1962b). *Learning from Experience*. London: Maresfield Library.

Bion, W. R. (1963). *Elements of Psychoanalysis*. London: Maresfield Library.

Bion, W. R. (1970). *Attention and Interpretation*. London: Maresfield Library.

Blum, S. (2012). My youngest co-analyst: the baby in the consulting room. *Journal of the American Psychoanalytic Association, 60*: 509–515.

Dennett, D. E. (2013). Personal communication.

di Ceglie, G. R. (1987). Projective identification in mother and baby relationship. *British Journal of Psychotherapy, 3*: 239–245.

Fairbairn, W. R. (1944). Endopsychic structure considered in terms of object relationships. *International Journal of Psychoanalysis, 25*: 70–92.

Fraiberg, S. (1982). Pathological defenses in infancy. *Psychoanalytic Quarterly, 51*: 612–635.

Freud, S. (1909b). Analysis of a phobia in a five-year-old boy. *S. E., 10*: 5–147. London: Hogarth.

Glucksman, M. (1987). Clutching at straws: an infant's response to lack of maternal containment. *British Journal of Psychotherapy, 3*: 340–349.

Joseph, B. (1948). A technical Problem the treatment of the infant patient. *International Journal of Psychoanalysis, 29*: 58–59.

Kite, J. V. (2012). A case for analysis with the baby in the consulting room. *Journal of the American Psychoanalytic Association, 60*: 501–508.

Kris, A. O. (1981). On giving advice to parents in analysis. *Psychoanalytic Study of the Child, 36*: 151–162.

Loewald, E. L. (1982). The baby in mother's therapy. *Psychoanalytic Study of the Child, 37*: 381–404.

Loewald, E. L. (1985). Psychotherapy with parent and child in failure-to-thrive—Analogies to the treatment of severely disturbed adults. *Psychoanalytic Study of the Child, 40*: 345–364.

Lyons-Ruth, K. (2006). The interface between attachment and intersubjectivity: perspective from the longitudinal study of disorganized attachment. *Psychoanalytic Inquiry, 26*: 595–616.

Magagna, J., N. Bakalar, H., Cooper, J., Levy, C., Norman, & C. Shank (2005). *Intimate Transformations: Babies with Their Families.* London: Karnac.

Magagna, J. (2013). Personal communication.

Norman, J. (2001). The psychoanalyst and the baby: a new look at work with infants. *International Journal of Psychoanalysis, 82*: 83–100.

Norman, J. (2004). Transformations of early infantile experiences: a 6-month-old in psychoanalysis. *International Journal of Psychoanalysis, 85*: 1103–1122.

Ogden, T. H. (2003). On not being able to dream. *The International Journal of Psychoanalysis, 84*: 17–30.

Ogden, T. H. (2004). On holding and containing, being and dreaming. *The International Journal of Psychoanalysis, 85*: 1349–1364.

Pruett, K. D., & Leonard, M. F. (1978). The screaming baby: treatment of a psychophysiological disorder of infancy. *Journal of the American Academy of Child Psychiatry, 17*: 289–298.

Salomonsson, B. (1998). Between listening and expression: On desire, resonance and containment. *Scandinavian Psychoanalytic Review, 21*: 168–182.

Salomonsson, B. (2006). The impact of words on children with ADHD and DAMP: consequences for psychoanalytic technique. *International Journal of Psychoanalysis, 87*: 1029–1047.

Salomonsson, B. (2007a). "Talk to me baby, tell me what's the matter now": semiotic and developmental perspectives on communication in psychoanalytic infant treatment. *International Journal of Psychoanalysis, 88*: 127–146.

Salomonsson, B. (2007b). Semiotic transformations in psychoanalysis with infants and adults. *International Journal of Psychoanalysis, 88*: 1201–1221.

Salomonsson, B. (2009). Mother–infant work and its impact on psychoanalysis with adults. *Scandinavian Psychoanalytic Review, 32*: 3–13.

Salomonsson, B. (2014). *Psychoanalytic Therapy with Infants and Parents: Practice, Theory and Results.* London: Routledge.

Stuart, J. (2012). Introduction: babies in the consulting room: what happens when analyst, mother and child meet? *Journal of the American Psychoanalytic Association, 60*: 493–500.

Stuart, J., & Ayeni, K. A. (2012). Babies in the consulting room: discussion. *Journal of the American Psychoanalytic Association, 60*: 527–531.

Winnicott, C., & Shepard, R. D. (1977). Preface. In: *The Piggle: An Account of the Psychoanalytic Treatment of a Little Girl* (p. viii). Madison: International Universities Press.

Winnicott, D. W. (1960). The theory of the parent–infant relationship. *International Journal of Psychoanalysis, 41*: 585–595.

Zeavin, L. (2012). The analyst's unconscious reactions to the baby in the consulting room. *Journal of the American Psychoanalytic Association, 60*: 517–525.

CHAPTER SEVENTEEN

Teleanalysis and teletherapy for children and adolescents?

Caroline M. Sehon

My aim in this chapter is to consider the use of teleanalysis and teletherapy with children or adolescents. Given that there is no apparent research and no literature that I could find on this, how can I proceed? First, I will refer to some of the adult literature and current research studies of teleanalysis with adults. I do not think of children as simply little adults, and so I know that not all those findings will be applicable, but they will create a base from which to develop analytic work with children who must live at a distance from a therapist. Then I will present some of my own work for discussion in hopes of starting a case study literature of teleanalysis with children and adolescents.

Analysts have become slowly more transparent about the extent of their use of teleanalysis in work with adults. They have begun to present their work at scientific meetings within their own local analytic institutes and at national and international association meetings. There is increased funding for large-scale research into the effectiveness of this work by reputable funding organizations, such as the National Institutes of Mental Health and the International Psychoanalytical Association (IPA). Two examples of such studies, currently underway and funded by the IPA but not yet published, include those by the Remote Psychoanalysis Research Team (formed by the Argentinean Psychoanalytic Association and Madrid Psychoanalytic Association) and the Teleanalysis Research Group of the International Institute for Psychoanalytic Training at the International Psychotherapy Institute.

Teleanalysis with adults is still an experimental process. To quote IPA President Stefano Bolognini: "The experiences of omnipotence fostered by the virtual sphere and the ease of remote communications open up new possibilities, but they also raise new methodological interrogatives for psychoanalysts, who are faced with requests for treatment over the phone or Skype, the credibility and limitations of which are now the subject of heated, theoretical-clinical debate." (Bolognini, 2013) Critics frequently question whether an analytic process can develop to a degree comparable to that of in-person work. They assert that unconscious communication is impossible because the body of analyst and the body of patient are not present in the same room, and that the transference cannot be analyzed as effectively (Scharff, 2013a). Others have offered illustrations of its effectiveness (Carlino, 2011; Scharff, 2013b). But a search on PEP-Web revealed no articles on the effectiveness of teleanalysis or teletherapy with children and adolescents and only one glancing reference: "Teenagers are comfortable with teleanalysis, but I know of no instances where it was workable with a child, primarily because children need to play in the presence of the therapist" (Scharff, 2013b, p. 504). I think we should not assume that this is the case. Instead we should investigate the possibility of teletherapy and teleanalysis where indicated.

A starting point for examining the question, therefore, about whether teleanalysis has potential or limitation in working with children would be to study analytic process notes when analysis is conducted using various kinds of distance technology. Out of an abundance of caution for children and adolescents, I have studied the clinical impact of analytic work using technology as a temporary or intermittent measure rather than a primary mode of work. In the absence of scientific evidence of its comparative effectiveness in this population, we should titrate the dose of technology carefully, ever vigilant to the evolving risks, benefits, side-effects, and varying process outcomes for a given patient at a particular time in the therapeutic relationship. Finally, any child treatment requires steady support from the parents who consent to the treatment on behalf of their children.

New questions about the effectiveness of teletherapy and teleanalysis will be addressed:

Is the work any less analytic—or does it actually enhance the process?
Is it possible to play therapeutically with a child across a screen?
If it is possible, is it less or more effective than in-person work?
Does a young person's body enter the therapeutic arena even though the patient is not in the actual room with the analyst?
Can transference be analyzed?
Since children cannot legally provide informed consent, is it unethical to offer them an experimental method such as teletherapy or teleanalysis?

As we explore these questions, we will begin to develop a body of case literature to define indications and contraindications for conducting teletherapy and teleanalysis with young people, to examine its effectiveness, and to develop best practices.

From time to time, young people are going to need access to this treatment option. A parent may be unable to drive the child to a session. The child may be ill. A soccer game may switch to a distant pitch, meaning that the child cannot do both activities in sequence as usual. When the child cannot attend in person, the clinician relies upon the parents to ensure that the conditions of technology-assisted treatment can be met (such as providing a secure technological platform and a private room, for example). A strong alliance between clinician and parent is an essential prerequisite to meet the standards of care in delivering this experimental procedure. Respecting the ethical challenges, and legal and regulatory requirements of dealing with this vulnerable population, we need to assess with the young person and the responsible family members how teletherapy or teleanalysis compares to treatment with a temporary substitute, an alternative therapist, or the "no treatment" option in select situations.

Today's youth who grew up with technology at hand—often referred to as digital natives—are much more comfortable navigating virtual environments than the youth of yesterday, who learned to use a computer as adults, now referred to as digital immigrants (Prensky, 2001). How does this important reality factor into their experience of teleanalysis or teletherapy? Might there be an advantage for some young people to have teleanalysis, and not only when logistical circumstances require distance technology? Conceivably, a child or adolescent might more readily encounter the world of frightening emotions when relating to her therapist in a virtual arena that is familiar to her and feels safer and more trustworthy than in a traditional clinical setting.

The field of pediatric medicine adheres strongly to the adage that "kids are not just little adults". In other words, we cannot assume that we can simply carry over our repertoire of theories and techniques and impose them on our young patient population. Our research with children should not have to wait until we have more data on the effectiveness of teletherapy or teleanalysis with adults. If we were to discover that the research findings on adult teleanalysis were that it is less effective than in-person work, why should we assume that these findings automatically translate to young people? Such an unfounded leap may be incorrect. It may unfairly deprive children and adolescents, who, because they are digital natives, may actually respond better than adults to analytic treatments carried across a screen. Questions like these abound without clear answers and call for well-designed research studies. In the meantime, study groups, clinical conferences, and individual case studies are required to expose the practice of teletherapy and teleanalysis to scrutiny and open a dialogue on its use.

I will describe two clinical situations concerning a girl I will call Violeta, and a boy, Jonathan. Violeta, a pre-adolescent, is regularly in four-times-weekly in-person analysis. When preparing to attend camp abroad, she faced the choice of no treatment or teleanalysis. The first summer Violeta chose no treatment. The second summer, she opted to use three-times-weekly teleanalysis using an online video connection for a two-month period at camp. Jonathan, a thirteen-year-old boy, is in twice-weekly analytic therapy in person. When his parents' work periodically limits their ability to drive him, Jonathan elects to use a videoconference (VC) session rather than miss a week. In both situations, the digital screen forms a bridge between our separate locations, preserving the continuity of our work. Sometimes I inquire into the patient's response to working across the screen, and sometimes I do not. Whether to raise it, or not, can be a difficult question of technique. When a shift has taken place from in-person work to meeting across the screen, or vice-versa, I often explore the impact upon the patient of such a change (as I would ask about the impact of a missed in-person session), unless it would seem to intrude into the discourse in an unhelpful way.

I have selected clinical material in which the subject of VC came up naturally in the context of the work. I will reflect on the rationale for this experimental modified treatment approach with such young people, the particular set of circumstances that strongly supports this way of working with them, and the reasons that this plan appears to have actually catalyzed their growth in ways that exceeded my expectations.

Clinical example one: Violeta

Violeta is a Hispanic girl born in the Washington DC area after her parents emigrated from Uruguay to pursue their professions in the United States. Violeta has two older brothers, and one younger sister. She and I first met when she was only nine. Always an anxious child, Violeta had been seeing various therapists since the age of six. Her separation anxieties escalated following a house fire caused by an electrical fault. Fortunately, Violeta didn't sustain any physical injuries, but her mother suffered inhalation injuries and required a two-week hospitalization. This traumatic event led to a massive, sudden loss for Violeta—a worry-filled separation from her mother and the sudden displacement of the family from their home.

When I met Violeta, she greeted me with a compliant smile and a furrowed brow. Small for her age, I thought she seemed much younger than nine. Yet, she walked pensively with a labored stride, like a pseudo-mature adolescent who seemed to carry the world on her shoulders. A striking feature from the outset was her shifting demeanor within and between sessions. Sometimes, she was quite engaging, creatively playful, and articulate. At other times, she avoided eye contact, appeared preoccupied and extremely distant, and became mute. Having floundered for many years, by the time she was nine Violeta was gripped by fears of terrorism, disasters, and death. Her parents thought she had seemed much more anxious and clingy since the house fire. She commonly lapsed into dissociated states that pulled her away from everyone, and interfered with her learning and socialization.

Since Violeta's infancy, her parents felt as if "she had come from another family." An artistic and musical child, she was said to be clumsy on the soccer field, in contrast to her competitively athletic siblings. However, she loved all computer-related games available to her, including SIMS, snapchat, musical podcasts, and Wolverine High. For her eighth birthday, her parents had given her a Kindle. Violeta thoroughly enjoyed surfing the net and watching various videos on YouTube.

In her first session of treatment, which at that time consisted of twice-weekly psychotherapy, Violeta revealed her loneliness and longing to meet with me. She said, "I feel lonely. It's a kind of stranded, lonely feeling—the kind of frightened feeling 'cause there is no one to talk to about these things." In her play, she enacted recurrent narratives of people affected by varying kinds of life-threatening situations, conveying her sense of herself as helpless, impotent, and frightened. In her drawings, she figured alone as a "super-powerful, super-wealthy, and super-strong" character who was invulnerable and invincible, as a defense against her sense of powerlessness. After a year of psychotherapy, I observed that, in contrast to the times when Violeta could play creatively, her mind was often in a state of psychic retreat, reflecting dissociative defenses and schizoid mechanisms of anxiety. I was concerned that her counter-phobic, omnipotent stance masked fears and anxieties, and that unless addressed in analysis, a character armor would harden and be less easily transformed in later years. I recommended a more intensive treatment to help her reach her deep-seated conflicts and traumatic experiences, and we began at a four-times-weekly analytic frequency.

As the analysis took hold, Violeta began to find words for the household fire that shattered her already vulnerable sense of security. She said, "That day, before the fire, the day was fabulous. It's like, all good things eventually come to a screeching halt. You know how in dreams, you're the cameraman, and you're the third person. You don't control what you do, what you say. It was so different than playing with SIMS, where you control what happens. You're in the first person. The scariest thing after we got into the ambulance was when the emergency crew said, 'You're lucky that the fire happened on the other side of the house, far from your bedroom. Otherwise, you might have been seriously injured.'"

Upon arrival at the local emergency department, Violeta was immediately separated from her mother who required medical stabilization and admission to the hospital. Violeta later told me of her fears she might have died. Much later, she wrote a creative story in which the protagonist had survived a house fire that she had caused and that had killed her parents. This brought to my awareness her death wishes towards her parents who she felt had inadequately protected the family long before the fire.

From the outset, she formed a strong, positive contextual transference. She readily accepted the frequency of analysis. She neither questioned it, nor expressed worries about what others would think about her need to attend so often, as many children do. Her focused transference was idealizing of me, but it broke down into negative transference expressed directly by pouting and pulling away in a prolonged silence, or displaced into destroying various toy characters.

Within a few months of the start of her analysis, as summer approached, the family tradition of children going to summer camp loomed ahead. Violeta desperately wanted to join her cousins there but she grew anxious about whether she could manage alone for two months at camp. Her parents worried that canceling or shortening her camp experience would cause her a crushing disappointment. I worried that time without analysis, as well as without her family, would leave Violeta in an anxious, dissociated state of mind. I thought about offering to continue our analytic sessions using VC. But I was concerned about the potential risks and side-effects of conducting teleanalysis with such a young person. So I researched the legal, regulatory, ethical and clinical issues. Having carefully assessed the pros and cons, I discussed the idea of a trial of teleanalysis with Violeta's parents. They warmed to the idea and worked with me to assess the availability of resources at camp to support the teleanalysis. We learned that there was a sound-proofed office in the home of the music director. I was told that this room could be reserved reliably for Violeta's analytic sessions, and that these could be scheduled during her rest hours after lunchtime three days each week. Violeta's parents gave informed consent to this revised treatment contract as a temporary measure to be used only over the summer. Violeta and I talked at length about this option, but in the end she decided against doing this, unless an emergency arose. She feared that she would come to feel more homesick were she to see landmarks through my office window, which would have reminded her of home and only exacerbated her longing and desperateness. It was a difficult fork in the road to assess what would be the best way to proceed, balancing many factors, such as Violeta's own capacity to know what she needed, her desires for autonomy, her parents' wishes for Violeta, and my clinical concerns for how a two-month hiatus from her analysis could be experienced as abandoning and destabilizing to Violeta at the infancy of our work together. Although she tried videoconference sessions in advance of her first camp experience, and she was readily able to converse across the screen, she chose not to use it during that summer camp. Her parents and I went along with her decision, knowing she was aware that she could change her mind during camp if urgent circumstances warranted.

Four months preceding her next summer camp leave, Violeta asked me to supply the office with Play-Doh, which would allow her to form easy-to-shape, multi-colored, and various shifting shapes and designs. She began to use the Play-Doh in a highly obsessional manner, pulling away into a force field of the play when aroused affectively by strong emotions that she could not tolerate, and sometimes for unknown reasons. We worked on understanding the transitions between her sometimes conversing readily and playing creatively, and other times retreating into the play in a monotonous remaking of various shapes.

In anticipation of her leaving for camp, Violeta decided that she wanted to preserve the link to me and to her analysis. In rehearsal, we tried meeting computer to computer, with each equipped with a webcam for some sessions while she was still at home, and we reviewed what it was like to meet in person versus online. She and I talked about which art and play materials she would like to bring with her to simulate the range of options she had in the office. She brought a camera to photograph some of her work for our record and later to review. Since she, her parents, and I all considered this at-home trial to be successful, we were all in agreement to use VC to maintain the continuity of Violeta's work with me the following summer.

The following material was taken from sessions during the last week of her camp, following a four-day separation in the analysis. Unlike her usually punctual arrival, she initiated the call two minutes late, which she attributed to a camp activity that ran overtime. She began the session in an uncharacteristically animated way, narrating excitedly how she and her cabin buddies were happy to have won a camp-wide contest on field day. As we had just had a break and were about to make the transition from doing analysis across the screen to meeting in person when she returned from camp in a week, I thought it was important to open a space for her feelings and reactions to the change and the upcoming shift.

SEHON: I was thinking that it's been a few days since we met, because you had your field days instead. What's it been like for you?

VIOLETA: It's been fine. [She stared at me with an intense and prolonged gaze. Silence ensued. Then she began rubbing her eye for a couple minutes.]

SEHON: It seems like there's something in your eye that's bothering you.

VIOLETA: Yeah, it seems better now.

SEHON: Hmm, what was it like?

VIOLETA: I think it was a piece of dust.

SEHON: [Thinking of the short break that had just occurred] Something barely noticeable, that bothered you a lot.

VIOLETA: [Nodding, her affect changed strikingly such that she seemed much more pensive and calm. Then she picked up the Play-Doh.]

SEHON: Violeta, I think you're working with the Play-Doh, though at the moment I can't see what you're making.

VIOLETA: [She repositioned the Play-Doh so I could see it, but then most of her face went out of view from the screen. Given her facility with working on screen, I wondered whether she had intended to create a partitioned view of herself, as if to symbolize our short separation, or whether this was an unconscious way of hiding her expression from me while needing me to see her play.]

SEHON: Ah, now I can see what you're making, but now I can't quite see your face.

VIOLETA: [She moved the camera so I could see her and the Play-Doh.]

SEHON: Good. [Silence] Oh, you've made a hexagon.

VIOLETA: [She nodded, and then lifted the hexagon in front of her face, once again blocking her line of vision. Then she kneaded the hexagon to fold it in half, and lowered it away from her face.]

SEHON: For a moment, when you held it up against your face, it was kind of like a barrier between you and me.

VIOLETA: [She nodded, then started rolling the Play-Doh, and sighed deeply. Suddenly there was a radical change in her affect again, and she became quite excited.] I just can't believe it!

SEHON: What?

VIOLETA: I come home in four days!

SEHON: It's right around the corner. You seem a bit stunned, all of a sudden.

VIOLETA: [She used a mold to make two rings which she aligned side by side. Then she attached them to each other to form a bracelet. Swinging the bracelet from side to side, she took on a kind of dazed expression. Then she squinted her eyes, sighed heavily, and finally lapsed into a long silence. I was closely attuned to Violeta's moment-to-moment shifts in her play, and nonverbal expression, as if I were conducting an infant observation. I wondered if I would have been as focused on her ever changing and subtle changes in affect had she been in my office.]

SEHON: That realization really seems to have thrown you.

VIOLETA: [Nodding] I don't know. It's just weird. It's going so fast.

SEHON: Hmm, maybe too fast?

VIOLETA: Maybe. [She made various shifting Play-Doh shapes, and sighed. She seemed more intensely withdrawn. I recognized a familiar feeling of disconnection in my countertransference that helped me understand something of Violeta's sense of not being held in mind by her parents.]

SEHON: There will be things that will be different when you're back, like how you and I meet.

VIOLETA: [Nodding, she formed another hexagon with the Play-Doh, and then again folded it in half. She seemed lost in thought and play, immersed in making and remaking various shapes.]

SEHON: Maybe you have a preference to meeting online or in person.

VIOLETA: [She shook her head] I don't have a preference. [Then the screen froze momentarily.]

SEHON: Hmm, that glitch just happened as we were talking about whether you had a preference.

VIOLETA: I don't really have a preference.

SEHON: I wonder if you would have said that last summer.

VIOLETA: I don't think I would have known that last summer. It was the first time we were going to do it online. I feel like it would have been too little time in person to realize what I would prefer. And now I feel they're about equal. I do feel more comfortable online than last year, because I know what to do. It's easier. I was a beginner then.

SEHON: And now you're quite experienced. We've figured out how it can work well.

VIOLETA: Yeah.

On the following day, Violeta arrived on time to the session, stating she had had to seek help at the infirmary earlier that day.

VIOLETA: I noticed that I felt dizzy and tired. I don't know why I keep feeling sick, over and over. It has got me worried. I can't see very far in front of me. Everything is just a blur, and I can't really focus on anything because it's like staring at something that's constantly moving, and your stomach—I mean, my stomach—is really upset, and I just don't know how to describe it. [Immediately, I was reminded of Violeta having had one prior experience of somatic distress at camp, which also took place at a point of separation and transition. On that occasion, she felt sickly right before she was about to take a trip with her peers, which would have necessitated a longer separation between her VC sessions.] That's all I can do ... like I can walk in a straight line, but I can't, I can't like, I can't really. [She sighed and then lapsed into a long silence. Picking up the Play-Doh, she layered one color upon the next.]

SEHON: You can't really ...?

VIOLETA: I can't really tell that I'm going there. I don't really notice that I'm getting there.

SEHON: Like you're putting one foot ahead of the other, but there's no sign that you're actually moving forward?

VIOLETA: Yeah, exactly.

SEHON: That might feel confusing, maybe even frightening.

VIOLETA: It's scary. It's like you are putting one foot ahead of the other. You know exactly where you're going but you don't know how you're going to get there. I don't know if that's a problem, or if it's temporary, but it's got me worried. I don't know how to describe it. [She started making more Play-Doh shapes, sighed, and then entered another long silence.]

SEHON: Hmm, all this is happening right at the time when you're about to leave camp—right when we're about to stop meeting online.

VIOLETA: [Silence]. It's a good point. [She sighed, reclined back in her chair. Looking straight at me, she raised the neck of her blouse over her mouth. I found myself wondering if she were retreating from the prospect of returning. Raising her head, she maintained her gaze, and then rested her head against the wall. She nodded again.]

The session continued with a discussion about the upcoming changes, including returning home, starting back at school, and a shift to meeting in person at our usual four-times-weekly frequency.

Reflections

Violeta is at home in the virtual world. The digital screen represents a concrete transitional space that offers her a playful and generative area for continued analytic work. The positive results for Violeta from continuing analysis using VC have been clear to her, to her parents, and to me. For example, Violeta used to have much more trouble with separations over weekends and longer vacations before our first trial of teleanalysis. In contrast, she became much more engageable and expressive, and her periods of retreat became less intense and frequent, during our second trial meeting via VC. These treatment effects were sustained when we later resumed our in-person sessions. Unlike the omnipotent characters in Violeta's play, she became more capable of tolerating heightened aggressive and loving affects, feelings of helplessness, and anxiety.

Violeta and I continue to reflect upon the meaning of our decisions to have combined teleanalysis with in-person work, and what effects this approach has had on her, on me, and on the analytic field. Recently she said, "I wish we'd met online the first summer too. That's when I needed it more than ever." Yet, it is possible that we would not have realized the same gains from the teleanalysis had we commenced this phase of the work after a short phase of in-person work.

Clinical example two: Jonathan

Jonathan is a thirteen-year-old only child who came to therapy when he was eleven, on the heels of his maternal grandmother's death. He was an obsessional boy with intense separation anxieties manifesting mainly at bedtime, when he had always needed his parents, alternately, to lie with him in bed until he fell asleep much later. Jonathan felt overwhelmed with guilt that he had not visited his grandmother more before she died. To make matters worse, he was consumed with anger at his grieving mother who seemed to him to have become even more emotionally unavailable than before.

Jonathan began meeting with me in twice-weekly, in-person analytic therapy. He was suffering from a traumatic and intrusive replay in his mind of the grandmother's demise, and an unshakeable grief response that persisted months after she died. He occasionally produced current-day dreams, but more often, he would reflect back to dreams he recalled having had as a young child. He came to rely on his sessions, and would fly into a rage when at times his parents would cancel the sessions unexpectedly. About once a month, the father would send me a last minute email to say that he would be unable to bring his son due to conflicting work obligations. Jonathan's mother did not work, but she felt too anxious to risk driving if the weather forecast predicted a snowfall or even a minor shower. After I recognized the pattern of this recurring situation and experienced Jonathan's frustration at being dependent on his parents' ability to drive him, I scheduled a parent meeting to explore alternative options on those days, so that he would not lose out on his scheduled sessions. Amongst these options was the possibility to meet via VC. They all agreed to try it.

A striking feature of the VC sessions was Jonathan's tendency to recall more dreams, to associate more deeply to his dreams, and to show a real interest in our work at understanding them together. This phenomenon reminds me vividly of a teleanalysis experience with a former young adult patient who began bringing in prolific dreams soon after we shifted our primary way of working to teleanalysis when he moved away to attend college. In the following clinical material, I will present two VC sessions that are separated in time by several months. The excerpts illustrate the ways in which Jonathan's dreams enter the work, and shows that work in the transference-countertransference can occur. In my view, these sessions with Jonathan, over the Internet, are comparable to the work we do in person in terms of content and analytic process.

SEHON: So we're meeting online today.

JONATHAN: Yeah, it's so frustrating. It's also kind of good, 'cause I have a ton of homework and this way, I save time with the drive there and the drive back. I had this dream two days ago. I was in my room and it was still dark outside. I saw some green light. So I got out of my bed, and I walked out of my room. I was walking like a zombie. I look downstairs and the green light was really, really bright. I walked halfway down the stairs, and then I saw my parents at the bottom of the stairs. They told me they captured Wolverine—you know, the superhero that's really menacing. It was the one that gets really, really angry. Then I saw its face. It didn't have much expression. I saw him and then I smiled at him.

SEHON: Hmm, its face was subdued? Despondent? Kind of numb?

JONATHAN: Yeah, kind of like that.

SEHON: What's occurring to you?

JONATHAN: I just have no idea.

SEHON: You were in pursuit of the green light.

JONATHAN: Yeah, you know in Green Lantern, when he's using his ring to shine light?

SEHON: Yes.

JONATHAN: That was my mindset. I was following it without thinking.

SEHON: Aimlessly, thoughtlessly. You were curious where it would lead. It sounds like you were sort of sleepwalking in your dream.

JONATHAN: Yeah, I think I was half awake and half asleep.

SEHON: I wonder what you were feeling as you had that dream.

JONATHAN: Not much. Like, I was okay. I didn't really understand why they did that, why they captured the Wolverine.

SEHON: It sounds like you were trying to figure that out. Okay, this might be a clue to helping us understand more about your dream.

JONATHAN: Oh! This might be about my anger! The Wolverine is like really angry. I used to get really angry at my mom. I guess my parents captured my Wolverine. It's like a lot of my built-up anger is gone. The anger is a lot of what was in the Wolverine's sad face.

SEHON: Hmm, that's a very helpful idea. Well, you and I have been talking off and on about how your worries sometimes mask or disguise your anger.

JONATHAN: Yeah! Yeah, that's good!

SEHON: A superhero is a mask of an actual person, just like your worry masks your anger sometimes. So let's think more about this together. When your parents captured the Wolverine, I think you're saying that the Wolverine became sad. The Wolverine embodies anger, so maybe the anger didn't go away but just went under cover. How can we circle back to Jonathan? The Wolverine's face might be telling us something about what happens to your anger when it gets trapped inside—sometimes then you feel sad or angry at yourself.

JONATHAN: I keep thinking about the green light. The Wolverine was actually in the kitchen, so I couldn't see it, but I could see the green light coming from it.

SEHON: The green light was illuminating it. Hmm. What comes to your mind as you think about a green light?

JONATHAN: Green stands for go! It got me to go after it.

SEHON: As if you could go after the Wolverine from a safe distance, without actually running into it. [Silence] The green light makes me think of the expression, green with envy? Maybe the Wolverine was angry, and green with envy.

JONATHAN: I don't think I'd be jealous of the Wolverine! [He started eating.]

SEHON: You just started eating something.

JONATHAN: Yeah, they're popcorn kernels, because I ate all the popcorn.

SEHON: There used to be a time when you'd feel ashamed for me to know about your anger, when we'd talk about your anger towards your mom and how you showed it.

JONATHAN: I'm not that angry these days. I feel more organized, that helps. I still get mad but I don't hit her. There was another thing that I wanted to tell you about. Today, I found out that I got third place in drumming for the county. I was really disappointed. I'm just a third, and I'm top of my age group. I've never been a third drummer.

SEHON: It makes you feel badly about your accomplishment, even when you've had a considerable success.

JONATHAN: I always have this feeling that I'm not doing enough, and that I should be better and better. I worry that I'm not going to get into the best college, the one I want to go to. I think I'm so consumed by it.

SEHON: It's hard for you to enjoy the success of being in the top three drummers of the entire area. It seems you feel angry with yourself.

JONATHAN: I used to get really stressed out before I would play. Now, I don't get stressed out, but I get so upset with myself when I find out how I did. I'm still getting the same grades at school, but I just don't feel I'm trying as hard as I used to. My friends don't work as hard as me. They have lots of time after school to hang out with each other. I guess it's nice that I'm getting good grades, but it feels unfair that I still have to work harder than them, and I'm mad at myself that I can't be satisfied with how I do.

SEHON: So I think we're seeing that there's a part of you inside that's like the Wolverine, angry and jealous at what others get for the efforts they put in.

JONATHAN: Yeah.

SEHON: And, maybe you want someone to capture that part of you so you wouldn't be so hard on yourself.

JONATHAN: Yeah.

SEHON: [Guessing that his anger may have been stirred by not getting to meet in person] I wonder what it's been like for you to meet today online instead of meeting in person.

JONATHAN: It's so frustrating that my mom couldn't drive me there. [I noticed that he didn't talk about what it was like for him to meet online, but he did address the feeling of irritation.]

SEHON: Maybe you wish you could have driven yourself here.

JONATHAN: My life would be so much easier if I could drive.

SEHON: So today, we've been talking about your very colorful and evocative dream.

JONATHAN: Yeah.

ANALYST: And how your worries disguise your anger that is captured inside and that you're wanting to find ways to express. We've also been seeing how you want someone, maybe me, to help you see the ways you can be so hard on yourself.

JONATHAN: It would be so much easier if I was one of those people who didn't care so much. They seem to be so much more relaxed than me.

SEHON: You want to feel more carefree. Okay, we will plan to meet in the office next week.

A few months later, Jonathan needed to meet online again to preserve the continuity of the work.

JONATHAN: I'm not feeling that good. Right now I got an 84.2 in math. So that's really frustrating. I want 90. And on top of that, I didn't get the position I wanted on the basketball team, and I don't think the coach likes me. I gave it my all. The coach was being really tough with me. I feel so disappointed in myself.

SEHON: You're so disappointed. This reminds me of a time not long ago when you felt so angry that you got third place in drumming.

JONATHAN: Yeah, I feel like I'm staying put in school. Everyone says, "Don't worry. You did great!"

SEHON: You feel you're held back compared to where you want to be. All their reassurances just don't cut it.

JONATHAN: I feel like people aren't being honest. In one way, I feel I'm doing enough. In other ways, I feel I'm not doing much. I don't know who I am trying to impress. Why am I doing all this? For a laptop? I asked my mom if she would get me a laptop if I got straight As. She said, "You don't need straight As to get a laptop", so who am I doing this for? If my parents expected me to get As, I could understand this, but they don't.

SEHON: Yes, this is a very important question. Could you be doing that for me? [Although Jonathan seemed to experience me as supporting him, I did wonder if he might have felt that I was also pushing him. For example, I was aware that he felt I was expecting him to verbalize his feelings in ways that were often quite difficult for him. In his identification with me in the transference, he would refer to the endless years of graduate school if he were to become a pediatric neurologist. I wondered if he experienced my offer to meet online, as an arduous alternative to an afternoon off, had I simply canceled the session when his mother informed us that she could not bring him.]

JONATHAN: For you?

SEHON: For me?

JONATHAN: I don't think I need to impress you.

SEHON: [I sensed that he was relating to me as his deceased grandmother who was devoted to him.] We've talked before about how you might be trying to please your grandma.

JONATHAN: It's either for her or me.

SEHON: Or both?

JONATHAN: [He started crying.] I never know what she would think is enough. [Sobbing] All I know is that she told me, "You can do better. You could be in the higher reading class."

SEHON: Yes, then you thought you failed in her eyes. That was in reading class. I noticed that although you were upset at the beginning of the session, it's really hitting you hard now, and shortly after I asked you if you might be trying to impress me. [He was crying uncontrollably.]

JONATHAN: I feel like I can't fully rejoice about happy things I've done. I just wish I could know what she thinks. Even before that conversation with her, I felt the same way. My grandma told me that they were saving money for me, for college. Besides their savings account, they have a special account. She was always saying, "You could go anywhere. It doesn't really matter what it costs." I feel like I'd have to go to the best college.

SEHON: Which might explain why you're looking into colleges always.

JONATHAN: I've been thinking of college since kindergarten.

SEHON: You were saying earlier that when people try to reassure you, it doesn't really help.

JONATHAN: It made me feel better, but just for a little while.

SEHON: I think you're saying that when you're struggling with these kinds of disappointments, reassurances don't really cut to the core of the issue. Do you think you're wishing your grandma was here for you?

JONATHAN: Yeah, it's that she can't be here.

SEHON: You feel sad she's not here, and sad that your mom seems less available to you. [At this juncture, I tried to explore the negative maternal transference in the displacement, particularly in the context that I was not available to him by meeting with him in person. When he did not confirm my hypothesis that he was experiencing these feelings of unavailability to me in the transference, particularly given that we were meeting via VC, I decided to hold off pursuing this possibility more directly on this occasion.]

JONATHAN: Yeah. I have three friends who are hanging out after school. I can't do that because I have all these extracurricular activities till 5 pm. You know I'm vice-president this year.

SEHON: Yes. [Once again, I did wonder if he was letting me know unconsciously that his therapy was interfering with his time to relax with friends, while at the same time I know he very much values his sessions.]

JONATHAN: I'm running again.

SEHON: Again?

JONATHAN: For next year.

SEHON: This year hasn't ended yet.

JONATHAN: No one's running against us. It's uncontested.

SEHON: So you get a break from all these disappointments. [He calmed noticeably.]

All of a sudden, we heard a very loud noise.

JONATHAN: Our cleaning woman just dropped something.

SEHON: How loud!

JONATHAN: How dare she! This is a private meeting!

SEHON: I think we're seeing that we need more room in here to explore your relationship with your grandma. Although she's not alive, you still have a relationship to her inside.

JONATHAN: [Gazing intently at me] A part of me always wonders—if she hadn't been so sick, we may not have met, or maybe we would have.

SEHON: I think we needed to meet regardless, because you had been having so many difficulties for such a long time. [I was very moved by Jonathan choosing to address our relationship, so directly and intimately. I wished I might have replied at a more affective level. Noticing that my response seemed somewhat intellectualized, I wondered if I would have expressed myself in a more attuned way had I been meeting in-person with Jonathan.]

JONATHAN: [Nodding] Yeah.

Reflections

Jonathan has mixed feelings about meeting via VC. He typically expresses a preference to meeting in person. On a recent occasion, he elaborated, "I'd much rather be there. It's not the same sitting in my house. [Sighing] My attic is such a huge room. When I am there, it is just a different feel. It's not the same. It's like more comfortable, not homey, but I don't know how to describe it. [Sighing] Not that I'm not, like, free here. I would express the same emotions if I was feeling sad in here as if I was there, but I'm just more comfortable there. Plus, it just feels really far away because I am thirty minutes away from you." Despite his preference to meeting in person, he would much rather meet via VC than suffer the loss altogether, particularly when we cannot find an alternative time that week. From my perspective, I have been unable to appreciate a significant difference in the nature of the analytic therapy work whether we met via VC or in person. Furthermore, I do wonder whether the virtual setting has catalyzed the emergence of dreams in his work. Of course, I cannot prove this idea, as he may well have begun to bring in more dreams without the introduction of this way of working. I am uncertain whether he is more likely to report his dreams when we meet via VC than when we meet in person, so this is a question yet to be examined. I feel that his transference to me as his devoted but absent grandmother is evoked particularly by my being with him on screen though absent in person and can be worked with effectively in the teletherapy setting.

Conclusion

My experimental move to use video communication technology to continue analytic work with Violeta and Jonathan was eased by previous clinical experience and collegial support. To them, meeting online was non-controversial, just a matter of convenience. Jonathan clearly preferred meeting in person if possible and yet worked well with dreams in teletherapy, while Violeta felt comfortable meeting via VC and had no preference. They each regarded it simply as a temporary bridge to preserve the continuity of the work when they were away. My prior experiences treating adults by teletherapy and teleanalysis reassured me and equipped me with skills that were necessary for working across a distance with these young patients. Also useful was the knowledge and understanding I gained from studying the theory and technique of distance analysis in the context of the International Psychotherapy Institute's teleanalysis research group. Although I could not predict how Violeta and Jonathan would respond to these trials, or promise success, it appeared to me that the risks of interrupting their treatments outweighed the known risks associated with providing analytic work via VC.

Now, I would like to address the questions which I posed in my introduction about the effectiveness of teletherapy and teleanalysis as I reflect upon my work with Violeta and Jonathan.

• Is the work any less analytic—or does it actually enhance the process?

I regard my work with Violeta and Jonathan as no less analytic when conducted across a screen relative to when we meet in person. Either context is constructed as a securely-framed setting, in which I hold an analytic attitude and where I listen analytically to my patient's unconscious self. In my view, the screen does not compromise or lessen my capacity to analyze my patients' dreams, to play therapeutically, to study their positive and negative transferences, to work within my countertransference, and to investigate my patients' symptoms and conflicts.

• Is it possible to play therapeutically with a child across a screen?

Violeta and I commenced our work across the screen after we had already established a sturdy therapeutic alliance. Further, she had already demonstrated her capacities to play imaginatively. I expected she would use this foundation of our work to express herself verbally, and via her play across the screen. Predictably, the results may have been less favorable had I been working with a child who could not play like Violeta, or who had greater limitations in her capacity to communicate, or with whom I had not formed as strong a therapeutic alliance.

• If it is possible, is it less or more effective than in-person work?

I found it possible, and no less effective. In Violeta's case, I often wondered if the screen actually served to catalyze her development in ways that we had not anticipated. Of course, her camp experience gave her a reprieve from other family stresses and academic pressures, and these factors, along with her ordinary growth, may well have accounted for some of her progress. Violeta and I were quite invested in finding ways to relate to each other across the screen. Moreover, I had the impression that Violeta derived a sense of efficacy in navigating the virtual world, at times more effectively than me.

Prior to our meeting via VC, Violeta tended to rely heavily upon me to access her when she would slip into prolonged silences, or when she could not find ways to express overwhelming feelings. In the context of her remote analysis while she was at camp, she had, in a certain sense, to step up to the plate to take charge of elements of the analytic setting that we built together. For example, she needed to assume responsibility to secure her play materials, to adjust the screen from time to time, and she would need to have her mobile phone at hand in case we needed to switch from one form of VC to another, to obtain an improved Internet connectivity and hence the tele-video communication quality). In contrast, the environmental provisions for our in-person meetings were established and maintained largely by me. It seemed to me that her desire to bridge the electronic interface may actually have helped her to occupy a relatively more active, engaged, and communicative stance.

- Can transference be analyzed?

Jonathan appeared equally willing to bring dreams into the therapeutic hours, whether we met in person or across a screen. From early in his therapy, he produced dreams, and he seemed to enjoy working on them with me. As illustrated by the preceding clinical material, I thought it was possible to work effectively with his dreams, and to analyze his transference to me as his grandmother during teletherapy sessions. In the office, Jonathan typically likes to lie down on the couch, curl up comfortably, and look at me as he talks. Although he has access to a couch in his attic, he prefers to use a swivel chair resembling my office chair. When we work remotely, we have wondered if he uses such a chair to create a greater symmetry, or to feel closer to me.

- Does a young person's body enter the therapeutic arena even though not in the same room as the analyst?

Violeta brought her bodily distress into the sessions for us to decode together, symptoms that heralded points of transition and separation in our meetings. Although she did not wander about the room at camp—as she occasionally did in my office—she communicated powerfully through shifting movements of the Play-Doh, by changes in her body positioning, like when she rested her head against the wall or reclined back in her desk chair. Jonathan's body figures importantly in the work, whether he is gazing at his image appearing on the VC screen, sighing heavily, or collapsing on his desk in a flood of tears, for example. Sometimes the bodily symptoms of Jonathan or Violeta are communicated unconsciously across the analytic field, so that I come to experience their bodily symptoms within my countertransference, such as when I "catch" a fleeting headache, or a stomach-ache that passes shortly after the close of that session.

- Is it unethical to offer children a treatment approach that is still considered experimental?

In my view, each clinical situation ought to be evaluated on its own merit, considering the particular features that characterize that child patient-analyst relationship within that family context. Ethical decision-making involves examining many separate and related questions rather than arriving at an all-inclusive, absolutist position, in which it is concluded that an experimental treatment approach must be unethical simply by virtue of its experimental nature. Related questions might include, for example: How long has the child's treatment been in person, prior to the point when online work is being considered? How effective has in-person therapy or analysis been? What supports are available to the patient in the event of an emergency? What is the quality of the analyst's alliance with the parents or other caregivers in case their support becomes necessary to mitigate the impact of any adverse events?

There are many instances within medicine and the healing arts when experimental treatments are offered to minors (or when "off-label" medicines are prescribed), in the context of less desirable, or even hazardous, alternatives. The unknown risks of an experimental method ought to be compared against the known risks of interrupting the established treatment (if any), and the risks of alternative options, if available. The question as to whether it is ethical to provide a therapeutic approach is not determined, *de facto*, by whether the treatment is experimental or not, but by carefully evaluating the entire spectrum of factors, for and against, using that approach at that time. Conversely, it might actually be unethical to deprive a child or adolescent of teletherapy and teleanalysis when substantial clinical justification exists to warrant its use in that specific clinical context, for that particular analytic partnership between the patient (family) and analyst, and at that precise "moment" in time.

I am not recommending teleanalysis or teletherapy for all children and adolescents, as a sole treatment approach or combined with in-person work. I cannot generalize my clinical findings to other children, adolescents, or adults, who have a different complement of vulnerabilities and strengths than Violeta and Jonathan. Well-designed research studies are needed to establish whether teleanalysis and/or in-person psychotherapy or analysis can lead to equally effective clinical outcomes, or whether one method is superior. In the meantime, Violeta and I, and Jonathan and I, are reflecting on past, present, and future experiences, to see what we can continue to learn about the indications and contraindications of continuing this approach for them. We need to remain open to the possibility that we may calculate the risk/benefit ratio differently in the future, as these patients continue to grow and develop, as the nature of these relationships evolve, and as I gather more skills and knowledge from new published literature on this subject.

Commentary: experiment, really? Or just good clinical work

Sharon Zalusky Blum

In reflecting upon Caroline Sehon's chapter, what remains particularly noteworthy is the level of co-operation and collaboration that has been established between Dr. Sehon, her patients, and their families. The examples reveal her talent for dealing sensitively and empathically with children and their parents. Her work is an example of how treatment is co-constructed by each party. Together parents, analyst, and child created a treatment that would work for each child. Both Jonathan and Violeta were ready to be involved in their own therapy. Each seemed to hunger for connectedness, which Dr. Sehon provided in a thoughtful manner. Her commitment to their well-being was continually demonstrated by the close attention she paid to the special, changing needs of each individual child. Dr. Sehon was open to explore alternatives to office sessions in order to keep the special therapeutic contact intact. She put it nicely when she wrote, "… the digital screen forms a bridge between our separate locations, preserving the continuity of our work." Unlike working with adults, Dr. Sehon had the additional task of bringing these caring parents on board. I say caring even in the case of Jonathan, whose parents at times chose not to bring him to session, much to his chagrin, because of their conflicting needs. Nonetheless, his parents still appreciated and validated Jonathan's wish to stay connected to his therapy and to his analyst, and they agreed to sessions online. Both children were, as Dr. Sehon noted, accustomed to using the computer, which made psychotherapy or psychoanalysis online an obvious alternative to office visits. They liked the computer. They felt *competent* using it.

Not practicing with children as young as Violeta, I found the work between Violeta and Dr. Sehon particularly touching. Here is this young girl who could appreciate the difference between the summer she went to camp without the benefit of her therapy and this summer, when she knew she could count on her therapist to help her through. I found her ability to play with her Play-Doh as if she were in the office a testament to their special relationship. Violeta felt so attended to in her sessions on the Internet that she allowed herself to play alone in the presence of Dr. Sehon (Winnicott, 1958), even if the presence was a virtual one. I appreciate Dr. Sehon's way of understanding Violeta's disappearing from the screen as a symbol and a struggle with separation, but I also see it as her complete comfort with Dr. Sehon's presence. Violeta knew she was out of sight, but not out of mind (Zalusky, 1998). She knew her therapist was on the other side of the screen watching her play. Being able to continue her work with Dr. Sehon was a gift for Violeta. It was a recognition on the part of her parents and her analyst that being able to go to camp and see her cousins, separate from her family for the summer, was an age-appropriate achievement. The pain and anxiety of being away was mitigated by knowing her therapist was available. She was able to go and to stay at the same time. Who could deny, other than a psychoanalytic purist, that Violeta being able to be like her friends, to go away for the summer, added to her developing sense of self?

For Jonathan, working in teletherapy was more complicated, even though he was able to use it very well. To accept a session on the Internet rather than in person meant that someone else's needs were more important than his desire to be taken to his appointments. It was bittersweet, yet adaptive. It is part of a lesson we all need to learn. At times adaptation is the best of what is available to us. The Rolling Stones (1969) said it well in their popular song, "You can't always get what you want." People (therapists included) limit growth when adherence to abstract ideals blinds them to the possible. Not all our patients (nor all our colleagues) are capable of making adaptions. Jonathan, no matter how disappointed he felt not being able to sit with Dr. Sehon in her actual office, continued to be aware that his analyst was thinking about him, concentrating and trying to help him make sense of his dreams, both literally and figuratively. Though Dr. Sehon attempted to attend to Jonathan's negative maternal transference, it seemed appropriate for her to back off when he did not agree. Even if Dr. Sehon's hypothesis might be partially true, what seemed more significant was the fact that unlike his dead grandmother and live mother, Dr. Sehon was actually there with him in a direct present way albeit through a virtual bridge.

It seems to me that psychoanalysis and psychotherapy online at the right, propitious times can help children and adolescents be more integrated with their friends and peers. In a city such as Los Angeles, where I practice, traffic can take enormous time out of one's life. Children who are seen multiple times a week, still need to play sports, join clubs, create music, do a myriad things with their friends after school. It makes sense that when these young patients are able to do kid things, they feel less like there is something wrong with them. Therapy adds to their life whether it takes place in the office or on the computer. It doesn't take away from it. Their parents too may feel less conflicted about the price that is being paid when therapy or analysis can be integrated into the young child's growing life.

The commentary that follows is directed more at our field than at Dr. Sehon's paper directly. My concern has to do with the question mark after the title, "Teleanalysis for children and adolescents?" It is obvious that Dr. Sehon has answered the question for herself. There is no doubt she thinks teleanalysis is both possible and helpful, and wants to share her experience in print. And there is no doubt I agree with her.

I have a different question however. When do we stop calling a treatment an experiment? It's now been over twenty-five years since I personally have been thinking and writing about psychoanalysis by telephone. Long before I published my first paper "Telephone analysis: Out of sight but not out of mind" in *Journal of the American Psychoanalytic Association* (1998), I wrote several drafts, discussed the topic with supervisors, and presented the idea in seminars and programs throughout the country. Some years before my own interest in telephone analysis, John Lindon (1988) a seasoned training analyst from my institute wrote "Psychoanalysis by telephone" in the *Bulletin of the Menninger Clinic*. He wrote about a patient who had been a famous musician traveling the world. Though I did not know it at the time, Lindon's patient was someone I knew personally. The patient revealed himself to me when he learned of my interest in the subject. He knew I had been conflicted about working on the phone because of the past traditions and prejudices of our field. He personally told me how meaningful it was that Lindon was there for him when he needed him most. For the patient, there was no conflict. He was able to work, travel, and maintain the bond with his therapist, which allowed him to heal and become a more thoroughly functioning person. It would be hard to believe Violeta and Jonathan wouldn't feel similarly.

Since Lindon's article there have been many contributors to the topic. To name just a few, Joyce Aronson (2000) edited a book *Use of Telephone in Psychotherapy* with chapters by twenty-one contributing authors, three of whom dealt specifically with working with parents, children, and adolescents. Leffert (2003) wrote "Analysis and psychotherapy by telephone: *Twenty years* of clinical experience" (my emphasis). Having changed cities several times in his life, Leffert had the opportunity to appreciate the difference between transferring all his patients early on in his career when he moved versus continuing the therapeutic work with many of his patients on the telephone following a later move. Leffert wrote about his considerable long-term experience conducting therapy and analysis with many different patients on the telephone over extended periods of time. In his important article Leffert explains, "My experience with telephone work falls broadly into four kinds of clinical situations: (1) intermittent or partial telephone treatment occurring as a result of plan or circumstance to meet the needs of patients living at a distance from the office, (2) extended periods of work over the telephone with patients away for business reasons, (3) the continuation of eight analyses and five psychotherapies via telephone following my move, and (4) the beginning by telephone of an analysis that continues in person following that move" (pp. 102–103). He is one of the few in our field who has written about starting an analysis on the telephone with someone he had never met before (and who later transferred to his office). It is important for us to think about that possibility. For the most part, the literature in our field emphasizes the need for an established relationship with a patient as a precondition to even thinking about conducting treatment on the phone or the Internet. Usually that is a rational way to proceed. Even so, there may be times when it makes sense to start first on the telephone or online and later continue the work in the office. One could imagine a pregnant woman on bed-rest who wishes to deal with her depression, anxiety, or relationship problems before she is physically able to come to the analyst's office. What about a latency age child who has had a bone marrow transplant that makes it physically dangerous to be exposed to people while the immune system is still weak? Most of us would agree that the young child might benefit from having a therapist. We could imagine a family moving from one city to another with a child who has need for therapy. Rather than starting in one city and having to terminate early before the therapy is completed, would it not make sense for the child to meet online or on the telephone with a therapist/analyst in the city where the family is planning to move? It might help with the actual transition.

Ten years after Leffert's article in *Journal of the American Psychoanalytic Association*, Jill Scharff (2013b) published in the same journal "Technology-assisted psychoanalysis", and in the same year edited, *Psychoanalysis Online: Mental Health, Teletherapy, and Training* (Scharff, 2013a). In her edited book there were twenty-two contributors. By no means is the above list a complete reference of what has been discussed in the psychoanalytic literature. In addition to the written literature, programs throughout the world in the last two decades have dealt with technology and psychoanalysis. It is because of the vast attention that has been given to this new evolving format for psychoanalysis that I disagree profoundly with Dr. Sehon's statement, "Teleanalysis with adults is still an experimental process." We do not need consensus from the whole field to know that at times teleanalysis can be the best option available. There will always be analysts who cannot or choose not to work analytically on the telephone or online. Some analysts may simply not like the experience. Some may find it difficult to concentrate without the actual presence of the other in the room. Others might be more visual by nature. Technological glitches may feel too disruptive to their process. In some cases analysts may truly hate the phone, or the computer. Nobody is directing any analyst to do teleanalysis if unable to conduct a viable treatment. But the problem comes when analysts, rather than acknowledging personal preference, feel the need to justify their feelings by cloaking their discomfort in a heated, theoretical-clinical debate. Many older analysts traveled hours and hours every day—some in cars, some in trains, and some in airplanes—for many years to be able to complete their training at enormous costs to themselves and to their families. It is no wonder, with such enormous personal sacrifices, that some may have idealized their own suffering and rationalized it into theory. Self-justification has always been part of our tradition, beginning with the reason for having analyands lie on the couch looking away from the analyst. Writing on beginning the treatment, Freud (1913) explains his first reason for arriving at the idea of the couch: "The first is a personal motive, but one which others may share with me. I cannot put up with being stared at by other people for eight hours a day (or more). Since, while I am listening to the patient, I, too, give myself over to the current of my unconscious thoughts, I do not wish my expressions of face to give the patient material for interpretations or to influence him in what he tells me (p. 133)." Having made his choice of the couch, Freud used his experience in that setting to develop his ideas on theory and practice. Many of teleanalysis's greatest critics have no experience doing it.

In a similar light there are those patients who do not like conducting sessions over the phone or online. There are some patients who are unable to create for themselves a quiet space where the work can take place. They need their analyst to provide an actual office to protect them. Some patients are easily distracted without the presence of the other concretely in the room. I once had a young patient who was away in Europe for junior year abroad. We continued talking twice a week online. She would lean in towards the computer. It felt like she was trying to get close to me in a way she never had before. In my office she would often attend to her cell phone when it beeped. She was easily distracted. Online she felt more present until I realized her leaning in towards the camera/computer had nothing to do with new ways of being in the world but rather she was reading instant messages that appeared on the screen while we were in session. Our work online continued, as it had in the office, dealing with her distractibility. The only difference was that she, like Violeta though a bit older, was able to manage her anxieties for the first time and go away to school. Today she is a world traveler. And sometimes we have office visits and sometimes we have sessions on the telephone.

Rather than thinking of teleanalysis as experimental, analysts should retain an experimental approach to technique in general (Renik, 2004). In psychoanalysis, one size cannot fit everyone. Explaining the problems involved when we conduct treatment on the basis of received wisdom, Renik writes, "… psychoanalysts cannot assume the virtue of any particular set of procedures—use of the couch, frequency of sessions, even the method of free association. These are techniques, and in the progressive development of any scientifically based clinical practice, techniques will alter, even alter dramatically, as empirical evidence accumulates; some prove valuable and are retained, others are discarded" (Renik, 2004, e-book [in keeping with our emphasis on technological changes], Ch. 1, para. 5). All good treatment seems to me to start as an experiment. We can only know retrospectively who we can help.

Our field may be slow to change, but Caroline Sehon's chapter may add just another little nudge to help it on its way into the twenty-first century.

Commentary

Virginia Ungar

It is truly a pleasure to have the opportunity to comment on this chapter concerning teleanalysis and teletherapy for children and adolescents, its title accompanied by a question mark. This way of presenting the topic invites us to enter ground that, as Dr. Sehon says, has as yet no bibliographic history. And even if there is literature on the distance treatment of adult patients it is, of course, quite recent. As a child and adolescent analyst, I recognise that it is precisely these young patients who take us adults—"digital immigrants", as the author puts it, quoting Prensky—to that world in which young people reside with such ease—being, as they are "digital natives"—a world of technology with all its amazing advances in which the new never ceases to appear. Whereas some years ago we were amazed by the conquests of the Internet in all regions, today we are continually surprised that the space of interchange for young people—that of virtual reality—fits into devices which are seemingly getting smaller by the day. I think it is no exaggeration to say that, for these kids, their world is increasingly to be found in a mobile phone, a piece of technology which itself comes with more and more features.

Taken from this perspective, the subject matter of this chapter is the natural evolution of life online to analysis online. If technology provides the medium and the platforms where young people spend much of their lives—listening to music, studying, watching TV, chatting, connecting to social networks, "speaking" on web chat sites, WhatsApp, Twitter, Snapchat, and all the rest—why should we think that this will in some way have no effect on our practice? I believe that we should be very careful in dealing with this topic and neither idealise nor demonize technology. Any tendency to demonize must be taken into account in our practice with children and adolescents. Analytic work with these patients demands that we strike a difficult balance in holding the analytic attitude, because the child's absorption with technology affects the most primitive unconscious levels of the therapist, which could throw us off. This requires us to work very closely on our countertransference and process it carefully in order to avoid being tied up in enactments or in unconscious alliances which then lead to possible impasses.

I think it important to pay attention to the questions the author asks herself and not try to answer immediately, but rather take them as starting points for reflection. She presents two clinical situations (one with a girl and one with a boy) of teleanalysis with patients who had previously worked with the analyst in face-to-face sessions. In both cases, the patients were hypersensitive to separation related to traumatic situations of different types in the past. In response to these cases, Dr. Sehon chose to use "technology as a temporary or intermittent measure rather than a primary mode of work." To allow us to enter completely into the chapter, she presents her own notes on analytic processes and her reflections on them.

In the case of the girl, nine-year-old Violeta, who wanted to go to sleep-away camp for a couple of months in the summer, Dr. Sehon carefully evaluates a factor which is often ignored: that analysis may prevent a child from going to camp at a point in development where interaction and integration with peers and learning from new experience away from home is of utmost importance. In the case of the prepubescent boy, thirteen-year-old Jonathan, Dr. Sehon takes account of the impact on him of having to miss sessions when his parents are unable to take him to the analyst's consulting room.

In the first clinical example, Dr. Sehon meticulously prepared the setting in coordination with Violeta's parents and the organisers of the camp, ensuring that there was a private room available for the sessions at a time that would not interfere with the girl's activities at the camp. The parents gave informed consent for the treatment. The first summer, Violeta decided against sessions online. Prior to the second summer, a lot of work was done trying out online sessions, and Violeta was able to go to camp and continue her analysis online. The analyst presents detailed material from the sessions during the last week of that camp. In these sessions, we can see Dr. Sehon working in an analytic mode, exploring the here and now of the transferential-countertransferential situation. In addition to this, she explores the consequences of the change of modality from in-person analysis to teleanalysis and its effects on both patient and analyst. We see this, for example, when Dr. Sehon says, "I wondered if I would have been as focused on her ever-changing and subtle changes in affect had she been in my office."

We see Violeta express, in the most beautiful of ways, the difference between real life, with all its hazards, and life in virtual reality in which whatever happens is controlled. Of real life, she says, "You are in the first person." We also see how the patient follows the analyst in the exploration of the change in modality when getting closer to her return to the normal face-to-face sessions. She admits that a year previously she wouldn't have been ready for this experience. As she herself puts it, comparing teleanalysis to in-person sessions: "And now I feel they're about equal. I do feel more comfortable online than last year, because I know what to do. It's easier. I was a beginner then." We see an analyst and a girl working in an analytic way and thinking together about the effect on each of them of the change in modality. The chapter leaves it quite clear for us that the decision to meet online helped Violeta continue in the analytic work. She is a girl who cannot cope with prolonged separations: separation evokes in her a traumatic situation involving danger that, as the analysis had only recently started, had yet to be worked through fully. This modality of online analysis allowed the patient to continue with the life experiences necessary at that moment for her development and for the analyst to accompany her closely, exploring analytically how she was living these experiences.

In the second clinical example, the young male patient made use of the online modality where, for various reasons, it was not possible for him to be taken to the analyst's consulting room for sessions in person. Jonathan suffers from very intense separation anxieties with traumatic roots related to the very painful loss he suffered when his grandmother died. In the detailed sequence that Dr. Sehon presents to us, we can see the thorough analytic work on a dream that, in the sequence of dreams, can be related to the traumatic experience. The analyst is able to help the young man connect his anger and frustration at coming third in a drumming competition, his "green anger" or envy, and his reaction at having to replace his face-to-face session with one online.

Here the analyst is able to cover the three levels of the complete interpretation, as described by Dr. Horacio Etchegoyen (1991), when she addresses the current and historical conflicts together with that of the transference. We are able to appreciate the pressure exerted by a superego constructed from a number of identifications, including one with the patient's late grandmother. The analyst, in treating this in the transference, allows the patient to deal with this internal demand, locating it on the path towards the working through of the root of his conflict. Also of great interest is Dr. Sehon's going on to connect the whole issue to the fact of working online, something that she had suggested so that the patient would not miss any sessions.

There is a particular point where analytic contact is made, and this turns out to be very moving for the reader. The author has the ability to get the atmosphere across; she is able to communicate the mood of the session where Jonathan, exploring his internal relationship with his grandmother in response to an interpretation, refers in a direct manner to the analytical relationship and to his need of analysis. Yet she asks herself if she could not have expressed her own affect better in a face-to-face session. This shows us the questioning attitude which the analyst constantly takes concerning the effectiveness of teleanalysis. This makes the chapter an excellent example of how an analyst can work analytically inside of the session and, outside the session, can engage in research into the effects of variations on the classic method on the patient and the analyst.

It is not my intention here to respond to all the questions posed by the author and, moreover, it would seem to me that there are some which must remain open, so as to guide the path of research. However, I believe that the episode in the treatment of Jonathan that I pointed out—one that for me was very moving to read—speaks for itself in terms of the possibility of maintaining an intimate space within the therapy, of being close to the patient, of maintaining a state of listening, observation, and receptivity, and of deep work carried out in the transference-countertransference. I am drawing attention to the components of the analytic attitude evident in Dr. Sehon's presentation, which has allowed the reader to appreciate what was lived in the therapeutic relationship.

In her commentaries on the case, Dr. Sehon says that despite the patient's openly expressed preference for in-person sessions, Jonathan would much rather meet online than not at all. Dr. Sehon goes as far as to ask if the fact of working online actually acts as some form of stimulant to the appearance of dream material. Similarly, with respect to Violeta, the analyst asks if the work on screen acted as a catalyst in her development in ways that had not been anticipated.

Coming to the end of the chapter, the author considers ethical questions in relation to this type of treatment with children and adolescents. It is clear that in setting out her position Dr. Sehon is not making a recommendation in favour of remote analysis, but rather is just relating her particular experience in two situations where such a modality was better than missing sessions with young people who felt certain vulnerabilities concerning separation. This chapter provides an excellent example of a situation where an analyst who has firmly internalised the analytic attitude is able to do "the most psychoanalysis possible" in a non-traditional setting.

Although what I am pointing to in the chapter can be seen as a general affirmation of tele-analysis, I want to emphasize that the real point of the chapter is the evaluation of the effects of the modality of teleanalysis with children and adolescents. I believe that, with this chapter from Dr. Sehon, we now have the starting point for establishing a case study literature of teleanalysis with children and adolescents, a goal to which she refers at the beginning. In both of the cases presented, we can appreciate the analytic work carried out in sessions conducted online yet using all the classic tools, such as the careful construction of the setting, the strong alliance forged with the patients' parents, the use of interpretation, the work in the transference, and the monitoring of the countertransference. The use of the online modality for analytic sessions is permanently included in the analytic field.

Taking these last points together, we have, here, evidence of profound and sustained psychoanalytic work and of a clinical base, which may well bring us to the conclusion that it is indeed possible, even in so-called virtual reality, to construct an intimate space for work towards the formation of symbols and analytic understanding of unconscious communication.

Once again, we are exposed to the amazement of discovering, every day, in a new way, our psychic reality as human beings tied to the unconscious.

References

Aronson, J. K. (2000). *The Use of the Telephone in Psychotherapy*. Northvale, NJ: Jason Aronson.

Bolognini, S. (August, 2013). Inaugural speech by President Stefano Bolognini and Vice-President Alexandra Billinghurst. International Psychoanalytical Association Retrieved from http://www.ipa.org.uk.

Carlino, R. (2011). *Distance Psychoanalysis: The Theory and Practice of Using Communication Technology in the Clinic*. London: Karnac.

Etchegoyen, R. H. (1991). *The Fundamentals of Psychoanalytic Technique*. London: Karnac.

Freud, S. (1913). On beginning the treatment (Further recommendations on the technique of psycho-analysis 1). *S. E., 12*: 121–144. London: Hogarth.

Leffert, M. (2003). Analysis and psychotherapy by telephone: Twenty years of clinical experience. *Journal of the American Psychoanalytic Association, 51*: 101–130.

Lindon, J. A. (1988). Psychoanalysis by telephone. *Bulletin of the Menninger Clinic, 52*: 521–528.

Prensky, M. (2001). *Digital Natives, Digital Immigrants: A New Way to Look at Ourselves and Our Kids*. On the Horizon. MCB University Press, Vol. 9, No. 5, pp. 1–6.

Renik, O. (2004). *Practical Psychoanalysis*. New York: Other Press ibook.

Scharff, J. S. (2013a). *Psychoanalysis Online: Mental Health, Teletherapy, and Training*. London: Karnac.

Scharff, J. S. (2013b). Technology-assisted psychoanalysis. *Journal of the American Psychoanalytic Association, 61*: 491–509.

Winnicott, D. W. (1958). The capacity to be alone. *International Journal of Psycho-Analysis, 39*: 416–420.

Zalusky, S. (1998). Telephone analysis: Out of sight, but not out of mind. *Journal of the American Psychoanalytic Association, 46*: 1221–1242.

CHAPTER EIGHTEEN

Cyberspace as potential space

Yolanda de Varela

Technology offers a way of extending the resource of psychoanalysis to those patients who choose teleanalysis because of their circumstances in the modern world. We are familiar with travel, migration, illness, and geographic disadvantage as indications for teleanalysis. I propose that the patient's preference for technology is another indication for the use of teleanalysis. We are facing a new generation of young adults, many of whom prefer to communicate across cyberspace. The mere idea of communicating across such a space places us very quickly between two possibilities: That the space will be full or empty. But if we think of space and time together as holding potential for development, as Winnicott did, then in cyberspace the analytic pair has a space where something that has not yet taken place may now happen in the future.

My idea stems from Winnicott's concept of potential space, "the hypothetical area that exists (but cannot exist) between the baby and the object (mother or part of mother) during the phase of the repudiation of the object as not-me, that is, at the end of being merged in with the object" (Winnicott, 1971b, p. 107). Winnicott describes it as a space for relating to transitional objects that are me and not me (1951); a space for creative living, play, and cultural experience (1971a). Drawing on Winnicott, I want to develop the idea that cyberspace can offer the analytic pair a potential space in which the patient can seek a non-represented past by finding it as a lack in the analytic relationship, looking for the experience that was missed, and finding it in the future of the analytic relationship. Like cyberspace, potential space is, according to Winnicott's idea, an intermediate area of experiencing that lies between (a) the inner world, "inner psychic reality" (Winnicott, 1971b, p. 106) and (b) "actual or external reality" (1971c, p. 41). When the analytic pair communicates in sessions that are technology-assisted, cyberspace becomes like the potential space that "both joins and separates the infant (child, or adult) and the mother (object)" (1971b, p. 108). The essential feature of the potential space is "the paradox, and the acceptance of

233

the paradox: the baby creates the object, but the object was there waiting to be created" (1967b, p. 89). Similarly, the analyst is there at the end of the telephone line or on the computer screen during online transmission, but the patient has to create the object represented in the analyst.

Socio-cultural changes pull us farther and farther away from the type of patients described and treated by Freud in the twentieth century, a time of sexual repression, protected personal privacy, and identity under worldwide threat of death from persecution and war. Acknowledging the changes in his time and their impact on the individual, Freud expanded his theory and technique accordingly. He moved from drive psychology, the seduction theory (Freud & Breuer, 1893–1895), and the technique of suggestion in the treatment of hysterics to ego psychology, conflict, and defense (Freud, 1923) in order to address the needs of neurotic patients, and later on developed his theory of construction (Freud, 1937) to lead him to a new method for treating those who suffered from conflicts beyond neurosis.

Now, in the twenty-first century, analysis must respond to a world that comes with a new baggage of experience and ways of thinking and relating, driven by rapid communication and endless information, and changing boundaries and sense of self. Widespread use of the Internet is the underpinning of these changes. Young people communicate constantly through the use of electronic devices. They chat with their friends, do their homework, arrange group outings, apply for college, and find intimate partners, all online. Dating is not confined to meeting a person in the same neighborhood, city, or hemisphere, nor even in the same time zone. Education, professional conferences, business meetings, loving encounters, and casual sex can all happen in cyberspace.

Cyberspace is a space that is difficult to represent. To some, it is a space of freedom and endless possibility. To others it is a *desmentida,* a place of disavowal that negates reality and at the same time accepts its own reality as *the* reality. For the practice of teleanalysis with the kinds of patients I have in mind, Green's (1993) concept of the work of the negative can be helpful. Green (1997) wrote of the absent object in relation to the mind as a frame: "… when the baby is confronted with the death experience, the frame becomes unable to create substitute representations—it holds only the void. This means the non-existence of the object or of any substitute object. The negative hallucination of the object cannot be overcome; the negative does not lead to an alternative positive substitution. Even the badness of the object and fantasised destructiveness will not do. It is the mind, that is, mental activity giving birth to representations, which is under the threat of being destroyed, in the frame. At other times it is the framing structure itself that is damaged: here we have disintegration" (Green, 1997, p. 1080). To put it another way, for the object to be there is the same as its not being there because the negative has made its indelible mark on the psyche. Analysts need to think more about the nature of cyberspace, the new patients who inhabit it, and the negative and positive types of objects they find there, so as to develop a new type of analysis in synchrony with their mores and habits, and to train analysts in theory and technique relevant to the needs of the new generation.

What kinds of patients seek a distant analysis supported by videoconference when they have the option of an in-person analysis? My first thought is that this mode is probably favored by people with schizoid features. On further reflection, I still think that is true. I also think that we are facing a schizoid generation, the product of a worldwide crisis of depression. The World Health Organization, WHO (2012) places depression as the principal cause of work incapacity worldwide. I see this as a global depression over object loss caused by the distractions of a fast-moving rate of societal change due to technology. In our modern world it is not unusual to find mothers who use electronic equipment to simulate lively interaction and excitement between them and their babies in place of steady maternal preoccupation and finely attuned mirroring (Winnicott, 1956, 1967a). I am not talking about the early use of electronic devices as one way, among many, of introducing stimulating games. I am referring to the use of these devices as if they are a substitute mother or caregiver. What kind of environment is this for a child to grow up in? The emptiness left by the lack of an affective link with the mother is substituted by a device offering infinite possibilities of manic, omnipotent activities that serve to deny the loss of the primary object.

Let's imagine now that time has passed. The child is an adult seeking analysis and choosing to undergo distant treatment through the videoconference. What is the patient's transference to the cybernetic space as the medium for analytic communication? What is the analyst's countertransference to it? Is there a sense that out there we can somehow find what we require? Maybe there is an illusion that out there in the future we will find an as yet to be experienced encounter? The experience of transference and countertransference in the treatment of patients like the ones I am trying to describe is one of floating in space, the patient looking for a way to link to the analyst, and the analyst free-floating without destination and without thinking about the possibility of finding someone to link with. In a situation like this, in which the transference is yet to be addressed because what is being evoked is preverbal, and maybe fixed to the negative, the analyst relies on the techniques of construction (Freud, 1937) and psychic figurability (Botella & Botella, 2005). Construction refers to the recreation, in the actual experience of the treatment, of something that happened during the preverbal life of the patient and therefore could not be represented. This early phase of life is created in the actuality of the patient-analyst relationship and is then connected to the primary experience. Figurability refers to a way of working with patients who could not verbalize an unrepresented early experience, using mental images or figures that form in the analyst's mind as a response to the actual state of "no transference" in order to establish, through these figures, a link with the patient. This type of work is not easy with in-person analysis, but it is even harder when doing analysis using videoconference.

Our consulting rooms are full of personal objects and books that surround us and hold us within a feeling of security, like a good environmental mother. Feeling held, feeling secure, allows us to offer our patients a secure base, which they experience in their contextual transference (Scharff, 2005, p. 96). But much of this sense of safety gets lost in distance analysis: We are in our consulting rooms but we cannot physically include the patient within our environmental holding. The patient is far away, creating his own environment, providing his own handkerchief to dry his tears. The analyst feels disconnected, on the verge of death anxiety. The likelihood of enactments grows. Looking for distraction by connecting to the objects that surround us is our defense against death anxiety provoked by the lack of linking. The predictably unpredictable failures in Internet communication evoke early environmental failures, creating lack of trust in both members of the analytic dyad in respect of the reliability of the Internet as an environmental facilitator.

The patient also protects himself from anxiety about connection. He utilizes omnipotent defenses that make him feel in control of the analytic cyberspace. He could be late in placing the call, even though he sees on his screen that the analyst is online waiting for it. He could reduce the fully engaged analyst in his mind to a bi-dimensional figure or a dehumanized screen. Because of trauma, he could collapse the multi-dimensional analytic space to a bi-dimensional space with no possibility of expansion. When the space is so contracted, the analytic experience is perceived as falling into the infinite without any possibility of the center holding. The only relief he can imagine is the omnipotent management of technology with which to disconnect the analyst and throw her into the void.

"Although potential space originates in a (potential) physical and mental space between mother and infant, it later becomes possible, in the course of normal development for the individual infant, child or adult to develop his own capacity to generate potential space. This capacity constitutes an organized and organizing set of psychological activities operating in a particular mode" (Ogden, 1985, p. 129). The internal space of the patient's mind, a product of the internalization of the external space between mother and child, is expressed in analysis. When this analysis takes place using videoconference, the experience of communicating primitive affect emphasizes both the potential and the failure of the mother–infant relationship. This is especially true when an early trauma has provoked the collapse of the potential space under the weight of the actual, concrete experience. Maybe these patients seeking analysis through the videoconference are trying to replay an early trauma between themselves and their mothers, by choosing to place the analytic-couple relationship within cyberspace.

Cyberspace seems to me to be similar to interstellar space where there is the possibility of finding something that we do not already know or cannot comprehend yet, namely the possibility of establishing new contacts. The image of the astronaut walking in zero gravity, linked through a plastic duct to his oxygen supply, is like the image of the fetus floating in his amniotic fluid, linked to his mother through the umbilical cord. Similarly in teleanalysis, analyst and patient are connected to the energy supply of their computers. The patient could be under the illusion that he has found the object in the screen, but this found object is not a real object linking with a real subject. It is an invisible subject in search of an object in hiding that he cannot find because of his omnipotent fantasy. Here is the dream of a man in analysis online with web camera:

"I am alone eating seated at a table in a huge dining room. Behind me and surrounding the whole area, instead of walls, there is a huge water tank full of fish observing me."

This man is starting to have the experience of being seen and of being surrounded by something. The context is not human, but it offers him some sense of companionship and safety. But whatever it is, it is still behind the glass, behind the screen, far away from any chance of instinctual discharge or object relating. Above all, this dream shows the anxiety behind the defense and the fear of being drowned by the object if he gets too close, and it eliminates the distance between them.

Concerning the function of electronic devices for this man, I think that his wish to win an online game may represent a wish to conquer the mother, get her approval, or succeed in understanding her. The player never gets any response other than the exact moves determined by the creator of the game. This is one-way relating, and it remains unsatisfying (and therefore somewhat addictive as the search for satisfaction continues) because in reality it never happened, nor will it ever happen, that this object substitute can offer a true and real response to the subject.

Another patient shares his feelings of being inside what he calls a "pensieve", a term drawn from his reading of a Harry Potter novel (Rowling, 2000). A pensieve is an object like a flat bowl into which a memory has been poured and stored. When a character submerges his head in the pensieve, he instantly develops perfect memory. He is able to observe everything, as if he were present at the moment when the situation stored in the memory actually occurred. But he is invisible to the characters living inside the memory: they can even walk through him as if he were ethereal. For this patient the link is not possible, because he could never be seen or found by the primal object. A space that could offer so many possibilities fades as if it were a dream. The analyst is behind the screen, but so far away. Can the analyst really see him?

From the patients' point of view, they are in total control of the space. The computer screen and familiar websites provide a containing frame. I have observed that patients like this rarely go out of their houses, or out of their rooms, not because they are agoraphobic and cannot go out, but because they prefer not to. They choose to be surrounded by a boundary where they will feel held. Here we could start thinking that the early maternal failure occurred not only with the object mother, but also with the environmental mother (Winnicott, 1975).

One patient had a history of traumatic separations, including his being sent abruptly to a wilderness camp and from there, without warning, to boarding school when he was eleven years old. When he came back from school on vacation, he never returned to the house that he left because the family had relocated. Not only that, the new house was in a country where the language was unknown to him. He would close himself inside his new bedroom, in communication with his friends on the Internet, mainly playing war games. His analysis was conducted online with web camera, five times a week, lying on the couch. The treatment was very difficult as the analyst's efforts to link with him, both emotionally and on the web, were attacked and rejected. For instance, at times he would not connect to the analyst while she waited on line for forty-five minutes, seeing on the screen that he was on line. He could not allow her into his space; he needed to maintain control of it. And when he did connect and allow them a common space to work on his issues, he ruthlessly attacked the link, dehumanizing his analyst and treating her as if she was just another avatar of his games.

As I mentioned earlier, doing teleanalysis with this type of patient is not merely an option because of distance but, because of the nature of his defense system, I will dare to say, it is the best treatment option that we could offer. I think that videoconference is better for these particular patients than just using the phone because the actual image of the analyst on the screen is like an anchor that holds them fast and prevents them from mooring themselves to nothing. In science fiction novels the future is presented as something amazing that might happen. Like Captain Kirk in the Star Trek saga commanding "Beam me up, Scotty" or "Warp speed, Dr. Sulu" and finding himself and his spaceship instantaneously transported to another space, these patients continue their search for the lost object inside cyberspace, a space to conquer.

In teleanalysis, the screen-to-screen connection at the boundary of this new analytic frame is particularly suited to convey by projection into cyberspace the experience of emptiness and loneliness with the primary object. Within that field of deprivation, made so vivid in teleanalysis, there lies an opportunity for the patient to discover the object in the potential space of the online environment. "The potential space is at the interplay between there being nothing but me and there being objects and phenomena outside omnipotent control" (Winnicott, 1967b, p. 100). How does this movement take place? Hernández puts it this way: "creative illusion is as vital to the subjective existence of the present object, as destructive illusion is to its being placed outside omnipotent subjectivity" (Hernández & Giannakoulas, 2001, p. 158). In their search for a meaningful relationship within cyberspace, analyst and patient both need to create the illusion of the other. For his part, the analyst succeeds by using his capacity for psychic figurability. When will the move from narcissistic relating to object usage occur? After enough experience of the analyst's dependability and understanding, the cyberspace of loneliness and omnipotent control can become a place of awareness of the reality of the other and of appreciation. In the near future we may find ourselves referring patients for teleanalysis as a modality specifically appropriate for these interpsychic conflicts, in the same way that today we suggest traditional psychoanalysis or psychotherapy.

References

Botella, C., & Botella, S. (2005). *The Work of Psychic Figurabiliy*. Hove, Sussex: Brunner-Routledge.

Freud, S. (1923). *The Ego and the Id. S. E., XIX*. London: Hogarth.

Freud, S. (1937). Constructions in analysis. *S. E., XXIII*. London: Hogarth.

Freud, S., & Breuer, J. (1893–1895). *Studies on Hysteria. S. E., II*. London: Hogarth.

Green, A. (1993). *Le Travail du Negatif*. Paris: Editions de Minuit.

Green, A. (1997). The intuition of the negative in *Playing and Reality*. *International Journal of Psychoanalysis, 78*: 1071–1084.

Hernández, M., & Giannakoulas, A. (2001). On the construction of the potential space. In: M. Bertolini, A. Giannakoulas & M. Hernández (Eds), *Squiggles and Space: Revisiting the Work of D. W. Winnicott. Volume 1* (pp. 146–167). London: Whurr.

Ogden. T. H. (1985). On potential space. *International Journal of Psychoanalysis, 66*: 129–141.

Rowling, J. K. (2000). *Harry Potter and the Goblet of Fire*. New York: Levine.

Scharff, D. E., & Scharff, J. S. (2005). *The Primer of Object Relations*. Lanham, Boulder, New York: Jason Aronson, Second Edition.

Winnicott, D. W. (1951). Transitional objects and transitional phenomena. In: *Playing and Reality*, (pp. 1–25). New York: Basic Books, 1971.

Winnicott, D. W. (1956). Primary maternal preoccupation. In: *The Maturational Processes and the Facilitating Environment* (pp. 29–36). New York: International University Press.

Winnicott, D. W. (1967a). Mirror role of mother and family in child development. *Playing and Reality*, pp. 111–118. New York: Basic Books, 1971.

Winnicott, D. W. (1967b). The location of cultural experience. In: *Playing and Reality* (pp. 95–103). New York: Basic Books, 1971.

Winnicott, D. W. (1971a). *Playing and Reality*. New York: Basic Books.

Winnicott, D. W. (1971b). The place where we live. In: *Playing and Reality* (pp. 104–110). New York: Basic Books.

Winnicott, D. W. (1971c). Playing: A theoretical statement. In: *Playing and Reality* (pp. 38–52). New York: Basic Books.

Winnicott, D. W. (1975). *Through Paediatrics to Psychoanalysis*. London: Hogarth.

WHO (2012). *Depression*. Fact Sheet Na 369, October 2012. WHO Int.

CHAPTER NINETEEN

One analyst's journey into cyberspace

Glen O. Gabbard

Perhaps the biggest surprise of my analytic career has been the impact on psychoanalytic practice brought on by the introduction of Internet technology. As early as 1995, I was chairing an Internet discussion on psychoanalytic papers with an international group of colleagues. In retrospect, I was remarkably naive. I experienced the use of email to discuss papers as an isolated phenomenon. It hadn't occurred to me that the medium of Internet discourse would eventually enter into my practice in ways that I would never have predicted. In this contribution I will provide a chronology of my experience over the last seventeen years with email, texting, social media, virtual reality, and the availability of information on the Web. I will describe how it has affected my practice and my thinking. I will also share some of my still-evolving thoughts about the long-range clinical implications of these technological changes.

1998—email in the analytic setting

I was in my office going through the usual daily routine of seeing patients and wrestling with the transference and countertransference demons that make our work interesting. As I took a look at my email, I discovered a message from Rachel, a patient I had been seeing for some time in analysis:

> You have undoubtedly noticed that I clam up at times, and you probably attribute it to embarrassment. Actually, while I am only mildly reluctant to share personal feelings with you, I am utterly unable to talk about them. I seem to have a real taboo on speech. It helps if you put words in my mouth. Once the topic is on the table, I can usually elaborate, to some degree.

I was not sure how to respond except to take up her email with her in the next session. So I did not reply to her email. What ensued was an analytic process that occurred partly in cyberspace and partly in person. When she arrived at the next session, Rachel asked if I had read her email message. I acknowledged that I had, and she then requested that I help her find the words she needed to express herself. I told her I could probably be more helpful by analyzing with her what made it difficult for her to talk. She said she was terrifically "turned on" but just couldn't talk about sex. "I just do not have the vocabulary for it," she said. "I've never been able to use words for sex organs or intercourse." Since she was unable to speak about her intense erotic transference, she continued to write emails between sessions that were sexually charged and explicit. I chose not to write her back when I received these messages. Instead, I simply read them and then brought them up in the following session. I became aware of a risk—namely, that she was trying to establish a split-off email process. She would have been perfectly content to let it go unaddressed and unanalyzed. I told her that we could not leave those communications out of our analytic process in the office even if that were her wish. As we analyzed the meaning of her email correspondence, she observed that "email is a direct line to you—always—wherever you are. I don't have to risk interrupting you at home with your wife and kids, as I would on the phone. I always felt overheard by my mom as a kid when I spoke to friends over the phone. But email seems more private."

My receipt of sexually charged emails from Rachel felt illicit in some way. There was a part of me that felt I needed to close my door while I read her messages. What would a colleague from down the hall think if she dropped in unexpectedly and saw what I was reading? At times, I felt I was reading pornographic communications, and I noted a distinct sense of embarrassment. I recalled news stories of corporate employees who had been fired for accessing pornographic sites during work hours. I would feel a pressing need to delete her emails from my computer as soon as possible, in order to avoid discovery, partly in the name of preserving the patient's confidentiality, but partly to deal with my own sense of shame and even excitement at reading them. Moreover, I recognized a countertransference part of me that wanted to collude with Rachel in a subtle subversion of the analytic task that she was staging in cyberspace, where "no one would ever know". I recognized that she had created a split self—the erotic Rachel on email and the inhibited Rachel who showed up in my office.

With the help of a thoughtful consultant, I was able to find a way to conduct the analysis that brought the split-off cyberspace part of the analysis into the office so it could be analyzed. I have described this case in detail in a previous publication (Gabbard, 2001).

2004—virtual-reality relationships

Six years later I was contacted by two worried parents. They wanted to send their nineteen-year-old son Bob to me for psychotherapy because he spent many hours a day in his room playing multi-player video games with unseen individuals who lived elsewhere. He had no social life and no interest in college or working. His parents were at a loss. They told me that if they insisted he go to college, he would simply continue his games in his dormitory room and eventually flunk out. If they insisted that he work, he could refuse to go to work and get fired. Of considerable interest to me was that they could not see how they were enabling his behavior.

Bob reluctantly came to my office for an appointment. He told me that he much preferred virtual reality to the reality of his parents. I asked him if he had any friends. He wished for me to clarify if I meant "friends that he saw" or "online friends." I told him I'd like to hear about both. He said that he really didn't get out much because he spent all his time from morning till night playing games. But he said he had three or four good friends online. I asked him if he had ever had a girlfriend. He said "One of my online friends is a girl. At least I think she is." I responded "You think she is?" He explained, "Well, her characters in the games are always female." I recognized that if I were to enter his intrapsychic world and attempt to help him, I would have to accept that his object world was one that existed in virtual reality, where gender and sexuality could be elusive.

I saw Bob for a few sessions, but he had no interest in therapy whatsoever. He looked at his watch during the sessions and counted the minutes till he could go back home to his games. He had no curiosity about his devotion to the games and certainly did not view his behavior as problematic in any way. I asked him if he would consider going to a program that could help him find a way to cut down on his games and pursue a life outside of his room. He became desperate, and told me that it would be a catastrophic mistake to cut off his access to the games. In fact, he told his parents that evening that he would commit suicide if he were forced to go somewhere for treatment. He said he would not continue seeing me because I was on his parents' side. He talked his parents into pulling him out of treatment with me, and I never saw him again.

I learned from this experience that our view of object relationships required some re-thinking. Specifically, relationships with objects in cyberspace were just as powerful as those in the real world. Indeed, in some cases they provided meaning for those who might otherwise be isolated and despairing. Who was I to suggest that they needed to be modified? Yet my heart went out to the distressed parents who were essentially held hostage by their son's demand to remain in a situation where the developmental tasks of young adulthood were entirely avoided.

2007—social media and the self

In the first decade of this century, I was hearing a great deal about Facebook, Twitter, and other forms of social media. A young woman I was seeing came to a session one day and announced that she was distressed because her boyfriend had broken up with her. She was clearly worked up and distraught, and she said to me, "I have been obsessing all night long about what I'm going to say on Facebook. This is so embarrassing. What do I do about the photos? How should I list my status now? What will everyone think? I made it sound like marriage was around the corner." As she continued to talk, I realized that she was actually much more concerned about how to present her image on Facebook than about losing the man with whom she had been involved. I shared this impression with her, and I asked her how she actually felt about losing him. She replied in a matter-of-fact way: "I was expecting it. He wasn't really right for me."

I began to appreciate that the psychoanalytic construct of the self was also changing in our cyberspace era. We watch ourselves from an "outside" position when we sit in front of our computer and read Facebook entries. A transformation is occurring. One observes a virtual version of the self that can be shaped by one's desire to create a new persona that strips away unwanted characteristics. More importantly, this cyberself is an amalgam of what one would like to be and what one imagines that other denizens of social media would like to see. Facebook, Google, and other forms of social media may assist in shaping this new persona. Social networking coaches advise their flock to "be authentic" on social media. The contemporary young adult must decide which version of the self should be represented on social media to have the greatest chance of *appearing* "authentic" to others. However, appearing authentic and being authentic is not the same thing. Moreover, authenticity usually implies a depth of character and a variety of facets to the personality, attributes that may be left behind in the pursuit of an "image."

2008—the decline and fall of analytic anonymity

In 2008 I received an email from someone in another state that I do not know. She was seeking my advice regarding how to deal with her obsession about her analyst:

> After 18 months of analysis, I'm still terrified to talk to him, but I am desperate to see him in between appointments. I'm technologically savvy, and I told him that I was able to gain entrance to the "members only" section of the American Psychological Association website. I also told him I had seen his family photos on Facebook. He has teenage boys, and I'm very attracted to one of them in some strange way. His wife seems sweet and beautiful. I'm not jealous of her in terms of wanting her relationship with my therapist, but she's also a psychologist, and she's successful, has a great family, and a good life. I'm 35, twice-divorced, still working on my dissertation and I have nothing to show for myself. I've had the photos for a few months, and he knows at least that I saw them. But tonight I sent him an email with the ones I have, and a brief summary of what I think about them. Now I think he will hate me, try to push me away, to protect his family from me.

When I read this account from a complete stranger, I was startled by the ease with which she could see into her analyst's life and invade his privacy. Having been trained in an era where self-disclosure was discouraged in deference to the analytic value of exploring the patient's fantasy, I felt a vicarious sense of violation. I chose not to respond to this email to avoid becoming a *de facto* consultant to a messy situation.

Shortly thereafter, a patient came to my office for the first time and told me that she wanted to be in therapy with me. She said she had Googled me and was impressed with my writings. She also told me that I looked a lot like my father. Stunned by this comment, I asked her how she knew what my father looked like. She replied, "Oh it's easy to get photos on the Internet now. Your dad had a nice smile." Her use of past tense clearly indicated that she was aware of his recent death.

Privacy is disappearing. Is our analytic anonymity gone? As we all know, what I experienced in 2008 is now commonplace. It is the rule rather than the exception for patients to Google us before deciding to see us. They come to their first session with lots of information about us— some accurate, some inaccurate. How can we defend ourselves against these intrusions? The answer, unfortunately, is that we can't. While we can feel violated, we have to recognize that what is on the Web is public information. Were we to forbid our patients from Googling us, it would backfire. Like a child told not to enter a particular room in one's house, the curiosity would be overwhelming. Even an obedient patient would be dying to know what the analyst was hiding. Moreover, the patient can taunt the analyst with what he finds on the Internet. He can access a photo of the analyst's house, look up what the analyst paid for it, and even critique the analyst's choice of shutters.

2009—the permanence of Internet information

Another disconcerting aspect of the information about us is its permanence. The self in cyberspace may be fluid in some ways, but it is also indelible (Rosen, 2010). It is not easy to change what is there. Postings of photos on social media sites have been viewed during deliberations about whether to offer an academic training position to young professionals (Gabbard, 2012). Similarly, there has been a mushrooming of web sites that invite patients to rate their doctor. Criticisms that appear on these sites may remain for years, perhaps deterring future patients from seeking help from a particular clinician. When critical ratings appear, clinicians have little recourse. It would be unethical for them to post a rebuttal, as they would be publically violating doctor–patient confidentiality. In fact, a new breed of experts is now emerging who spend their time identifying negative information about their clients and doing what they can to prevent it from appearing on Google searches.

False information can also appear to be indelible. Individuals with the same name can be confused so that negative attributions associated with a particular John Smith are linked to another John Smith. Unfortunately, we are increasingly finding it difficult to exonerate ourselves from false information or accusations. In a truly clever op-ed piece in the March 12, 2011 *New York Times*, entitled "How the Internet killed me," Zick Rubin, an American social psychologist, wrote about how he recently Googled himself and discovered the following Wikipedia entry: "Zick Rubin (1944–1997) was an American social psychologist."

When he informed one of the Wikipedia co-founders of this error, she insisted that an authoritative source had informed her that the Wikipedia entry was, in fact, correct. Rubin, with considerable wit, said that he began to question his own existence and recognized that he was perhaps too close to the situation to be objective. He noted, "Now that I had been made aware of my death fourteen years ago, I began to feel some twinges, starting in my right elbow and extending to my fingertips." With persistence, however, he was finally able to convince the powers that be at Wikipedia that he was still breathing. They ultimately resurrected him on the pages of Wikipedia, making him the Lazarus of cyberspace.

One is also subject to pranksters who enjoy entering false information on Wikipedia and seeing how long it takes before their prank is detected. One day in 2009 a colleague asked if I had checked my Wikipedia entry recently. I said I had not, and she recommended that I take a look. I had a start when I read it. After accurately recounting my publications and my career path, the entry ended with "Dr. Gabbard is currently an Awesome Ranger at the Cub Scout camp in Port Huron, New York." In fact, I had never set foot in Port Huron, New York, I did not even know what an "Awesome Ranger" was, and I have no connection with the Cub Scout organization. I was able to eliminate this sentence from my entry, but it is disconcerting that one's identity may be shaped by false information.

2010—texting to the analyst

It was a Friday night around 10:30pm. I was about to go to bed and suddenly noticed that my iPhone had a text message on it. The message came from Alice, a thirty-five-year-old patient of mine. It said "Do you think I should sleep with Bill tonight?" My first reaction was "How should I know?" My second reaction was, "In any case, I'm not going to respond to this at 10:30 on a Friday evening!" As I thought it over, I realized that if I did respond, I would be giving a message to my patient that I am available for free instant consultation anytime, even when I'm relaxing at home with my wife and perhaps having a glass of wine. I chose to do nothing, but brought it up at the next session for discussion.

Over the last several years, a sea-change has occurred in the expectation that one should be able to text professionals. Several colleagues have complained that even if they have policies about prohibiting the use of texting by patients, they regularly receive text messages about appointment changes and such because it has become a universal assumption that text is convenient, acceptable, and professional. While initially wary of receiving texts, I now find myself appreciating the time-efficiency of texting to arrange appointment changes.

However, texting by patients is not limited to administrative matters. With some patients, the practice goes well beyond those limits. Ms. B, a twenty-eight- year old investment banker, came to analysis because she was highly successful at work but was deeply troubled by her romantic relationships. She routinely texted me to let me know whether she were running late or would be on time for the session. In one particular session, I received a text saying "Traffic jam. Will be late. Maybe 10 minutes." About fifteen minutes later, I received another text: "Parking now." Then about three minutes later, I received one saying "In waiting room now." During the sessions with me, she reclined on my couch with two smartphones at her side. When she received a text, she briefly checked it, sometimes apologizing for interrupting her associations, and then returned to the analytic process. On her Wednesday session, an important report from the stock market was issued around 2.00am. Her phone vibrated, and she said, "Just a minute," checked the phone, and returned to our discussion. She frequently read me text messages from her new boyfriend. For example, one morning she came into my office, lay on the couch, and said: "I'm really liking Brian. He is always sending me sweet little texts. I just got one. I'll read it to you: 'thinking about last night and can't concentrate at work'. Isn't that lovely? He is thinking about me right now". She then raised the phone so I could see it, and said, "Here's another one: 'Quick—which star would make you want to see a film more—Brad Pitt or Ryan Gosling?'"

The reading of the texts and the frequent interruptions in the sessions presented me with dilemmas that were not easily resolved. As I have argued in my writing (Gabbard, 2000), there is not one "correct" way to do analysis. Each patient must do analysis the way that he or she must do it. Hence, an effort to set limits on the use of texting or access to the iPhone potentially may create problems for the analysis. The patient might well feel that he or she is doing analysis incorrectly and thus conform to the analyst's wishes or rebel against them. Psychoanalysis is not coercive—we allow our patients to show us who they are without controlling what they say or do. On the other hand, an analyst cannot simply ignore the use of texting or the interruption of the session to check one's smartphone. One must attempt to analyze whatever is taking place in the analytic discourse, just as I insisted that the emails from my patient Rachel in my

"Cyberpassion" paper (2001) had to become part of our analytic work. The analyst must make an effort to integrate the split-off virtual world with the here-and-now real world. Indeed, the use of a smartphone has become an essential part of our real world.

Hence I made an observation to Ms. B: "Sometimes I have the impression that it's difficult for you to be fully present here, as though you have one foot in my consulting room and one foot in the virtual world of cybercommunication." She was puzzled by my comment. Her reply was, "What do you mean?" I pointed out that her full engagement in the analysis was perhaps compromised by her attention to the messages bombarding her through her iPhone. She laughed and said, "Oh no, these are no problem. I can do both the analysis and check my texts at the same time. It doesn't take me out of the room." I recognized that from my perspective, I was trying to call attention to something that was unusual in the context of psychoanalytic work. From her perspective, she felt it was somewhat jarring for me to call attention to a routine part of her daily existence typical of virtually everyone she knew in her age group. Her response was to attempt to help me understand that I was simply old-fashioned. She finally said to me: "Oh come on, Dr. Gabbard, this is 2010. Everyone is texting these days. Phone calls are obsolete. Sometimes you sound like a dinosaur." In other words, what she was doing was utterly normal and required no analytic reflection.

As I drove home that evening, I was doing some self-analysis in my car. Her designation of me as a dinosaur took me by surprise. I associated to Loewald's classic paper on the waning of the Oedipus complex (Loewald, 1979). He suggested that the succession of generations is a key component of analytic work. In a reconsideration of the Loewald paper, Ogden (2006) noted, "For Loewald, the Oedipus complex is at its core a face-off between the generations, a life-and-death battle for autonomy, authority, and responsibility" (p. 655). Ogden explicitly states that to some extent we analysts must allow ourselves to be killed off by our patients lest we diminish them. It is the natural order. We must not attempt to force our analysands to submit to our preferred ways of doing things. We must understand that change has been set in motion, and we cannot stop it. We must adjust as we take our ultimate place as ancestors to our analysands.

Reflections in 2015

Looking back on this journey into cyberspace, which is still unfolding within me, I recognize that there is no turning back. We cannot stop the juggernaut. Life as we know it is being transformed before our eyes. Each week I am trying to figure out how to expand what we think of as the analytic frame to encompass the new world we live in (Gabbard, Kassaw, & Perez-Garcia, 2011). Where do we go from here? Do we print up guidelines on email and texting for new patients? Wouldn't that imply that we expect them to use these new tools? Should we wait until they text us and then hand out such guidelines? Should we simply allow patients to relate to us in the way they wish to and attempt to analyze it?

As Indiana Jones once said, "We are making this up as we go along." I do not know the right answer. But I do know this: the death knell is not sounding for the kind of work we do. Analysis assumes a special role in a society where we are tethered to our iPhones and there is no time for reflection. We are the only remaining sanctuary for quiet reflection where we can discover who we are and where we are going. We will accommodate this brave new world in our own way as we stumble into the future and deepen our understanding of the human condition.

References

Gabbard, G. O. (2000). On gratitude and gratification. *Journal of the American Psychoanalytic Association*, *48*: 697–718.

Gabbard, G. O. (2001). Cyberpassion: e-rotic transference and the Internet. *Psychoanalytic Quarterly*, *70*: 719–737.

Gabbard, G. O. (2012). Clinical challenges in the Internet era. *American Journal of Psychiatry, 169*: 460–463.

Gabbard, G. O., Kassaw, K. A., & Perez-Garcia, G. (2011). Professional boundaries in the era of the Internet. *Academic Psychiatry, 35*: 168–174.

Loewald, H. (1979). The waning of the Oedipus complex. In: *Papers on Psychoanalysis* (pp. 384–404). New Haven, CT: Yale UP, 1980.

Ogden, T. H. (2006). Reading Loewald: Oedipus reconceived. *International Journal of Psychoanalysis, 87*: 651–666.

Rosen, J. (2010). The web means the end of forgetting. *New York Times Magazine*, July 21, 2010.

Rubin, Z. (2011). How the Internet killed me. *New York Times*, March 12, 2011.

INDEX

247